PENGUIN BOOKS

NELSON AND HIS CAPTAINS

Lud   Kennedy is one of Britain's foremost journalists and broad-
cast   Born in Edinburgh, Scotland, he was educated at Eton
Col   e and Oxford University. During the Second World War he
serv   i in the Royal Navy and took part in the pursuit of the *Bismarck*.
Afte he War he became a newscaster for BBC radio and television.
In i dition to his long and widely acclaimed career in broadcast
jou alism (which includes the documentary *Who Killed the Lindbergh
Bai ', shown in the United States on PBS), he was a columnist for
Nei veek International as well as writing for other newspapers and
ma   zines. He was knighted in 1994 and in 1995 he was elected
Pre lent of the Voluntary Euthanasia Society. He is married to the
bal : dancer, Moira Shearer, and they have a son and three
da: hters.

Lu¹ vic Kennedy is the author of many of works of non-fiction,
inc ding *Nelson's Band of Brothers* (1951), now published as *Nelson and his
Caf ins* (Penguin, 2001); *Ten Rillington Place* (1961); *The Trial of Stephen
Wa (1964); *Very Lovely People* (1969); *Pursuit: The Chase and Sinking of the
Bis. rck* (1974); *A Presumption of Innocence: The Amazing Case of Patrick
Me: n* (1975); *Wicked Beyond Belief* (1980); *The Airman and the Carpenter*
(19!), re-published in the United States in 1996 as *Crime of the Century*;
Eut nasia: The Good Death (1990); *In Bed with an Elephant: A Journey
Thr gh Scotland's Past and Present* (1995); and *All in the Mind: A Farewell to
God 999). He has also written an autobiography, *On My Way to the
Club 989) and a play, *Murder Story* (1954), which includes an essay on
capit punishment. He is at present completing a book called *Thirty-
Three Murders and Two Immoral Earnings*, a résumé of his previous books
on m arriages of justice.

NELSON
and his Captains

LUDOVIC
KENNEDY

PENGUIN BOOKS

PENGUIN BOOKS

Published by the Penguin Group
Penguin Books Ltd, 80 Strand, London WC2R ORL, England
Penguin Putnam Inc., 375 Hudson Street, New York, New York 10014, USA
Penguin Books Australia Ltd, Ringwood, Victoria, Australia
Penguin Books Canada Ltd, 10 Alcorn Avenue, Toronto, Ontario, Canada M4V 3B2
Penguin Books India (P) Ltd, 11 Community Centre, Panchsheel Park, New Delhi – 110 017, India
Penguin Books (NZ) Ltd, Cnr Rosedale and Airborne Roads, Albany, Auckland, New Zealand
Penguin Books (South Africa) (Pty) Ltd, 24 Sturdee Avenue, Rosebank 2196, South Africa

Penguin Books Ltd, Registered Offices: 80 Strand, London WC2R ORL, England

www.penguin.com

First published by William Collins Sons & Co. Ltd 1951
New revised edition published by William Collins Sons & Co. Ltd 1975
Published as a Classic Penguin 2001

2

Copyright © Ludovic Kennedy, 1951, 1975
All rights reserved

Printed and bound in Great Britain by Cox & Wyman Ltd, Reading, Berkshire

CONTENTS

ILLUSTRATIONS

Illustrations

'I had the happiness to command a Band of Brothers.'

Nelson to Howe, January 8th, 1799

'Great captains they assuredly were;
bright they have made our annals;
each ship was a perfect school.'

Tucker: *Life of St Vincent*

ATLANTIC OCEAN

FRANCE

PORTUGAL

SPAIN

Genoa

Marseilles

CORSICA

Rome

MINORCA

SARDINIA

Port
Mahon

C. St. Vincent

Cadiz

Algeciras

Cartagena

MEDITE

Gibraltar

Tetuan

Algiers

MOROCCO

ALGERIA

SICILY

TUNISIA

0   50   100 Miles

Trieste

Genoa

Nice

Toulon

CAPRAJA

Leghorn

HYERES IS

C. Corse

Vade

Marseilles

St Fiorenzo
Bay

Porto Ferrajo

Bastia

ELBA

Calvi

Civita-Vecchia

Ajaccio

Rome

CORSICA

Gaeta

MADDALENA IS

Capua

Naples

ISCHIA

Salerno

PROCIDA

SARDINIA

C. Marittimo

Messina

Palermo

SICILY

Augusta

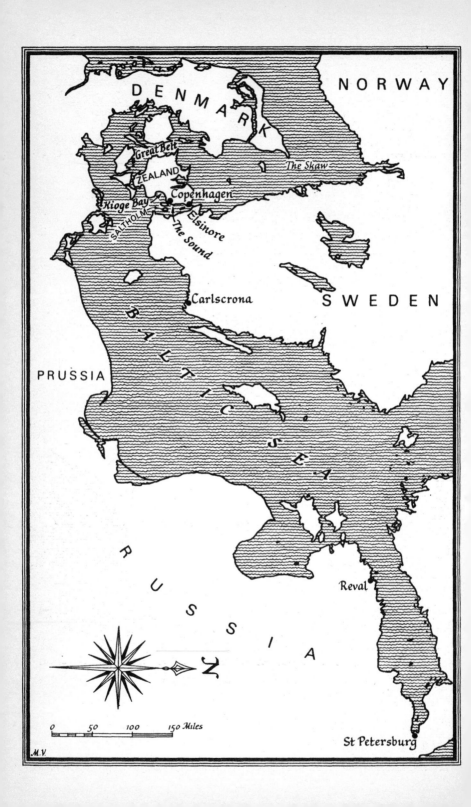

PROLOGUE

'I have just been amusing myself,' wrote Captain Byam Martin of the *Implacable* to his brother in 1808, 'in ascertaining the diversity of human beings which compose the crew of a British ship of war, and as I think you will be entertained with a statement of the ridiculous medley, it shall follow precisely as their place of nativity is inserted in the ship's book: English 285, Irish 130, Welsh 25, Isle of Man 6, Scots 29, Shetland 3, Orkneys 2, Guernsey 2, Canada 1, Jamaica 1, Trinidad 1, St Domingo 2, St Kitts 1, Martinique 1, Santa Cruz 1, Bermuda 1, Sweden 8, Danes 7, Prussians 8, Dutch 1, Germans 3, Corsica 1, Portuguese 5, Sicily 1, Minorca 1, Ragusa 1, Brazil 1, Spanish 2, Madeira 1, Americans 28, West Indies 2, Bengal 2.'

This extraordinary list (which, Byam Martin added, was typical) gives some idea of the difficulties of manning the warships of Nelson's time. It was one of the Admiralty's greatest problems. Service afloat gave no guarantee of employment beyond a single commission; and men who could keep their families from starving on bread and cheese were not inclined to give up jobs that would at once be filled by others. There was also a very real horror of life in the Navy. Conditions of service had not changed radically since the days of Charles II, and the severity of the discipline was proverbial.

A few did volunteer. Some were attracted by the glib posters in the seaport towns advertising free grog and plenty of prize-money: they soon regretted their decision. Others came to avoid a worse evil ashore; criminals booked for the gallows, absconding debtors, and what were known as the Lord Mayor's Men – youths of good family who had been found in bawdy-houses or drunk in the street and feared to see their names in the papers.

But these produced only a handful, and the majority were raised by other means. The most successful was the press-gang, which, throughout the Napoleonic wars, terrorized the inhabitants of seaport towns. The captain of a ship commissioning would send ashore, usually after dark, a lieutenant and six seamen, armed with heavy cudgels. These roamed the waterfront taverns and back-streets, picking up all able-bodied men. The victims seldom gave in .without a fight in which their womenfolk often joined. They were then taken on board and examined by the ship's surgeon. Those found unfit for service and apprentices carrying bona-fide papers were discharged: the others, whatever their situation, were hustled below to the gun-decks.

But even the press-gangs could not satisfy the demand for men, and in 1795 the quota system was introduced. A law was passed requiring every county to furnish annually a stated number of men. At first the sheriffs welcomed the bill as a means of getting rid of poachers, vagrants and gipsies; but when this supply was exhausted they were forced to offer bounties, some very high, to induce men to come forward. Many of them were found to be diseased and verminous and quite unfit for duty: 'truly wretched and unlike men' was how one writer described them.

These were the types who made up the crew of an eighteenth-century ship of the line – criminals, debtors, vagrants, men impressed against their wills and foreigners who had deserted from their own ships and been picked up in the world's seaports. It was estimated that of every ship's company one-third were landsmen and one-eighth foreigners. 'In a man-of-war' wrote Commodore Edward Thompson, 'you have the collected filth of jails: there's not a vice committed on shore that is not practised here.' Dr Johnson could not understand what made people go to sea when there were prisons ashore. The Admiralty's manning policy was not only morally wrong but practically short-sighted. As long as men could be obtained, reform was neglected: while reform was neglected only the worst men could be obtained.

Natural disaffection was aggravated by wretched living conditions. Shore leave was practically non-existent. Pay, which had remained on the same scale for a hundred years, was negligible. An ordinary seaman received 25*s* a month, a landsman 22*s*: by the time they had been defrauded by the purser for slop clothing and by the Jews who exchanged their pay-tickets there was little left. The food was an abomination. Biscuits were made of wheat, pea-flour and bone-dust: they were incredibly hard and thick and invariably harboured weevils. The meat was 'fibrous, shrunken, dark, grisly and glistening with salt crystals'; the sailors carved fancy articles out of it, and the flesh was said to have taken on a good polish 'like some close-grained wood'. Another food was 'burgoo,' or oatmeal mixed with water, which was usually found inedible and thrown to the pigs. The butter turned rancid within a few weeks of commissioning and was given to the boatswain for greasing the shrouds and rigging.

On such a diet sickness was unavoidable. Lack of fresh fruit and vegetables and the external damp of the gun-decks brought on typhus, scurvy and ulcers – horrible sores which appeared all over the body and defied attempts at healing. The work of the surgeons was hampered by the excessive economies of the Navy Board. Lint was considered too expensive for dressings, so sponges were used instead. There were not enough sponges to go round, so inevitably infection spread. No anaesthetics were available for amputations, and many ships were without proper sick-bays.

But the worst aspect of the life was the discipline. For minor offences junior officers could award certain punishments without the captain's authority. One of these was 'gagging'. A heavy iron bar was placed in the offender's mouth and kept in position by a length of spun yarn knotted behind his head: he was then secured to the rigging some way above the deck and left until ordered to be cut down. Another punishment was 'starting' a man, or ordering the boatswain's mate to beat him about the head and shoulders with a heavy rattan.

For more serious offences such as drunkenness or stealing the standard punishment was flogging. Although floggings could only be ordered by the captain, they were a common feature of the routine: during the twenty-seven days before Trafalgar the log of the *Royal Sovereign* recorded twenty-five such punishments. They took place on the quarter-deck in the presence of the ship's company. The offender took off his shirt, and with hands held above his head, was secured by his wrists to the gratings. The captain read the Articles of War and then called on the boatswain's mate, with the cat-o'-nine-tails, to do his duty. Normal punishment was anything up to four dozen lashes. Even this made the back a bloody mess; but for desertion, sedition and sodomy, two, three and sometimes five hundred lashes would be given. A man who underwent one of these cruel punishments has left his impressions of it.

'I felt an astounding sensation between the shoulders under my neck, which went to my toe-nails in one direction and my finger-nails in another, and stung me to the heart as if a knife had gone through my body . . . He came on a second time a few inches lower, and then I thought the former stroke sweet and agreeable compared with that one. I felt my flesh quiver in every nerve from the scalp of my head to my toe-nails. The time between each stroke seemed so long as to be agonizing, and yet the next came too soon . . . The pain in my lungs was more severe, I thought, than on my back. I felt as if I would burst in the internal parts of my body . . . I put my tongue between my teeth, held it there, and bit it almost in two pieces. What with the blood from my tongue and my lips which I had also bitten, and the blood from my lungs or some other internal part ruptured by the writhing agony, I was almost choked and became black in the face . . . Only fifty had been inflicted, and the time since they began was like a long period of life; I felt as I had lived all the time of my real life in pain and torture and that the time when existence had pleasure in it was a dream long long gone by.'

Sometimes, as a reprieve from the death sentence, courts martial awarded a flogging round the fleet. So terrible was this punishment that many asked for the swifter justice of the yard-arm. The prisoner, accompanied by the ship's surgeon, was placed in the longboat and lashed by his wrists to the capstan-bar. The boatswain's mate came down the gangway and inflicted fifty lashes. The longboat cast off and, attended by guardboats sounding half-minute bells and the rogue's march on the drums, was rowed to the next ship in the line. Here and alongside every other ship in the harbour the performance was repeated. Few men survived. Those that did seldom recovered from the effects: their self-confidence was gone, they took on a premature senility and died young.

Such were the rigours of the naval life of the times.

It would not have been surprising if the men who had endured them had become broken in spirit and reduced to little better than animals. But this was not so. They managed somehow to adapt themselves, to remain spirited and cheerful. They never lost the gift of laughter; contemporary writings are full of their good-natured and bawdy witticisms. In their leisure moments they sang and danced, and much of their music has lasted to this day. Nor were they the ruffians they have sometimes been painted. Many proved their bravery and loyalty time and time again. It is true a few were ready for violent measures, and because of them the rigorous discipline was maintained. But the patriotism of the majority was never in doubt. The great mutiny of 1797 was no more than a protest against the infamous conditions of service. The ringleaders declared they would not obey orders until their just demands were satisfied: but they added that if the French Fleet was reported at sea they were ready to sail at once.

What these men needed were leaders. In the past the Navy had suffered from two types of commander: the 'aristocrats' whose knowledge of sea affairs was often pitiful but whose natural authority the sailors recognized; and later the 'tarpaulins', rough, uneducated men who were born seamen but understood little of human nature or civilized life. These men, instead of mitigating the severity of the discipline, perpetuated it.

But towards the end of the eighteenth century a new type of officer was arising. Unlike the tarpaulins, who had been bred in seaport towns, they came mostly from middle-class country families. They owed their entry into the Navy either to senior officers who were their fathers' friends or to one of the great local landowners who was often their fathers' patron. They shared the tarpaulins' seamanship and bravery, but lacked their crudeness and bigotry. They were simple, decent men, direct in speech and manner, reasonably well educated but with no intellectual pretensions; they had a high sense of morality and honour and an appreciation, which the tarpaulins never had, of the wider events in which they were taking part. Such men were Ball, the son of a Gloucestershire squire, Hardy who came of a respected Dorset family, Berry and Troubridge whose fathers were London tradesmen, Foley from Wales, Fremantle from Buckinghamshire, Saumarez from the Channel Islands, and Nelson, the son of a Norfolk parson and the greatest humanitarian of them all. These were the captains for whom the seamen had been waiting, men who understood and cared for them and to whom in turn they could give willing service.

They could not have appeared at a more opportune moment: for in 1793 the ambitions of Revolutionary France were loosed suddenly upon the world. How the captains, with the seamen supporting them from below and the genius of St Vincent and Nelson guiding them from above, met, withstood and overthrew this menace is the central story of this book.

PART I

The Retreat from the Mediterranean

CHAPTER 1

14 July 1795, was an important day in the life of Captain Horatio Nelson. For one phase of his career – that of endurance and subordination – was at an end, and another – that of command and fulfilment – was about to begin. Two years' strenuous Mediterranean campaigning had cost him the loss of his right eye and an impaired constitution, and brought in return little satisfaction or reward. Lord Hood, a Commander-in-Chief whom he worshipped, had spoken too plainly to his Government the year before and been ordered home. Nelson was disconsolate. 'Oh, Miserable Board of Admiralty,' he wrote, 'they have forced the best officer in our service away from his command.' Hood's place was taken by Hotham, a weak man whom Nelson openly despised. Under his command the Fleet lost two great opportunities on 14 March and 13 July of destroying the French Fleet at sea and thereby altering the whole course of the Mediterranean War. In the first action, after the *Ça Ira* and *Censeur* had struck their colours, Nelson went on board the flag-ship to urge Hotham to pursue the rest of the enemy. 'No', replied Hotham, 'we must be contented, we have done very well.' 'Had we taken ten sail,' commented Nelson, 'and allowed the eleventh to escape, I would not have called it well done.' And in the skirmish off the Hyères Islands

on 13 July, Hotham's premature signal of recall again deprived the Fleet of a much-needed victory.

For Nelson, with his extraordinary perception, saw what Hotham with his limited vision ('their intentions are for the moment frustrated') could not see – the wider picture of the whole war. With the Toulon Fleet destroyed or disabled the British Fleet could range the Riviera at will and help the Austrian armies first to check and then drive back the French forces massing on the Italian frontier. 'The British Fleet,' he wrote five years later, 'could have prevented the invasion of Italy: and if our friend Hotham had kept his fleet on that coast, no armies from France could have been furnished with stores or provisions: even men could not have marched.'

What Nelson feared came to pass. France made peace with Spain and Bonaparte from his office in Paris saw the opportunity it offered: 'Peace with Spain makes offensive war in Piedmont certain'. But to launch an effective attack certain small obstacles had first to be removed. The Riviera port of Vado was in Austrian hands and from it de Vins, the Austrian general, was sending out privateers to harass the trade between France and the neutral port of Genoa. 'By intercepting the coasters from Italy,' said Bonaparte, 'it has suspended our commerce, stopped the arrival of provisions and obliged us to supply Toulon from the interior of the republic. Communication with Genoa must be promptly opened.' For the Allies it had equally promptly to be stopped. Even Hotham saw the need for some action, and on 15 July he gave Nelson command of a squadron of frigates to co-operate with the Austrian Army along the Riviera.

This was Nelson's first independent command. His mission required courage, ability, perseverance and especially diplomatic tact if he were not to offend the neutral Genoese. Some of his frustration must have been dispelled at the sight of the eight frigates taking station on the *Agamemnon* as she slipped out of the fleet-anchorage of St Fiorenzo Bay in North Corsica and stood to the northward. 'What a change in my life,' he wrote to his wife a few days later. 'Here I am having command and co-operation with an old Austrian General, almost fancying myself charging at the head of a troop of horse. Nothing will be wanting on my part towards the success of the Common Cause. I have eight sails of Frigate under my command: the service I have to perform is important.'

The service was important, and in more ways than Nelson knew; for the ships now under him were the training ground for the fleets of England he was later to lead to victory, their captains the genesis of his Band of Brothers. Few of them achieved distinction in later years and most are now forgotten. But among them was one destined to share many of his battles. His name was Thomas Francis Fremantle.

* * *

Fremantle was the third son of John Fremantle, of Aston Abbots in Buckinghamshire. He was twelve when he went into the Navy and as midshipman and lieutenant served in the West Indies under Hyde Parker in the War of American Independence. On the outbreak of the French War in 1793 he was given command of the *Tartar* in time to come out with Lord Hood to the Mediterranean. Nelson had already formed a high appreciation of his abilities, first at Bastia, and later in the first of Hotham's abortive actions, when his brilliant seamanship and gunnery led to the taking of the *Ça Ira*. While the French Fleet were being pursued, the *Ça Ira*, by an overpress of sail, ran on board one of her consorts and lost her topmasts. She might have had time to repair the damage and slip away had not Fremantle in the *Inconstant*, far in advance of the leading British columns, run down on her and brought her to action. The *Inconstant* was only a frigate and the *Ça Ira* an 80-gun line-of-battle ship, but by keeping in the enemy's wake and avoiding the fire from his broadsides, Fremantle was able to inflict much damage on his opponent, while suffering little himself. The *Ça Ira* was engaged later that day by Nelson in the *Agamemnon*, and next day, after she had been taken in tow by the *Censeur*, by other ships including the *Illustrious* and *Courageux*. Both French ships struck, but the *Courageux*, Captain Benjamin Hallowell, was so badly damaged Fremantle had to take her in tow. Both ships eventually reached Leghorn Roads. In his report Fremantle paid tribute to the exertions of his master, Mr Fryer, who had been Bligh's carpenter in the *Bounty*.

At this time Fremantle was just thirty. He was a short, stocky man, with small rounded features expressive of determination and authority. He was, according to a lady who met him at this time, 'not handsome, but there is something pleasing in his countenance and his fiery black eyes are quite captivating. He is good-natured, gay and lively, in short he seems to possess all the amiable qualities that are required to win everybody's heart the moment one sees him.' This lady, as will be seen, had some reason to be biased, but there is no doubt that Fremantle was a smart, efficient officer, popular afloat and ashore. Nelson was happy to have him under his command.

* * *

Nelson, as usual when undertaking a new mission, set out with high hopes. His natural enthusiasm led him to place the same confidence in others as he did in himself. At the Austrian headquarters at Vado Bay he conferred with Mr Drake and Mr Trevor, the British Ministers at Genoa and Turin, and found they thought as he did. Even the Austrian Commander-in-Chief, de Vins, who came on board the *Agamemnon* creaking with age and weighed down with ribbons, impressed him. 'He is an officer,' he told the First Lord, 'who perfectly knows his business and seems disposed to act with vigour.' But there was one difficulty. Included in Hotham's instructions was an Admiralty letter instructing all captains 'not to give any just cause of offence to the foreign powers in amity with His Majesty'. This clearly pointed to Genoa and the trade with France. But to Nelson the main point of the naval co-operation was preventing supplies reaching the enemy. 'If we are to finish the war in France,' he wrote to a friend, 'we must not stop at trifles.' He therefore distributed his ships along the Riviera west and east of Genoa; their orders were to stop all trade between Italian and French ports. After a month the blockade began to tell and even the enemy had to admit the precariousness of their position.

Yet despite every precaution, a number of coasters and small boats, by hugging the cliffs at night, succeeded in breaking the blockade. His next plan was to establish a landing-point west of the French armies on their line of communication with Nice. He took the *Agamemnon* on a reconnoitre along the coast, chose San Remo as the most suitable place, and on return to Vado told de Vins that if he could provide 5000 men with field-guns he would guarantee to land them, maintain them with supplies and if necessary cover their withdrawal: if this force could hold out for a few weeks the French would have to abandon their lines for want of supplies and the way to Nice would be open.

It was, as Hotham said when he heard of it, 'a wild scheme'. But Nelson, whose restless mind missed no opportunities, wanted to show that the fleet, which he knew would be blamed for any subsequent reversals, was ready to co-operate. De Vins was lukewarm and non-committal, and Nelson was now beginning to see him in his true light. 'At my first coming on this station,' he told Hotham, 'he seemed very anxious to get to Nice: and indeed I had very little doubts as to the accomplishment of it. However, week after week has passed without his Army having removed one foot to the westward of where I found them'. Baulked in one direction, Nelson tried another. He went to Leghorn to see Hotham and demanded more ships. Hotham not only refused but reduced his squadron and ordered him to reconnoitre Toulon – 'while he,' wrote Nelson in disgust, 'lies quiet in Leghorn Roads'.

Things went from bad to worse. Hotham struck his flag and was succeeded by Hyde Parker, another indecisive character to whose flag at Copenhagen Nelson later turned a blind eye. Hyde Parker reduced the squadron further and forbade Nelson to attack a fleet of supply-vessels gathering in a bay behind Borghetto. The climax to this policy of indecision came when 300 Frenchmen from the frigate *Brune* in Genoa harbour made a landing at Voltri nine miles down the coast, seized a magazine of corn and captured from the local inn an Austrian emissary carrying £10,000 pay for the troops. Next day the French captain, exhilarated by his success, flaunted Genoese neutrality by enlisting troops for the French Army on the steps of the Genoa Exchange. Two days later he embarked 700 men to make a landing between Voltri and Savona. As soon as Nelson heard of this incident he sailed for Genoa. He found the *Brune* with a dozen merchant ships alongside the outer mole and he put the *Agamemnon* across the harbour mouth to prevent their leaving. This had the desired effect: the captain of the *Brune*, fearing a more effective breach of neutrality by his adversary, warped his ship into the inner mole where port regulations obliged him to discharge his powder.

A week later the French armies, now regularly supplied by a strong fleet of their own and Spanish coasting-vessels, launched an attack all along the line. At the battle of Loano the Austrians lost 7000 in killed and wounded, and tumbled in defeat across the Apennines into Piedmont. Nelson had been disconsolate at leaving Vado, but with his squadron reduced to a skeleton he had no choice. By remaining at Genoa he had thwarted the plans of the captain of the *Brune*, kept open the Bocchetta Pass and saved de Vins and several thousand of his troops from destruction. He made one more journey westward to look at the French in possession of Vado Bay, then at the close of the year stood south for Leghorn because 'the ship, ship's company and myself are all out of repair'.

The campaign had been a failure, but for Nelson it had had compensations. He had been spared the boredom of swinging round an anchor in St Fiorenzo Bay and had been given an opportunity of operating in a wider field than he had yet experienced. 'The campaign here,' he wrote to his friend Collingwood, 'is so far pleasant as it relieves me from the inactivity of our fleet which is great indeed as you will soon see.' Further he knew that in the responsibilities of a detached command and the carrying out of delicate diplomatic negotiations he had enhanced his already growing prestige. His actions had earned the full approval not only of Mr Drake and Mr Trevor but of the Commander-in-Chief against whose orders he had acted.

During the campaign his captains had carried out his orders

with an efficiency he must have found pleasing. In an attack on Alassio in which the squadron captured or destroyed twelve French ships, he told his admiral he was indebted to every captain and officer. Among the latter was one of the *Agamemnon*'s midshipmen, young William Hoste, in whom Nelson took a particular interest and with whose father, the Rev. Dixon Hoste, he corresponded regularly. In taking out one of the enemy vessels Hoste fell down a scuttle and broke his leg. He was rowed over to the *Agamemnon* and put to bed. 'Don't you think I was very unlucky to lose the command of my vessel so soon?' he wrote to his mother, adding, 'Captain Nelson often comes down to see me and tells me to get everything I want from him'. Nelson also had a word for Fremantle, who had executed his orders 'in the most officer-like manner'.

Nelson's relations with his captains and officers were based on loyalty, trust and love. He once extravagantly said of them: 'They are my darling children,' a phrase which sums up his extraordinary sense of personal, almost paternal, responsibility. It is interesting that, on the first occasion of his commanding a detached squadron, this responsibility should have been challenged. A report had gone round the Riviera that the commanders of the squadron were conniving at the entrance of supply-vessels into French ports. This reached Lord Grenville, the Foreign Secretary, who forwarded it to Mr Drake. Drake showed the documents to Nelson, who could hardly contain himself. This was something which touched at the very roots – the honour of a sea-officer, ('The honour of an officer,' Lord St Vincent once said, 'may be compared to the chastity of a woman, and when once wounded, may never be recovered.') In a white heat of passion he wrote to Lord Grenville:

'Having received from Mr Drake a copy of your Lordship's letter to him of October, enclosing a paper highly reflecting on the honour of myself and others of His Majesty's Officers employed on this coast under my orders, it well becomes me, as far as in my power lies, to wipe away this ignominious stain on our characters.

'I do therefore in behalf of myself and much-injured

brethren demand that the person, whoever he may be, that wrote or gave that paper to your Lordship do fully and expressly bring home his charge; which as he states that this agreement is made by numbers of people on both sides, there can be no difficulty in doing. We dare him, My Lord, to the proof . . .

'Perhaps I ought to stop my letter here; but I feel too much to rest easy for a moment when the honour of the Navy and our country is struck at through us; for if nine captains whom chance has thrown together can instantly join in such a traitrous measure, it is fair to conclude we are all bad.

'As this traitrous agreement could not be carried on but by concert of all the captains, if they were on the stations allotted them, and as they could only be drawn from those stations by orders from me, I do most fully acquit all my brother captains from such a combination, and have to request that I may be considered as the only responsible person for what is done under my command, if I approve of the conduct of those under my orders, which in this most public manner I beg leave to do; for officers more alert and more anxious for the good and honour of their King and Country can scarcely ever fall to the lot of any Commanding Officer: their names I place at the bottom of this letter . . .'

* * *

On arrival at Leghorn 'to make the *Agamemnon* as fit for sea as a rotten ship can be,' Nelson immediately fell prey to the depression which usually assailed him when faced by inactivity after great exertion. The arrival at St Fiorenzo of Admiral Sir John Jervis, whom he had met once casually in the Treasury passage of the House of Commons, but whose reputation as 'a man of business' he well knew, did little to cheer him. 'Our new Admiral is at sea,' he wrote to his brother. 'I hear he is willing to keep me with him. He has wrote to me, I am sorry to say, a most flattering letter and I hear I am to be offered *St George* or *Zealous*, but in my present mind I shall take neither.

My wish is to see England once more and I want a few weeks rest, as do everyone in my ship.'

But Nelson's spirits could revive quickly when there was a chance of active service. Early in 1796, when the *Agamemnon* had been refitted, he sailed for St Fiorenzo and saw Jervis in person. The Admiral took him into his confidence, talked to him 'more as an associate than as a subordinate,' told him without reserve of his future plans and concluded by asking Nelson if, when his promotion to the flag came, he had any objection to serving under him. Nelson, to whom flattery from anyone was gratifying and from someone he respected irresistible, replied that he had none, adding to save pride that if promotion did not come he would prefer to return to England. Two days later Jervis, appreciating the importance of keeping such a valuable officer occupied, detached him with another squadron to the Gulf of Genoa 'to prevent any small number of men from making a descent upon Italy'. Captains who had been kicking their heels for months in St Fiorenzo Bay, watched his departure with envy. One said to him: 'You did just as you pleased in Lord Hood's time, the same in Admiral Hotham's and now again with Sir John Jervis: it makes no difference to you who is Commander-in-Chief'. 'To this speech,' commented Nelson, 'I returned a pretty strong answer.'

His hopes of giving practical help to 'the common cause' did not receive much encouragement. Neither the French nor Austrian armies were disposed to move while the bitter weather lasted and the snow lay thickly on the Rivierà. Deprived of active service, Nelson consulted with Mr Drake and Mr Trevor as to what he should do if the French armies, as he expected, broke into Italy in the spring. He also discussed co-operation with General Beaulieu, the new Austrian Commander-in-Chief, whom he found even more aged (he was seventy-one) and indecisive than de Vins. Nor did he neglect the care of the squadron. 'The *Blanche* is returned,' he wrote to Jervis, 'but with very few stores: not canvas enough to mend our sails – 10 lbs of twine, no tar, not a spar. We want much and I must beg you will give me your orders to purchase stores.' There was also time to think about his health. Writing to his brother from Genoa Mole with the superscription 'Deep snow. Intense cold,' he said: 'I shall not be very sorry to see England again. I am grown old and battered to pieces and require some repairs.' But to Drake he admitted: 'I hope a good opening to the campaign will set me quite to rights'.

But the campaign was disastrous. A few days before it opened Midshipman Hoste, now recovered, wrote to his mother that Nelson had been made a Commodore. 'His Broad Pendant is now flying and therefore I must beg my dear father to draw an additional cork in honour of our gallant countryman.' Even this news could not compensate Nelson for what followed. On the evening of the 10th April, Beaulieu informed Nelson he intended to attack the French at Voltri at daylight next day. Nelson sailed from Genoa during the night so as to be in a position to harass the enemy as they retreated along the sea-road. But an unauthorised skirmish started by the Austrians made the enemy fall back, and by daylight they were out of sight to the westward. Nelson was incensed at such inefficiency and wrote to Drake: 'I beg you will endeavour to impress on those about the General the necessity of punctuality in a joint operation'.

But there were to be no more joint operations that year. Like de Vins, Beaulieu was old and distrustful and proud: he had missed his opportunity and now it was the turn of the enemy to take theirs. Unknown to him or Nelson a new and terrible figure, whose name was soon to be feared throughout Europe, had slipped quietly into the Riviera to take over command of the French armies. At the beginning of March, Bonaparte, aged twenty-seven, had been at the Directory in Paris. At the end of the month he was at Nice inspiring the miserable troops he found there with the flame of his genius. 'Soldiers, you are half-starved and half-naked. The Government owes you much but can do nothing for you. Your patience and courage are honourable to you, but they procure you neither advantage nor glory. I am about to lead you into the most fertile valleys of the world: there you will find flourishing cities and teeming provinces: there you will reap honour, glory and riches.' Now he waited the opportunity to put into practice the lessons of history he had so industriously studied. Beaulieu, by his advance to Voltri and away from the centre of his own army, gave it to him. On 11 April Bonaparte struck. His first success, at Montenotte, was followed by others, at Millesimo, Dego, Ceva and Lodi. Most of the fighting took place in the mountains so that Nelson, moving restlessly about between Genoa and Leghorn 'in extraordinary weather – fogs, heavy swells and calms,' was powerless to act. Only once at Loano was he given an opportunity of retaliating when the boats of his squadron cut out four vessels lying beneath the batteries. Otherwise he watched the fighting go by him.

On the 18th May Nelson decided that co-operation with the Austrians was no longer possible and wrote to Jervis that as the service for which his Broad Pendant had been hoisted was now at an end, he was ready to strike it. Inevitably his thoughts turned again to his health. His reaction to the same situation three months earlier had been to ask permission to go home. Now he was not so sure. The admiration he felt for Jervis personally, the knowledge that Jervis had written repeatedly to the First Lord asking for his further services, the remembrance of Jervis's words: 'We cannot spare you, either as Admiral or Captain,' above all the exaltation of having a squadron under him and power to act on his own, all tempted him to remain. Moreover, he believed that under Jervis there might be a chance of a fleet action, and his heart, as he confessed later, would have broken to be absent at such a time. He adopted a compromise. 'My health,' he told Jervis, 'certainly is not bad; on the contrary I believe it is better than what medical people assert; but I believe a little rest and the baths of Pisa, the same nearly as those of Bath, would render me great benefit. If I could without any impediment to the service, take twenty days to fit me for another winter, I should not dislike it; and yet perhaps I shall do without it.' Could there have been more indecision? He knew it himself, for his letter ended: 'I do not much like what I have written'.

The day Nelson wrote this he was joined by the frigate *Comet*, newly arrived from England. Aboard her was the *Agamemnon*'s new first lieutenant, Edward Berry, another of his future captains. Berry was one of seven children, five of them girls. Their father, described as 'a respectable member of the London mercantile community,' had died young and left his widow and family badly off. Berry was fortunate in getting an education at an academy at Norwich through the influence of Lord Mulgrave, then a Lord of the Admiralty, who had once been a pupil there under the mastership of the Rev. Titus Berry, Berry's uncle. Also due to Mulgrave Berry was accepted as a volunteer into the *Burford* until the end of the American War in 1783. In 1793 he was signal midshipman of the *Duke* when she attacked the batteries of St Pierre at Martinique. William Hotham (the Admiral's nephew), who was also in the *Duke*, relates how Berry was standing on the poop 'when a shot across him deprived him of all sense and feeling so that he was carried down into the poop as dead, and intense was the surprise of those around him when he recovered the shock'. In 1794 Berry was promoted to lieutenant for gallantry in boarding, and he is also said to have distinguished himself on the Glorious First of June.

In course of time Berry's conduct came to the notice of Jervis and through him he was appointed to the *Agamemnon*. At the time of joining her he was twenty-eight. Of all of Nelson's captains he is one of the most attractive, certainly the most handsome: of slim, light build with pointed chin, fair hair and bright blue eyes; brave to the point of foolhardiness and irresistibly impulsive.

This impulsiveness, although useful in times of crisis, severely limited his judgment and he was of no great intellect. But his imagination was strong and many of his letters are a delight. He made a great impression on Nelson who wrote to Jervis soon after he joined: 'I have as far as I have seen every reason to be satisfied with him both as a gentleman and an officer. I had a few days ago a plan for taking the French Brig-of-War out of Vado and intrusted the execution of it to him: it miscarried from an unforeseen and improbable event, but I was much pleased by Mr Berry's strict attention to my instructions.' And Jervis, in forwarding the report to the Admiralty, said: 'Lieutenant Edward Berry, of whom the Commodore writes so highly, is a protégé of mine and I know him to be an officer of talents, great courage and laudable ambition'.

* * *

Nelson's disappointment at being deprived of further co-operation with the Austrian Army was partly compensated for by a successful attack on a French convoy carrying supplies for Mantua, then about to be invested by Bonaparte. The squadron took or destroyed every ship; and the booty included guns, gun-carriages, shells, 'wheelbarrow and intrenching tools,' provisions and a parcel of books. 'I have got,' Nelson told Jervis, 'the charts of Italy sent by the Directory to Bonaparte, also Maillebois's *Wars in Italy*, Vauban's *Attack and Defence of Places*, and Prince Eugène's *History*: all sent for the General.' This studying the lessons of past campaigns was one of the secrets of Napoleon's generalship. 'If Bonaparte is ignorant,' commented Nelson, 'the Directory it would appear wish to instruct him: pray God he may remain ignorant.'

The success of this action, coupled with Jervis's repeated requests to him to remain on the station, brought Nelson to a decision about his future. He admitted that when he was actively employed his health was not so bad: he would therefore postpone the trip to Pisa. Next day, 'not less anxious for having slept since my last letter,' he showed his true feelings for the first time: 'I cannot bear the thought of leaving your command'. But one thing worried him. The *Agamemnon* was capable of another three months' service but she would have to return to England before the winter: the state of the *Diadem*, the only other 64 available was not much better. If the Admiralty intended to send out his flag, he would be ready to move to whatever ship the Admiral thought proper.

Overjoyed at this news, Jervis lost no time in complying. Only five days later Nelson was telling Sir Gilbert Elliot, the Viceroy of Corsica – with whom in view of the French advance he was now regularly corresponding – that he had been ordered to transfer to the *Captain*, 74. He sailed for St Fiorenzo Bay to join her and on 11 June shifted his pendant. He took most of his old officers, including Berry and Spicer. Young Hoste was not with them, for soon after recovering from his broken leg he had succumbed to a fever, and through Nelson's kindness was being nursed at Leghorn by Mrs Pollard, wife of an English merchant.

As soon as the transfer to the *Captain* was completed Nelson sailed for Toulon, which for six weeks Jervis had been blockading with twelve sail of the line. The Admiral, whom he found 'in great spirits,' ordered him back to Genoa. On arrival he found that his exertions during the past few months 'had so completely alarmed the French that their coastal trade is at an end'. But Genoese trade had suffered too and under French pressure the Genoese government was becoming increasingly unfriendly. They served him with a long catalogue of complaints 'so ridiculous that I hardly know what to say'. Among them was an accusation that on various occasions Nelson's squadron had violated Genoese neutrality, captured Genoese vessels and ill-treated the crews. Again Nelson took up his pen to rally to the defence of his captains and in a long, angry letter to Jervis refuted all the charges. If anyone was to be censured, it was the Genoese who had consistently broken their neutrality by firing on British ships and killing and wounding the crews. 'So far from my conduct having been oppressive,' Nelson concluded, 'it has been constantly marked by a forbearance and humanity never exceeded. These facts, most truly related, will show who has real cause for complaint.'

Bonaparte meanwhile had not been wasting the time granted him by Beaulieu's need to re-equip his defeated army. Having occupied Verona at the beginning of June, he now despatched Augereau into the Papal States. These quickly surrendered and the terrified Pope agreed to deliver up 'one hundred pictures, busts, vases, statues, including the bronze bust of Junius Brutus and the marble bust of Marcus Brutus together with five hundred manuscripts'.

Another division under Vaubois crossed the Arno below Florence, then swung westwards. When Nelson heard this at Genoa Mole on 23 June, he became uneasy. As long ago as March he had written: 'The enemy possessing themselves of Leghorn cuts off all our supplies such as fresh meat, fuel and various other most essential necessaries; and of course our fleet cannot always in that case be looked for on the northern coast of Italy'. More worrying was the threat to Corsica, only a hundred miles away and the Fleet's main Mediterranean base. Without waiting for orders, he sailed from the harbour that evening. He was delayed in his passage by light winds and did not sight Leghorn lighthouse until the morning of the 25th. By this time the French were already in the town. But there was no need for regret. As he stood into the Roads he saw the sail of forty merchantmen proceeding slowly seawards under the care of the *Inconstant*. Fremantle had got there before him.

*   *   *

Nelson and Fremantle were not the only Englishmen in Italy whose destinies at this time Napoleon was deciding. There was residing in Florence a Mr Wynne, a good-natured, ineffectual Englishman who had sold his estates in Lincolnshire seven years before and taken up permanent residence on the Continent with his family. This consisted of his Catholic wife, one grown-up daughter married to an Italian, and four other daughters: Elizabeth seventeen, Eugenia sixteen, Justina eleven, and Harriet ten. Elizabeth (known to her family as Betsey) and Eugenia both kept diaries, which have been preserved by their descendants. Betsey's is the more regular (she hardly missed a day between 1789 and her death in 1857) and the more sophisticated: her comments are witty, intelligent, even (where her own heart is not concerned) a little cynical. Eugenia's attitude to life was more charitable.

On 20 June 1796, Betsey wrote: 'Nothing can be compared to the alarm in which Papa and Mamma were set on their hearing that the French were at Bologna, that they wanted Leghorn and that they searched an occasion of breaking their neutrality with the Grand Duke'. The next two days were spent in a fever of indecision, Mr Wynne giving orders to the family to pack for Leghorn one moment and cancelling them the next. Finally, and against the family's wishes, he decided to go. Betsey, who hated the idea of leaving Florence and had no wish for a sea voyage, was consoled by the British Minister's assurances that the French would by-pass Leghorn, and they would all be back in Florence in a few days. On the evening of 23 June, while Nelson was warping out of Genoa Mole, the Wynnes left for Leghorn. They travelled by coach all night and arrived at eleven the next morning. At the house of Mr Udney, the British Consul, there was 'a most terrible bustle and noise – all packing up and getting on board the ships'. The family hardly had time to swallow breakfast before being hurried down to the docks and put on board the *Inconstant*. In these new and strange surroundings Betsey soon forgot her longings for Florence. 'I found the *Inconstant* so fine, so clean and comfortable, so many civil persons, that I was quite delighted and regretted no more the French had obliged us to run away.'

Fremantle impressed her. 'How kind and amiable Captain Fremantle is,' she wrote, 'he pleases me more than any man I have yet seen.' Having once accepted the new situation, Betsey's next thought was for entertainment; 'We were very gay,' she wrote; 'the captain, though excessively busy and persecuted by everybody, took the greatest pains to amuse us. He had promised to make us dance but something came in the way that prevented it. He had Mr Udney's harpsichord come on board and we all had a little music.' Poor Fremantle's thoughtfulness did not end there: 'he did the honours so well that we all got a good Bed or Cot, while he had none'.

Early next morning Fremantle was called on to appease another demanding female. This was Lady Elliot, the wife of the Viceroy of Corsica who had arrived post-haste with her children from a holiday at Lucca. He succeeded in getting the family embarked in the *Dolphin* store-ship; but the captain was ashore and there were not enough men to weigh the anchor. Responsibility for viceroyalty induced Fremantle to send men from the *Inconstant* to move her, and order the ship to sail without the captain.

Tired and hungry he returned to the *Inconstant* for dinner. Then, said Betsey, 'most alarming news arrived which put everybody in the greatest confusion'. This was the approach of the French to the outskirts of the town. The Wynnes had to leave the *Inconstant* hurriedly and go on board a merchantman. Betsey was miserable. 'One does not easily quit a place where one received so many marks of friendship and civility – not only the Captain but every one of the officers was equally kind and amiable': and she found Captain Parish's *Achilles* 'rather small and unpleasant'.

That evening, under Fremantle's direction and assisted by Mr Udney, Mr Pollard and young Hoste, the work of evacuation went on. By midnight everything salvageable from the English factory and private houses had been put on board. At four in the morning the convoy sailed. They left none too soon, for there was little wind, and by daylight they were not clear of the port. At one o'clock the French entered the town. The *Inconstant*, last to leave, was becalmed, and firing from different quarters went on all day. 'Papa was very uneasy as he was sadly afraid of the Privateers.' His daughter was not. 'All the guns, musquets and pistols were loaded and all prepared to make a vigorous defence but we have nothing to fear and I went quietly to bed without having the least apprehension.'

The next day, wrote Betsey, the *Inconstant* proved *inconstant*, as she kept so far away they could not see her without a glass. During the night the wind got up. 'The motion in the ship was terrible. It made Mamma sick and I was very near being it myself – I did nothing but eat and drink to prevent my being so and I found that a very good remedy.' In the morning Fremantle came on board with Lord Garlies, captain of the *Lively* frigate, to say he was going to report to the Commander-in-Chief at Toulon, and if ordered to England would ask permission to take the Wynnes with him. Betsey watched his departure with mixed feelings: although hardly conscious of it, something was happening to her heart. Fremantle's suggestion was flattering and the prospect of a long sea voyage in the *Inconstant* pleasing; but even this could not compensate for his few days' absence. 'I cannot say how many marks of friendship we received from that excellent young man. He has an open, noble, fine character. I wish we would meet him again.'

For Fremantle the evacuation of Leghorn had been a personal triumph. Nelson, who remained in Leghorn Roads to prevent any English ships from entering, told Jervis: 'The exertions of Captain Fremantle must have been very great, for the Consul told me that except bad debts and the loss of furniture, nothing of any great consequence was left in the town'.

On the last day of June Nelson sailed from the port, leaving the *Blanche* to guard the roads. On arrival at St Fiorenzo Bay he found all the convoy safely at anchor. Betsey, after a stormy passage in the *Achilles*, was regaining her land legs in a walk with some of Fremantle's fellow officers, whom she found 'complaisant and good-natured, they live like brothers together and give all they have'. That evening the *Inconstant* swept into harbour from her flying visit to Toulon. For Betsey, Fremantle brought word that he had permission to carry the family to Toulon and establish them in a first-rate until a passage to England could be arranged. For Nelson he had rather different news. The *Captain* was to return to Leghorn and commence a close blockade. Corsica and British sea-power in the Mediterranean were in danger.

CHAPTER 2

Nelson did not sail immediately. He wrote to Elliot telling him of Jervis's instructions, and sent Fremantle with the letter across the peninsula road to Bastia. Betsey, disconsolate at his sudden departure, was comforted by the knowledge that he would be back next day, and had promised a ball in the *Inconstant*. She dined with Lord Garlies, whom she found to be 'rather more a man of fashion' than Fremantle. A Mr Foster, a lieutenant, was unpleasant. 'He has very free ways and I dislike him exceedingly.' Next day Fremantle arrived back from Bastia with Elliot's reply, and the ball was held in the *Inconstant* that evening. 'The deck was most elegantly dressed up and looked really like a charming large Ball-room, all the guns being removed. We had a lively gay dance. Mrs Pollard, Miss Wood and Miss Berry and me were the only ladies, the gentlemen were in vast numbers.' Lord Garlies's conduct suffered a relapse. 'He is an amiable man but not at all of an equal and steady temper. One moment he is serious, the other quite foolish and he proved to me at supper the greatest borer in the world, for he quizzed me in a most tedious manner and I never could put an end to his unpleasant jokes. It is quite the reverse with Fremantle . . .'

Next day the Wynnes transferred from the *Achilles* to the *Inconstant*. Mr Wynne gave Captain Parish £70 for his trouble, which Betsey thought too much. After dinner Fremantle received orders from the Viceroy to sail immediately. 'It seems to be something of great consequence for Captain Fremantle looked very much disappointed, busy and occupied: he was in such a hurry that he could not wait for some of his officers that were on shore and remained behind.' The Wynnes' curiosity as to their destination remained unsatisfied for Fremantle would divulge nothing. However, Betsey, whose affection for him was growing stronger every day, regarded the immediate future with indifference. 'As long as we stay on board the *Inconstant* with this excellent man, I do not care what part of the world we go to.'

The *Inconstant* weighed anchor and stood out to sea; and Betsey soon learned their destination. Sir Gilbert Elliot had decided that the French occupation of Leghorn constituted a threat not only to Corsica but to Corsica's gateway, Elba; and the island was to be occupied. 'Fremantle is Commodore,' wrote Betsey, as the *Inconstant*, having embarked troops, set course for Porto Ferrajo; 'and he is quite in a fever, as the success of this enterprise depends on him.'

Fremantle arrived at Porto Ferrajo on the morning of the

9th to find Nelson, who had since received duplicate orders from Elliot, already awaiting him. 'This,' said Betsey, 'has been a great relief to Captain Fremantle and is likewise a great increase in forces.' Nelson and Fremantle went ashore to present capitulation terms to the Governor. These, backed by the presence of the *Captain* which Berry took to within half pistol-shot of the grand bastion, were speedily accepted; and Major Duncan and the 800 troops from Bastia took formal possession of the town. It had been a swift and successful operation. Nor did the Tuscans resent the intrusion. Betsey, who went ashore in the afternoon with Fremantle, Mr French and Mr Boger, remarked: 'Satisfaction and happiness appeared in all the inhabitants' countenances, the English were welcome and received with the greatest demonstrations of joy'.

In the evening the *Inconstant* sailed to join the Fleet where, according to Jervis's promises, the Wynnes were to be transferred to a first-rate. 'I do not wish to go to the Fleet,' wrote Betsey desperately, 'I cannot bear the idea of leaving this excellent man. He looked to be likewise sorry to part from us. Why don't he keep us with him? All this is a riddle I should like to answer.' There was some consolation as the *Inconstant* headed northwards through rough seas, for Fremantle also conscious of the coming parting, showed his feelings for the first time. 'By what he says he seems to share the pain this separation gives us. He certainly is much attached to us and if I didn't think it too vain on my part to presume to have such ideas I might guess the reason.' During the next two days the confines of ship-life brought matters to a head; Betsey's entries speak for themselves:

'*Tuesday, July 12th.* It blew again very hard to-day and Mamma was seasick, the motion in the ship being great. I did not feel it at all, but though I could not complain of my health, what happened to-day filled my heart with such a mixture of pleasing and painful feelings that I found myself in a situation I never had been in before. The many proofs of kind friendship I had received from Captain Fremantle, the attention he paid to me filled me with gratitude and cause

36

me to be excessively sorry in the idea of quitting him soon and perhaps never see him again. . . . He acknowledged to M. that he was partial to me, and as his fortune at present was not sufficient for him to maintain a family, he said he could not keep us any longer with him, for he feared that the later we would part the more unfortunate he would feel the separation. I was very much astonished at all this, I do not know how it will end but I regret very much that ever we knew this man, for as he cannot stay with us it certainly is very painful for us to part in this way.

'*Wednesday, July 13th.* Most luckily for us the wind continued so unfair that we did not get to the Fleet to-day, but alas there is no doubt but we will be there to-morrow. C. F. wrote a letter to M., in which he says the same things as yesterday. How very few men would have behaved like he did. We are all very dull, even all the gentlemen of the *Inconstant* are sorry that we are going to leave the ship. They are very good honest creatures and were very kind to us. We paid them a visit to-day in the gunroom and went to see once more the ship. It is astonishing in what good order it is kept. I am sure it is not possible to attend better to Duty than C. F. does. He is active and always ready to do his business. Everybody agrees to say that his ship is one of the best kept in the Mediterranean. Indeed, he is very far advanced for his age and has reason to flatter himself that he will reach to the highest, for he is on a very good way. But, as he says, an imprudent match at present would be his ruin and make him lose the fruits of eighteen years' service and pain. What can be done? wait with patience!'

Next morning the *Inconstant* came into the Fleet. Betsey was up early and went on deck, where she found 'the poor C. F. who was still more afflicted if possible than I was. We both looked mighty stupid for we could not speak two words.' Breakfast was a grim meal, eaten in a silence broken only by the sobs of her mother and Harriet. Afterwards Fremantle went over to the *Victory* to call on the Commander-in-Chief. It had already been arranged that the Wynnes were to be transferred to the

Britannia, 100 guns, and although Fremantle had said that to introduce Captain Foley, the *Britannia*'s captain, to Betsey would break his heart, he had no option but to bring him back in the barge. When Betsey saw Foley coming into the cabin she made a 'very wry face'. Fremantle also brought news that Jervis would arrange a passage to Gibraltar as soon as Captain Cockburn arrived in the *Meleager*. That morning the family moved their baggage over to the *Britannia*. Betsey, who had never seen so large a ship, was delighted. 'It is like a castle.' The ship being built for a flag, Foley was able to offer them Admiral Parker's late quarters in the poop. Their spaciousness impressed Betsey. 'We will have there as good accommodation as we would have in any house on shore.'

The Fleet, as usual, was short of frigates, and Fremantle had orders to sail again in the evening. He dined with Foley in the *Britannia* and afterwards 'had much discourse with Mamma'. His heart was too full to say much to Betsey, but they agreed to correspond and he gave her a ring. 'We parted,' wrote Betsey 'with a broken heart.' Back in the *Inconstant*, Fremantle set down on paper what he had been unable to express in words, and sent the message over to the *Britannia* before sailing. This made Betsey 'exceedingly happy'. In the evening the *Inconstant* stood out to sea; Betsey watched her until she had dipped below the horizon, then retired to her cabin to set down in her diary her troubled thoughts: 'Now I have nothing to do but pray night and day – that his cruise may be short and that he may soon be restored to our wishes. But that is not all, for if we cannot get a fortune, the whole will be worse and worse. I trust in the Almighty, who ever recompenses the virtues, and indeed I may flatter myself that this man will be happy, for he certainly deserves it better than any other man in the world.'

* * *

Nelson remained at Porto Ferrajo to see the British garrison settled in, then stood over to Leghorn to continue the blockade. The town, lying on the edge of a long coastal plain, depended on shipping for its existence. The strength of the French garrison was not great, and Nelson hoped that, as the privations of the inhabitants increased, they would rise against the French and drive them out. The blockade was strict: no ships except local fishing boats were allowed to enter or leave. A Dane, who came out to test its efficacy, told Nelson: 'I am a neutral. You may take me but I will not return.' Nelson at once took possession, and informed the master that he would hand him over to a Corsican privateer: whereupon he begged to be allowed to return. These measures soon began to tell, and from the fishing boats which came alongside the *Captain* on their way out of harbour, Nelson learnt of the growing unrest in the town. The French were being treated with increasing contempt and their discipline was beginning to suffer. 'The other night an officer and twenty cavalry went off. We will not go to Mantua to be killed is their common talk.' From such reports, Nelson had hopes of an early rising.

Besides the blockade, there was other and more active work for the squadron. One or two ships kept in touch with Genoa where the Government, under French pressure, was becoming increasingly hostile to British interests: others were employed on the shuttle service to Toulon and Bastia, carrying the Commodore's voluminous correspondence to Jervis and Elliot. Nelson watched the movements of his captains with a father's eye, and if ever he thought they had been ill-treated or their wants not supplied he took up their cause as his own:

'If I write too much', he told Jervis, 'say so, and I will hold my pen; for myself, I feel a comfort in knowing everything on which each Vessel of my squadron is employed; and as but few of my letters require answers, I hope you do not think it gives you too much trouble to read them, occupied as I know you are with greater concerns. I would not stop the *Comet* one moment, as I was anxious she should find *Peterel* at Bastia. As to stores she is just come from Ajaccio but was absolutely refused those supplies which she stood in need of . . . I would not have every captain take what stores he pleases; but at the same time, the fair wants of a Vessel, whatever is the rank of her Commander, ought to be supplied, and the officer treated with civility. You well know, Sir, what to do,

39

to settle both sides of the question, therefore I shall say no more; the *Peterel*'s sails are rags, and none have been supplied her.'

There was also the condition of his own ship. 'The *Captain* has her wants,' he told Jervis, 'but I intend she shall last until the autumn, for I know when once we begin, our wants are innumerable.' He must have been pleased to hear that on 11 August he had been promoted full Commodore, with Captain Ralph Willett Miller as his flag-captain. He had been on the look-out for a flag-captain ever since Jervis had spoken of his promotion, and as far back as June he had told his brother of his choice. Miller, he said, was 'about thirty-five years of age: in my opinion a most exceeding good officer and worthy man'.

By birth Miller was a New Englander. He had been sent to England for his education, and at the age of fourteen committed to the care of Admiral Gambier in the *Ardent*. This ship took part in the American War, and Miller was said to have been in all the actions fought by Admirals Barrington, Rodney, Hood and Graves, and three times wounded. In 1781 he was promoted by Rodney to lieutenant. On the outbreak of the French War in 1795, he was appointed lieutenant of the *Windsor Castle* and came out to the Mediterranean. He distinguished himself at the evacuation of Toulon by remaining behind to help Sir Sidney Smith destroy the arsenal and shipping. Some of the French ships, loyal to the Royalist cause, had left the harbour before the evacuation, and later that year the *Windsor Castle* found herself near one of them, the *Scipion*, 74, in Porto Especia harbour. The captain of the *Scipion*, de Goa, was a staunch Royalist, but many of his crew were Jacobins and ready for violent measures. In a letter to his wife Miller records how the officers of the *Windsor Castle* were drinking their first glass of wine after dinner when the officer of the watch hurried down to say that smoke was issuing from the *Scipion*, and she appeared to be hailing them. 'We all rushed on deck, manned such boats as were in the water, and hoisted out the rest, and in five minutes there was not a lieutenant left in the ship but Dalby.'

But they were too late. Before the boats could reach the ship, 'such a body of fire ran up her main mast and burst out of her central ports, that all the powers of a million men with every possible assistance would have availed nothing'. The *Windsor Castle*'s boats picked up more than four hundred Frenchmen, Miller's alone saving one hundred and forty: the French captain was not among them.

In 1794 Miller was at the reduction of Calvi and Bastia where, like Fremantle, he met Nelson for the first time. Next year a rumour reached him that his name had gone forward to Hotham on a confidential list of officers not recommended for promotion; much distressed, he sent Elliot a record of his services, and asked him to intercede. Soon after Jervis arrived and it did not take his penetrating eye long to see Miller's worth. He appointed him first to the frigate *Mignonne* and then to the *Unité*, which he sent into the Adriatic to bolster up Austrian resistance. There, Jervis told the First Lord, he had answered the description given him by all the officers of character, 'and raised the minds of the people at Trieste from abject despair to perfect confidence'.

Miller's life was short and he has left few records, but he seems to have been a man of extraordinarily high principles and much charm. Nelson twice called him the only truly virtuous man he ever knew – high praise even from him, and Captain Brenton described him as 'a man of rare talents and amiable manners'. His mind was quick and imaginative, like Berry's, but unlike Berry's tempered by judgment and good sense. Any novel idea appealed to him, and he was often at work thinking out some unusual way of discomfiting the enemy. He had an aptitude for drawing and painting, and used to make sketches of the places he visited and send them to his wife.

Owing to his commitments in the Adriatic, Miller was unable to join the *Captain* immediately; but it was a relief to Nelson to know he would be on his way. The blockade of Leghorn was not being the success Nelson had hoped. 'Sometimes I hope and then despair,' he told Collingwood, 'of getting

these starved Leghornese to cut the throats of this French crew.'
What he had not appreciated was that a small number of well-
armed troops can control an unorganized mob indefinitely.
Impatient at the delay, he drew up a plan for storming the
town by sea, and sent it to Elliot for comment. Hardly had he
received Elliot's approval when a more pressing problem
arose. Rumours of a Spanish war had been filtering through to
the Mediterranean for some time: Nelson knew that if it came
about, the strength of the combined French and Spanish
Fleets would be such that Corsica might have to be abandoned,
and the British Fleet withdrawn from the Mediterranean.
Intelligence had already reached him that small parties of men
and guns were slipping across to the island daily; and now that
Elba was in British hands, the tiny island of Capraja, half-way
between Leghorn and Bastia (where Boswell had been stranded
on his visit to Paoli thirty years before), was being used by the
insurgents as an advance base.

What was Nelson to do? Should he continue with his plan
for an attack on Leghorn? Should he, as Elliot wished, attack
Capraja instead? His Commander-in-Chief answered these
questions for him. Believing the enemy might appear in
strength at any moment, Jervis ordered Nelson to shift his
broad pendant to a frigate and send the *Captain* to Toulon.
Nelson could hardly disregard this order, and yet to risk missing
a fleet action was impossible. In the absence of Miller he found
the excuse he needed: Berry's proved abilities could be forgotten.
'As there is no captain joined her,' he told Elliot, 'I think it
advisable to go in her myself.' On 26 August 1796, he gave
orders to Berry to prepare the *Captain* for sea, and set course for
Toulon.

* * *

Betsey and her family meanwhile were settling down to life
in the *Britannia*. On the day she had watched the *Inconstant* sail
away from the Fleet the last entry in her diary had concerned
her new host. 'Captain Foley behaves with the greatest kindness towards us. He is a man between thirty and forty and
seems very good-natured and gay.'

Thomas Foley was born in 1757, at Ridgeway, near Narberth, in South Wales. His father, like Fremantle's, was a country gentleman of modest means. His estate had belonged to the family since 1383: during the sixteenth century their right to it had been challenged, but a meeting of the Court of the Star Chamber at which Henry VIII had presided, upheld their claim. Many of Foley's ancestors had been serving officers: five had been killed fighting for the King at the Battle of Colby Moor, near Ridgeway, in 1648, and an uncle, another Captain Thomas Foley, had been with Anson on his voyage round the world.

Foley entered the Navy in 1770 when he was thirteen, as midshipman of the *Otter*. In 1773 he moved to the *Antelope*, flag-ship of the Admiral at Jamaica in which he saw much active service in West Indian and American waters, including a trip up the Mississippi to New Orleans. His next appointment was as lieutenant of the *America*, Captain Lord Longford, in which he took part in Keppel's famous action off Brest. Next year he transferred to the *Prince George*, 98, Admiral Digby's flag-ship on the Channel Station. One of his messmates here was another of Nelson's future captains, Richard Keats, and the two of them were responsible for the work and conduct of the young Prince William, their future king, newly joined as a midshipman. 'But for His Royal Highness's infinite good fortune in meeting such men as Foley and Keats,' wrote Byam Martin, 'his youthful spirits and propensities might not have been checked with such good judgment.' In 1780 the *Prince George* was attached to the fleet sailing for the West Indies, and Foley was present at the Battle of St Kitts and the Saints.

On the outbreak of the French War in 1793, Foley went out to the Mediterranean as flag-captain to Admiral Gell in the *St George*. He took part in Hood's pursuit of the French Fleet in June, 1794, and next year was in both of Hotham's abortive actions. In January, 1796, he shifted from the *St George* to the *Britannia*.

At the time of meeting Betsey, Foley was already a captain of some seniority. Her guess at his age was only just correct, for he was then a few months short of his fortieth birthday, or two years older than Nelson. His appearance was striking: his height (he was 6 feet 2 inches), his firm good-humoured features and his eager blue eyes all gave him authority and presence. His hair, once brown, was rapidly turning grey: in other ways he seems to have shown the weight of his years, for Betsey (who lumped everyone over the age of thirty-five into one single category 'ancient') frequently refers to him as 'the old gentleman'. His manner was bluff, and his talk rather *risqué*: also he spoke very loudly. But if he lacked social finesse, it was not wanting to him as a seaman. Jervis considered him one of his ablest captains and Midshipman George Elliot, the Viceroy of Corsica's second son, who passed 'not one unhappy day' during the five years he served with him between 1795 and 1800, said, 'We were all obedience and respect for our captain. His kindness only increased as years rolled on'.

In the admiral's quarters of his ship, the Wynne family settled down to their new life. Betsey pined for Fremantle, but as usual found it easier to adjust herself to the change than the others. 'Captain Foley keeps an excellent good table,' she wrote the day after joining; 'his ship is a little town – you get all your desires in it.' The life was 'very regular'; breakfast at eight, dinner at half past two, supper at nine and bed at ten. The officers were good-natured, but not as amiable as those in the *Inconstant*.

In the mornings the girls drew sketches of the Fleet and the hilly coastline behind, practised music on Mr Udney's harpsichord, and improved their languages. (Once they were sent for by the flag-ship to act as interpreters for some Austrian deserters whom Jervis hoped to enlist as recruits – 'all stupids and idiots,' was Betsey's comment.) During the afternoons there was a succession of callers. The girls had little idea of the stir they had caused in the Fleet, nor of the effect of their presence on men who for months had shared no company but their own. 'To have ladies on board is thought quite a rarity,' wrote Betsey innocently; 'every minute we have a new visitor and we are looked upon like curiosities.' Like bees to the hive, the captains of the Fleet clustered on board to pay their respects.

Calder and Grey, the two captains of the *Victory*, were among the first. Betsey liked Grey more than any, 'for he is a very intimate friend of C.F.'s'. Later came the fiery Troubridge and the gallant Hood of the inshore squadron, Sir Charles Knowles, the 'old bachelor' of the *Goliath* and 'a real bore', the domestic-minded Dacres of the *Barfleur*, and the ephemeral frigate captains – the teasing Garlies and the 'sprightly fashionable' Cockburn, who were in the Fleet one day and gone the next.

Many of the captains stayed to dine, and often in the evenings there was dancing on the quarter-deck. Once the Fleet ran too close to the shore, and the French batteries opened fire on the *Britannia* and *Goliath*. Midshipman Elliot wrote: 'The third shot passed through the canvas screens on each side of the deck, a few feet over the heads of the dancers, but it was not allowed to interfere with the dance – perhaps the ladies may not have been aware of what took place.' It seemed not, for Betsey makes no mention of it: all her time was taken up watching the shot falling round the *Goliath*, and keeping a weather-eye on Foley who had threatened to send her to the cockpit. On the anniversary of Robespierre's death the French ships in Toulon were dressed with flags. 'It looked indeed very pretty.' A fornight later it was the turn of the British, who expressed themselves more noisily. 'This being the Prince of Wales's birthday, it was celebrated in the evening by all the Fleet. Every ship fired eighteen guns and a vast number of musquets. We went on the poop to see the firing and were not at all frightened at the noise, but the smoak was mighty unpleasant.'

Sir John Jervis, although sending the girls 'a mighty gallant' message on their arrival, bided his time before welcoming them in person. His views on women were well known. He had been heard to say that an officer who married was damned for the Service, and he once asked the First Lord to send a captain who had plighted himself to 'a very bad party,' to the East or West Indies to consume his flame. On the day of the Wynnes' arrival Jervis issued a general memorandum admonishing the women in the Fleet on their wicked waste of water, and threatening future offenders with being shipped to England by the first convoy.

When, some time later, the *Victory* was passing close by the *Britannia*, Jervis sent word that he wished to see all the ladies in the stern gallery. He then repaired to his own, and from a decent distance surveyed them. The result must have been satisfactory, for a few days later (in a note headed 4 a.m.) he invited them to dinner.

Betsey's nervousness was dispelled as soon as she set foot in the *Victory*. 'The Admiral was on deck to receive us with the greatest civility and kindness, nothing stiff or formal about him and we were not at all embarrassed, as I feared we should be.' Jervis led the way to his cabin, which, according to one of his midshipmen, was divided into three parts: a servant's room, a dining-room and a sitting-room. 'He desired we should pay the tribute that was due to him at our entering his cabin, this was to kiss him, which the ladies did very willingly.' Lord Garlies arriving a few minutes later, 'the Admiral abused him for not having yet saluted us, the consequence was that we were kissed a second time'. The dinner-party was a large one, most of the captains being present. 'We were very gay,' wrote Betsey, 'laughed much, and made a monstrous noise at table.' She took an immediate liking to old Jervis, 'Nothing can express how kind, gallant and friendly the Admiral was to us, he is a fine old man, though past seventy[1] he is as fresh and brisk as if he was only thirty.' He told Betsey she could remain in the *Britannia* as long as she wished. To her parents he spoke highly of Fremantle, and said that he very much approved of the match. Mr Wynne complained that Fremantle had no fortune, but Jervis, without divulging where he had gone, said he might be in a good way to get one. After dinner Betsey and Eugenia sang a duet and then the party broke up, 'for as Admiral Jervis gets up at two o'clock in the morning, he goes to bed at half past eight': also there was to be a grand dance in the *Britannia*. On the way back from the *Victory* the Admiral's barge passed close by the *Courageux*, and the party stopped to

1. He was sixty-one.

46

listen to the famous band of Captain Hallowell (whom Betsey called Hallow). 'They played the charming tunes,' wrote Betsey, 'and the flutes and bugle-horns made a most delightful effect.'

The dance in the *Britannia* should have been the end of a perfect evening. Unfortunately for Betsey it brought to a head a matter which had been troubling her almost since her arrival. This was her relationship with Foley. At first his attitude towards her had been one of studied chivalry. 'The pains he takes to amuse us,' she wrote three days after joining, 'are quite surprising: he is an excellent creature.' But as the days passed Foley found his attitude towards Betsey becoming less and less disinterested. It was not surprising that a man who had not set foot ashore for six months, and then found himself in the daily company of a pretty intelligent girl of eighteen, should find her presence disturbing. At first his attentions had taken the tedious form of 'quizzing' her on her relations with the junior officers; later they became more direct. By taking charge of the conversation whenever it was heading for danger, Betsey succeeded in avoiding a collision. To her the idea of Foley as a suitor was laughable: he was still 'the best creature that ever lived,' but she could think of him only as a grandfather. Things might have continued peaceably enough if it had not been for Lord Garlies. Betsey's account of the evening speaks for itself:

'Lord Garlies was as usual remarkably merry, good-humoured and amiable. He danced with me all the evening, and though he quizzed me and tormented me all the time, I must own I found him very pleasant. At supper we had famous fun, but which finished bad and vexed me not a little. This all comes from his Lordship; he told me that the Admiral had asked him whether Captain Foley was not much attached to me, whether I was engaged to him. [1] On hearing this I screamed very loud, and said it was the most ridiculous, foolish nonsense that ever could be imagined. I should not have minded it if Captain Foley had not come to know what it was. I was then puzzled to the highest degree, and indeed the old man was not a little embarrassed.

1. This was an untruth in view of Jervis's remarks to Betsey at dinner.

47

Lord Garlies told me *en confidence* many other things concerning Captain Fremantle, and finished by saying to take care of him for he was a cunning, well-speaking fellow, etc. This I must own I did not at all like from his Lordship. If he was in Joke it was a very stupid one, if serious it would give me a bad opinion of Lord Garlies. With all the nonsense we set late at supper. At last Lord Garlies went away; he is going back to Bandol. I long for the arrival of the *Meleager*; since this Joke with Captain Foley I am impatient to leave the *Britannia*. Mamma and myself had guessed this long ago, but now that it has been said out, though laughing, it has quite made me angry. How can such ideas come into that old Gentleman's head, especially since he must know all that has passed on board the *Inconstant*.'

The next day, 'I looked mighty stupid, and Captain Foley seemed likewise to be embarrassed. I wish Lord Garlies had held his tongue.' There were no more complaints during the next few days and it seemed as though Foley, having learnt where he stood, had decided to let things be. A week later Jervis, convinced of the certainty of a Spanish war, sent word it would now be impossible for the Wynnes to go to Gibraltar, but he could arrange a passage to Naples instead. Mr Wynne agreed, and plans were made for the family to go there in the *Barfleur*, Captain Dacres. When all the luggage had been placed on board and good-byes made to the *Britannia*'s officers, Foley, desperate at the thought of losing Betsey, privately interceded with Jervis to allow the family to remain. The result was a note from Jervis to the second captain of the Fleet: 'The Amiables may remain on board the *Britannia*. All that had been said of their leaving the Fleet is to be buried in oblivion'.

Betsey was furious. 'I should like it very well if it was not the reason that makes us stay which displeases me to the highest degree. I have friendship for that man, but it does not flatter me in the least that he should pay more attention to me than any of the rest of the family.' Things went from bad to worse. Betsey's shallow parent impressed on her that he recognized no arrangement with Fremantle, and made it plain he considered

Foley a more suitable match. Encouraged by this unexpected support, Foley ventured more boldly into the open. It was a foolish move, and brought down on him all Betsey's pent-up wrath. 'I really do not know how to behave towards this old fool. I find his jokes insupportable. I avoid speaking to him as much as I can.' In spite of deliberate snubs he persisted in his attentions, and poor Betsey, thinking only of Fremantle, grew daily more desperate. 'I wish,' she wrote, 'I had never, *never* come on board the *Britannia*. It would have spared me many painful and unpleasant things. What is to be done? What will happen? God knows. C. Fremantle's answer will decide the whole thing. If he says, as it in reality is, that his circumstances do not permit him to think of a match at present, then this *unwelcome gallant* will doubtless offer himself. I am resolved not to have him.' Not even the arrival of Rear-Admiral Man's reinforcing squadron and a meeting with Fremantle's brother-in-law, Captain Wells of the *Defence*, nor the certainty of the Spanish war and its promise of prize-money, could cheer her spirits. Her continued hostility at last began to affect Foley. 'He is very ill-humoured,' she wrote with triumph. 'I believe he is sorry to find out that I am partial to an absent person. Of this I want to persuade him that he may bury his own schemes in oblivion.'

Such was the unhappy state of affairs in the *Britannia* when Nelson and Berry sailed into the Fleet in the *Captain*.

CHAPTER 3

Nelson stayed in the Fleet only one night. Another crisis had arisen elsewhere, and again his services were wanted to deal with it. The Genoese had issued an order closing their harbours to British shipping, and had confiscated a number of bullocks, already paid for, which were awaiting shipment to the Fleet. Nelson sailed to Genoa to get a revocation of the order and a permit of clearance for the bullocks. Despite lengthy negotiations, which included a memorial to the Senáte and an audience with the Doge ('he was very curious about me: he asked me my age'), he got no satisfaction on either score; and when a French supply-ship fired on his boats and in retaliation he sent a party to take it, the Genoese forts opened up on him. Frustrated, he returned to Leghorn; but this open hostility gave Elliot the excuse he wanted for ordering Nelson to seize Capraja (a Genoese possession) and putting an end to its use as an arms base.

Having seen a military garrison established in the island, Nelson left to Leghorn to resume the blockade. He did not stay long. On 19 August France and Spain signed a mutual treaty of offence and defence; and the British Government, having taken this and the sweeping victories of Napoleon along the northern Mediterranean seaboard into account, regretfully decided that 'the blessings of the British Crown' must be withdrawn from Corsica, and the British Fleet sent down the Mediterranean. Porto Ferrajo alone was to be retained as a garrison for arms and supplies. Nelson received the news with bitter disappointment. It was, he told his wife, a measure which he could not approve. 'They at home do not know what this fleet is capable of performing: anything and everything. Much as I shall rejoice to see England I lament our present orders in sackclothes and ashes, so dishonourable to the dignity of England whose fleets are equal to meet the World in Arms: and of all the fleets I ever saw, I never beheld one in point of officers and men equal to Sir John Jervis's, who is a Commander-in-Chief able to lead them to glory.' Nor was his bitterness relieved by an order from Jervis to leave Cockburn in command at Leghorn, and proceed to the island at whose taking he had sacrificed his right eye, to superintend the evacuation personally.

It was fortunate that the evacuation was ordered when it was. News of the Franco-Spanish Alliance had already reached Corsica, and the Corsicans, believing the island would soon be restored to the French, were anxious to avoid charges of collaboration. As soon as Elliot gave out news of the evacuation, the Municipality of Bastia seized the government from his hands and delegated it to a Committee of Thirty. Then a gale sprang up, and the warships and transports in the harbour were driven from their anchors. Encouraged by this confusion, the Corsicans insisted on mounting equal guard in the citadel, and then, growing bolder still, began impounding British property. At this juncture Nelson arrived. He sent an officer ashore to tell the Committee of Thirty that unless they allowed the evacuation to proceed he would batter down the town with his guns. This soon restored order and during the next five days more than £200,000 worth of British property was safely embarked in the ships.

The work was completed not a moment too soon. Late on 18 October a large body of French landed near Cape Corse and began marching towards the capital. Nelson continued the evacuation until the evening of the 19th, by which time everything of value had been embarked. At midnight the British garrison marched out of the citadel: at 1 a.m. the French marched into it. In the early morning Nelson and General de Burgh, the Army commander pushed off for the *Captain* in the last boat from shore: Elliot, fearing assassination, had embarked the previous evening. Before nightfall the convoy was safely in Porto Ferrajo.

A few days later Nelson sailed for St Fiorenzo Bay where, in view of the changed situation, Jervis had recently brought the Fleet. Troubridge in the *Culloden* had been left to keep watch at Toulon: otherwise the French roadstead was empty.

*   *   *

Since Nelson's visit to the Fleet two months earlier Betsey had grown more and more miserable. In spite of every discouragement Foley had persisted in his attentions and, when thwarted, indulged in petty retaliations such as forbidding Betsey to dine in the wardroom. Her parents too had clearly shown on whose side they stood. 'Mamma says that I am not in the least engaged to Fremantle and that the matter is far from settled. Papa forgets his promise and says he will not go home in the

Inconstant, for as he would never give his consent to the marriage, it would be imprudent to be again some time together.' Her only consolation lay 'in the happiness I shall enjoy when I see Fremantle again, when I shall be compensated for all I suffer now'. Before the Fleet left Toulon, Jervis confided to her that Fremantle had gone to fetch the trade from Smyrna, but was expected back within a week or ten days. From this moment Betsey lived in expectation. 'Every time I hear a strange boat is in sight I feel my heart beat with double force.' Once a ship was sighted, which everyone in the *Britannia* swore must be the *Inconstant*. On closer inspection it turned out to be the *Sardine*. 'A most cruel pain seized my heart. I blushed and turned pale; it was at table and did not pass unnoticed.'

Betsey was not the only person anxiously waiting for a sail. Jervis was in a precarious situation. Spain had declared war on England early in October, and a Spanish fleet of twenty-six sail of the line, under Don Juan de Langara, had passed into the Mediterranean and recently been sighted off Cape Corse. Jervis's fleet consisted of only fifteen sail of the line but every day he expected the return of Admiral Man's squadron which he had sent to Gibraltar to reprovision. The latest orders from home had urged him to keep open Porto Ferrajo, and remain in the Mediterranean as long as possible. If Man arrived soon, with his seven sail of the line and extra provisions, he might challenge the Spanish Fleet to action.

But Man never came. Instead he behaved in a manner which astonished the whole Navy. On his passage down to Gibraltar he fell in with de Langara's fleet entering the Mediterranean, and in a brief skirmish lost a brig and a transport. He revictualled the squadron at Gibraltar, and then proceeded to cruise off Cape St Vincent. On 10 October he received instructions from Jervis to rejoin immediately. Despite this and knowledge of de Langara's entry into the Mediterranean, Man calmly called a council of war of his captains to decide on a plan of action. Several of the captains wishing to return to England, this motion was put to the vote and carried. What justification was claimed for it is not recorded. The squadron continued cruising off St Vincent for some time, then sailed for Spithead where they arrived at the end of December. Man was ordered to strike his flag and come on shore; and he was never employed again.

The French and Corsicans having made St Fiorenzo Bay untenable, Jervis moved his fleet into the outer anchorage of Mortella Bay. Here he hung on until the end of October, when he heard that de Langara had taken his ships into Toulon thus making the strength of the combined fleet thirty-eight sail of the line, 'the largest fleet of men-of-war ever seen in that port.' Then, certain that some accident had happened to Man, and with his crews victualled at two-thirds allowance he gave orders for his fleet and the transports to begin the long journey down the Mediterranean. This was one of the most shameful moments in the history of the British Navy and, as Jervis and his captains knew, one which need never have arisen. During the three years it had been in the Mediterranean the Fleet had sacrificed much and effected little. What it needed was an immediate and decisive victory; and Jervis and Nelson, who between them had brought it to a state of unparalleled fighting efficiency, knew that despite the odds in numbers such a victory was possible. The withdrawal of the Fleet meant the loss not only of Corsica but of Italy, and with it Napoleon's mastery of the Mediterranean.

On this scene of gloom appeared two small rays of light. During the last days of October, when the First Lord of the Admiralty, Lord Spencer, was writing to Jervis from Whitehall that 'Captain Fremantle's spirited and active conduct on all occasions has made me very desirous of his acquaintance and of shewing him every possible mark of attention,' the young frigate-captain sailed into the Fleet with the trade from Smyrna, and on board the *Britannia* was united again with Betsey.

Betsey's diary for the last quarter of 1796 has been lost, so it is only possible to conjecture the happiness of the meeting. It seems to have been complete in every way; and the pair so succeeded in convincing Betsey's parents of their love that, when Fremantle was ordered to remain behind with the garrison at Porto Ferrajo, it was arranged the family should go with him. The other happy event was also a reunion, also on board the *Britannia*. For the first time for many months Gilbert Elliot met and talked again with his son George: he found him well, he told his wife, and a great favourite with everybody.

But there was one person in the *Britannia* who was experiencing not reunion but the pangs of parting. As the great three-decker obeyed the Admiral's signal to proceed to sea, and took up her station in the line, a large and lonely figure paced her quarter-deck. For him the sun had lost its warmth and the sea its colour: and the empty cabins below still rang with the clamour of familiar voices. As his ship lumbered out to sea, past the ruins of the great Martello Tower which Sam Hood of the *Zealous* had blown up a few days before, then past where the *Inconstant* swung lazily at anchor, one wonders what were Foley's thoughts.

*   *   *

After a long and difficult passage Jervis and his fleet anchored in Gibraltar Bay on 1 December, and for the first time in generations there was not an English ship of the line on the face of the Mediterranean. On the same day Villeneuve and de Langara put to sea from Toulon. On the 6th de Langara with his twenty-six sail of the line and twelve frigates entered Cartagena. Villeneuve, unaware that Jervis had reached Gibraltar, had orders to push through the Straits with five sail of the line and three frigates, and proceed to Brest. When he arrived in the Straits a hurricane was blowing from the eastwards. The force of this wind carried his squadron rapidly through. From the Rock Jervis saw them go by, but was powerless to act: the gale not only made pursuit impossible, but was driving his own ships towards the rocks. Not all escaped; and Ben Hallowell's ship, the *Courageux*, met disaster.

Hallowell has already been introduced into this story, first when Fremantle towed the *Courageux* to Leghorn after the first of Hotham's two actions, and more recently when Betsey stopped to listen to his band. He was a Canadian, his father having been the last Commissioner of the American Board of Customs. Like most of his contemporaries he entered the Navy young, and took part in the Battle of the Saints as a lieutenant in the *Alfred*. From the outbreak of the French War he was continually in the Mediterranean, first in the *Robust* at the evacuation of Toulon, and later in temporary command of the *Courageux*. In 1794 he served ashore at Calvi in Corsica, and took twenty-four-hour turns with Nelson in command of the advanced batteries. 'Hallowell,' said Nelson 'is as good and active as ever,' and on another occasion he spoke of his 'indefatigable zeal, activity and ability'. On the fall of Corsica Hallowell was given command of the frigate *Lowestoffe* when her captain was sent to England with Hood's despatches; but on applying to Hood for a ship of the line he was again posted to the *Courageux*. He served with the main body of the Fleet all through 1795, and when Jervis began his long watch off Toulon in January, 1796, joined the inshore squadron with Troubridge and Sam Hood. In his reports to the Admiralty Jervis frequently mentioned the appalling state of the *Courageux*'s copper; 'but', he added, 'it would break Ben Hallowell's heart to go home'.

Hallowell is said to have been a man 'of gigantic frame and vast personal strength'. His features, as one biographer has pointed out, resemble those of a prize-fighter: but behind a tough expression lay much kindliness and humour. His contemporaries speak of his bravery and skill, but they chiefly remembered him for his generosity and thoughtfulness. Lady Shelley, whom he met in later years, called him 'a thorough sailor and a most intelligent, blunt and entertaining being'.

On the afternoon of 10 December, while Villeneuve was scudding through the Straits, Hallowell was ashore at a court martial. Hearing the *Courageux* was in difficulties, he asked the President of the Court, Vice-Admiral Thompson (who had just moved into the Wynnes' quarters in the *Britannia*), permission to return to his ship. Because of the weather he was refused. His ship meanwhile had parted from her anchors and was being driven rapidly across the Bay. She succeeded in pulling up clear of the Spanish batteries, and Lieutenant Burrows, the first lieutenant, decided to stand over to the Barbary Coast under close-reefed topsails until daylight. At about eight in the evening, 'the night being very dark, the wind blowing a hurricane, and much thunder and lightning,' officers and men, who had not eaten since daylight, went below for refreshment. By some mishap a Lieutenant Ainslie, who had never held a watch before, was left in charge on deck. The rest of the melancholy tale is described in Jervis's report to the Admiralty. 'A little before nine the land was seen ahead and Mr Ainslie, instead of putting the helm-a-weather and easing the mainsheet, sent down to the first lieutenant and master to acquaint them of the danger. Mr Burrows, who, though an experienced officer, was a nervous man, burst into hysterics while the master made every effort to wear the ship, but it was too late, for the bowsprit struck against the precipice and the ship going bump ashore, swung alongside it; her foremast went overboard, and she divided into two parts very soon.' This precipice was the almost sheer Apes Hill on the Barbary Coast. The *Courageux* was a total wreck: out of a ship's company of 593, only 129 were saved.

This was not the only accident to the Fleet. The *Gibraltar*, Captain John Pakenham, and the *Culloden*, Troubridge's ship, were also driven ashore, the *Gibraltar* damaging herself seriously, and a few days later the *Zealous*, Captain Sam Hood, struck a rock in Tangier Bay.

About this time Jervis received orders from home for the evacuation of Elba, and he appointed Nelson to supervise it. With the Fleet reduced to eleven sail of the line there could be no question of sparing the *Captain*, and he ordered Nelson to shift his broad pendant to the *Minerve* frigate, Captain Cockburn. At the same time Captain Miller, having returned in the *Unité* from the Adriatic, took command of the *Captain*. Nelson's instructions were to sail with the *Blanche* frigate to Porto Ferrajo, and evacuate the naval and military garrisons and their equipment and stores. 'I am going,' he told his wife, 'on a most Important Mission which with God's blessing I have little doubt of accomplishing.'

On 15 December 1796, he weighed anchor, and with the *Blanche* sailed eastwards into familiar waters. The next day, in view of reports of French and Spanish designs on Portugal, Jervis took his ships through the Straits to the Tagus. By that evening there was not a ship of the line left in Gibraltar Bay.

* * *

On board the *Minerve* Nelson was meeting for the first time an officer whose name was to go down with his into history – Lieutenant Thomas Masterman Hardy.

Hardy's ancestors were Channel Islanders, originally le Hardi, who in the fifteenth century had migrated to Dorset. Hardy was born in 1769 in Kingston Russell House, a bleak building with an imposing classical façade, once a seat of the Dukes of Bedford. His father was a small country landowner and he had six sisters and two brothers. Later the family moved to the nearby village of Portisham, which Hardy always called 'Possum.' For his education his father sent him and his brothers over the Somerset border to Crewkerne Grammar School; the curriculum included taking part in cock-fighting under the supervision of the masters. In 1781, at the age of twelve, 'having expressed a determination to go to sea almost as soon as he could speak,' Hardy entered the Navy as captain's servant of the brig *Helena*. Soon he was writing to say that his dog Bounce was well, and that Captain Roberts had promised to send him home 'to learn navigation and everything that is proper'. Captain Roberts, writing at the same time, said: 'Am glad to inform you that Thomas is a very good boy and I think will make a complete seaman one day or other'. He next joined the *Carnatic*, as captain's servant, then the *Hebe* frigate as midshipman. In 1795 he went out to the Mediterranean as midshipman of the *Amphitrite* frigate, and was present at the operations before Toulon. At the end of the year he was promoted to lieutenant, and joined the *Meleager*, Captain Cockburn. He was present at both of Hotham's actions and took part in the operations of Nelson's squadron in the Gulf of

57

Genoa. In the autumn of 1796, when Cockburn was appointed to the *Minerve*, he took Hardy with him.

At the time Hardy was twenty-seven years old. He could hardly have been more different to Nelson, in appearance and temperament. Nelson was small, wiry, almost fragile, but Hardy, like Hallowell, was a tall, weighty man, with heavy features and broad shoulders. In character, Nelson was passionate and fretful, Hardy ponderous and placid; and it was Hardy's serenity in later years that Nelson was to find so soothing. Hardy had little imagination: his conversation was of the bluntest, and his letters, where they are not illiterate, are mostly of a deadly dullness. 'The desk,' said Hotham feelingly, 'was not his *forte*.' But Hardy had something else. Sir William Parker called it 'the very soul of truth,' but Codrington was probably nearer the mark when he said 'Hardy has not beauty, but he is very superior'.

Hardy did not have to wait long before distinguishing himself. Late on the night of 19 December, abreast of Cartagena, the *Minerve* and *Blanche* fell in with two Spanish frigates. Nelson directed Cockburn to attack the one carrying a poop-light. A fierce action began, and continued for three hours, when the enemy struck. She was the *Santa Sabina* of forty guns, commanded by Don Jacobo Stuart, a great-grandson of James II of England. The losses in the *Minerve* were negligible, but more than half the Spanish crew of 286 were killed or wounded. The Spanish captain came on board the *Minerve* to present his sword, and lieutenants Culverhouse and Hardy, with forty men, were put into the *Sabina* as prize-crew. About four in the morning another Spanish frigate came up, which the *Minerve* engaged for about half an hour, when the Spaniard sheered away. It was then seen that two Spanish line-of-battle ships were in pursuit, and Nelson had no choice but leave the *Sabina* to her fate and run for it; the *Blanche*, to which the other Spanish frigate, the *Ceres*, had surrendered, was also obliged to fly. Culverhouse and Hardy, in the wrecked *Sabina*, diverted the attention of one battleship by hoisting English colours over the Spanish ones and steering to the southward: the other battleship and the two frigates continued chasing the *Minerve* and *Blanche* till dark. It was, as Nelson told Jervis, an 'unpleasant tale,' for instead of taking two new Spanish frigates, he had to report the capture of two gallant officers and forty badly needed men.

Nelson also wrote to the Captain-General of Cartagena.
'Sir,

The fortune of war put *La Sabina* into my possession, after she had been most gallantly defended: the fickle dame returned her to you, with some of my officers and men in her.

I have endeavoured to make the captivity of Don Jacobo Stuart, her brave Commander, as light as possible; and I trust to the generosity of your nation for its being reciprocal for the British officers and men.

I consent, Sir, that Don Jacobo may be exchanged and at full liberty to serve his King when Lieutenants Culverhouse and Hardy are delivered into the garrison of Gibraltar.'

This was written on Christmas Eve, 1796. On Christmas Day Eugenia Wynne, in her room overlooking the harbour of Porto Ferrajo, wrote in her diary: 'While we were at dinner Fremantle sent to tell us that the *Minerve* was come in with Commodore Nelson, who was going to take the command of the place'.

*   *   *

On Christmas Day there was a ball given by General de Burgh, the Army Commander, and on Boxing Day Nelson got down to the business of evacuation. From Fremantle he learnt that Sir Gilbert Elliot was touring the Italian States but would be back in Naples by the New Year. He decided to send the *Inconstant* to fetch him. 'Fremantle sails on Thursday morning,' he wrote to Elliot, 'he shall stay forty-eight hours at Naples: this is the full stretch I can allow him, and I trust you will find it sufficient; if not I will send something else for you, but I feel I have nothing so pleasant.' There remained the question of the Wynnes: now that the garrison was to be evacuated they could not stay on in Elba. Nelson advised them to go to Naples in the *Inconstant,* and after some deliberation Mr Wynne agreed.

Eugenia's feelings at being in the *Inconstant* again were mixed. The ship was full of happy memories for her and Betsey, but the day was not far off when she must leave it for ever. She dreaded Naples, which would be 'adieu to all that is English and to all those we have known in the Navy to whom we owe sentiments of everlasting regard and friendship.' The passage to Naples was very slow, and the girls passed the time exploring the ship. 'When the people were at quarters,' wrote Eugenia, 'I saw the light-room, a place very deep under water where the candles which are to light the magazines are kept. It is very narrow, lined with tin, and the candles are kept within a sort of tin grate with so many precautions you should think it impossible that ever a ship could be blown up, and yet it frequently happens. The descent to the magazines being too difficult for us damsels, we could not see it.'

Eugenia also plucked up courage to sound Fremantle on his feelings for Betsey. He told her his love was as strong as ever, but he was no richer than when he had first met her, nor had any prospect of becoming so. In view of Mr Wynne's fearsome declarations he had not dared risk asking for Betsey's hand, and had almost begun wondering whether to give up the idea of marrying her.

Yet matters between the young couple were moving to a head. Fremantle's orders were to stay at Naples only long enough to embark Elliot, and then return to Elba; and there was no question of the Wynnes returning with him. If he did not make an effort to win Betsey now, she might be lost to him for ever.

The day after they arrived there was an expedition to the grottoes at Posilipo. Fremantle, totally unconscious of his surroundings, spent the day working up the courage to tackle Mr Wynne. He was, both sisters agreed in their diaries, 'quite stupid'. After dinner, in the Hotel Grand Britannia, he firmly announced to Betsey that he would speak to her father in the morning. He landed early the next day, bringing Mr French the surgeon to bolster him up, and they began walking towards the hotel. At the last moment his nerve failed him. The man who could cheerfully take the little *Inconstant* under the guns of the great *Ça Ira* and harry her into surrender, could not bring himself to ask a muddle-headed, middle-aged Englishman for his daughter's hand. He produced from his pocket a letter (which he had prepared for this emergency), and asked Mr French to hand it to Mr Wynne. Betsey and Eugenia were in the room when their father received it. He read it but said nothing. He continued to say nothing all day so that Betsey concluded he had refused. She waited anxiously for Fremantle's return in the evening. Her father, who she knew had written a reply, 'was serious and silent'. Very late in the evening Fremantle arrived. 'My surprise and happiness were beyond expression,' said Betsey, 'at hearing Papa had given a very favourable answer.'

The next two days were spent in a flurry of preparations. Fremantle, his courage restored, had a long talk with Mr Wynne who, according to Eugenia, 'behaved very handsomely in granting him and my sister 8,000 pounds'. Then Sir William Hamilton, the British Minister, and his wife called and insisted that the wedding should take place in the Embassy the next day. The famous Emma made an instant impression on both girls. Eugenia called her beautiful and amiable. 'She showed the greatest interest to us all, she is a charming woman.' More than her beauty she admired her attention towards her husband. 'Sir William is passed seventy, she is four or five and twenty, in the bloom of youth and beauty, full of talents, graces and accomplishments, and yet her gratitude towards her husband is so great that she is always employed in making him happy.' Betsey was as full of praises. 'It is not possible to express the many civilities she has shown us. There never was a woman more affable, civil and amiable.' On the eve of her wedding Betsey wrote in her diary: 'For the last time I shall write as Miss Wynne. What a day tomorrow is. I dread it.'

Shortly after one o'clock Betsey and Eugenia, dressed in white crêpe, drove from their hotel to the Palazzo Sessa, the British Embassy. There they found the Hamiltons, Prince

Augustus of the Royal House of Naples, who was to give Betsey away; Sir Gilbert Elliot and his aide-de-camp, Colonel Drinkwater; Mr Lambton, 'one of the richest private gentlemen of England',[1] and Mr Lambton's chaplain, who was to marry them. 'The ceremony was soon performed,' says Eugenia, 'it was awful, and was gone through in great style,' Betsey was briefer still. 'What I felt was not to be described.'

Two days later the *Inconstant*, with Mrs Fremantle on board, warped out of the harbour and set sail for Elba. She was in sight of Naples the next morning, but Eugenia at her window in the town 'would not see her'. Soon Naples and its hills became a purple smudge astern. In the open sea the ship ran into heavy weather. Sir Gilbert Elliot was seasick, but Betsey, by now a thorough sailor, felt only an increase in appetite.

After an uncomfortable passage of seven days they arrived at Porto Ferrajo. Elliot went ashore to discuss the evacuation with Nelson and de Burgh. De Burgh was against it, saying he could do nothing without military orders. Elliot supported him, but Nelson, for the Navy, was adamant. 'My instructions,' he told de Burgh, 'both verbal and written, are so clear it is impossible to mistake a tittle of them.' Whatever de Burgh might decide for the Army, he intended to evacuate the naval garrison.

Betsey, meanwhile, was accustoming herself to her new life. The social side was quite strenuous. There were numerous dinner-parties to attend, including several on board the *Inconstant* at which she had to act as hostess. One evening she entertained 'a noisy party' consisting of Nelson, Cockburn, the Commissioner and Captain Hope. 'Old Nelson very civil and good-natured,' she remarked, 'but does not say much.' On other evenings Fremantle went off on bachelor parties of his own. One night he dined in the *Minerve*, for a drinking party. 'He assured me when he returned on board at nine that he was tipsy, but I found him perfectly sober; even had he been tipsy he behaved so kind and good-humoured to me and begged I

1. He died at Pisa later that year, leaving a five-year-old son who became the first Earl of Durham and the founder of modern Canada.

should forgive him with so much good grace that it could not have given me the least uneasiness.' Another evening there was 'a rioting-party' of captains, led by Cockburn and Colonel Drinkwater. Then it was the turn of the ship's company, 'who got very drunk and behaved horridly ill.' It was this 'horridly ill' which marked the dividing line between their drinking bouts and the captains'; and the inevitable floggings followed. From the little cabin which Fremantle had had built for her, Betsey missed nothing. 'I could distinctly hear the poor wretches cry out for mercy. A man broke his leg.' A few days later she was an unwilling spectator of a flogging round the Fleet. This, she admitted, made Fremantle ill.

A week after the *Inconstant*'s return, Nelson had completed the naval side of the evacuation. De Burgh confirmed his decision to stay on with the troops, and Nelson decided to leave the *Inconstant* to assist them, an arrangement that suited Betsey and Fremantle admirably. Two convoys of transports, under the *Dido* and *Southampton*, were to steer separate courses for Gibraltar, so that if the enemy's fleet were at sea a part might escape. The *Minerve* and *Romulus* would sail to Gibraltar, looking in at Toulon and Cartagena on the way.

On the morning of 29 January 1797, both parties sailed. Nelson and Hope remained with the convoy until evening, then parted company. They looked in at Toulon where everything seemed normal, then sailed to Cartagena, where to Nelson's horror they found the Spanish Fleet had sailed. At Gibraltar, which they reached on 9 February, they learnt that twenty-seven Spanish sail of the line and twelve frigates had passed through the Gut four days before. The Spaniards had detached two sail of the line into Gibraltar Bay to supply their lines there, and in one of them, the *Terrible*, were Culverhouse and Hardy. Nelson stayed at Gibraltar only long enough to welcome them back, and make his respects to the Governor before sailing westward. The great moment for which he had waited so long – a fleet action – was, he believed, close at hand, and he dared not delay a minute.

He had intended to leave Gibraltar on the 10th, but the

wind was foul and he was not able to weigh till the morning of the 11th. When clear of the Bay it was seen that both Spanish ships of the line were in pursuit and that one, the *Terrible*, was gaining. About this time the officers went down to dinner. Colonel Drinkwater found himself next to Hardy, and was congratulating him on his release from captivity when there was a cry of 'Man overboard.' Hardy was on deck in a flash, and threw himself into the jolly-boat which was already being lowered. The falls were cast off, and there being a strong current, the boat was soon far astern. In a little while Hardy signalled that they could not find the man, and the jolly-boat began pulling towards the ship. Against the current they made little progress. The *Terrible* was now gaining fast, and Nelson saw that before long she would reach the jolly-boat. 'By God I'll not lose Hardy,' he shouted, 'back the mizen-topsail.' The sail was backed, and the wind filling it, the *Minerve* drifted rapidly down on the boat. The captain of the *Terrible*, suspecting some trickery, also shortened sail and waited for his consort to join him. This saved the *Minerve* from almost certain destruction. The jolly-boat was soon alongside and hoisted inboard: then to the astonishment of the *Terrible*, the *Minerve* began to draw away. 'In a short time,' wrote Colonel Drinkwater, 'we had the satisfaction to observe that the dastardly Don was left far in our wake; and at sunset, by steering further to the southward we lost sight of him and his consort altogether.'

Danger was not quite over yet. That night the *Minerve* found herself in a fog, surrounded by tall shapes. It was the Spanish Fleet labouring towards Cadiz. Cockburn skilfully threaded his way through them, unobserved by the sleeping look-outs, and by daylight they were all out of sight astern.

On the afternoon of 13 February Nelson found Jervis and fifteen sail of the line cruising off Cape St Vincent. He and Elliot waited on the Admiral, and gave news of the enemy fleet. Then Elliot transferred to the *Lively* under sailing orders for England, and Nelson, after an absence of nearly two months, returned to the *Captain*. A new captain and first lieutenant were waiting to welcome him. Miller was standing on the quarter-deck, and beside him, to Nelson's surprise, was young Spicer. He looked round, and to his delight saw Berry standing slightly apart from the rest, wearing the uniform of commander. During his absence, and as a result of Jervis's repeated recommendations Berry had been promoted; now, while waiting for a new appointment, he had been granted the status of 'passenger'.

As day ended the wind shifted to the westward: soon, borne down upon it, came the sounds for which Jervis and his officers had been listening – the minute-guns of the Spanish Fleet. Late that night, the eve of St Valentine's Day, 1797, and the day on which the retreat of the British Fleet from the Mediterranean was completed, Jervis threw out a signal: 'Prepare for battle'.

PART II

The Elite of the Navy
of England

CHAPTER 4

The ill-luck which had befallen Jervis's fleet at Gibraltar had
continued during Nelson's absence, to follow it. Entering the
Tagus on 21 December the *Bombay Castle*, Captain Sotheby,
struck hard on a sandbank at the mouth of the river, and after
several fruitless attempts to move her, had to be abandoned.
The rest of the fleet proceeded up river to Lisbon where they
spent a festive Christmas and New Year. 'Received on Board a
Present from the Queen of Portugal to the Ship's Company,'
reads the log of the *Britannia*. 'Eight Oxen, Sheep, Fowls,
Hogs, Oranges etc, with 3 Pipes of Wine.' Over this scene of
rejoicing loomed the grim figure of Jervis. No boat was to be
sent ashore unnecessarily, 'to prevent quarrels with the
Portugese which always leads to assassination': a post-captain
accompanied by a boatswain's mate with a length of rope, was
to visit the hospital daily 'to see that the patients conduct
themselves properly and orderly,' and, if not, 'to punish them
agreeably to the rules of the Navy'. On their way down river in
the New Year to escort the Portugese trade to the westwards,
the fleet met with another disaster. The *St George*, Captain
Shuldham Peard, a first-rate of 98 guns, ran foul of a Portugese
frigate and swung on to the South Cachops. She was refloated
two days later, but had to return to Lisbon for repairs.

Jervis's fleet was now reduced to ten sail of the line. They were the *Victory*, Captains Calder and Grey; *Britannia*, Captain Foley; *Barfleur*, Captain Dacres; *Blenheim*, Captain Frederick; *Captain*, Captain Miller; *Goliath*, Captain Sir Charles Knowles Bart; *Excellent*, Captain Collingwood; *Egmont*, Captain Sutton; *Culloden*, Captain Troubridge; and *Diadem*, Captain Towry. Hallowell was serving as a supernumerary in the *Victory*, where Jervis had appointed him temporarily, and Captain Hood was in the *Tagus*, repairing the *Zealous*. With these ships Jervis saw the Brazilian convoy into the Atlantic, then sailed to his cruising station off Cape St Vincent. On 6 February, he sighted a reinforcement of five sail of the line sent out from England as a result of Man's return. He was glad of their support, but knowing how much depended on individual captains, wondered uneasily who they were. They turned out to be old friends: Rear-Admiral Parker and Captain Irwin in the *Prince George*, Captain Whitshed in the *Namur*, Captain Martin in the *Irresistible*, Captain Sir James Saumarez in the *Orion*, and Captain George Murray in the *Colossus*. Jervis was delighted. 'I thank you very much for sending so good a batch,' he told the First Lord. 'They are a valuable addition to my excellent stock.' Jervis's fleet now numbered fifteen sail of the line – what it had been before the loss of the *Courageux*. With it he continued cruising off Cape St Vincent.

The Spanish Fleet had entered Cartagena in early December. It remained there two months, when the Directory decided that it should proceed by easy stages to Brest, there join the French Fleet under Morard de Galles, and cover the passage of the French army of invasion to England. Don Juan de Langara was relieved of the command by Don Jose de Cordova. The Fleet sailed from Cartagena on 1 February, and passed the Straits on the 5th. In the Atlantic they encountered strong easterly winds which pushed them far out, and it was while trying to work back to Cadiz that the *Minerve* passed through them. Not until the evening of Nelson's return, when the wind shifted to the westwards, were they able to make sail towards the land.

During the night the sound of their minute-guns grew

louder. At 2.30 a.m. a Portugese frigate commanded by a Scot, Captain Campbell, brought word they were only five leagues – about fifteen miles – distant. At 5.30 a.m. Captain Foote in the *Niger* frigate reported they were nearer still. Jervis, who had not been to bed all night, received these reports with his usual calm. At dinner the evening before, with Nelson, Elliot, Hallowell and Calder, he had proposed a toast to victory in the battle he knew was imminent; and after the departure of his guests he had made his will. Now, restlessly pacing the deck, he waited only for the dawn. It came slowly, a cold, foggy morning, and with mingled feelings of relief and pride he saw the ships of his fleet standing to the southwards in two perfect columns. He turned to those about him and murmured: 'A victory to England is very essential at this moment'.

The leading ship of the British line was the *Culloden*. Two days before she had run foul of the *Colossus*, sustaining damage which would have driven any other captain but Troubridge into harbour. At about 6.30 a.m. she made the signal for five enemy sail in the south-east, and with the *Blenheim* and *Prince George* stood towards them. At this juncture Jervis had no clear idea of the strength of the enemy fleet. They began to appear in one's and two's out of the fog, 'thumpers,' said the signal lieutenant of the *Barfleur*, 'looming like Beachy Head in a fog'. On the quarter-deck of the *Victory* Calder and Hallowell counted them.

'There are eight sail of the line, Sir John.'

'Very well, sir.'

'There are twenty sail of the line, Sir John.'

'Very well, sir.'

'There are twenty-five sail of the line, Sir John.'

'Very well, sir.'

'There are twenty-seven sail of the line, Sir John.'

'Enough, sir, no more of that; the die is cast, and if there are fifty sail I will go through them.'

'That's right, Sir John,' shouted Hallowell, in the enthusiasm of the moment banging the Admiral on the back. 'That's right! And, by God, we'll give them a damned good licking.'

Soon it became apparent that the Spanish Fleet were in no order, but proceeding raggedly towards the land in two loose divisions, one to windward of about eighteen ships, the other, nearer the British Fleet, of nine, Jervis formed his ships into a single line, the *Culloden* in the lead, the *Victory* in the centre, the *Captain* towards the rear, and steered for the gap between. The Spanish weather-division, seeing they could not join their consorts in time, hauled their wind and approached the British ships on opposite courses. As the two fleets closed the British ran up their colours.

The first part of the battle belongs to Troubridge. As the *Culloden* let fly a broadside at the first Spaniard that passed, her first lieutenant saw that her course would bring her down on a huge enemy three-decker. He told this to his captain. 'Can't help that, Griffiths,' said Troubridge gruffly, 'let the weakest fend off.' This was the Spaniard who, fearful of collision, suddenly went about. As Troubridge passed her he poured in two double-shotted broadsides, 'fired', it was said, 'as if by a seconds-watch, and in the silence of a port-admiral's inspection'. This brought Troubridge to the end of the enemy's line and he brilliantly anticipated the next order. Before Jervis's signal to follow the enemy round had reached his own mast-head, Troubridge had broken the repeating signal and put down his helm. The manoeuvre was not lost on the Admiral. 'Look at Troubridge!' he cried, 'he tacks his ship to battle as if the eyes of all England were upon him; and would to God they were.'

Meanwhile the rest of the British Fleet were coming into action one by one. The Spanish leeward division, seeing their consorts could not reach them, suddenly put about in order to cut the British line and rejoin them. Soon Jervis's ships were being hotly engaged on both sides. In the smoke of the gun-decks the crews fired broadside after broadside. 'We gave them their Valentines in style,' wrote a gunner of the *Goliath*. In the *Victory* Jervis was spattered by the remains of a marine. Captain Grey, seeing his Admiral covered in blood, rushed up in agitation. 'I am not at all hurt,' said Jervis decidedly, 'but do you, George, see if you can get me an orange.' Ahead of the *Victory* the *Colossus* had her topmast shot away and had to wear instead of tacking. This put her in a dangerous position, and Sir James Saumarez in the *Orion*, next astern, gallantly backed his topsail to support her as she went round. Serving on board the *Orion* was Nancy Perriam, one of whose duties was 'to make and mend the dear Captain's clothes,' and she recalls that as the ship went into action she had just begun a flannel shirt. She divided her time between helping her husband serve out powder in the magazine and assisting the surgeon in the cockpit.

By now the British line was in the shape of a U: the rear section was clear of the Spanish rear at one end, and the van had not reached it at the other. This left what James calls 'an open sea' between the two Spanish divisions; and the weather-division, seizing the opportunity of joining their comrades, swung suddenly to starboard. Nelson in the *Captain*, the third ship from the rear, realized that unless this manoeuvre could be thwarted everything so far gained would be lost. In deliberate disobedience of orders he told Miller to wear the *Captain* out of the line, and passing between the *Diadem* and *Excellent* astern of him, headed straight for the leading Spanish ships. These were in a bunch and consisted of the huge *Santissima Trinidad* of four decks and 130 guns, the largest fighting ship in the world, the *Salvador del Mundo* and *San Josef*, first-rates of 112 guns, and the *San Nicolas* 84, and *San Isidro* 74. As soon as the *Captain* was within range Nelson opened fire on the *Santissima Trinidad*. A little later he was joined by Troubridge, and together the two British 74s took on the three Spanish first-rates and two sails of the line. Calder, fearful for their safety, suggested they should be recalled. 'No,' said the Admiral, 'I will not have them recalled. I put my faith in those ships. It is a disgrace they are not supported.'

Support was not long in coming, for Nelson's plan suddenly bore fruit. Demoralized by his audacity, the Spaniards gave up all idea of joining their comrades and turned again northward. This lost them valuable sea-way, and enabled the *Prince George*, *Blenheim* and *Orion* to come up from astern, and the *Excellent* which Jervis had ordered to the *Captain*'s support, to cut across from the British rear. After an hour's heavy fighting the *Salvador del Mundo* struck to Saumarez. A little later the *San Isidro* surrendered to Collingwood, 'who,' in Nelson's words, 'disdaining the parade of taking possession of beaten enemies, most gallantly pushed up with every sail set to save his old friend and messmate.' The *Captain* was now hotly engaging the *San Nicolas*. Collingwood ranged up between the two ships, so close he said, 'you could not put a bodkin between us,' and poured in a broadside. In endeavouring to avoid it the *San Nicolas* ran foul of the *San Josef* on her other side. There now occurred the most glorious incident of the battle. With the genius he had already shown once that day of seeing what the occasion demanded and acting on it, Nelson ordered Miller to put down the helm. Then as the *Captain* with guns still bellowing, drew alongside the *San Nicolas*, he gave the order for boarders.

The first man over the side was Berry. So far he had spent a rather wretched battle helping where he could, but having no particular duty. This was an occasion after his heart. He leapt into the enemy's mizen-chains, followed by Lieutenant Pierson and soldiers of the 69th Regiment who were serving on board as Marines. Miller was about to join them when a voice stopped him. 'No, Miller,' said Nelson, 'I must have that honour myself.' With the help of several soldiers and sailors Nelson broke through one of the stern windows, and after a scuffle with some Spanish officers, reached the quarter-deck. There he found Berry in possession of the poop and already engaged in hauling down the Spanish ensign.

Hardly was the surrender of the *San Nicolas* completed when a burst of musketry from the port side drew the attention of the boarders to the *San Josef*. Nelson called over to Miller for more men, and then raced across to where the huge three-decker towered about him. 'Westminster Abbey or Victory,' he shouted as Berry helped him into the main chains, and began clambering up towards the deck. But the defence of the *San Josef* was even briefer than her consort's. 'At this moment,' said Nelson, 'a Spanish officer looked over the quarter-deck rail and said they surrendered.' On deck the news was confirmed by the Spanish Captain who presented him with his sword and said that his Admiral, Don Francisco Xavier Winthuysen, was dying of wounds below. The story ends in Nelson's own words:

'. . . and on the quarter-deck of a Spanish First-rate, extravagant as the story may seem, did I receive the Swords of vanquished Spaniards; which, as I received, I gave to William Fearney, one of my bargemen, who put them with the greatest Sangfroid under his arm. I was surrounded by Captain Berry, Lieutenant Pierson, 69th Regiment, John Sykes, John Thomson, Francis Cook, all old *Agamemnons*, and several other brave men, seamen and soldiers: thus fell these Ships.'

Although a certain amount of fighting continued, the capture of the *San Josef* and *San Nicolas* marks the end of the battle. The only one of the division to escape was the *Santissima Trinidad*. The last ship to engage her was the *Orion*, and for the second time that day Saumarez had the satisfaction of seeing a Spanish first-rate strike to him. But as his best boats had taken a prize-crew to the *Salvador del Mundo* and the others were wrecked, he could not take possession; and soon after he had the mortification of seeing her re-hoist Spanish colours and escape. The time during which her colours were struck was so short that many officers did not believe it. Nelson was one of them, and years afterwards when it was known the Spaniards had struck, he mentioned it to Saumarez. 'Who ever doubted it, Sir,' replied Saumarez, whose feelings were easily wounded. 'I hope there is no need for such evidence to establish the report of a British officer.'

Nelson remained on board his prizes while they were secured, the ships of the Fleet cheering him as they went by. He returned to the *Captain* to thank Miller for his help and present him with the sword of the captain of the *San Nicolas* and a large topaz ring: then, as his cabin was a shambles, he shifted his pendant to the *Irresistible*. At the close of day, his face black with smoke and his uniform in tatters, he went on board the flag-ship where, in his own words, 'the Admiral received me on the quarter-deck, and, having embraced me, said he could not sufficiently thank me, and used every kind expression which could not fail to make me happy'.

The Fleet slowly made its way back to Lagos Bay to repair and re-equip itself. Jervis wrote several despatches which Calder was to take to England in the *Lively*, and in one he singled out Nelson, Troubridge and Collingwood for special praise: Saumarez, of whose action with the *Santissima Trinidad* he was then ignorant, he did not mention. There was also a word for Hallowell, 'whose conduct on board the *Victory* during the action has made him more dear to me than before,' and an earnest request to give him a frigate on the station. Nelson, in the *Irresistible*, had several letters to write; to his 'dearest friend' Collingwood to thank him for sparing the *Captain* from further loss, to Elliot to say that Miller was making him two sketches of the action, and to the Rev. Dixon Hoste, that the gallantry of brave William could never be exceeded. From the *Captain* Miller sent details of the ship's casualties, 24 killed and 56 wounded, nearly a third of those of the Fleet. Berry wrote that he had collected all the Spanish officers' swords; the Admiral's he had put in a safe place 'for you and you only'. There was a chivalrous touch to the P.S. 'I would not touch an article of the officers' – neither charts nor glasses – they behaved so well.'

News of the battle reached London two weeks later, and was received with acclamation: the House of Commons heard it towards the end of the afternoon and insisted on its thanks being made that night. The victory was not overwhelming but decisive, and it came at a necessary moment. It had pricked the balloon of the Spanish Alliance and restored the confidence in the fleet which the retreat from the Mediterranean had shaken. The country was not slow in showing its gratitude. Jervis was created Earl of St Vincent with a pension of £3,000 a year, Admirals Thompson and Parker were made baronets,

Nelson made a Knight of the Bath, Calder knighted, Berry promoted to post-rank. Every admiral and captain of a ship of the line received a gold medal. Collingwood refused to accept his until he was also given one for the Glorious First of June (when a number of captains had been omitted). And a grateful country sent him both medals, and a letter of apology.

* * *

Captain Thomas Troubridge, who had shared with Nelson the honours of St Vincent, was also his 'honoured acquaintance of twenty-five years' standing,' the two having first met as midshipmen in the West Indies. Troubridge was Nelson's senior by one year, and except for Saumarez the senior captain in the fleet. Unlike many of his brother officers who were the sons of country gentlemen, he came of humble parentage: his father was a baker in the Strand. His promotion was steady but unspectacular. Cornwallis had noticed him in Indian waters in 1791, but it was not until Jervis took over the Mediterranean Fleet that he first came into the limelight. 'I never saw him before my arrival at St Fiorenzo,' Jervis told Spencer, 'his merits are very uncommon.' His admiration grew, and soon hardly a letter to the First Lord passed without some praise of his abilities. 'He is capable of commanding the Fleet of England and I scarce know another when Lord Howe is gone': and later, 'the best Bayard of the British Navy; the ablest adviser and best executive officer, with honour and courage bright as his sword.' Soon Nelson and Troubridge became the two officers on whom Jervis relied for every important operation away from his flag. He first gave Troubridge command of a squadron in the Levant, then of the inshore squadron off Toulon, where, owing to his 'unremitting vigilance' for five months, not one French ship escaped. Nelson, too, admired Troubridge as an officer, but also loved him as a man. He constantly refers to him as 'dear Troubridge,' and often began letters to him, 'My dear friend'. Troubridge had a quick temper and vivid imagination and in Nelson's stormy, feminine nature he found a counterpart to his own. Yet although older than

Nelson, he always remained the subordinate, Nelson the leader. Both were passionate, excitable, moody; both shared a devastating single-mindedness in pursuit of a common ideal; both hated the French with a savage, personal hatred, and were ready to give their lives to defeating them.

An incident which illustrates this side of Troubridge's character occurred during the battle of the Glorious First of June. A few days before the action Troubridge's ship, the *Castor*, was captured by Nielly's squadron and he was taken on board the French Admiral's flag-ship, the *Sanspareil*. When the English Fleet was first sighted, it made no attempt to engage. Troubridge noticed that Lord Howe had hoisted the breakfast pendant, told this to Nielly, and they went down to breakfast themselves. Some time went by and still the British held off. Nielly remarked that they did not seem disposed to fight. Troubridge 'in the act of helping himself to a large brown loaf,' gripped Nielly by the shoulders and said fiercely: 'Not fight! I know John Bull damned well, and when his belly is full you will get it'. Not long after, Howe bore up to engage. During the action Troubridge was put in the boatswain's store-room, 'where he amused himself in pouring forth every invective against the French and the man appointed to guard him'. When he heard the *Sanspareil*'s mainmast go overboard 'he began to jump and caper with all the gestures of a maniac'. Soon after, the *Sanspareil* surrendered and Troubridge had the ironic satisfaction of commanding her into port.

On the evening of 11 April 1797, Nelson, now a rear-admiral and in command of the inshore squadron off Cadiz, entertained Troubridge to dinner in the repaired cabin of the *Captain*. Miller was also there, but Berry had left for England. He was going to spend part of his leave with a married sister at Tofts, in Norfolk; and as Nelson's parson brother lived close by at Hillborough, had promised to call. Nelson told his brother of Berry's proposed visit. 'You will find him, a very pleasant and gentleman-like-man.'

Nelson had invited his old friend to dinner to discuss two schemes he had been turning in his mind. During the five

75

weeks since the battle of St Vincent, Nelson had been cruising first with Saumarez, Martin and Thompson of the *Leander*, secondly with Troubridge, Cockburn and Hood ('whose exertions in forwarding the repairs of the *Zealous*,' said Jervis, 'would have exhausted an ordinary mind'), in search of some Spanish treasure-ships. This fleet was said to be on its way home from South America with the Spanish Viceroy and six or seven million in sterling. They had not found them and Nelson guessed that, having heard of the arrival of the British Fleet off Cadiz, they had taken refuge at Santa Cruz in the Canary Islands. This harbour was a focal point of the Spanish trade routes and a storehouse for their South American trade. Nelson had formed the idea of making an expedition against the island, capturing the treasure-fleet and raiding the warehouse. The expedition would require troops; and this led him to the other idea – the evacuation of the military garrison at Elba. Their safety and Fremantle's had been on his mind, and he had several times told Jervis of his willingness to cover their withdrawal. There were in Elba about 3700 troops, just the number he needed for Santa Cruz: they would, he thought, 'do the business' in three days.

Nelson discussed these plans with Troubridge far into the night: then, when his guest had gone, he wrote a detailed memorandum on them to Jervis.

The first scheme was to be put into action sooner than he anticipated. The very next day Jervis ordered him to hand over command of the inshore squadron to Saumarez, take the *Colossus*, *Leander* and three frigates under his orders, and proceed to the evacuation of Elba.

The second was to wait a little longer.

* * *

For Betsey and Fremantle left behind in Porto Ferrajo, life had not been as smooth as they might have wished. Fremantle was now senior naval officer in the Mediterranean, and his responsibilities allowed him little private life. There was much entertaining and Betsey found the 'tiresome long suppers' exhausting, and longed to escape to Inconstant Cottage, the little house they had taken overlooking the bay. She was glad to see Fremantle's brother officers, even if the stupidity of Lord Proby and the stinginess of Captain Hotham (who went on a cruise and captured only a chest of oranges – 'he feels the disappointment more sensibly than other people') vexed her. The real 'borers' were the Army officers and their wives: General Horneck, 'drunk and would never go away, we did not get rid of him until twelve o'clock'; and Mrs Dunlop, 'talked of nothing but her pregnancy, of children, etc.'. Fremantle also had difficulties with the Army. His opposite number held the equivalent of flag-rank, a delicate position which de Burgh did nothing to respect. When the General decided to fit out his own privateers, a right exclusively the Navy's, Fremantle told him that if they captured any prizes he would order the Navy to retake them. There was a full-blown row which Fremantle, by reason of *force majeure*, won. The General was furious, broke off social relations with Fremantle and threatened to report him to Jervis.

The strain of all this had an effect on Fremantle's relations with Betsey; now that the first flush of marriage was over, he made her the target for some of his pent-up feelings. 'Fremantle attacked me for some nonsense or other. I am too inanimate. I see that very little is required to make him uneasy'; and a week later, 'Was unhappy all the morning as I saw I had given F. real cause to be angry'. Happily these tiffs did not last long. At other times Fremantle was 'full of attentions,' and for her sake gave up snuff. The night of a masked ball they spent quietly in Inconstant Cottage. 'Last year I should have been distressed and miserable to finish the carnival in my room, but now I am never so happy as alone with Fremantle.'

She found relief from the social hurly-burly in various ways. Sometimes she retired to her room to play on the piano or Mr Udney's harpsichord; at others she went for long rides in the country. There was the comfort of corresponding with her family, though the news from her sister was not happy. History had been repeated by her father encouraging a match between

Eugenia and a Count Senft, and at the eleventh hour forbidding it. 'Everybody says he behaved very ill; poor Eugenia is in great distress.' Betsey was happiest when the *Inconstant* went to sea. There were drawbacks here, such as duty dinners with the midshipmen in the gunroom where she was always ready to fall asleep, and 'restless miserable nights' caused by the noise of the bulkhead. But there were compensations too. The excitement of strange sails on the horizon, of capturing prizes and sharing out the money, even the 'confusion and botheration' of examining ship's papers, she found immensely satisfying. Best of all was the luxury of the two little cabins Fremantle had fitted out for her below his own.

At the beginning of April despatches arrived from England with orders for the evacuation. On 16 April Fremantle embarked General de Burgh and his staff in the *Inconstant*, and put to sea with forty sail of transports and men-of-war. Outside the harbour he formed up the convoy and his small squadron and began the long journey down the Mediterranean. A few days later Betsey was writing in her diary: 'This was my birthday. I am an Old Lady of nineteen'. Two days afterwards she wrote: 'Several strange sail in sight, which alarmed everybody as they were known to be not only frigates but line-of-battle ships'. But she need have had no fears. The same evening Nelson was sending a despatch to Jervis: 'You will rejoice to hear I am with the convoy, all safe and well'.

The junction of the convoy with the squadron was a great relief, both to Nelson and Fremantle. Betsey was able to have her piano and harpsichord brought up to the cabin, which had been cleared for action. Here she whiled away many evenings accompanied by a Major Brindley on the flute, who played at first 'quite well', but later 'sadly worse'. But the arrival of the squadron meant more entertaining. She was glad to see Nelson, looking better than ever, and Captain Murray of the *Colossus*; but General Horneck was a less welcome guest: 'Both Generals together is rather too great a bore'. One night Fremantle was required in the *Captain* for consultations, and did not return until the morning. 'I slept alone in the cabin, the first night I have slept alone since I have been married, did not like it.'

The last part of the journey was very uncomfortable. The annoyance caused by the continued presence of the Army officers in the cramped cabin was aggravated by a storm, which blew hard for a week and made progress almost impossible. The dishes and plates rolled off the table, and everybody ate off chairs. Most of the Army officers were sick. Major Campbell 'had a dreadful fall at dinner and hurt himself': the General was 'quite stupid'.

At the beginning of May the convoy sighted the Rock of Gibraltar. Nelson, having 'only overshadowed the convoy with his wings,' ('its charge and arrangement,' he told Jervis, 'could not be in better hands') made sail through the Straits. He came into the Fleet off Cadiz on 24 May, the day after Fremantle, labouring against foul winds and adjusting his speed to that of the slowest ship, arrived at Gibraltar.

* * *

Captain Sir James Saumarez of the *Orion*, to whom Nelson had handed over command of the inshore squadron two months earlier, came of an old Guernsey family originally called de Saumarez, who settled in the island at the time of the Norman conquest. His father, Matthew de Saumarez, was a doctor, but two of his uncles had served in the Navy with distinction. One, Captain Philip Saumarez, was Anson's first lieutenant on his voyage round the world, and in 1756 introduced the first standard naval officer's uniform; the other, Captain Thomas Saumarez, won a brilliant action off Lundy Island in 1758 when his ship the *Antelope*, 54, captured the French *Belliqueux*, 64. Saumarez began his education at a school in London and continued it in his first ship under Captain Goodall, 'who gave him constant access to his cabin, allowed him to write there and make extracts from the best authors in his possession'. French, which was still in common use in the Channel Islands, he spoke fluently.

Saumarez's abilities came to the notice of Lords Howe and Hood and his promotion was rapid. At the Battle of the Saints, at which many of Nelson's captains were lieutenants or midshipmen, he found himself, aged twenty-five, in command of a line-of-battle ship. During the peace he married a Miss le Marchant, daughter of another old Guernsey family, by whom he had several children. On the outbreak of war he was appointed to command the *Crescent* frigate, and won one of the most brilliant early actions of the war by capturing the French frigate *Réunion*, for which he was knighted. Soon after, while cruising to the south of Guernsey, he sighted five French men-of-war: they were on one side of him, to windward, the land on the other: escape seemed impossible. Saumarez ordered the helm to be put down, and steered straight for the shore. The Frenchmen – and some of his own crew – thought that he was going to run the *Crescent* on the rocks rather than risk capture. But Saumarez had remembered from childhood a narrow creek which gave access to a safe anchorage. As the ship raced through, the land almost touching on either side, he asked the master if he could see the marks. 'Why, yes', replied the master, pointing, 'for there is your house – and there is mine.' A year later Saumarez was appointed to the *Orion*.

Saumarez was an interesting character. People who knew him spoke of his 'erectness' of bearing and his 'formal ceremonious manner'; and Betsey called him the 'civilest' man she ever saw – impressions which his portrait by Phillips confirm. This rather unbending attitude, which many, including Nelson, who never liked or understood him, mistook for aloofness, was the mask for an almost pathological sensibility. This did not show itself in his dealings with his subordinates, who worshipped him; his crews were mostly Guernsey volunteers and – almost a unique distinction – there was not a pressed man among them. But his reactions with his superiors were less happy. A slur on character or ability was the worst indignity a naval officer could suffer; and a series of unhappy incidents beginning with Jervis's omission to mention his part at St Vincent led Saumarez to a lifelong delusion that his services were being ignored. Nelson and Troubridge were also quick to react to criticism, but whereas, with their extravagant emotional natures, they vented their grievances aloud, Saumarez brooded on his alone. Byam Martin says his fits of depression almost unhinged him, and at times he was hardly fit to be entrusted with his duties. One instance of his touchiness has already been shown: another occurred in 1781 when, having been rebuked on watch by Hyde Parker – unjustly as he thought – he refused an invitation to dine with him; an action which led the Admiral to say tersely: 'Can't you put up with the fractious disposition of an old man?'

Saumarez's command of the inshore squadron was marked by a correspondence between himself and the Spanish Port-Admiral, Don Josef Massaredo, reminiscent of the chivalry of another age. Their first exchange of letters had concerned the return of Spanish prisoners captured on 14 February. Jervis had initiated the correspondence, but later told Saumarez: 'You prove yourself so able in the diplomatique you need no assistance from me.' The letters had grown more and more trivial. Captain Martin captured a Spanish frigate, the *Ninfa*, returning from South America. On board were found three boxes containing dissections of birds and plants consigned to the Spanish Royal Family. With exquisite courtesy Saumarez forwarded them to Massaredo under a flag of truce. Massaredo assured Saumarez he would send them at once to the King, 'in whose Royal Breast the thoughtfulness of the Admiral will meet due attention': if a chest of clothes belonging to a lady who had taken passage in the *Ninfa* came to light, he would also be glad to have them. 'Be assured,' he concluded, 'I love thee.' The last act of this ludicrous comedy was a letter from Saumarez informing Massaredo that Jervis had a beautiful woman, a Mrs Mansfield, on board the *Ville de Paris* who was very anxious to see Cadiz before leaving for England. To this Massaredo gave a polite but firm refusal. The people of Cadiz, he explained, having 'confined ideas,' might not be able to reconcile their respect for individuals with their notions of what constituted war. However, he hoped to be more fortunate in granting future requests, kissed Saumarez's hands, and prayed God to guard his life many years.

After this Saumarez must have been glad to receive a letter

from a more honest correspondent. This was his small son James. The boy had written an earlier letter in which he said his mother had sent him a cake, that he was taking bark for his health, and that he had finished his Latin Grammar. Now he wrote that his baby sister Carterette had begun to recognize him, that it only wanted three weeks to the holidays, and that he had just recovered from the measles.

CHAPTER 5

In April and May the Channel Fleet had been paralysed, and England shocked, by the great mutinies of Spithead and the Nore. Whispers of it had already reached the Mediterranean Fleet, and among some officers caused great uneasiness. When letters arrived from England which Captain Dacres of the *Barfleur* knew contained exhortations from the Channel Fleet to mutiny, he suggested to Jervis they be withheld. 'Certainly not,' replied the Admiral, 'I daresay the Commander-in-Chief will know how to support his own authority.'

In the iron discipline he exerted on his men, Jervis had absolute faith. But he also trusted in something else – the characters of the captains he had placed over them. He knew that much of the trouble had arisen from the bad living conditions; but he also knew, and never tired of repeating, 'The present indiscipline of the Navy originated with the licentious conduct of the officers'. Nelson had said he did not care to what ship he was appointed, so long as he had the stuff to work on. Jervis knew that while he had captains of Nelson's calibre he need not worry about the discipline. Since taking over the Fleet he had been testing them one by one. Many had proved themselves: 'Troubridge, Hood and Hallowell abound in resources and are very great characters: they will achieve important services to their country when I sleep with my fathers'. Foley was 'a valuable officer'; Miller 'an excellent example for a young man'; Fremantle's 'spirited and active

JOHN JERVIS, EARL OF ST. VINCENT

From the painting by Carbonnier engraved by Turner. The
decoration is the Star of a Knight Grand Cross of the Bath. The
portrait was painted when the admiral was in his eighties. It has
been chosen in preference to more complimentary ones because it
shows the extraordinary mixture of severity, wisdom and humour
which were his chief characteristics.

THOMAS FREMANTLE
From the painting by Pellegrini at Swanburne in Buckinghamshire, showing undress uniform of a captain of over three years' seniority. Fremantle sat for this portrait early in 1800. His wife's diary for April 11th, 1800, reads: 'After Church walked with Fremantle to Pellegrini's, his picture is excessively like and very well done.'

conduct on all occasions cannot be too much praised'; Saumarez 'I have known long: he will never complain'. Others, who were less satisfactory, he did not hesitate to remove. Sam Hood was appointed to the *Zealous* because her previous captain, Lord Harvey, had got the ship 'in a most undisciplined state, the people incessantly drunk'. Hood 'found it necessary to call upon the officers to make exertions which from other habits they were little inclined to do. Dissatisfaction, of course, followed, and the captain, whose whole soul is wrapped up in his profession, had been obliged to appear upon all occasions as the only means of enforcing discipline and good order, which he has most effectually done.'

Sir Charles Knowles of the *Goliath*, whom Betsey had found 'a real bore', Jervis described as 'an imbecile, totally incompetent, the *Goliath* no use whatever under his command,' and made an order for him to change with Foley. The result was that Foley 'soon restored the *Goliath* to order,' while Knowles was 'so feeble that the very first night he received the *Britannia*, the ship's company took the command from him and have been in a state of licentiousness ever since'. Worst of all ships was the *Theseus*, newly arrived from England. Spencer had warned Jervis she was a hot-bed of mutiny and intrigue, a view which the Admiral soon confirmed. 'She is,' he told the First Lord, 'an abomination.' For the worst ship nothing would do but the best officers. The day he arrived back from Elba, Nelson was ordered to shift his flag to her. That night he told Miller to transfer his gear 'with Midshipmen Hoste and Bolton and such men as came from *Agamemnon*, as they like it'. 'Nelson and Miller,' Jervis told Spencer confidently, 'will soon put the *Theseus* to right.'

Two weeks later his prophecy was fulfilled. A dirty scrap of paper was found on the *Theseus*'s quarter-deck. On it was printed in thick, clumsy lettering:

'Success attend Admiral Nelson! God bless Captain Miller! We thank them for the Officers they have placed over us. We are happy and comfortable, and will shed every drop of blood in our veins to support them, and the name of

the *Theseus* shall be immortalized as high as the *Captain*'s.
SHIP'S COMPANY.'

These measures and others, such as segregation of the
marines and the forbidding of the speaking of Irish, helped to
forestall a mutiny, though they did not entirely prevent it.
Among the ships commanded by Jervis's chosen band there
was not a whisper of trouble; but a squadron newly arrived
from the Channel Fleet contained several disaffected ships and
in these there was a small rising.

Typical of Jervis's attitude towards mutineers was his
treatment of a seaman of the *Marlborough*. This man was the
ringleader of a plot to wrest the ship from the officers and sail
her to Ireland. He was seized, court-martialled and sentenced
to death. Jervis, to make clear his authority to the Fleet,
made an order for the prisoner to be executed at eight o'clock
the following morning by his own shipmates, 'no part of the
boats' crews from the other ships, as had been usual on similar
occasions, to assist in the punishment'.

On viewing this order, Captain Ellison ('an old officer,
suffered severely in the service and lost an arm in action,')
waited on the Admiral in the *Ville de Paris*. He found the officers
and ship's company drawn upon the quarter-deck and that he
had to address the Admiral in front of them. Hesitatingly he
told him he did not think his men would allow the sentence
to be carried out. Jervis, 'standing with his hat in his hand, as
was his Lordship's custom when anyone, even a common
seaman, addressed him,' listened to Ellison in silence and then
replied: 'Do you mean to tell me, Captain Ellison, that you
cannot command His Majesty's Ship the *Marlborough*; for if
that is the case, Sir, I will immediately send on board an officer
who can'. Ellison returned to the *Marlborough* and on Jervis's
instructions gave orders for the gunports to be closed and the
guns run back and housed. At half past seven the next morning
the ports were opened and the *Marlborough* found herself
surrounded by boats armed with carronades under the command of Captain Campbell of the *Blenheim*. If any signs of ·
mutiny or interference with the execution showed themselves,

Captain Campbell had orders to take his boats alongside the *Marlborough*, commence firing through the open ports, 'and continue to fire until all mutiny or resistance should cease: and should it become absolutely necessary he should even sink the ship in face of the Fleet.' Confronted by this authority, resistance in the *Marlborough* collapsed. The prisoner was placed on the cat-head, the halter put round his neck, and as the watch-bells of the Fleet struck eight o'clock, run smartly up the yard-arm. An hour later the body was cut down, sewn in its hammock with a piece of shot, and dumped in the sea half a mile from the Fleet.

In the *St George* three mutineers were ordered to be similarly executed. Captain Peard, learning that a second plot had been contrived to prevent it, told his men he knew of their intentions. 'Finding that this did not produce the desired effect, he and his first lieutenant rushed amidst the crowd, resolutely seized two of the people whom they knew to be the promoters, dragged them out by main force and put them in irons. Order was immediately restored.' The original mutineers had been convicted on a Saturday evening and asked for five days to prepare – 'in which,' commented Jervis, 'they would have hatched five hundred treasons'; and he ordered them to be executed next morning. At this desecration of the Sabbath Vice-Admiral Thompson publicly protested, for which Jervis removed him from the Fleet. Nelson approved: 'Had it been Christmas Day, instead of Sunday, I would have executed them'.

By the end of July all signs of serious trouble had disappeared, and Jervis wrote a private line to Lord Garlies:

'We have had five executions for mutiny and a punishment of 300 lashes given alongside two disorderly line-of-battle ships and the frigate to which the mutineer belonged. He took it all at one time and exhorted the spectators to mind what they were about, for he had brought it upon himself. Two men have been executed for sodomy and the whole seven have been proved to be most atrocious villains, who long ago deserved the fate they met with for their crimes. At present there is every appearance of content and proper subordination.'

To divert the attention of the Fleet during this critical period, Jervis ordered the inshore squadron to make nightly bombardments of Cadiz.

The squadron now consisted of the *Theseus*, Nelson and Miller; *Orion*, Saumarez, and *Goliath*, Foley. At the beginning of July they were joined by the *Seahorse* frigate from Gibraltar, now under the command of Fremantle who had made an exchange with Captain Oakes, invalided home. Betsey had had a hectic month in Gibraltar. She had seen all the sights, including a climb to the top of the Rock, breakfasted, dined and danced with the officers of the garrison from the Governor – 'Old Cock of the Rock' O'Hara – downwards, gone to dinner at The Convent 'at which fifty-eight people sat down and *such* figures some of them,' studied perspective with a Mrs Parish, learnt to sing with a Mr Hale, 'vexed' Fremantle, made caustic comments in her diary on everybody and everything she met; and in the *Seahorse*'s cabin conceived her first child.

The *Seahorse* joined the inshore squadron in time to take part in the first attack on Cadiz on the night of 3 July. The bomb *Thunderer* went close up to the town walls and began a heavy bombardment. The Spaniards sent out launches to capture her and these were met by barges commanded by Nelson, Fremantle and Miller. The launch containing the Spanish Commandant, Don Miguel Tyrason, and twenty-six men engaged the barge containing Nelson, Fremantle and fifteen men. There was a long and bloody contest at the end of which the Spaniards retired with eighteen men killed and all the others wounded. Losses in the British boats were one killed and twenty wounded including Fremantle and Hoste, neither badly. Their retreat to the squadron was covered by Foley in the *Goliath*. The launch of the *Ville de Paris* was badly holed but managed to reach the *Culloden* where Troubridge saved her from sinking. Two nights later another attack took place, and Betsey again sat up miserably into the small hours waiting for Fremantle's return. A third attack was planned but postponed owing to the weather. 'Thank God,' was Betsey's comment; 'it was sacrificing men for nothing.'

Between these fierce engagements the social round of the Fleet went on. Betsey and Fremantle dined with Jervis, whom she found 'very gallant as usual,' and later with Saumarez in the *Orion*. Then it was her turn to play the hostess, and soon hardly a day passed without some of the captains coming to dine or spend the evening. To the lives of these men, often tired, often lonely, never seeing any other company but their own, little Betsey brought a gaiety and warmth they had almost forgotten: her femininity and gentleness stood as a symbol of all they had left behind. Nelson, Miller and Martin were her most frequent visitors. She saw Foley again for the first time since their parting: if the meeting was at all delicate, she refrains from mentioning it. Whether Foley had succeeded in cooling his flame it is impossible to say; but from his nightly visits to the *Seahorse*, it would seem his admiration remained undimmed. The rejected suitor became, as sometimes happens, the warm friend.

Meanwhile in the *Ville de Paris* preparations were pushing ahead for the expedition against Santa Cruz.

*   *   *

The First Lord was not long in granting Jervis's request to give Hallowell a frigate. As soon as Lord Garlies, after landing Sir Gilbert Elliot and Captain Calder at Spithead, had paid off the *Lively*, Hallowell was appointed to succeed him. After a short refit he sailed for Lisbon, and there found orders from Jervis to proceed with Cockburn in the *Minerve* on a cruise to the Western Islands.

On 28 May 1797, standing in to Santa Cruz, Hallowell observed a brig-of-war at anchor which, as he approached, hoisted French colours. He decided she could be cut out, and the next day the boats of the frigates, under Hardy, attacked her. Although heavily outnumbered and outgunned, they succeeded in boarding and carrying her. The French colours were lowered and the English hoisted, much to the mortification of Captain Xavier Pommier who had gone ashore the previous day and not troubled to return to his ship. A heavy fire was opened from the shore batteries, which Hardy and his party endured until they had worked the ship out of the harbour. She proved to be the *Mutine* of 349 tons, mounting 14 guns. Jervis was so delighted at the exploit that he put her in commission, gave Hardy the command of her, and promoted him to commander . . . Hardy's 'desperate enterprise' also pleased Nelson. 'He has got it by his own bat,' he said, 'and I hope will prosper.'

Hallowell and Hardy brought no news of the Spanish treasure-fleet: but preparations for the expedition were so far advanced it was decided to carry on with them. The *Principe de Asturias* was known to have been at Santa Cruz at the beginning of May, and had not been sighted since: it was more than likely she had discharged her treasure in the storehouses ashore. By 14 July the expedition was ready to sail. Jervis had allowed Nelson to choose his own captains, and he had picked the cream of the Fleet: Troubridge and Sam Hood in the *Culloden* and *Zealous*, Thompson in the *Leander*, Fremantle in the *Seahorse*, Waller and Bowen in the frigates *Emerald* and *Terpsichore*: the *Fox* cutter and *Cacafuego* mortar-boat. The troops from Elba were not available owing to the obstinacy of General de Burgh, but Nelson told Jervis that with extra marines from the Fleet, 'General Troubridge' ashore, and himself afloat, he could do the business well enough. On 15 July the captains assembled in the *Theseus* for a final conference before sailing. A little later they returned to their ships and weighed anchor. 'God bless and prosper you,' was Jervis's parting message. 'I am sure you will deserve success. To mortals is not given the power of commanding it.'

Nelson, as usual, was full of high hopes, although he knew the obstacles were considerable. The harbour of Santa Cruz is formed out of an extinct volcanic crater: along the tall cliffs there are few suitable landing places and anchoring, except close inshore, is impossible; and from the mountain tops that surround the bay great winds sweep down to lash the waters into turmoil. But from all accounts there was not much of a garrison, and the surprise of the attack led Nelson to hope for speedy results. After a passage of five days during which there were captains' conferences, small-arms drills, making of scaling ladders and muffling of oars, the squadron sighted the high peak of Tenerife. While still out of sight of the bay the landing parties under the command of Troubridge, Hood and Miller transferred from the battleships to the frigates, and the battleships then stood over the horizon. The plan was for the three frigates to enter the bay after dark, approach as near to the shore as possible, and send away the boats with the landing parties. Troubridge had orders not to attack the town itself which lay in the centre of the bay, but to make for a fort to the right of it. Having stormed this with the scaling ladders he was to turn its guns on the town and send a summons to the Governor to surrender.

The first part of the operation proceeded according to plan. The frigates stood into the bay as far as they dared, the landing parties embarked in the boats and began pulling for the shore. Then one of the dreaded gusts came sweeping down from the mountains. By midnight the boats were still three miles from shore. They laboured bravely on but when dawn broke – the time planned for the assault – they still had a mile to go. Surprise had gone and it would now be impossible to storm the fort direct. However, Troubridge had spotted a beach nearby, and he believed that if his party landed there they could carry the heights above the fort and take it from the rear. He ordered the boats to return to the frigates while he went to the *Theseus*, now standing into the bay, to lay his plan before the Admiral. Nelson approved immediately and at nine o'clock, or three hours after their withdrawal, the boats went into the beach. But it was too late. The landing party 'scrambled up a steep hill' only to find the Spaniards facing them from the summit of another. 'There was a deep valley between us,' said the gunner's mate of the *Seahorse*, 'so that we could not well engage each other.' The two forces remained in these positions all day and then Troubridge, seeing his plan had failed, re-embarked his men and returned to the frigates. His party were angry and exhausted. When the detachment from the *Theseus* returned to the *Seahorse* Betsey found them 'noisy and mutinous,' Captain Miller 'very much dissatisfied,' Troubridge 'almost dead with fatigue'.

The three hours between six and nine o'clock mark the turning point between the success and failure of the operation. Captain Mahan cites Troubridge's action in going back to the *Theseus* for Nelson's approval as typical of the difference between the two men – 'between a really great captain and the best type of a simply accomplished and gallant officer'. Troubridge shared Nelson's gift of seeing in a flash what the occasion demanded, but where there was a senior officer he shunned the responsibility of acting on it. Their respective parts at St Vincent are typical of their difference in character: Troubridge's abilities were limited to a brilliant execution of orders, Nelson's allowed him to act in opposition to them. If Nelson had been in command of the landing parties he would, as he afterwards told a friend, have made straight for the heights above the fort; and 'complete success would have crowned our endeavours,' or, as he said elsewhere, he would have been 'in a confounded scrape'.

All the landing parties returned to their ships and the squadron stood out to sea. The expedition had been a failure, and any other commander but Nelson would have admitted it and returned chastened to the Fleet. But for Nelson to admit failure was to admit a lack of confidence in his own abilities, to admit personal defeat: there was a stubborness in his spirit which made return impossible. 'Thus foiled in my original plan,' he told Jervis, 'I considered it for the honour of our King and Country not to give over the attempt to possess ourselves of the town, that our enemies might be convinced there is nothing to which Englishmen are not equal to.' His resolve was strengthened by the arrival of the *Leander* which had been delayed in her passage from Lisbon. His new plan was to anchor the frigates near the beach so as to give the impression that a second assault was intended there; then, under cover of darkness, to send the boats direct to the mole-head in the centre of the town. This time Nelson was to lead the expedition himself: Troubridge, Miller, Hood, Thompson, Fremantle, Bowen, and Waller and a thousand men were to accompany him, with Lieutenant Gibson in the *Fox* cutter.

When the plan was made known a little shudder ran through the Fleet. Several officers made their wills. Nelson, aware of the hazards, wrote to Jervis: 'To-morrow my head will be crowned with laurel or cypress,' and he committed his stepson Josiah Nisbet to his care. George Thorp, aged nineteen and first lieutenant of the frigate *Terpsichore*, left a last letter for his family: 'Going to storm Santa Cruz. As I think there is a chance of my never returning, I leave this directed to you. As I never intentionally did wrong I do not feel afraid, and I think you will have the satisfaction of saying your boy has done his duty.' Alone in the Fleet Betsey, from whom Fremantle had kept back the dangers of the operation, thought it 'an easy and almost sure thing'; and after entertaining Nelson to supper, she went to bed 'apprehending no danger to Fremantle'.

The frigates took up their position at five o'clock in the evening. At eleven o'clock the landing parties embarked and started inshore. Although strict instructions had been given for the boats to keep together, the weather made it impossible, and the detachments of Troubridge and Hood became separated. At about 1.30 a.m. the main body, under Nelson, were close to the mole-head when the night was broken by the pealing of alarm bells. A devastating fire from thirty or forty cannon and musketry from troops massed on the beach was poured into the nearest boats. A large ball struck the *Fox* cutter between wind and water and sank her almost immediately, with the loss of her captain and ninety-seven men. Nelson, in the act of drawing his sword and leaping on to the mole-head, had his right arm shattered by a discharge of grape and fell back into the boat. Fremantle and Thompson were also wounded, the former like Nelson in the right arm. The rest of the party succeeded in carrying the mole-head and spiking the guns. They advanced towards the town, only to be met by a second murderous fire from the citadel and the houses on the waterfront. Captain Bowen of the *Terpischore*, George Thorp and half a dozen men all fell together. 'They lay,' said Miller, 'within the space of four square yards, as if one instant had determined the fate of all.'

Soon it became clear that further advance was impossible, and on Miller's orders the remnants of the party retired to the mole-head, re-embarked in the boats and pulled out to the frigates. Nelson, lying in agony at the bottom of the *Seahorse*'s barge, was taken alongside the *Seahorse*. On hearing the name of the ship he refused to go on board and directed the crew to make for the *Theseus*. When told that any further exposure might endanger his life, he replied, 'Then I will die; for I would rather suffer death than alarm Mrs Fremantle by her seeing me in this state when I can give her no tidings of her husband'. On reaching the *Theseus* he refused assistance in going up the side, and on deck called for the surgeon to amputate his arm. Fremantle was safe. He had managed to make his way to the *Zealous* where his wound was dressed; at daylight he returned to the *Seahorse*, where he found Betsey 'not a little distressed and miserable'.

Troubridge's party meanwhile had made a good landing to the south of the citadel, and began marching towards the rendezvous, the main square of the town. They were in a sorry condition. Their scaling ladders had been lost in the surf, their ammunition was soaked, they had no provisions; and by the terrible sights and sounds coming from the mole-head they knew they could expect little help. Hood and his party succeeded in joining them, making a total force of eighty marines, eighty pikemen and a hundred and eighty small-arms men. With this small band Troubridge proposed to storm the citadel without ladders. But having advanced a little way he found 'the whole of the streets commanded by field-pieces, and upwards of eight thousand Spaniards and one hundred French under arms approaching by every avenue.'

Troubridge then showed something of his true greatness. There was no senior officer to turn to, and the responsibility for further action was his alone: the way he accepted it would have done credit to Nelson. With superb impertinence he sent Hood forward with a flag of truce to the Spanish Governor to say that if the Spanish forces advanced an inch further he would burn down the town; but if the Governor would provide them with boats, they would make a peaceful withdrawal. The astonished Governor told Hood he would consider the matter with his officers and let him have an answer in an hour. To this Hood replied he could spare only five minutes, as his friends were anxiously awaiting to renew hostilities. After a short consultation, the Governor announced he would agree to the request. He entertained Hood and Troubridge to dinner, and afterwards allowed the little party to march with colours flying to the mole-head where he provided them with boats. Then, with a chivalry exceeding Massaredo's, he gave orders for his enemies to be provided with biscuits and wine, for their wounded to be admitted to the hospital, and as a final proof of magnanimity sent a message to Nelson that his squadron might purchase whatever refreshments they required – a gesture which Nelson returned by asking the Governor to accept a parting present of an English cask of ale and a cheese, and by an offer, also accepted, of carrying the despatches of his own defeat to the Court of Spain.

It was a sad and chastened squadron that made its way back to Cadiz. They had lost in killed and wounded 280 men. The death of Captain Bowen who had been about to retire was particularly felt. 'He was continually talking,' said Betsey, 'of the happy life he should lead when he returned home.' Anxious signals were passed as to the welfare of survivors. Nelson had many tender messages. 'He is much obliged for your kind inquiries,' Miller told Thompson, 'he is, as the ladies in the straw say, "as well as can be expected!" ' To Betsey Nelson sent a personal line – one of the first with his left hand: 'God bless you and Fremantle,' and a message that he was coming on well. Fremantle's wound, aggravated by the heat and the incompetence of his surgeon Mr Fleming, healed less rapidly, and all the way back to Cadiz he was unable to move from his cot: Troubridge, said Betsey, 'was quite angry to find him so low and weak'. Betsey herself, 'sick a little generally before breakfast,' and unable to divine the cause, was also in poor spirits. Nelson too, although showing a supreme contempt for his disability, was in great depression. He was convinced that his career was finished, and he sent on the *Emerald* with a note to Jervis: 'When I leave your command I become dead to the world; I go home and am no more seen,' and when, on 16 August, he came in sight of his flag: 'A left-handed Admiral will never again be considered as useful, therefore the sooner I get to a very humble cottage the better'.

But instead of the censure he feared, sympathy and approbation were awaiting him. The glorious failure of the expedition had stirred Jervis's imagination. 'Mortals cannot command success: you and your companions have certainly deserved it by the greatest degree of heroism and perseverance that ever was exhibited.' To Fremantle too, lying in pain in his cot, his brother officers hastened to show their sympathy. 'We had all the captains on board,' wrote Betsey, 'they were uncommonly attentive and kind.' A visit from Jervis himself was prevented by an earnest message that the patient was not well enough. For five days the *Seahorse* lay in the Fleet. Then Jervis, appreciating that two of his greatest officers were sorely in need of 'a change of climate,' ordered Nelson to shift his flag to the *Seahorse* and sail to England.

The passage home was particularly unhappy. Nelson and Fremantle were both restless and in pain, Betsey was suffering from an uncomfortable first pregnancy, and the sick and wounded of the *Theseus* who were also taking passage, 'did nothing but groan from morning to night'. On the evening of 1 September 1797, the *Seahorse* anchored at Spithead. Despite rough weather Nelson insisted on going ashore, and the same night he set out across country to where Lady Nelson was living in the quiet crescents of Bath. A few days later Fremantle, still in much pain, moved into lodgings in Portsmouth.

*   *   *

Two of the captains who had fought with Nelson at Santa Cruz and were to serve with him again were Samuel Hood and Thomas Boulden Thompson.

Sam Hood came of a distinguished naval family. He was a cousin of the great Lord Hood under whose wing he had entered the Navy, and of his brother Viscount Bridport; and his own brother, Captain Alexander Hood, was captain of the *Mars*. Hood's early career was packed with incident and he is one of the few officers of the time about whom his contemporaries have left a detailed record.

In 1787, at the age of twenty-five, he was appointed to the *Thisbe* frigate on the Halifax station where his senior officer was Prince William in the *Andromeda*. The young Prince had a reputation for good living and General Dyott, then a subaltern in the garrison, told of the dissolute habits into which he led them. 'In the course of my life,' said Dyott, 'I never saw such fair drinking.' At an evening at the Blue and Orange, a military dining club at which Hood and the Prince were guests of honour, the Prince brought his own claret. 'He took very good care to see everybody fill and he gave twenty-three bumpers without a halt. There was just twenty dined and we drank sixty-three bottles. Whenever any person did not fill a bumper HRH called out, "I see some of God Almighty's daylight in that glass, Sir. Banish it!"' Hood and Dyott must have been relieved when the Prince took away the squadron off on a cruise; but there was another dinner at the barracks to celebrate their return. 'After the Royal toasts, we had three times twenty-one and two bands playing "Rule, Britannia." We drank twenty-eight bumper toasts, by which time we were in pretty good order. At nine o'clock a *feu de joie* was fired by the garrison from the citadel. Those that could walk attended.'

Hood's next appointment brought him in touch with a less dissipated but equally demanding member of the Royal Family. This was to the *Juno* frigate ordered to attend on the Prince's father, George III, during his summer visit to Weymouth Bay. The King, who loved his Navy, came frequently on board; and Byam Martin, then a lieutenant in the ship, tells of the demands his visit made on the captain's purse. 'It became necessary to provide largely and handsomely for the royal table and the numerous train of attendants at lunch. This was no small affair and, as Captain Hood was at that time a very poor person, he had no alternative but to borrow the money; so that the honour of being selected for this service ended in his being £700 in debt.' One day when the King was on board, the *Shark* and the *Chesterfield* came into collision close by and the *Chesterfield* was severely damaged. 'The good old King,' said Byam Martin, 'took this to be a part of the designed exhibitions of the day and immediately called out in a rapturous tone, "Very fine, how beautiful, very fine indeed: I never saw anything finer." '

All the officers found attendance on the Royal Family a great strain, and when the *Juno* was at last ordered to sea, Midshipman George Thorp wrote to his family: 'I am exceedingly happy we are done with Weymouth. No one can conceive what trouble their Majesties gave us'.

The *Juno* sailed to Spithead, embarked the Spanish Admiral Gravina who had been on a tour of English dockyards, and took him and his staff to Corunna. Then the war with France broke out, and in striking contrast to Weymouth was the *Juno*'s taking of the French privateer *L'Entreprenante* and her prize the *Glory*. The *Glory*, a small merchant brig, had been captured a few days earlier and the Frenchman had treated the crew with appalling brutality. They robbed them of their personal belongings, put many in irons and lashed the captain to his sea-chest. 'I was in the most excruciating pain for four hours and a half,' he wrote. 'In this helpless condition one of the cowardly miscreants snapped a pistol at my breast and another made a thrust at me with a cutlass. They cut off my dog's head, for the purpose they said, of representing the fate of the whole crew upon our arrival in France.' Then the *Juno* bore up and the master and his crew were liberated. The terrible end of the story is told in his own words.

'It is difficult at all times to keep the passions within a due state of subordination; it was at the moment totally impossible for me to subdue my rage; and snatching a cutlass from the hands of the man who untied me, I almost at one stroke severed his arm from his body; when, fearing the further effects of my frenzy, he jumped out of the cabin window and was drowned. Another followed his example and jumped off the taffrail; and the captain, dreading the just vengeance which was awaiting him, took a pistol and shot himself through the head. I was not yet reduced to reason and just before the *Juno*'s crew could overpower me, had cut and lacerated three other of the Frenchmen so dreadfully that they were entirely covered with blood and now lie in the hospital without hopes of recovery.'

At the end of the year the *Juno* sailed to the Mediterranean station, and early in 1794 Hood narrowly avoided capture. He left Malta in January with a hundred and fifty supernumeraries for the Fleet, which he had last heard of lying in Toulon harbour, then held by French Royalists, under the command of his cousin. He entered the harbour on a dark rainy night and looked round for the flag-ship. A French brig hailed him and asked: 'What ship?' Hood replied: '*Juno*,' and asked where the English Admiral lay. The Frenchman did not seem to understand and called out: 'Luff, luff.' The helm was put over and the ship struck on a shoal. While they were trying to get off several French officers came on board, and told Hood he must go to another part of the harbour. Hood was about to reply when one of his midshipmen whispered that the Frenchmen were wearing National cockades. 'I looked at their hats more closely and clearly distinguished the three colours.' The French, seeing they were suspected, said: 'Keep calm, m'sieur . . . the English Admiral has been gone some time.' The awful news quickly spread through the ship. Then a gust of wind blew down the harbour and Lieutenant Webley, not relishing spending the rest of the war in a French prison, suggested the ship be got off under sail. Hood ordered everyone to their stations. The Frenchmen drew their sabres but were hustled below. All sails were set, the cable cut, and another gust of wind blew the ship clear. With brilliant seamanship

Hood turned the ship towards the harbour mouth and in the darkness made his way back along the channel. By now the alarm had been given and the *Juno* was fired on by several shore batteries. But their aim was erratic and soon after midnight the ship reached the open sea.

When Hood was appointed to the *Zealous* in 1796 to relieve the incompetent Lord Harvey, he was thirty-four years old. Apart from his great height (which required him in the *Weasel* brig to put his head through the skylight so the barber on deck could dress his hair), he was, with his loose-limbed build and kindly authoritative expression, not unlike Nelson. Captain Hotham says he was 'awkard and ungraceful in his figure, and his manners not very polished,' but Captain Basil Hall that 'his appearance and manners were at all time unspeakably winning'. His charm therefore seemed to lie in an absolute naturalness, 'in the peculiar sweetness of his voice and the benignant expression of his countenance'. 'He was,' says Hall, 'completely devoid of affectation.' Many of his contemporaries speak of his "gentleness", a quality reflected in his eyes and the humorous curve of his mouth. He shared with Nelson and Troubridge a professional singleness of purpose: Hotham said he was the only man he knew who liked sea-life *par excellence*. During the peace he spent two years in France to learn the language – a task which all their lives Nelson and Troubridge steadfastly refused – and he was an expert on astronomy, geography and shipbuilding.

*   *   *

If appearances by contemporary artists were anything to judge by, there could hardly have been a greater contrast to Hood than Thompson. His miniature by Engleheart shows a little, dark-haired, doll-like face, more Italian than English, more feminine than masculine. But this is misleading. We are told that he was 'above middle size, and of a vigorous make', and that he much enjoyed 'all the manly sports'.

Thompson's father had died young and he was brought up by his uncle, Commodore Edward Thompson, a friend of Garrick's and a famous character of the late eighteenth

THOMAS FOLEY

From the miniature attributed to Grimaldi, showing undress uniform of a captain of over three years' seniority. The medals are those of St. Vincent and the Nile.

BENJAMIN HALLOWELL

From the painting by Thomas, showing full-dress uniform of an admiral. The decorations are the Ribbon and Star of the Knight Grand Cross of the Bath, the Order of St. Ferdinand and Merit, and the Medal of the Nile.

century whose activities earned him the nickname of 'Poet Thompson'. An anecdote which shows his difficulties in reconciling naval and literary interests is recorded by the Naval Chronicle.

'*The Fair Quaker of Deal* as altered by himself was, by his direction, performed in the Plymouth theatre and his name was accordingly put in the bills. Fifty of the crew with their ladies, presented themselves at the door of the Playhouse and demanded admittance without the ceremony of paying; alleging that it was their Commander's play and that whatever was his they were welcome to. During the tumult which this occasioned at the door, a messenger was despatched to the captain who was then in the stage box (with a lady), requesting him to come out and pacify them. "Admit them directly, I will pay for them," said the captain. In the meantime the tars, roused by resistance, did not on this occasion wait for orders, but surmounted every opposition and rushed in. Observing their Commander they gave him three cheers and remarked, "There's His Honour, God bless him; he has got as good and tight a frigate as ever was manned in His Majesty's Navy." They concluded with one of the captain's admirable seasongs.'

In 1778, when Thompson was twelve, his uncle took him to sea, first in the *Hyena* frigate, and later in the *Grampus*. This ship was appointed to the African station and on the way home the Commodore caught a tropical fever. At the time the vessel was crowded with monkeys, parrots and other birds which the Commodore was bringing to England as presents for his friends. 'The surgeon appeared on deck and informing the crew that the stench arising from these animals had increased the virulence of their Commander's disorder, in an instant the sea around the ship was covered with bird-cages, birds, monkeys and other animals and every part of the ship thoroughly cleansed.' Notwithstanding, the Commodore's fever grew worse and in January 1786 he died. His death causing a vacancy in the squadron, young Thompson was appointed to command the sloop *Nautilus*. In her he returned

99

to the African coast the following year with a consignment of 'black poor,' and seventy English prostitutes with which to establish a British colony at Sierra Leone. On return to England the *Nautilus* was paid off and Thompson went to London, 'where,' says a contemporary, 'having passed so great a part of his youth at a distance from scenes of relaxation, it is not surprising he occasionally gave way to indulgence.' 'The captain,' he explains, 'was a man of gallantry, and by his figure, address and accomplishments well qualified to make an impression on the hearts of the fair.'

For the next six years Thompson was unemployed. He wrote repeatedly to the Admiralty for an appointment. Some letters Lord Spencer answered – 'I must beg you to have patience a little longer'; copies of others bear Thompson's angry comment: 'No Reply!' At last, in August, 1796, he was appointed to the *Leander*, convoying the Baltic trade. In 1797 he was ordered to Lisbon, and he joined Jervis's fleet in time to be detached with Nelson for the final evacuation of Elba.

On Nelson's departure for England, Hood and Thompson rejoined Jervis – now Earl of St Vincent – with the Fleet off Cadiz. By the end of the summer all Europe, exhausted by war, was ready for peace; and Malmesbury's mission to Lille to discuss terms led many in the Fleet to believe they would soon be home. St Vincent was certain of it and in August he bet Saumarez £100 that the preliminaries would be signed by 12 September. But Bonaparte's *coup d'état* of Fructidor made further negotiations impossible. Malmesbury returned home, and on 8 September Saumarez wrote in his diary: 'Received from the Earl of St Vincent 444 dollars and a half'.

During the autumn and winter the Admiral kept watch over the Spanish ships in Cadiz, never for a moment relaxing his iron discipline. Decks were to be scrubbed before daylight and not after, 'so that the ships may seize that favourable moment to get under way, chase, and fall suddenly on an enemy': the great guns were to be exercised daily; the seamen's bedding was to be regularly aired; slop clothing was to be soaked in tubs of salt water. On captains, officers and men the Admiral exerted his powerful personality, never hesitating to punish the wrongdoer nor omitting to reward the deserving. A captain whose ship was in a disorderly state he forbade to go on shore 'on what is called pleasure'. To another who complained that the Governor of Gibraltar had removed a number of troops acting as marines he replied: 'There are men enough to be got at Gibraltar, and you and your officers would be better employed in picking them up than lying on your back and roaring like bull-calves'. And yet to a frigate captain of modest means, who had done long service before Cadiz, he gave £100 to fit out for a cruise on which there would be a chance of prize-money.

To the junior officers he was equally discerning. Thinking the lieutenants were 'running to fat,' he ordered the entering port of the *Ville de Paris* to be blocked up for all except admirals and captains. One boisterous morning he made the signal for all chaplains, and when they arrived very green about the gills, ordered them to the wardroom 'to hold a conclave'. Officers who went ashore 'wearing round hats and dressed like shop-keepers' he threatened with arrest. But there was always the other side to him. One young officer made a brilliant parody of St Vincent's custom of attending morning divisions in full-dress uniform. 'The Earl of St Vincent, the Commander-in-Chief, made an image of blue and gold whose height was about five feet, seven inches and the breadth thereof was about twenty inches, and he set it up every ten o'clock a.m. on the quarter-deck of the *Ville de Paris* before Cadiz . . .' This came unwittingly into the Admiral's hands. He made the author read it aloud before a dinner-party of captains, and then sent him to England on three months' leave. To the men he was equally fair. A mutineer he would hang without compunction and at a moment's notice; but when poor Roger Odell, one of his best seamen, lost his savings of £70 while bathing, he refunded him the money out of his own pocket in the presence of the ship's company.

Those captains whom experience had taught him to trust he sent on detached missions. Troubridge and Hood went cruising and captured a large Spanish ship from Rio Plata, 'which I trust,' Hood told Bridport, 'will give Captain T. and myself two thousands each'. Thompson was sent to negotiate with the Bey of Algiers who was in one of his most recalcitrant moods. Saumarez commanded a boat attack on Cadiz. Collingwood was made a commodore during a shortage of junior admirals. 'My wits are ever employed,' he told his wife, 'to keep my people employed, both for health's sake and to save them from mischief.' His crew made several musical instruments and produced 'a very good band' (though one night the rats destroyed the bagpipes by eating the bellows). 'There seems as much mirth and festivity,' he concluded, 'as if we were in Wapping itself.' Under Miller's command the abominable *Theseus* became one of the best ships in the Fleet. 'We have a good captain,' said Hoste, 'and I mess in the wardroom with a jovial set of officers.'

So the life of the Fleet went on and the captains, reflecting on the crews under them the authority, efficiency and humanity of their Commander-in-Chief, continued to mould the Fleet into a weapon that before long was to challenge the French for the mastery of the seas.

CHAPTER 6

Back in England the two invalids were slowly recovering from their wounds.

Fremantle's was particularly obstinate and painful. The inflammation had spread to his hand and at times he was in agony; once on a walk he was so overcome by pain he had to go into a cottage and lie down. He was glad of the company of his mother, who showed Betsey every kindness and gave her 'an exceedingly pretty diamond ring,' but visits from his brothers William and Jack were less welcome. When they came to say good-bye he refused to see them. 'He was distressed about it afterwards and cryed much, what relieved him.' But the pain persisted, and at length Fremantle wrote to the Admiralty to be superseded. He and Betsey took a small furnished cottage at Purbrook near Portsmouth, and here Fremantle found the rest he needed. Fitzmaurice, the surgeon of Haslar Naval Hospital, came out regularly to dress his arm. Slowly the wound began to heal, although he knew it would be a long time before he would be fit for service. Betsey sent for a piano-forte from Portsmouth and there was a little entertaining. A Miss Fortnum, 'whose father keeps a grocer's shop in London,' came to dinner, and later Fremantle was well enough to dine at Southwick with Lady Calder, 'who talks of nothing but ships and sea-service and of the red ribbon that was given to Admiral Nelson instead of very properly bestowing it on the great Sir Robert.' They visited Porchester Castle and saw three thousand French prisoners. 'They are very industrious and make all kinds of little works. We bought a Guillotine neatly done in bone.'

A month at Purbrook improved Fremantle's health, and they set off for London. Betsey called at the Bond Street lodgings of the Nelsons, who had come up for a specialist's opinion on the Admiral's arm. Lady Nelson was not at home, but Betsey 'saw the good Admiral'. Fremantle called on Lord Spencer who promised him a pension subject to a medical examination at Surgeons' Hall. At this interview Fremantle was so 'pulled about by the surgeons' that in the evening he had to leave a performance at Drury Lane where they were playing ' – *A Wife and have a Wife, The Devil to Pay,* and *The Trip to the Nore.*' The examination was satisfactory. Fremantle was given a gratuity of a year's pay, and a pension of £200 a year. He and Betsey then left for Stowe, the great country seat of Lord Buckingham who was Fremantle's patron. Here they spent a happy Christmas Day (on which 'near 300 poor people dined in the house'), and there was an invitation from Lady Buckingham to stay on until Fremantle had fully recovered.

Nelson meanwhile was undergoing much the same ordeal. He had drawn up a memorial to the King and received a summons to Surgeons' Hall, though not for his arm but his eye. He refused to go at the inconvenient hour demanded and arrived in his own time in jocular mood. 'This is only for an eye,' he told the surgeons, 'in a few days I shall come for an arm; in a little time longer, God knows, for a leg.' He was granted a pension of £1,000 a year. The exposed nerve in his stump was giving him great pain, but his indomitable spirit rose above it and his mind was already on the new ship promised him as soon as he was well enough. The choice of a flag-captain did not take long to decide. Berry, now a post-captain, was in the country and temporarily unemployed: he liked him as a man and knew his abilities as an officer. The decision had already been taken when Berry came up from Norfolk on 23 September to be presented by Nelson at a levee. It was a splendid gathering at St James's Palace: the company included old Lord Howe resplendent in blue and gold, Malmesbury just back from Lille, and Captain Waller who had brought to England the Tenerife despatches. The 'good old King' was up from Kew for the day with two of his daughters. On approaching Nelson he exclaimed: 'You have lost your right arm!' 'But not my right hand, Sir,' replied Nelson, 'as I have the honour of presenting Captain Berry.'

For two months Nelson's stump continued to give him pain, and even the news of Duncan's great victory at Camperdown did little to cheer him. Berry, realizing it might not be long before he was called for, became engaged to his cousin, a Miss Forster of Norwich. 'I congratulate you on becoming one of *us*,' wrote Nelson, and added that the *Foudroyant* would most likely be their ship: she was to be launched in January, 1798, and commissioned in February. Five days later the ligature on Nelson's stump fell away and revealed a wound perfectly healed. He reported to Spencer that he was now fit for service and a few days later he was again writing to Berry:

'If you mean to marry, I would recommend your doing it speedily, or the to be Mrs Berry will have very little of your company; for I am well, and you may expect to be called for every hour. We shall probably be at sea before the *Foudroyant* is launched. Our ship is at Chatham, a Seventy-four, and she will be choicely manned. This may not happen, but it stands so to-day.'

In his new flag-captain Nelson had perfect confidence; but he did not neglect his friendship for the old. One of his first actions on arriving in England was to tell Mrs Miller that her husband was well and that he had the greatest regard for him; a gesture which, Miller gratefully told him, 'completely saved the torment of all those anxious fears to which the tenderness of a female bosom is so liable'. The two corresponded regularly. Miller brought news of the Fleet: Hallowell had left the *Lively* and gone to the *Swiftsure*, 74. Fremantle's wound worried him. 'I am sincerely sorry for his sufferings both on his own account and that of his amiable little wife.' Now Nelson wrote that he and Lady Nelson had been to see Miller's daughter and thought her 'a very fine little girl'; more important news was his appointment to the *Vanguard*, at Chatham.

On 17 December Nelson went to Chatham to see the *Vanguard* out of dock. 'She is ready,' he told the First Lord, 'to receive men whenever your Lordship is pleased to direct her being commissioned.' Next day Berry accompanied him to the great naval thanksgiving service at St Paul's for the victories of the First of June, St Vincent and Camperdown. Then, early in the New Year, Berry set off for Chatham and Nelson took his wife down to Bath until the ship was ready.

The commissioning of the *Vanguard* took longer than expected. On 25 February, Berry was writing that most of the work had been completed and he hoped to sail for the Nore early in March. 'I'm very anxious to get out, heartily tired of fitting.' All the powder had arrived and most of the stores and wood. The officers were satisfactory: 'Mr Kremer, the Hanoverian, towers above them all'. He had 'received the parson safe,' and sent Galway, the first lieutenant, 'on three or four days leave to take his farewell of the shore'. The main problem was finding men: despite frequent representations to the Port-Admiral he was still far short of complement. His wife and sister had been on board, and one evening it blew so hard they had to remain all night: 'They behaved very well and enjoyed the frolic'. Nelson's furniture had arrived safely, and he suggested a square looking-glass about two feet long for the after-cabin. There was a characteristic P.S. 'Despite all my care, there is *a* Rat on board.'

Berry's hopes of an early sailing were not fulfilled. Ten days later he was writing: 'There are 300 women on board and not less than 150 supernumeraries besides the ship's company. All the females go ashore to-morrow if we are paid. At all events I have set my face against taking *one* to sea.' Mrs Berry was in London and Berry was grateful to Lady Nelson for calling on her. 'She requires consolation after parting from me, but this is only teaching her discipline – of what necessarily must happen to sailors' wives.' The comfort of the Admiral's quarters was still on his mind. 'If a floor cloth would not be too expensive, I think one in the dining-room would be comfortable where the table stands – 16 feet in length and 13 feet, 5, 6 or 7 inches broad – also a carpet for the side of your cot, if you use one.' The looking-glass he had mentioned would require a deep, gold frame.

At last Berry succeeded in getting the men paid and the women disembarked and orders came to sail to Portsmouth. Writing to Nelson at sea off the Downs, having rounded the North Foreland 'in as rough a state as any ship of war can be supposed to be in,' he asked: 'Why not before? – but their Lordships know best. Perhaps I'm rather impatient.' Nelson's cabin still worried him. 'Have you thought of curtains for the quarter-galleries? They are necessary. Whether or not for the stern windows you will judge. There are shutters but no jalousies.' And he gave the measurements for both.

In London Nelson saw again the Fremantles, who had settled in a little house in Bolton Row at the end of Curzon Street: and on 28 February he took Fremantle to a levee. Fremantle's arm was mending but he was still much of an invalid; and Betsey was nearing the end of her pregnancy. She went shopping with Fremantle's sister and 'bespoke all the baby linen,' but was disappointed she could not get it under £30. Despite their disabilities the pair took a full share in the London social

round. One evening they visited Drury Lane to see Hamlet and
Blue Beard – it must have been a long programme:

'We had an exceedingly bad Box up one pair of stairs,
nothing but fine Damsels about us, which I found not a
little annoying. Blue Beard is vastly pretty but it was interrupted in the most interesting part by a great noise and cry
of fire. All the ladies fainted away and were greatly alarmed.
I was not much frightened. It proved to be nothing but a
boxing-match. Our Beaux chose to leave us alone in one of
the Lobby boxes whilst they went to look for the carriages.
Two drunken young men came in and were exceedingly
impudent, taking us for other sort of women. I was very
much alarmed but we got, however, rid of them.'

She heard regularly from her family at Naples, but 'P. is
more undetermined than ever, and as he won't avail himself of a
French passport I fear I have no chance of seeing them'. On
9 March Betsey dined at her brother-in-law William's where
the ladies told her she would soon be brought to bed. Two days
later, while Berry was rounding the North Foreland, 'to my no
small happiness and everybody's surprise I was brought to
bed by seven o'clock in the evening of a boy'.

Betsey soon recovered. By the end of the month when Nelson
was hoisting his flag in the *Vanguard* in Portsmouth harbour,
she was up and about and 'dining with F. in his little parlour'.
In the spring she heard that her father was 'determined to
come over to us very soon,' and finally the family arrived back
in London on 24 May 1798. That day a squadron of ten ships
of the line passed into the Mediterranean on an expedition
which was to end in one of Britain's greatest naval victories.

*   *   *

'Sir Horatio Nelson being on his return to Lisbon,' wrote
Saumarez's son James with all the sophistication of his
eight years, 'I am very happy to send a few lines by him.
The Figs and Plumbs arrived last night and we are very
thankful to you for them. Mary says she would rather see
you than all the Plumbs and I think so too. We had a party
the other day and all found me like you and I am very glad

of it. Carterette is a very pretty little girl and I wish you could come and see her.'

Nelson handed this letter to Saumarez when he joined the Fleet off Cadiz at the end of April, and was posted to the in-shore squadron where Troubridge, Miller, Hood, Collingwood and other old friends were awaiting him. There were letters and parcels for them too. 'On my visiting Sir Horatio this morning,' wrote Sam Hood to Lord Bridport, 'I was satisfied to find such good accounts of your Lordship's health.' Colling-wood had a batch of letters from his wife. 'I never saw my friend Nelson look so well,' he told her. 'He is really grown fat, and not the worse for losing an arm.'

But if Nelson and his old friends expected something of each other's company they were disappointed. During the early months of the year, while Nelson and Berry were waiting for the *Vanguard* to commission, the French had been preparing a great fleet in the northern Mediterranean ports, especially Toulon and Genoa. Speculation as to its destination had been rife: everyone had their own ideas and few coincided. The French, who made no effort to conceal their activities, gave out that it was intended against the Kingdom of the Two Sicilies. Lord Spencer thought Naples the first objective, but that the main plan was the conquest of Spain through Portugal or a landing in southern Ireland. Captain Sir Sidney Smith, recently escaped from two years in a Paris prison, favoured Egypt: Collingwood heard reports from American ships that England was the objective. St Vincent had no clear ideas.

As the weeks passed and the great armament grew, it became of prime importance to find out its intentions. At the moment that St Vincent was casting round for some suitable officer to undertake the task, Nelson arrived in the *Vanguard*. Nothing could have been more opportune. 'The arrival of Admiral Nelson,' St Vincent told Spencer, 'has given me new life. His presence in the Mediterranean is so very essential that I mean to put the *Orion* and *Alexander* under his command and to send them away to endeavour to ascertain the real objects of the preparations making by the French.'

Nelson had joined the Fleet on 30 April 1798. On 2 May he ordered Captains Saumarez and Ball to follow his motions, and accompanied by four frigates under Captain Hope made sail to the southward. The squadron passed through the Straits into familiar water and the Rock of Gibraltar dropped out of sight astern. Not for another five years was Nelson to sight it again.

* * *

Captain Alexander John Ball came of an old Gloucestershire family who for many years had lived at Stonehouse Court, near Stroud. He was educated at the Market School-house, and here at an early age his life nearly ended. One day after the execution of some thieves at Gloucester he and his friends 'played at hanging.' Ball was chosen as the victim and 'after being suspended for some time in mid-air, everyone thought his performance very life-like'. His younger brother said: 'Our Alick likes it: he won't speak'. An elder boy happened to pass by and seeing Ball black in the face, cut him down not a moment too soon.

On leaving school at the age of twelve Ball went into the Navy because, he afterwards told the poet Coleridge, of the deep impression made on him by Robinson Crusoe. At the Battle of the Saints he served as a lieutenant in Rodney's flag-ship, the *Sandwich,* and for his skill and bravery was promoted to Commander. Apart from a brief commission in the *Nemesis* frigate, he took little part in the French War until his appointment to the *Alexander* in 1797. He joined the Fleet in the early summer but was detached for duty at Gibraltar. Here he met Fremantle and Betsey, on the point of sailing for the Fleet in the *Seahorse.* While the *Seahorse* was taking in powder, Fremantle breakfasted with Ball in the *Alexander*; 'where, by the by' said Betsey, 'he got a very bad one'.

Neither in appearance nor temperament was Ball at all like his fellow captains. His portrait by Pickersgill, with the long dome-shaped head, wide reflective eyes and thoughtful expression give him the air of a university professor rather than a

sea-officer. The impression is borne out by his character, for
Ball was a 'bookish' man. The habit of reading, which he first
acquired during a long illness as a lieutenant, became a lifelong
pleasure. His favourite subjects, said Coleridge, were 'history,
political economy, voyages and travels, natural history and
latterly agricultural works; in short such books as contain
specific facts or practical principles capable of scientific application. Works of amusement as novels, plays, etc, did not
amuse him: and the only poetical composition of which I have
heard him speak was a manuscript poem written by one of
my friends which I read to his lady in his presence.' This was
Wordworth's *Peter Bell*. And yet Ball could not have been a
professor any more than a great sea-officer; for he was too
much a man of action for the one and of meditation for the
other. His contemporaries speak of his courteous speech, his
'conciliating' manners, the evenness of his temper and the
soundness of his judgment.

Ball did not enjoy Nelson's insight, Troubridge's seamanship, Hood's leadership; but he did not share their fretfulness.
There could be no greater contrast than Troubridge's and
Ball's handwriting, the one sprawling across the page in large
ill-formed lettering, often forged in a white heat of anger and
impatience, the other neat, legible, considered, a model of
punctuation and precision. In stability of temperament Ball
was nearer Hardy: but where Hardy, like Foley and Hallowell,
came of the traditionally bluff, solid type of officer who arrived
at decisions by a blend of instinct and experience, Ball acted
solely by his reason. 'An ignorant commander,' said Coleridge,
'terrified him.' When Ball took over the *Nemesis* her crew were
dissatisfied and mutinous. When he had to punish a man,
Ball would ask three questions: 'Did you commit the act? Did
you know it was a breach of the rule? Was it not in your power
to have avoided it?' 'By enlisting the reason and conscience
of his men on the side of the law,' says one of his biographers,
'he won his crew completely; and they became as fine a body of
loyal seamen as the Navy possessed.'

Ball's early relationship with Nelson was rather peculiar.

In 1783 Ball and his wife visited France and found themselves at St Omer where Nelson was also staying. Each expected the other to call, with the result that neither had, and there was a certain coolness. 'Two noble captains are here,' Nelson wrote home, 'Ball and Shepherd. They wear fine epaulets for which I think them great coxcombs. They have not visited me and I shall not, be assured, court their acquaintance.' The two did not meet again until Nelson's arrival off Cadiz in the *Vanguard* fifteen years later. But the incident had stuck in Nelson's memory, and when Ball came to pay his respects he was greeted roughly with: 'What, are you come to have your bones broken?' Ball, sensing in the remark as much sourness as jest, replied he had not, unless for the service of King and Country; and after an uncomfortable interview he returned to his ship.

On Thursday, 17 May, Nelson's squadron captured a French corvette and learnt that Bonaparte had arrived at Toulon, that 12,000 cavalry had embarked in the transports, and that fifteen sail of the line under Admiral Brueys in *L'Orient* were ready for sea. There was no news of their destination so Nelson bore up towards Cape Sicie, the headland guarding the approaches to Toulon. On the evening of Sunday 20 May, a violent gale sprang up. At two in the morning the *Vanguard*'s main topmast went over the side, followed a little later by her mizen topmast; and at three o'clock the foremast went by the board. Young Berry, shattered by this series of disasters on his first operational cruise, was at his wits' end. 'Our situation was really alarming,' he wrote, 'knowing we were driving on an enemy's shore.' There was a small rag of sprit-sail left, and by waiting for a favourable moment he was able to wear the ship on to the other tack and steer to the southwards. The gale continued all Monday and Tuesday, but by Tuesday evening when the squadron was close in to Sardinia, it had abated sufficiently to allow Ball to take the *Vanguard* in tow. By nightfall the wind had dropped, but there was a heavy swell which set the two ships in towards the shore. 'You may figure to yourself our situation,' wrote Berry, 'when I tell you I could easily distinguish the surf breaking on the rocky shore.'

Nelson, believing the *Vanguard* doomed, ordered Ball to slip the tow and make for safety. Ball refused; whereupon Nelson 'became impetuous and enforced his demand with passionate threats'. Ball then picked up his speaking trumpet and 'with great solemnity and without the least disturbance of temper' called out in reply: 'I feel confident that I can bring you in safe. I therefore must not, and by the help of Almighty God will not leave you.' At dawn the two ships were close in to the island of St Pierre. A slight breeze bore up which enabled them to weather the headland, and Saumarez went ahead to guide them into harbour. Here at midday they all came to anchor. Nelson lost no time in visiting the *Alexander*, and greeting Ball with 'a friend in need is a friend indeed,' gave him his unreserved thanks. From this moment a friendship sprang up which was to grow in intensity and end only with Nelson's death.

* * *

While Nelson's carpenters were labouring to make the *Vanguard* seaworthy, the British and French naval commands had, without his or each other's knowledge, already launched operations which were to have far-reaching effects.

Having made his peace with the Austrians by the treaty of Campo Formio, Bonaparte turned his attention elsewhere. The enormous conquests he had made had only whetted his appetite for more. But the stumbling-block to all his plans was England, and in particular England's Navy. The Directory made him Commander-in-Chief of an army of invasion: but it was an operation which he regarded as professionally impracticable and personally unsatisfying. As far back as February he had written to Bourienne: 'My glory has already disappeared. This little Europe does not supply enough of it for me. I must seek it in the East: all great fame comes from that quarter. However I wish first to make a tour along the northern coast to see for myself what may be attempted. If the success of a descent upon England appears doubtful as I suggest it will, the Army of England shall become the Army of the East and I go to Egypt.' He went to Dunkirk and the Flemish coast, and found his fears confirmed. Without a strong Navy he was powerless, and 'whatever efforts we make we shall not for some years gain the naval supremacy. To invade England without that supremacy is the most daring and most difficult task ever undertaken.' Another plan suggested itself. The Mediterranean was now a French waterway: there were no British battleships watching the roadstead of Toulon. By landing an army in Egypt and then pushing on to India, Bonaparte would be able to deprive England of the trade on which she depended and at the same time fulfil his ambition of creating a new and glorious Eastern Empire.

Having obtained the approval of the Directory, Bonaparte ordered the expedition to prepare, and during the winter and spring of 1798 it began assembling. On 3 May Bonaparte left Paris and five days later arrived in Toulon. The fleet consisted of thirteen ships of the line and some four hundred transports under the command of Vice-Admiral Brueys, with Rear-Admirals Villeneuve, Blanquet and Decrès, and Commodore Ganteaume as Captain of the Fleet. The military forces numbered 35,000 troops led by nine generals including Kleber, Davout, Lannes, Murat and Marmont. There was also a corps of scientists and professors. On 19 May, the day before the *Vanguard* was dismasted in the gale, the armada sailed.

The British Admiralty had been slower to act. Had it not been for Pitt they might not have acted at all. For a long time he had been considering sending a British squadron into the Mediterranean – not because of the preparations at Toulon, but because he thought it might induce the peoples of southern Europe to revolt against their oppressors. Spencer and the Board of Admiralty condemned the scheme out of hand. With the Spanish fleet to blockade in Cadiz, and rebellion threatening in Ireland, there were not the ships to spare. But Pitt persevered and at a Cabinet meeting in April carried his colleagues with him. On the day that Nelson arrived back in the Fleet, Spencer was writing to St Vincent 'of a plan of operation very different from what we have hitherto adopted'. 'The appearance of a squadron in the Mediterranean,' he continued, 'is a condition on which the face of Europe may at this moment be stated to depend.' The squadron was to be detached as soon as a supporting force under Sir Roger Curtis reached Cadiz from the west of Ireland. 'I think it almost unnecessary to suggest to you,' concluded Spencer, 'the propriety of putting it under the command of Sir H. Nelson, whose acquaintance with that part of the world, as well as his activity and disposition, seem to qualify him in a peculiar manner for that service.'

St Vincent received these orders on 10 May – nine days before Bonaparte sailed. He at once despatched Captain Hardy in the *Mutine* into the Mediterranean to look for Nelson and tell him that eleven sail of the line would join him as soon as the reinforcements arrived. He also gave Hardy a line for the British Ambassador at Naples.

'I have a powerful squadron ready to fly to the assistance of Naples the moment I receive a reinforcement from the West of Ireland, which is on its passage hither, and I hourly look for its appearance with the utmost degree of anxiety and impatience. Rear-Admiral Sir Horatio Nelson will command this force, which is composed of the *élite* of the navy of England.'

After dark on the evening of 24 May, Sir Roger Curtis brought his ships into the Fleet off Cadiz, and the squadron under Troubridge sailed. During the night Curtis's ships painted themselves with the same markings so that when daylight came there was nothing to arouse the suspicions of the watching Spaniards.

By 27 May, owing to what Nelson called 'the wonderful exertions of Sir James Saumarez and Captain A. Ball,' the *Vanguard* was ready for service. The squadron proceeded to sea, and next day took a prize from which Nelson learnt that the French Fleet had sailed. On 5 June, he fell in with the *Mutine*, and Hardy told him that Troubridge and the reinforcements were on their way. 'This intelligence,' said Berry, 'was received with universal joy throughout our little squadron.' Two days later Berry sighted 'ten ships of war standing upon a wind in a close line of battle, with all sails set'. One by one the ships displayed their pendants; those whom St Vincent had called 'the *élite* of the Navy of England' proved to be some of Nelson's old and most trusted friends: Troubridge in the *Culloden*, Miller in the *Theseus*, Hallowell in the *Swiftsure*, Hood in the *Zealous*, Foley in the *Goliath*, Thompson in the *Leander*; and other less intimate but equally reputable officers: Louis of the *Minotaur*, Gould of the *Audacious*, Peyton of the *Defence*, Westcott of the *Majestic* and Darby of the *Bellerophon*.

Nelson formed up his squadron in three divisions under himself, Troubridge and Saumarez, and stood to the eastward in chase.

* * *

The handicaps with which Nelson set out were considerable. Bonaparte had the advantage of nearly three weeks' sailing; he had no clear idea which way he had gone; there was practically no wind; and worst of all Captain Hope, imagining that the damage to the *Vanguard* would necessitate dockyard repairs, had returned with the frigates – 'the eyes of the fleet' – to Gibraltar. Against this he commanded a body of ships and men tested by five years of war in all weathers and conditions and brought by St Vincent and himself to a fighting efficiency unequalled. Saumarez spoke for the whole squadron when he wrote: 'The officers and crews in the several ships are all in the highest spirits; and I never remember going into action with more certain hopes of success.' And behind them, welding them together and driving them invincibly forwards, was the will of their Admiral; his own terrible inflexible purpose to seek out the enemy wherever they might be, and however long it took him. 'Be they bound to the Antipodes,' he told Spencer, 'your Lordships may rely that I will not lose a moment in bringing them to action.'

In light airs the squadron rounded Cape Corse and stood to the southward. Hardy was detached into Telamon Bay, and reported it empty. On 14 June Nelson ordered Troubridge to transfer to the *Mutine* and proceed ahead to the British Ambassador at Naples. Two things particularly he wanted of the Kingdom of the Two Sicilies: 'frigates and other fast-sailing vessels, for all mine have left me'; and an assurance that Naples and Sicily would be open to the fleet for supplies. 'Captain Troubridge,' he told Sir William Hamilton, 'is my honoured acquaintance of twenty-five years standing, and the very best sea-officer in His Majesty's Service. He is in full possession of my confidence and I beg that whatever he says may be considered as coming from me.'

During the night of 16 June the *Mutine* entered Naples Bay, and by six in the morning Troubridge and Hardy were with the Ambassador. From him they learnt that the French armada had passed by several days before, and was now reported on the point of attacking Malta. Hamilton took the two captains to see General Acton, the Prime Minister, and the Marquis de Gallo, Secretary of State. Troubridge's directness impressed them. 'He went straight to the point,' said Hamilton, 'we did more business in half an hour than we should have done in a week in the usual official way.' But although the diplomats were anxious to help, they could not conceal their terror of the French; and Troubridge was bound to reiterate that unless the Fleet could obtain provisions from Italy, it might have to be withdrawn from the Mediterranean. Acton refused to sanction the use of Neapolitan frigates – that was too near a declaration of war; but he gave a firm promise that the ports of the Two Sicilies should supply the fleet 'under the rose'.

Their business completed in less than two hours, Hardy and Troubridge re-embarked in the *Mutine* and made sail to where the squadron was lying to off Ischia. Nelson waited long enough only to write a final note to Hamilton about his need for frigates, and then crowded on sail to the southwards. On 20 June the squadron pushed through the Straits of Messina: the *Orion* led, guided by a local pilot from whom Saumarez learnt that the French were still off Malta; and the next day he wrote: 'To-morrow I think will bring us in view of the enemy's fleet.'

But the morrow brought different news. During the morning three French frigates were sighted and Nelson detached the *Leander* in chase. About the same time Captain Hardy captured a Ragusan brig which told him that the French had captured

Malta on the 16th and sailed the day after. 'This intelligence,' said Saumarez, 'has more than ever left us in perplexity as to their further destination.' Nelson, equally perplexed, signalled 'those captains in whom I place great confidence' – Troubridge, Saumarez, Ball and Darby – to come on board for a conference. His own peculiar genius had divined the enemy's purpose. 'If they pass Sicily, I shall believe they are going on their scheme of possessing Alexandria and getting troops to India.' Since the wind had blown steadily from the west his captains were forced to agree with him; although, as Berry pointed out, it was equally possible the enemy had gone up to the Adriatic. Nelson therefore recalled the *Leander* from her pursuit of the French frigates. 'They were not considered,' said Saumarez, 'of sufficient importance to run the risk of separating the squadron.'

This decision, which Nelson probably forgot as soon as he had made, was one of the most momentous in European history. For the report of the Ragusan had been false: the French had not left Malta on the 17th but on the 20th, and the frigates Thompson had been sent to chase were not, as Nelson and Saumarez supposed, on their own, but the outer screen of Bonaparte's huge fleet which was labouring eastwards just over the southern horizon. If Hardy had not captured the Ragusan when he did, if her master had given a true instead of a false report, if the French frigates had been sighted an hour or two earlier and Thompson had been able to catch up, if Captain Hope had not deprived Nelson of his own frigates – if any one of these small accidents had been avoided, the French Fleet would have been brought to battle that evening. And if that had happened, Trafalgar might have been fought seven years earlier and Waterloo not at all. The misfortunes which enabled Bonaparte to escape destruction by a few hours were, in the words of one historian, 'to cost Britain and the civilized world seventeen more years of war, waste and destruction'. That night the tracks of the two fleets, the one steering south of east, the other a little north of it, crossed. So close did they pass that Brueys heard the minute-guns of the British ships signalling and sheered away to the northward. By daylight the sea around Nelson's squadron was empty.

Although the decision to steer for Egypt had been unanimous, few had confidence in it. 'We are proceeding upon the merest conjecture only,' said Saumarez, 'and not on any positive information.' He himself was distressed and unhappy and beginning to realize what his fellow captains already knew, that he acted as second in command by virtue of rank not choice, and that in St Vincent's and Nelson's eyes Troubridge was the better man for the post. St Vincent had already put the *Orion* under sailing orders for England and given Nelson permission to detach her when the reinforcement under Troubridge joined. Nelson had refrained from this only because, having heard that Bonaparte had sailed, he wanted every ship he could lay hands on. His many conferences with Saumarez during the voyage had not improved their relationship. The spark which Nelson aroused in his other captains, in Troubridge, Ball, even the dour Hardy, was lacking in Saumarez. Nor was Saumarez's aloof, reserved manner protection against the moods of Nelson; and he confessed in his diary that the situation was almost more than his 'too irritable nerves' could bear.

On 26 June, the mouth of the Nile being 230 miles distant, Nelson ordered Hardy to go ahead to Alexandria to obtain news from the British Consul. 'Pray do not detain the *Mutine*,' he told the Consul, 'for I am in a fever at not finding the French.' Three days later off Pharos Tower, Alexandria, the *Mutine* rejoined with a blank report. 'The Consul was away on leave,' wrote Sam Hood, 'and all the information that could be obtained was from a stupid Vice-Consul, not an Englishman.'

Nelson, desperate at having missed the French and believing, as he always did when things went wrong, that the failure was his, wrote to St Vincent a long apologia. 'Where success does not crown an officer's plan,' it opened, 'it is absolutely necessary he should explain the motives which actuate his conduct.' And it ended: 'I am before your Lordship's judgment, and if it is decided I am wrong, I ought for the sake of our country to be superseded. I hold that I was right in steering for Alexandria and by that opinion I must stand or fall.' Before forwarding the letter Nelson sent it to Ball, whose judgment he now highly respected. 'I was particularly struck,' Ball replied, 'with the clear and accurate style as well as with the candour of the statement in your letter; but I felt a regret that your too anxious zeal should make you start an idea that you are not perfectly satisfied with your own conduct. I should recommend a friend never to begin a defence of his conduct before he is accused of error'. But Nelson could not be dissuaded. With his extra-ordinary perception he had sensed what in fact was true, that in London and off Cadiz people were saying that the failure to find the French was due to the appointment of so junior an officer to so important a command. Off Cadiz Sir John Orde, an admiral senior to Nelson, wrote a public letter to the Commander-in-Chief to protest; for which impertinence St Vincent ordered him home.

There now approached the second occasion of the long chase whereby Nelson missed the French Fleet by a few hours. His decision to make for Egypt had been correct. If he had had the patience to stand by it and remain a little longer off Alexandria he would have been rewarded. But he felt as always, 'that to do nothing was disgraceful'. 'His anxious and active mind,' said Berry, 'would not permit him to remain a moment in the same place.' According to Hood, he thought it possible the French were watering in Corfu; and using this yard-stick as an excuse for more 'active' service, he 'stretched the fleet over to the coast of Asia'. Hardly had the grey sails of his squadron faded out of sight to the north-east than the watchers on the Pharos Tower saw the hulls of Bonaparte's armada climbing over the horizon to the north-west.

Having sighted nothing off the coasts of Carmania and Crete, Nelson supposed he had been wrong in his conclusions, and began the long journey back to Sicily. He entered Syracuse on 20 July, by which time Bonaparte had landed his army, stormed Alexandria and won the Battle of the Pyramids.

From the Sicilians Nelson learnt that the French were not to the westward and must therefore still be behind him. 'The devil's children,' he wrote to Hamilton, 'have the devil's luck.' Depressed as he was, nothing could shake his determination. 'All my ill-fortune,' he told St Vincent, 'has proceeded from want of frigates. But if they are above water I will find them out and if possible bring them to battle.' The squadron sailed again on 25 July. On the 28th Nelson sent Troubridge into Coron to ask the Turkish Governor for news: he reported the French Fleet had been sighted steering to the south-east four weeks earlier. A vessel captured by Ball confirmed the news, and the squadron crowded on sail for Egypt.

On the morning of 1 August the *Alexander* and *Swiftsure*, which had been sent on ahead, arrived off Alexandria. Ball and Hallowell signalled to Nelson that the French flag was flying over the battlements, that the harbour was crowded with merchant ships, but there was no sign of the French Fleet. 'At this news,' said Saumarez, 'despondency nearly took possession of my mind, and I do not recollect ever to have felt so utterly hopeless or out of spirits as when we sat down to dinner.' Nelson, hardly believing it possible that he had missed the enemy again, recalled the *Alexander* and *Swiftsure* and turned the Fleet eastwards along the coast. This manoeuvre brought the *Goliath* and *Zealous* into the lead; but there was no order of sailing, each ship pressing onward as fast as possible to save time.

A little after two o'clock George Elliot, the son of the ex-Viceroy of Corsica and now Foley's signal midshipman, sighted from the royal yard of the *Goliath* a strange fleet at anchor in Aboukir Bay. They were moored in line of battle facing seawards, one astern of the other, and protected on their larboard sides by the western shoals of the bay: they consisted of thirteen ships of the line and four frigates. Not daring to hail the deck for fear the *Zealous* might overhear and gain the credit, Elliot slid down the backstay and reported his news to Foley. The signal 'enemy in sight' was hoisted, but owing to a faulty stopper came adrift. Hood, whose look-out had sighted the

French Fleet at almost the same time, hoisted his own signal and this, to Elliot's unspeakable disappointment, was first seen in the flag-ship.

The news that the enemy had at last been found quickly spread. 'The utmost joy,' said Berry, 'seemed to animate every breast.' Saumarez and his officers, sitting despondently at the dinner-table, heard the news as the cloth was being removed. 'Judge what a change took place,' he said. 'All sprang from their seats and only staying to drink a bumper to our success, we were in a moment on deck.'

From the yard-arm of the *Vanguard* a succession of flags broke out. The *Alexander* and *Swiftsure*, thrown astern by the turn to eastwards, were ordered to rejoin as quickly as possible: the *Culloden*, delayed by a prize, was also ordered to make sail. At 3 p.m. Nelson made the general signal: 'Prepare for battle and for anchoring by the stern,' and two hours later, when approaching the entrance to the bay, 'I mean to attack the enemy's van and centre'. Finally at 5.30 p.m. he signalled: 'Form line of battle as convenient'. On receiving this Elliot was able to get his own back on Hood. For Foley had anticipated the signal and already bent on his studding and staysails. As soon as Elliot reported the signal had left the flag-ship's deck, the sails were let fly; and before the *Zealous* could act on it the *Goliath* had shot half a ship's length ahead. 'Hood was annoyed,' commented Elliot, 'but could not help it.' As the two ships approached the island at the entrance to the bay, the *Vanguard* came up with the *Zealous* and Nelson asked Hood if there was enough water to bear up for the enemy. 'I cannot say, Sir,' shouted Hood, 'but if you will allow me the honour of leading into battle, I will stand in and try.' 'You have my leave,' said Nelson, 'and I wish you success'; and he waved his hat. Hood raised his in acknowledgment, but a gust of wind swept it overboard. 'Never mind, Webley,' said Hood to his first lieutenant, 'there it goes for luck. Put the helm up and make sail.'

The *Zealous* altered course to starboard, and almost immediately the *Goliath* did the same. By this manoeuvre Foley, who had the inshore berth, increased his lead to a ship's length. Hood tried to catch up, but at length saw it was useless. 'Well, never mind,' he said, 'Foley is a fine, gallant, worthy fellow. Shorten sail and give him time to take up his berth. We must risk nothing that will tend to the enemy's advantage and we shall all soon have enough to do.' The *Vanguard* dropped astern to speak to the *Mutine* and was passed by the *Audacious* and *Orion,* which took station astern of the *Zealous.* The *Theseus* also passed the Admiral, and Berry called to Miller to take station between him and the *Orion.* The rest of the fleet formed up astern in the order *Minotaur, Defence, Bellerophon, Majestic, Leander,* with the *Culloden, Alexander* and *Swiftsure* still some way astern.

In each ship officers and men prepared for action. Bulkheads were pulled down, loose furniture removed to the hold, galley-fires extinguished, livestock thrown overboard. Tubs of fresh and salt water were placed alongside each gun for the refreshment of the men and in case of fire, and wet sand sprinkled on the decks. Sails not in use were well damped: Ball gave orders for his to be rolled into tight non-inflammable cylinders. Hammocks were brought up from below and stowed in the nettings on the upper deck as a protection against splinters and small shot. Lower-deck hatches were battened down, except two fore and aft for the powder-boys going to and from the magazines: marine sentries stood guard over them to prevent skulkers seeking protection below. Officers and men moved confidently to their accustomed stations; the captain and first lieutenant to the quarter-deck, the lieutenants and midshipmen to their sections of the guns, the carpenters to the orlop-deck to plug the shot-holes, the purser to his store to issue battle-lanterns, the gunners to the magazine, the surgeon to the cockpit. The marines, equipped with small arms, took up positions on the quarter-deck to pick off the enemy's sharpshooters.

At the guns the men stood about in little groups. They had opened up the ports and run out the guns and now they only waited the order to fire. Most had stripped to the waist and tied round their heads black silk handkerchiefs to deaden the noise. Because they had always lived hard and set little value on life, they were not silent and afraid but talkative and expectant: many welcomed an action as a change to the daily routine and for the chance of prize-money. An officer stationed at one of the guns jotted down this conversation between two of them:

Jack: 'There are thirteen sail of the line, and a whacking lot of frigates and small craft. I think we'll hammer the rust off ten of them, if not the whole boiling.'

Tom: 'We took but four on the First of June, and I got seven pounds of prize-money. Now, if we knock up a dozen of these fellows (and why shouldn't we?) d–n my eyes, messmates, we will have a bread-bag full of money to receive.'

Jack: 'Aye, I'm glad we have twigged 'em at last. I want some new riggin d–bly for Sundays and mustering days.'

Tom: 'So do I. I hope we'll touch enough for that, and a d–d good cruise among the girls besides.'

Soon after six o'clock, as the sun was setting over the western sand-dunes of the bay, the *Goliath* and *Zealous* cleared Aboukir Island and the shore. Not hesitating for a moment, they made straight for the French van. At six twenty the enemy hoisted their colours, and a few minutes later the *Conquerant* and *Guerrier* at the head of the French line opened fire.

The Battle of the Nile had begun.

CHAPTER 7

Brueys had anchored his ships in what he thought an impregnable position. He had strung them out in a long slightly-curved line nearly two miles long, stretching from one end of the bay to the other: they were protected by shoal water ahead, astern, and all down their larboard side. So confident was he, that when Nelson's squadron was sighted many of his men were ashore getting water. He made the signal for their recall, but

according to Admiral Blanquet it was obeyed only by a few.
Brueys remained unperturbed, for he knew that before the
British could attack darkness would have fallen, and he did not
imagine they would attempt a night action in a strange anchorage infested with shoals. The same darkness, he hoped,
would enable his fleet to escape.

If Brueys had been dealing with an orthodox admiral his
presumptions might have been correct. But he could not reckon
with the tactical brilliance of Nelson. During the long chase
Nelson had forged his ships and men into a discipline and
understanding that was the single instrument of his will. Their
fighting efficiency, thanks to St Vincent, was as near perfect
as he could wish. 'He had the happiness to find,' said Berry,
'that to the captains he had no necessity to give directions for
being in constant readiness for battle. The decks of all the ships
were kept perfectly clear night and day, and every man was
ready to start to his post at a moment's notice.' Nelson therefore was able to devote all his attentions to problems of strategy
and tactics. Every day when the weather permitted he summoned his captains on board, 'in order,' said Berry, 'to fully
develop to them his own ideas of the different and best modes of
attack, and such plans as he proposed to execute upon falling
in with the enemy, *whatever their position or situation might be by
day or by night. There was no possible position in which they could be
found that he did not take into his consideration.*'

Chief among Nelson's plans, and one he emphasized time
and time again, was that of concentrating *all* his force on a
portion of the enemy's line, annihilating it in detail and dealing
with the rest later. Simple though this sounds, it was something
revolutionary in naval warfare. During the eighteenth century
it had been the custom in a fleet action for ship to grapple with
ship: and it had become an accepted dictum, laid down by
Clowdisley Shovell in 1702 and confirmed by Jervis in 1778,
that where two fleets of more or less equal strength were
matched, there could be no decisive result. This concentration
of fire-power was a thing Nelson practised all his life and the
key to most of his victories. Once, when sending two frigate

captains on a cruise, he advised them, if they fell in with two French frigates, to attack only one. 'If successful,' he added, 'chase the other; but if you do not take the second, still you have won a victory and your country will gain a frigate.'

There were two methods of achieving a local superiority, either by placing two ships on the bow and quarter of an enemy, or one on either side. When the *Goliath* was approaching the French van, Foley murmured he wished he could get inside the enemy's line as he was sure they would be unprepared on that side. The danger was the shoal. Foley did not know how near it was to the French line until he suddenly saw that the enemy ships were anchored only by the head. This told him that there must be clear water for a ship's length all round to enable them to swing, and that therefore there must be room for a British ship to anchor. He gave orders to the master to pass between the *Guerrier* (1)[1] and her buoy, and as soon as the *Goliath* was a ship's breadth inside, to let go the anchor. The responsibility for this manoeuvre was entirely Foley's, but it was in accordance with Nelson's general design. 'His projected mode of attack at anchor,' said Berry, '(formed more than two months before an opportunity presented itself of executing it) was minutely and precisely executed.'

It was fortunate that Foley led the British line and not Hood, for whereas Foley had a modern French atlas, Hood had an out-of-date English one; and he remarked that as the enemy's van was in five fathoms of water, he did not imagine Foley would pass inside. As Foley was letting go his anchor, the French frigate *Sérieuse* opened fire on him. A few broadsides soon silenced her. ('Our captain,' said one of his seamen, 'cried "Sink that brute. What does he here?"') This diversion caused more of the *Goliath*'s cable to run out than was intended, and she brought up between the *Conquérant* (2) and *Spartiate* (3). Hood seeing Foley had failed in his purpose, cut away his sheet anchor and came to abreast the *Guerrier* 'in the exact situation Captain Foley intended to have taken.' Saumarez, next astern in the *Orion*, followed Hood inside, passed him and

1. Signifies position in the French line.

Foley, and having finished off the *Sérieuse* anchored between the *Aquilon* (4) and *Peuple Souverain* (5). Gould in the *Audacious* cut across between the stern of the *Guerrier* and the *Conquérant* and fetched upon the *Conquérant*'s larboard bow, midway between the *Goliath* and *Zealous*. Miller followed Saumarez round the enemy's van and took the *Theseus* between the *Goliath, Zealous* and their opponents. As he passed down the line, the crews of all three ships cheered. 'The French,' commented Elliot, 'were ordered by their officers to cheer in return, but they made such a lamentable mess of it that the laughter in our ships was distinctly heard in theirs.' Having let fly a broadside at each ship that he passed, Miller anchored the *Theseus* astern of the *Goliath* and abreast the *Spartiate* (3).

Foley's belief that the French would be unprepared on their inner side proved correct. 'As we passed the *Guerrier*'s bow,' said Elliot, 'I saw her lower-deck guns were not run out and there were lumber such as bags and boxes on the upper-deck ports which I reported with no small pleasure.' As a result all her masts were shot down within a quarter of an hour of Hood's opening fire, while the damage to the *Zealous* was negligible. The *Conquérant* was able to inflict more damage on her opponents, but under the combined fire of the *Goliath, Audacious* and *Theseus*, her masts too went by the board, and after an action of only twenty minutes she became the first ship to surrender.

Nelson now approached the enemy line with the rear portion of his fleet. His first five ships having stationed themselves inside the enemy's van, he placed the remainder on the outside to effect a withering cross-fire. The *Guerrier* (1) and *Conquérant* (2) were already shambles. He therefore anchored the *Vanguard* abreast the *Spartiate* (3). Louis and Peyton in the *Minotaur* and *Defence* dropped down until they were abreast of the *Aquilon* (4) and *Peuple Souverain* (5). Darby in the *Bellerophon* intended to bring-to opposite the *Franklin* (6), but misjudged the distance and fetched up abreast *L'Orient* (7), Brueys's huge, three-decked flag-ship; and Westcott anchored the *Majestic* abreast of the *Tonnant* (8). Neither of these last two French

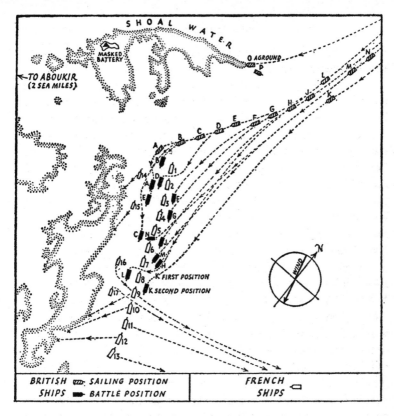

THE BATTLE OF THE NILE

	British Ships	Guns		French Ships	Guns	Result
A	GOLIATH	74	1	GUERRIER	74	taken and burnt
B	ZEALOUS	74	2	CONQUÉRANT	74	taken
C	ORION	74	3	SPARTIATE	74	,,
D	AUDACIOUS	74	4	AQUILON	74	,,
E	THESEUS	74	5	PEUPLE SOUVERAIN	74	,,
F	VANGUARD	74	6	FRANKLIN	80	,,
G	MINOTAUR	74	7	L'ORIENT	120	blew up
H	BELLEROPHON	74	8	TONNANT	80	taken
J	DEFENCE	74	9	HEUREUX	74	taken and burnt
K	MAJESTIC	74	10	MERCURE	74	taken and burnt
L	ALEXANDER	74	11	GUILLAUME TELL	80	escaped
M	SWIFTSURE	74	12	GÉNÉREUX	74	escaped
N	LEANDER	50	13	TIMOLÉON	74	taken and burnt
O	CULLODEN	74	14	SÉRIEUSE	36	sunk
P	MUTINE	14	15	ARTEMISE	40	burnt
			16	DIANE	44	escaped
			17	JUSTICE	44	escaped

127

ships was being engaged on her inner side. The *Culloden*, *Alexander* and *Swiftsure* were still some way astern.

For the next two hours the battle raged, as Berry put it, 'with an ardour and vigour it is impossible to describe.' Darkness had fallen as the action commenced, and the sultry night quickened to the roar of gunfire and flash of exploding powder. With his usual foresight Nelson had instructed his ships to wear white instead of blue ensigns to distinguish each other, and to hoist four horizontal blue lights at the mizen. With these to guide them, the British crews poured accurate and devastating broadsides into their opponents. The French, despite their unpreparedness and lack of training, fought back bravely. The casualty lists on both sides began to mount, and soon the upper decks became littered with dead and wounded. A boy in the *Goliath* who sat on a salt-box and gave out cartridges, 'was asked for one but gave none; yet he sat upright and his eyes were open.' One of the men pushed him and he fell on the deck. 'There was not a blemish on his body, yet he was quite dead and thrown overboard.' Among the senior officers the casualties were particularly heavy. Hood, Miller, Saumarez and Ball were all slightly wounded. Captain Westcott of the *Majestic* was killed. His opponent in the *Tonnant*, Captain Du Petit Thouars, having lost both arms and a leg, insisted on his trunk being put in a tub on the quarter-deck where he continued to fight the ship. Admirals Brueys and Blanquet were both wounded and nearly all their captains killed or hurt.

To those on deck the spectacle was 'grand and awful,' and a thing which few ever forgot; but to the men below it presented a different picture. 'I saw as little of this action,' wrote a seaman in the magazine of the *Goliath*, 'as I did of the one on the 14 February. Any information we got was from the boys and women who carried the powder. In the heat of the action a shot came right into the magazine, but the carpenters plugged it and stopped the water that was rushing in. I was much indebted to the gunner's wife who gave her husband and me a drink of wine every now and then, which lessened our fatigue much. There were some of the women wounded and one woman belonging to Leith died of her wounds. One woman bore a son in the heat of the action; she belonged to Edinburgh.' Another woman in the fleet was Nancy Perriam of the *Orion*, who helped the surgeon with his dreadful task in the cockpit as she had done at St Vincent. She records how a young midshipman, a protégé of Saumarez, had his arm taken out of the socket. 'The boy bore the operation without a murmur, and when it was over turned to me and said: "Have I not borne it like a man?" Having said this he immediately expired.'

The *Vanguard* and *Minotaur* were hotly engaging the *Spartiate* and *Aquilon* when at a little after eight o'clock Nelson, in the act of studying a map of the bay taken from a French prize by Hallowell, was struck on the forehead by a piece of shot. 'I am killed,' he said to Berry as he fell to the deck and then, in the style so dear to him, 'Remember me to my wife'. Berry helped him down to the cabin and into his cot. Believing his last hour had come, Nelson asked Berry to hail the *Minotaur* and summon Louis on board, as he could not have a moment's peace until he had thanked him for his support. 'This is the hundred and twenty-fourth time I have been in action,' he added, 'and I believe it is now nearly over with me.' Louis (a great-grandson of Louis XIV) came on board and was shown down to the cabin. 'Farewell, dear Louis,' said Nelson. 'I shall never forget the obligation I am under for your brave and generous conduct; and now whatever may become of me, my mind is at rest.'

About this time two welcome reinforcements arrived in the shape of the *Alexander* and *Swiftsure*. The *Culloden* was not with them. While bearing up to enter the bay, Troubridge had struck heavily on the shoal at the entrance; and only his prompt signals prevented Ball and Hallowell from following him. The *Mutine* and *Leander* went to his assistance but the rudder was torn away, there was quite a large hole in the keel, and it was clear nothing could be done till daylight. Here Troubridge passed a wretched night watching his fellow captains share the glory of a victory in which he could take no part.

As the *Swiftsure* approached the centre of the bay, an unlighted and disabled 74 drifted past her. The guns were brought to bear, but Hallowell ordered his crew to withhold their fire. It was as well he did, for the ship was the *Bellerophon* which had been engaging the huge *L'Orient* single-handed for over an hour, and had Darby and a third of her crew casualties. Making straight for the centre of the French line where there was now a lull in the firing, Hallowell brought up the *Swiftsure* abreast *L'Orient*, in the position Darby had quitted. Ball, passing beneath the French flag-ship's stern, anchored the *Alexander* close on her larboard quarter. At this moment a stray shot cut the cable of the *Peuple Souverain* (5) and she drifted away to leeward: whereupon Thompson anchored the *Leander* in her place and commenced a vigorous fire down the French line on the *Franklin* (6) and *L'Orient* (7).

By nine o'clock the first part of the battle was over. Under the combined fire of the *Zealous*, *Audacious*, *Goliath*, *Theseus* and *Orion* on one side, and the *Vanguard*, *Minotaur* and *Defence* on the other, the whole of the enemy's van was, in Miller's words, 'completely subdued.' The *Conquérant* (2) had already struck to Foley. The *Guerrier* (1), totally dismasted and with three-quarters of her crew killed and wounded, at last accepted Hood's repeated requests to surrender. The *Spartiate* (3) and *Aquilon* (4) had also been silenced, and the *Peuple Souverain* (5) was a wreck on the shoals to leeward.

Then it was the turn of *L'Orient*. Battered on three sides by the guns of the *Swiftsure*, *Alexander* and *Leander*, she suddenly caught fire. The flames, fed by barrels of paint left on deck when the action began, and by a combustible device thrown from the *Alexander* without Ball's permission, quickly spread. Soon the whole ship was enveloped in fire so bright that every ship in both fleets could be clearly distinguished. 'The moon,' said the chaplain of the *Swiftsure*, 'had just risen, and opposing her cold light to the warm glow of the fire beneath, added to the grand and solemn picture.' Nelson, to whom Berry brought the news in his cot, insisted on being led up on deck. Realizing that nothing could prevent her destruction, he sent away Galway in a boat for survivors. The captains of other ships took precautions against the impending explosion. Ball and Miller sluiced their decks with water. Saumarez closed the *Orion*'s gunports, furled the sails and secured the magazine. The French ships astern of *L'Orient* veered their cables. For about an hour the fire continued to grow in height and intensity. Then it reached the magazine. A little after ten o'clock Berry, standing beside Nelson on the quarter-deck, watched the ship blow up 'with a most tremendous explosion.' The noise was heard in Rosetta ten miles away and a seaman in the magazine of the *Goliath* thought a part of his own ship had gone. 'The wreck of the masts, yards, etc.,' said Berry, 'which had been carried to a vast height, fell down into the water and on board the surrounding ships.' A port fire set light to the *Alexander*'s rigging and only Ball's timely precautions prevented her sharing her opponent's fate.

L'Orient took with her to the bottom Vice-Admiral Brueys (who, after a shot had nearly cut him in two, had refused to go below, saying: 'A French admiral should die on his quarter-deck'), Commodore Casabianca and his son, nine-tenths of her crew, and half a million pounds' worth of treasure. Commodore Ganteaume escaped in a boat and lived to fight another day. A few survivors succeeded in swimming to the *Theseus* and *Orion*. An apparition which reached the deck of the *Swiftsure*, naked except for a cocked hat, was greeted by Hallowell with: 'Who the deuce are you, Sir?' He explained he was Lieutenant Berthelot, *L'Orient*'s first lieutenant, and that after swimming some way had returned to the wreck for his hat to convince his captors he was an officer. For some minutes after the ship had disappeared there was 'an awful pause and death-like silence'. Then the firing broke out again and shortly before midnight the *Franklin* (6), the only ship ahead of *L'Orient* still in action, struck her colours.

There now occurred a lull. The *Tonnant* (8), *Heureux* (9) and *Mercure* (10) had veered out of range of the British guns. Nelson, back in his cot, was too ill to give orders for pressing home the victory, and the ships' companies, having fought for six hours without pause, were too exhausted to execute them.

The crew of the *Alexander* asked Ball's permission to lie down, and this was granted. George Elliot fell asleep 'in the act of hauling up a shroud hawser'. Miller's ship's company 'were so extremely jaded that as soon as they had hove our sheet-anchor up, they dropped under the capstan-bars and were asleep in a moment in every sort of posture'. He himself was woken by Sam Hood, who came on board at daylight to propose that the *Zealous, Goliath* and *Theseus* should go down the line to help the *Alexander* and *Majestic*, then intermittently engaged with the enemy's rear. The same idea had occurred to Nelson who sent his flag-lieutenant Capel to order all ships on this service that were not disabled. Seeing the state of *Goliath*, Capel told Foley he did not suppose the order included him. 'Not so much disabled,' said Foley, 'that we cannot go down with the wind.'

These three ships went down the line, and having been joined by the *Leander* began an action with the enemy's rear. The *Heureux* soon surrendered to Miller. The *Artemise* frigate then poured a broadside into the *Theseus* and immediately struck her colours. Miller sent over a boarding-party who found her crew had fired and abandoned her. The *Mercure* also hauled down her colours and the *Tonnant*, dismasted and cableless, drifted away to leeward. The three remaining ships, the *Guillaume Tell* (11), *Généreux* (12) and *Timoléon* (13), now weighed anchor, and under the orders of Rear-Admiral Villeneuve stood out to sea. The *Timoléon* did not get far; crippled by a heavy fire from the *Theseus*, she ran herself on the beach and was wrecked. The other two ships, accompanied by two frigates, continued across the bay. Hood made chase after them, but as there was not a single ship to support him Nelson ordered his recall; and Villeneuve escaped to the open sea.

*   *   *

So ended the Battle of the Nile. It was, as Nelson said, 'a conquest'. Of the seventeen French ships which had begun the action, all but four had been captured or destroyed. The French casualties were impossible to compute, but estimated variously as between three and five thousand killed, wounded and missing. The British losses were just under a thousand killed and wounded. The worst hit ships were the *Majestic* and *Bellerophon*, which, for the first half of the battle, had engaged the *Tonnant* and *L'Orient* unsupported: they suffered two hundred each in killed and wounded. A few ships escaped lightly. Hood, who had anchored the *Zealous* so that the *Guerrier*'s fire was almost ineffectual, had only one man killed and seven wounded. The *Defence* had fifteen casualties, the *Theseus* thirty-five. 'Providence in its goodness,' commented Miller, 'seemed willing to make up to us for our heavy loss at Santa Cruz.'

The destruction of most of the Toulon Fleet was an achievement in itself. More important was its effect on the war. The Mediterranean was no longer a French waterway, but once again a province of the British Fleet. With their sea communications paralysed, Bonaparte and his Army of the East, the French garrisons at Malta, Corfu and in the Adriatic were all bottled up without hope or supplies or reinforcements. 'We have left France only two sail of the line in the Mediterranean,' said Saumarez. 'A squadron of five sail leaves us masters of these seas.' More important was the continued presence in the Mediterranean of the little Admiral and his battle-scarred ships, which in the months ahead were to become for the oppressed peoples of southern Europe a beacon of hope and liberty. 'The Battle of the Nile,' said the British Ambassador at Vienna, 'will be the saving of Europe.'

When the news of the victory reached England two months later, it was received tumultuously. The battles of St Vincent and Camperdown had helped to restore public confidence at a low ebb, but neither had been fought against the real enemy, nor did they reopen the Mediterranean to the British Fleet. With the news of the departure of Bonaparte and his armada from Toulon, depression had again settled in. In their disappointment many people blamed Spencer and Nelson for failure to bring the enemy to action; but in their hearts was an uncomfortable feeling that the French, invincible by land, were now proving the same at sea. News of the victory arrived when almost all hope had gone, and its splendour took the country by storm. When Lord Spencer heard from his secretary that not a single British ship was lost, he fell insensible on the floor. 'His joy,' said his wife, 'had mastered him.' The King at Weymouth, on reading the first words of Nelson's despatch – 'Almighty God has blessed His Majesty's Arms' – was so moved that he stood a moment in silence, his eyes turned to heaven. This was the effect everywhere: the magnitude of what had happened defied expression. Then suppressed feelings broke out in a wave of rejoicing. Up and down the country guns were fired, church bells rung, towns illuminated, banquets and bonfires and torchlight processions organized, free beer distributed by patriotic landlords. In London Betsey and Fremantle went to a play: 'God Save the King' and 'Rule, Britannia!' was sung twice with universal applause.

The country showed its gratitude in many ways. The Government raised Nelson to the peerage with the title of Baron Nelson of the Nile, presented him with the thanks of both Houses and a pension of £2,000 a year. The East India Company, thankful for the safeguarding of their Indian possessions, gave him £10,000. For the captains there were gold medals struck at the King's orders, and swords presented by the City of London. Medals were also struck by Mr Alexander Davison, agent for the prizes; gold for the captains, silver for the officers, copper for the seamen. The first lieutenants of all battleships engaged were promoted.

The arbiters of the victory had been conjointly Nelson and his captains. 'My band of friends,' he said, 'were irresistible.' They were so firstly because he had so wedded their minds to his that there was no problem of tactics they could not solve themselves, secondly because of their own distinguished merits as fighting seamen.

And Lord Howe, England's Grand Old Man of the Sea, said of the battle: 'It stood unparalleled and singular in this instance that *every* captain distinguished himself.' It was this all-embracing unity which bound the captains to their admiral and each other, and yet allowed complete freedom of action, that was the secret of their strength. 'I believe,' said Saumarez, 'greater unanimity never existed in any squadron.'

After the battle congratulations and enquiries about his health reached Nelson from every ship in the Fleet. 'He congratulates and thanks you,' Berry told Miller, 'and hopes your wounds are of no consequence.' Yet among the captains was a feeling that these expressions were inadequate, that the occasion called for something bigger. They all assembled in the *Orion*, and Sir James Saumarez proposed a resolution:

'The Captains of the Squadron under the Orders of Rear-Admiral Sir Horatio Nelson K.B., desirous of testifying the high sense they entertain of his prompt decision and intrepid conduct in the Attack of the French Fleet in Bequier Road, off the Nile, the 1st of August, 1798, request his acceptance of a Sword; and as a further proof of their esteem and regard, hope that he will permit his Portrait to be taken, and hung up in the Room belonging to the Egyptian Club, now established in commemoration of that glorious day.'

To which Nelson replied:

'Gentlemen,

I feel most sensibly the very distinguished honour you have conferred upon me by your Address of this day. My prompt decision was the natural consequence of having such captains under my command, and I thank God I can say, that in the Battle the conduct of every officer was equal. I accept, as a particular mark of your esteem, the Sword you have done me the honour to offer, and will direct my Picture to be painted the first opportunity, for the purpose you mention.'

On the day after the battle the ships' companies mustered on their quarter-decks to give thanks to God for victory and deliverance. Then they got down to refitting the ships and prizes. 'Employed splicing, knotting and rigging', run the entries in most logs. Several captains sent parties to enemy ships too badly damaged to be repaired. Foley ordered Elliot and a dozen men to salvage the *Sérieuse*, and here, in rather peculiar circumstances, Elliot first met Hardy. Having dived into one of the lower decks and discovered floating there a dead and much-swollen French marine ('by no means a pleasant companion'), Elliot pushed open a hatchway to let him out. Hardy, who had come on board by more orthodox means, was standing on the upper-deck when the corpse, apparently of its own accord, shot out. 'Shortly after,' said Elliot, 'up came a naked figure with a bandaged head and neck, which of course he thought was another dead body, but to his surprise it shook its head.' (Elliot had been slightly wounded in the action.) 'On asking my men who I was and hearing my name, he knew all about me and good-humouredly said as I was before him, he would not interfere with my wrecking.' Troubridge, having shipped a new rudder to the *Culloden* and succeeded in plugging the leak (which at one time was letting in 120 tons of water an hour), turned his inexhaustible energy to refitting the prizes, procuring fresh provisions for the wounded, and arranging cartels for the prisoners. Hallowell sent a party to salvage wood from *L'Orient*. Months later, when he was afraid that the adulation being heaped on Nelson would turn his head, he fashioned a coffin out of this wood and sent it to the *Vanguard* with a note:

'My Lord,

I have taken the liberty of presenting you a coffin made from the mainmast of *L'Orient*, that when you have finished your military career in this world, you may be buried in one of your trophies – but that that period may be far distant is the earnest wish of your sincere friend

BEN HALLOWELL'

This strange present delighted Nelson, who insisted on it always accompanying him. Once when it was lying on the gratings of the quarter-deck, he came upon his officers looking at it. 'You may look at it, Gentlemen,' he said, 'as long as you please; but depend upon it, none of you shall have it.' In this coffin his remains now lie in the vault of St Paul's Cathedral.

By 6 August the *Leander* was ready for sea and Berry, to whom Nelson had charged his despatches to St Vincent, set out with Thompson on the long journey to Cadiz. Hardy moved into the *Vanguard* as flag-captain until Berry's return. Capel was appointed to the *Mutine* in Hardy's place, and 'as an accident may happen to Captain Berry,' ordered to take Lieutenant Hoste and a duplicate set of despatches to Naples. On arrival he was to resign the command of the *Mutine* to Hoste, and proceed overland with the despatches to England.

A week later the prizes had been made seaworthy. These were the *Peuple Souverain, Spartiate, Aquilon, Franklin, Conquérant* and *Tonnant*. The *Guerrier, Heureux* and *Mercure* were too badly damaged to be saved, and Nelson, 'confiding that the Lords Commissioners will direct that a fair value shall be paid for those ships,' ordered them to be destroyed. He gave the command of the prizes to Saumarez, who, with the *Bellerophon, Majestic, Minotaur, Defence, Audacious* and *Theseus*, put to sea on the same day as Capel and Hoste left for Naples. This appointment suited both men. Saumarez was anxious to get back to England. Nelson, exhausted in body and mind and doubtful whether he could carry on much longer, was now in a position to hand over without offence to Troubridge, 'than whom,' he told St Vincent, 'we both know no person is more equal to the task. I should have sunk under the fatigue of refitting the squadron but for him, Ball, Hood and Hallowell; not but that all have done well, but those are my supporters.'

Finally on 19 August the *Vanguard*, accompanied by the *Alexander* and patched-up *Culloden*, set sail for Naples. The *Zealous, Swiftsure* and *Goliath* remained behind in the bay with orders to blockade Alexandria.

PART III

The Band of Brothers

CHAPTER 8

Saumarez and his squadron had hardly cleared the bay when the wind fell, and they were forced to anchor for the night. For Saumarez this was a happy misfortune. He was awoken at eleven o'clock with the news that a brig had arrived from the *Vanguard* with a bag of mail, the first for many weeks. There was a large batch for Saumarez with a covering note from Nelson: 'I hope Lady S. and all the little ones are well.' During his long journey home Saumarez kept a daily journal for his wife, to be posted home in sections; and the description of the arrival of his mail strikes a familiar note to all whom war has carried far from home.

'I soon had them sorted out, and out of about twenty for myself I selected four from you, which were read with an avidity you will better conceive that I can describe; before I had finished a page of one I flew to another, and so for near an hour, till at last I found their date and endeavoured to read them regularly; but it was not till daylight that I could bring myself to a sufficient degree of composure.'

During the long journey to Gibraltar Saumarez remained cheerful, although two unhappy incidents lingered in his mind. One had occurred the day after the battle, when he went on board the *Vanguard* to congratulate Nelson on the victory. Saumarez had never approved of Nelson's plan of doubling on the enemy, saying it did not require two British ships to sink a French one. Knowing that a number of casualties had been caused by the cross-fire of British ships, he opened his remarks with: 'It was a pity that . . .' Nelson, sensing what Saumarez was going to say, cut him short with: 'Thank God, there was no order,' turned his back and went below. Saumarez's remark was ill-timed and the rebuke justified, as he must have seen.

What he had less cause to forget was St Vincent's original order to Nelson to detach the *Orion* to England. Try as he would, he could not get this out of his head. 'It was merely to favour Captain Troubridge,' he wrote in his journal, 'with whom I clashed from seniority. Judge what must have been my feelings had I been thus deprived of my share in this action.' Nor was it any compensation to know that he had the sympathy of many officers. 'I most sincerely congratulate you upon the success of the great event that has befallen you,' wrote Admiral Sir William Parker from Cadiz, 'and more particularly as you have reaped honours that were meant you should have been deprived of.'

At this time Saumarez's resentment was mainly against St Vincent who had given the order, rather than Nelson who, whatever his motives, had refrained from executing it. His relationship with Nelson remained cordial, even friendly. When the squadron was overtaken by the *Vanguard*, *Culloden* and *Alexander*, Saumarez called on Nelson and was 'happy at finding him in perfect health'. (He feared the scar on Nelson's forehead would remain for life: his own wound, he confessed delicately, was 'not quite in so distinguished a place.') After they had parted Nelson wrote to him: 'I can say with truth there is no action of your life, as far as relates to me, but what must be entirely to my approbation'. What Saumarez did not then know was that once again his name had been omitted from the despatches of an action in which he had played a distinguished part. What made it worse was that Nelson was on the point of writing frenzied letters to the Admiralty, insisting that whatever honours were given for his captains should also include Troubridge. Troubridge's conduct had been beyond reproach; and if Saumarez's name had been also included in the despatches, he would later have had no cause for complaint. But to single out the name of a captain who had taken no part in the action and ignore that of his second-in-command was most unjust.

Of these things however Saumarez was ignorant. 'It is now exactly three weeks since the Battle of the Nile,' he wrote on 21 August; 'it appears almost an age.' Past grievances were forgotten in the pride of his new command and expectations of an early home-coming. 'My situation is exactly as I could wish – the command of a respectable squadron escorting the trophies of our victory. I am now, thank God, as well as ever; and when I consider that every day shortens my distance from you, my happiness is daily increasing.' His officers were 'in rapture' at the ship's part in the battle: Lieutenant Barker was commanding the *Peuple Souverain*, 'happier than a prince'. The ship's company were in good health and the wounded rapidly recovering. Two French officers, one the second captain of the *Tonnant*, were living in the wardroom and he occasionally invited them to dine. More frequent guests were the captains of the squadron, whom he entertained in rotation.

At the end of September the squadron reached Malta, which they found blockaded by a Portuguese squadron under the Marquis de Niza, a French Royalist. Inside the harbour were the *Guillaume Tell* and the two frigates which had escaped from Aboukir: no one knew the whereabouts of the *Généreux*, but she was thought to have foundered. Having consulted with de Niza and a deputation of Maltese, who reported the French garrison was in the greatest distress, Saumarez sent a flag of truce demanding surrender. It returned with a firm rejection. 'You have clearly forgotten,' wrote General Vaubois, 'that it is Frenchmen who hold Malta.' Saumarez landed all the guns and ammunition he could spare; and having detached the *Minotaur* and *Audacious* to Naples on Nelson's orders, continued on his way to Gibraltar.

On 10 October, Saumarez fell in with *L'Espoir* frigate, ten days out from Gibraltar, and learnt that the *Leander*, which had sailed with the despatches two months earlier, had not yet arrived. On approaching the Rock he received a letter from St Vincent (who, owing to failing health, had shifted his flag there) expressing the hope that she might have been dismasted and taken refuge in one of the Greek islands: but he could not help writing in his journal: 'Great is our uneasiness for the fate of the *Leander*'.

At Gibraltar the squadron received a tremendous welcome. St Vincent was warm in his praises. 'I request you will convey to your brave companions-in-arms that in my judgment they stand foremost in the page of naval history.' But after what had gone before Saumarez found the homage embarrassing. 'The solicitous attention he shows to me almost overwhelms me,' he wrote, 'and I wish to keep clear of laying myself under obligation, except as far as concerns the promotion of my officers.' The Governor gave a ball, and there were invitations to dinner from the officers of the garrison. The sick and wounded were taken to the naval hospital, which Dr Harness had specially purified for the occasion.

With the arrival of the *Colossus* from Naples, Saumarez received two letters, one from Nelson approving 'very highly of your officer-like behaviour relative to Malta,' the other from Ball, with whom he had struck up a friendship during the four days at St Pierre in May. Ball wrote from off Malta, where he had taken over the blockade from de Niza: he sent also some things Saumarez had asked for – 'six fan-mounts, two boxes of perfumery, four large and two small of Naples soap'. There was definite news of the *Leander*. She had been captured after an action with the *Généreux* and taken as a prize into Corfu. Ball had no details of the action, nor of the fate of Thompson and Berry. The news from Egypt was happier. Foley had captured a French colonel, 'who says that the whole army must soon perish'.

Saumarez remained at Gibraltar a week, then with the *Theseus* sailed for Lisbon where the prizes were to be repaired. Just before leaving the *Transfer* brig came into harbour and confirmed the news of the *Leander*'s capture. There was still no news of survivors, but as the ship was said 'to have well supported the fame of the Nile Squadron,' Saumarez felt uneasy about Berry and Thompson.

At Lisbon Saumarez handed over the prizes, and found various people waiting for passage to England. Room was found for the Duc D'Havre, an exiled French Royalist, and his suite, but others had to be left behind. They included a Miss Raikes of Gloucester with whom Thompson had reached 'an understanding' during his last visit to the Tagus. 'She will not be sorry to hear the *Leander* is at least heard of,' wrote Saumarez, 'although in possession of the enemy.'

On 25 November 1798, the *Orion* anchored at Spithead. Saumarez despatched Lieutenant Dumaresq to Newport to fetch his son James, and a day later ('having placed Monsieur le Duc and the rest of the party at cards to send these lines') he wrote to Lady Saumarez at Bath: 'James is by my side and glows with thankfulness at being so soon likely to embrace his beloved Mamma.' Then, Saumarez set out for London, where he found Captains Berry and Thompson.

* * *

At daybreak on 18 August the *Leander* was off the western coast of Crete when she sighted a sail which Thompson soon identified as a French ship of the line. Being eighty men short of complement and having many wounded on board, he decided not to seek action with an enemy so superior and stood away. The *Généreux*, however, had the advantage of the wind and bore down. At eight o'clock the enemy was within range and Thompson 'immediately commenced a vigorous cannonade on him which he instantly returned'. By ten-thirty the two ships were almost interlocked and for five hours, in a flat calm, continued to fire into each other at point-blank range. By three-thirty the *Leander* was totally dismasted: most guns had been disabled by the wreckage of the spars, her hull was cut to pieces and a third of her crew, including Thompson who had been hit four times, were casualties. Berry, looking at the scene afterwards, 'wondered how any of us escaped'. M. le Joille, the French captain, hailed to know if they surrendered. Thompson consulted with Berry, and both agreeing further resistance was useless, replied that they did; and after a gallant action of six and a half hours, the *Leander*'s flag was hauled down.

The humanity of the British towards their prisoners at the Nile was in striking contrast to the brutality of the crew of the *Généreux*. They plundered everything they could lay hands on. Berry was robbed of all he possessed, including six sets of uniform. 'My poverty was such,' he wrote to Nelson, 'that I had not a second coat and would have been literally *sans culotte* had not Captain Thompson furnished me with that necessary article.' Thompson lost all his belongings, including a miniature of his mother. When he remonstrated, the French captain coolly replied: 'I am sorry for it, but the fact is the French are expert at plunder'. More dreadful was the treatment of the wounded. 'The French,' said Berry, 'actually trod over the wounded English and plundered the surgeon's instruments at the time he was performing amputations.' In this way Thompson nearly lost his life.

The two captains had asked for themselves and the *Leander*'s officers to be sent to Naples, subsequent to an exchange of prisoners; but M. le Joille put them instead in a small French coasting vessel. The only provisions he allowed them out of Thompson's large stock were two gallons of port, a few pieces of salt meat and a bag of the *Leander*'s bread-dust. After an uncomfortable passage of four weeks, during which they touched in at Zara and learnt of Nelson's triumphant arrival at Naples, they reached Trieste. Both captains wrote accounts of the action to Nelson. Thompson's was a formal letter of proceedings which he sent through the British Ambassador at Naples. 'It makes one's heart bleed,' wrote Hamilton to Nelson, 'for what he and Captain Berry must have suffered; but it is plain they did all that gallant officers possibly could do.' Berry's letter was more intimate and full of the intense personal admiration he always felt for Nelson. 'The success of your glorious victory seems to have the most salutary effect throughout the Mediterranean, and the name of Nelson is held dear by everybody.' He was not happy about chances of employment, though he still hoped to command the *Foudroyant* for the flag. 'How I shall stand at present on my arrival, I do not pretend to say – but for my own part I shall always advert that I was *your* captain on 1st August, '98.'

On 24 October, the two captains left Trieste for Vienna, where Berry again wrote to Nelson. Their journey (he first wrote 'passage' then crossed it out) had not been comfortable and they had spent all but one night in the coach; Thompson however was better. From the British Ambassador, Berry had news of Nelson's peerage. 'I hardly know whether or not to congratulate you. If it is to lead to a Viscountcy on your arrival in England, I shall be satisfied. Otherwise I am not.' This was the opinion of many others including Lord Hood, who wrote to Nelson: 'Mr Pitt told me the day after Captain Capel arrived that you would certainly be a Viscount. But it was objected to in a certain quarter because your Lordship was not a Commander-in-Chief. In my humble judgment a more flimsy reason was never given.'

From Vienna Berry and Thompson proceeded to Cuxhaven, embarked in the Harwich packet and, after a stormy passage of fifty-six hours, reached England on 25 November – the same day that Saumarez was bringing the *Orion* into Spithead.

Although the news of the Nile victory had reached England nearly two months before, Berry found the excitement had not died down. At Norwich, his own and Nelson's home-town, he was given a hero's welcome. 'The people,' he told Nelson, 'received me with mad joy. In short, I'm so great a man that I'm very *in and out* everywhere to the great annoyance of my pocket and distress of my feelings.' In London it was the same. Lady Nelson was still besieged by so many callers that she was *at home* only to Berry and his wife. 'She and your father,' Berry told Nelson, 'are both well and get through the amazing bustle of congratulations wonderfully.' At Kensington Berry found his father-in-law, Dr Forster, 'and all hands, like everybody else, incessantly talking of you'. He was knighted by the King at a levee, and at Guildhall received the freedom of the City of London in a gold box. But amid all this rejoicing Berry was

struck by the national ignorance as to the details of the battle
and the demand for an account of them. Seeing no alternative
but to write it himself, Berry enlisted the help of Mr Heriot,
editor of the *True Briton*, and made his first excursion into
literature. This was published under the title of '*An Authentic
Narrative of the proceedings of His Majesty's Squadron under the
command of Rear-Admiral Sir Horatio Nelson from its sailing from
Gibraltar to the conclusion of the glorious Battle of the Nile, drawn up
from the Minutes of an officer of Rank in the Squadron.*' 'Everyone is
pleased with the Narrative,' Berry told Nelson, 'and it sells
with great avidity.'

Saumarez had also arrived in London, bringing two plants
he had collected at Aboukir for the King. These were accepted
by Sir Joseph Banks, the famous president of the Royal Society,
and despatched to the head gardener at Kew. 'His Majesty
will be informed,' replied Sir Joseph in a flowery letter of
thanks, 'that Sir James, in gathering those never fading laurels
brought home from Aboukir, did not forget to bring home
something more for the garden of his King; and Sir Joseph is
confident that His Majesty will receive more pleasure from the
recollections which the sight of these plants will present to his
mind than all the other plants in the Royal Gardens will ever
be able to afford to him.'

With Berry and Thompson, Saumarez discussed the design
of the sword the Egyptian Club was to present to Nelson, and
they placed the order for it. They also ordered one for each of
the captains, on the same plan but without the costly ornaments: the hilt was to be in the form of a crocodile with an
emblematical figure of the Nile, and the shell engraved with a
sketch of the action drawn by Miller. 'I hope,' Saumarez wrote
to Ball, 'that it will soon be finished and we shall all have the
happiness soon to meet in the Egyptian Hall.' Another matter
which exercised them was the granting of prize-money for
those French ships burnt after the battle. Nelson's letter explaining that they were destroyed only to save time and
expense, had been lost in the *Leander*, and he had not sent a
duplicate in the *Mutine*. They therefore wrote a joint letter to

Davison, the prize-agent, saying that as Captain Berry was 'in full possession of the sentiments of Lord Nelson,' which were that a fair value should be paid for the ships, they hoped that the Government would make indemnity. This was promptly done, though Saumarez told Ball he thought the ships had been much undervalued.

Thompson had now nearly recovered from his wounds, but since his arrival home the shadow of the court martial for losing his ship had been hanging over him. This took place on board the *America* at Sheerness. The verdict went better than he could have hoped: 'The gallant and almost unprecedented defence of Captain Thompson of His Majesty's late ship, the *Leander*, against so superior a force as that of the *Généreux* is deserving of every praise his country and this court can give'. The thanks of the court were also given to Captain Sir Edward Berry. On return to the shore the boat carrying the two officers was cheered by all ships in the harbour.

Back in London Thompson learnt he had been granted a pension of £200 a year and was to be knighted. On 13 February 1799, he wrote to Miss Raikes (since returned from Lisbon) that he had just come from the levee at St James's Palace. The King had been 'kind and most gracious. . . . Upon my saying that in the action with the *Généreux* I had at one time strong hopes of succeeding in taking her, he, without the smallest hesitation, declared: "You would not have gained a scrap more credit than you have already achieved if you had." '

Next day, the second anniversary of the Battle of St Vincent, was a red-letter day for Nelson and his captains. He was promoted to Rear-Admiral of the Red. Saumarez, after a month's leave at Bath, was given a vacant Colonelcy of Marine and appointed to the *Caesar*, 84, fitting at Plymouth. Thompson, having been exchanged with a Captain Audouard of the *Immortalité*, living on parole at Tiverton, was posted to the *Bellona*, 74, also at Plymouth. Two weeks later he went to Gloucester, where he married Miss Raikes. St Vincent, in a congratulatory letter to the bride's uncle, said he had no knowledge where the *Bellona* would be stationed, 'but as Lord

EDWARD BERRY

From the portrait by Copley painted in 1815, showing undress uniform of a captain of over three years' seniority. Berry is wearing the badge of a Knight Commander of the Bath, and the Medals of the Nile, Trafalgar and St. Domingo.

THOMAS TROUBRIDGE

From the portrait by Beechey painted between 1804 and 1806, showing the full-dress uniform of a rear-admiral. Troubridge is wearing the Order of St. Ferdinand and Merit, and the Medals of St. Vincent and the Nile.

Spencer knows how desirous I am to have all the officers who served under Lord Nelson's orders – the *élite* of my fleet – returned to me, I flatter myself with the hope of seeing Thompson again here: with honour and glory he overflows'.

Only Berry, confined to his room with jaundice brought on by a chill caught at Sheerness, remained inactive. But a letter from the far-off Mediterranean must have cheered him:

'The defence of the *Leander* was glorious and does Thompson and you the highest credit. I rejoice that we are now Brother-freemen of London as we have before been in serving our Country. I shall never forget your support for my mind on the 1st of August. As to my stay here, in truth it is uncertain; but if you can get the *Foudroyant* out here, if I should go home for all next summer to rest me, she will be a good ship for you.

We have got Leghorn. Malta is blockaded by Ball. Hood commands in Egypt and Troubridge on the North Coast of Italy. We are all united in our Squadron: not a growler amongst us.'

England's reception of the news of the Nile was matched by that of the people of Naples. When Capel and Hoste arrived with the duplicate despatches, the Queen and Lady Hamilton fainted: they had recovered later for the one to receive the two young captains at a levee and for the other, wearing a bandeau with the words 'Nelson and Victory,' to parade them in an open carriage through crowded streets until dark. Next day Capel set off for Vienna, and Hoste took command of the *Mutine*, 'You can have no idea,' he wrote home, 'of the rejoicing made throughout Naples at this time. Bonfires and illuminations all over the town. We went to the opera and were in the Minister's box with him and his lady. Not a French cockade was to be seen.' For her part Emma took 'dear little Captain Hoste' to heart. 'He is a fine good lad,' she wrote to Nelson when the *Mutine* sailed with the Ambassador's despatches; 'Sir William is delighted with him and I say he will be a second Nelson. If he is only half a Nelson, he will be superior to all others.'

But Naples' welcome to the messengers of the victory was only a dress rehearsal for that given to its chief participants three weeks later. The first ships to enter the bay were the *Culloden* ('the whole ship is rotten,' Nelson told St Vincent, 'and nothing but a Troubridge could have kept her afloat') and the *Alexander*. Ball, whom Nelson had decided was 'the polite man' to entertain enemy officers, had on board Admiral Blanquet and Bruey's Captain of the Fleet. Blanquet had spent the voyage writing a report of the battle for his Admiralty. ('One of my officers copied them, unknown to him,' Ball wrote to Saumarez, 'but his aide-de-camp allowed everybody to read them.') Ball was met by a procession of boats headed by the King in his state galley and the Hamiltons in their barge. With the Ambassador were a Miss Cornelia Knight and her mother, widow of a rear-admiral, who had spent the last twenty years travelling on the Continent. She described Ball as one of the most gentlemanly men breathing, and found him 'very courteous' to the prisoners. Her apartment ashore was next to that of the French Consul, and when Admiral Blanquet reported there she eavesdropped on their conversation. 'How delighted I am to see you, Admiral, out of the hands of those abominable Englishmen,' said the Consul. 'Say nothing against the English, Consul,' she heard Blanquet reply. 'They fight like lions and they have treated me and my officers and men most kindly.'

The *Vanguard*, having been dismasted in a gale, did not reach the bay until four days later. She arrived in tow of a frigate and escorted by the *Minotaur* and *Audacious*, which Saumarez had sent from Malta.

It was a perfect Italian morning of late summer, with a hot sun and blue cloudless sky. To starboard was the purple hump of Vesuvius; ahead, along the curve of the bay, the white and terracotta roofs of the houses, screened by palm and oleander and bougainvillaea, rose tier upon tier to the grey summit of Castle St Elmo. Between the flag-ship and the shore the sea was dotted with small craft – eye-witnesses estimated over five hundred. Many carried bands, among them the orchestra of the San Carlo Opera House, which had learnt for the occasion 'Rule Britannia!' and 'See the Conquering Hero Comes.' The first boat to come alongside the *Vanguard* was the Ambassador's barge, carrying the Hamiltons and the Knights. On arrival on board Emma cried: 'Oh, God, is it possible!' and fell swooning into Nelson's arms. The next visitor was the portly hedonistic Ferdinand, King of the Two Sicilies. He hailed Nelson as 'Deliverer' and 'Preserver' and, with a warmth which his host must have found embarrassing, expressed a wish that he could have served under his orders during the battle. Another visitor was Commodore Caracciolo, flag-officer of the Neapolitan Navy, whom Nelson once said he 'loved' and whom, before a year was out, he was to hang from the yard-arm of his own flag-ship.

Ashore Nelson was greeted by a crowd of shouting fishermen, who released from wicker baskets hundreds of multi-coloured birds. He, the Hamiltons and Miss Knight entered a waiting carriage and drove through streets crowded with cheering *lazzaroni*, past houses decked with flowers and flags and bunting, to the tall, grey Palazzo Sessa, official residence of the British Ambassador. That night, in the long drawing-room where eighteen months earlier Fremantle and Betsey had been married, and surrounded by pictures, vases, marble statues and other *objets d'art*, the fruits of a lifetime's collecting, Nelson and his captains attended a reception. Outside on the façade the words 'Nelson of the Nile' and 'Victory' blazed from the light of three thousand lamps.

This was only the beginning. The King held a dinner-party, which Ball described to Saumarez as 'very select', on the poop of one of his ships. Sir John Acton, the Prime Minister, gave a state banquet, and Prince Esterhazy a ball. The driving force behind all this rejoicing was Emma Hamilton. This robust, beautiful, talented, vulgar, utterly unpretentious woman of thirty-three, once a serving-girl, seduced when still a child, herself the mother of two illegitimate children, foisted by her previous lover, Charles Greville, on to his uncle, her present husband, a man more than twice her age, was the dominant figure in Neapolitan society. Those who did not know her were apt, in an age which set store on rank and breeding, to belittle her; but those whom she met invariably fell under the spell of her magnetic, warm-hearted personality. Betsey and Eugenia had found her 'civil, amiable and affable; a charming woman'. Lady Malmesbury, less easy to please, wrote: 'She really behaves wonderfully well, considering her origin and education,' and this was not meant unkindly: Sir Gilbert Elliot said she was 'all Nature and yet all Art'. Nelson was captivated. In his limited experience of what he called 'high life' he had never met a woman like her. Her attitude towards his victory, which aroused in her full-blooded nature the most primitive feelings of pride and adulation, was in striking contrast to that of his thin-lipped, conventional little wife who, after the glories of St Vincent, had urged him 'to leave boarding to captains'. His first meetings with her were a new and exciting emotional experience, and his heart quickened to the warmth of her flattery and attention.

Nor was Nelson alone in his admiration. Ball had arrived at Naples ill and tired and still suffering from the effects of his wound, and she nursed him back to health. On leaving for Malta to take over the blockade, he wrote: 'I cannot let slip this occasion to address a few lines to the best friend and patroness of the Navy and to assure you and Sir William Hamilton that I shall ever retain a most lively sense of the attention and hospitality we all received at Naples through your goodness'. To Troubridge also, whose brief appearance with Hardy at the Palazzo Sessa in June she clearly remembered, she showed every kindness and attention. Troubridge was in need of some sympathy. Off Stromboli he had had news from England that his wife had died; and he was, Nelson wrote to Hood, 'in much distress'. Nor could he forget his bitter disappointment at being deprived of the glories of the Nile. 'How I felt for poor Troubridge,' Lady Hamilton wrote to Nelson before his arrival, 'he must have been so angry on the sandbank, so brave an officer': and after she had met him: 'What a dear good soul he is'.

Troubridge had taken the damaged *Culloden* to the dockyard at Castellamare, on the other side of the bay. Nelson visited him there in early October. He found him, he told St Vincent, better than he expected. 'The active business and the scolding he is obliged to be continually at does him good.' Lady Hamilton wrote to Troubridge that she would like to present him to the Queen. 'I shall be highly flattered by the introduction your ladyship mentions,' he replied, 'for I really am very partial to the King and Royal Family of Naples. Indeed, I begin to think you will spoil us all.' The meeting took place at the Royal Palace at Caserta four days later. 'We have had our good Troubridge here a day and a half,' Lady Hamilton wrote to Nelson. 'I presented him and Captain Waller to the Queen. We staid with her two hours. Poor dear Troubridge was affected at seeing her with her children. He thought of his own.'

But although the captains were grateful for the welcome shown, the entertaining soon began to cloy. Nelson was at his wits' end to know how to get through correspondence which, since the squadron had dispersed, had nearly doubled. There were despatches to answer from Alexandria on the subject of the Turks, whom Hood described as 'as horrid a set of allies as ever I saw'. Hallowell had led a party of them on an attack of the Castle of Aboukir, but owing to their cowardice it had to be abandoned. 'I kept in my boat ahead of them to lead them on,' he told Hood, 'sometimes coaxing, sometimes dancing and swearing at them for poltroons, but to very little effect.' Another day a Turkish boat refused an order to anchor. Hallowell sent some men over to enforce it: there was a scuffle and one was wounded; the others, 'having no arms to defend themselves, had recourse to their handspikes with which they beat one Turk's brains out and wounded the captain. Had I not got on board instantly, I believe every Turk would have been murdered.' 'Captain Hallowell,' Hood wrote to Nelson, 'manages the Turks very nicely.'

Besides his normal correspondence Nelson had to answer a stack of letters on his peerage. 'I was fortunately a witness of your conduct on that glorious day,' wrote Ball, 'it made such an impression on my mind as will be a source of happiness to me through life'; and Louis, assuring Nelson that everything 'stood firm' in *Minotaur*, thanked him for the pleasure 'of serving with the man I have the greatest regard for'. Lady Hamilton wrote in different vein: 'If I was King of England, I would make you the most noble present, Duke Nelson, Marquis Nile, Earl Aboukir, Viscount Pyramid, Baron Crocodile, and Prince Victory . . .'

With the run of naval business pressing on one side, and Neapolitan Society on the other, Nelson hardly knew which way to turn. His active, disciplined mind was already beginning to revolt against the indolence and corruption around him. The climax came at a fête given by Lady Hamilton in honour of his birthday – a gala evening at the Palazzo Sessa to which over a thousand guests were invited, and at which his step-son, Captain Nisbet, got so drunk that he had to be removed by Troubridge. 'I trust, my Lord,' he wrote to St Vincent the next day, 'in a week we shall be at sea. I am very unwell and the miserable conduct of this Court is not likely to cool my irritable temper. It is a country of fiddlers and poets, whores and scoundrels.' This did not include his feelings for Emma, which he never attempted to conceal. 'I am writing opposite Lady Hamilton, therefore you will not be surprised at the glorious jumble of this letter.' Equally, he knew there was danger in the relationship: 'Naples is a dangerous place and we must keep clear of it'; and 'We are killed by kindness'.

Many of the captains too, who shared Nelson's view of the Neapolitan Court, did not allow it to dim their admiration for Lady Hamilton. Ball and Louis who, after their first visit to Naples saw little of her again, thought of her always with gratitude and affection: Foley liked her, and Fremantle had much to be grateful for. But to Hardy and Troubridge, whose attendance on Nelson brought them into closer touch with her, she appeared in a different light. Her demands on their time, which they could not with delicacy refuse, seemed a permanent barrier against preparing the squadron for sea. Troubridge especially had reason for changing his opinions. At Caserta, Emma sang to him her own version of a popular song.

> *'See our Gallant Nelson comes*
> *Sound the trumpet, beat the drums*
> *Sports prepare, the laurel bring*
> *Songs of triumph, Emma sing*
> *Myrtle-wreath and roses twine*
> *To deck the Hero's brow divine.'*

A few days later Troubridge was writing to Nelson: 'I long much to see you. God send I may never see this degenerate place again.'

In October Nelson sailed with the *Minotaur* and *Audacious* for Malta, where he found 'not such an immediate prospect of getting possession of the Town as the Ministers of Naples seem to think'. Having taken the island of Gozo, he left Foley and Gould with Ball to continue the blockade, and sailed again for Naples. He ought and was expected to have remained at Malta longer; but the Court of Naples, he told St Vincent, 'thinks my presence may be necessary and useful in the beginning of November'. Lady Hamilton was not the only reason for his return. In September General Mack had arrived from Austria to take over command of the Neapolitan armies. The French garrison in Italy covered Leghorn and the Roman State. The Emperor of Austria promised Ferdinand that if he attacked them he would give support. Nelson, puffed up by the flattery of the Neapolitan Court, had given 'the firm and unalterable opinion of a British Admiral' (on a subject of which he knew nothing) that Mack should march, and was warmly supported by the Queen.

Nelson found Mack and the Neapolitan Army in camp at St Germano. He inspected them and thought the troops well-found but 'wretchedly officered'. A day or two later word came from Vienna that Austrian support was now conditional on the French instituting hostilities. This was too much for Nelson. 'I ventured to tell their Majesties directly,' he wrote to Spencer, 'that one of the following things must happen to the King, and he had his choice – either to advance, trusting to God for His blessing on a just Cause, to die with *l'épée à la main,* or remain quiet and be kicked out of your kingdom.'

Swayed by this impolitic advice (for the French had no intention of attacking Naples), Ferdinand gave the order to march, and joined his troops in the field. Nelson in the *Vanguard,* accompanied by the *Culloden, Minotaur,* and Portuguese Squadron under de Niza, embarked 5000 troops commanded by General Naselli, and sailed for Leghorn. He reached the port on 28 November, sent in a summons for unconditional surrender which was accepted, and landed the troops and their equipment. Leaving Troubridge in command, he sailed again for Naples. Mack meanwhile had advanced northwards with 30,000 Neapolitans, whom he styled '*la plus belle Armée d'Europe.*' On their reaching Rome, the French General Championnet withdrew, and Ferdinand marched in state to the Farnese Palace.

His success was shortlived. Britain's Mediterranean allies invariably proved more trouble than they were worth, and from Troubridge's angry despatches, Nelson had an inkling of what was to come: 'Such an old woman for a General I never saw before. How the King of Naples could place such a thing in such an active situation, I am at a loss to conjecture. One Genoese (vessel) attempted to push out: however I caught him and made a famous fire which burnt and amused the people on shore for eight hours. The General sent off to know *if I burnt the people in her.* I told the Messenger *it was not customary the first time.* The men belonging to the *Flora* all deserted. I immediately pressed him to give directions for all English seamen to be taken up, and to-day he sent to Mr Wyndham that twenty-two were sent to the *Culloden* – an infamous falsehood, not one has been taken up. *The true Neapolitan shuffle* on all occasions.' This news was the forerunner of worse from Rome. The French Army, which had retired to Castellana, suddenly advanced; whereupon the Neapolitan Army, although greatly superior in numbers, collapsed without firing a shot. The cause, as Nelson had feared, was the officers.

Some dashed off to join the enemy, others turned and fled; among the former was General San Filippo, who was shot by one of his own sergeants, among the latter Ferdinand, who returned to Naples disguised as a peasant. 'They have not lost much honour,' commented Nelson, 'for God knows they had but little enough to lose; but they lost all they had.'

On reaching his capital Ferdinand stoutly declared he would wait for the French surrounded by his loyal subjects; but a despatch from Mack announcing that he was in full retreat made him hastily change his mind. Preliminary arrangements for evacuating the Royal Family and Court to the 'other' Sicily were already being carried out. Lady Hamilton had received from the Queen two and a half million pounds' worth of treasure, which, under Hardy's tireless direction, was shipped to the *Vanguard* in relays. On 19 December the King decided to leave immediately, not so much for fear of the French as of republicans in his own capital: for the same reason he chose to embark in the *Vanguard* rather than a Neapolitan man-of-war. Nelson sent summonses to Troubridge at Leghorn and Foley at Malta to join him, but he knew there was small chance of their arriving in time. On the night of 21 December, attended by the armed barges of the *Vanguard* and *Alemene*, Nelson landed at the Mola Figlio, and having entered the Palace by a subterranean tunnel, conducted the Royal Party to the molehead and embarked them in the waiting boats. During the next forty-eight hours the English residents and various foreign *émigrés* were taken on board the *Vanguard*, the ships of the Portugese squadron, and several small merchant-vessels. Miss Knight and her mother, arriving too late alongside the *Vanguard*, were told by Captain Hardy there was no more room, and embarked in de Niza's flag-ship. At 7 p.m. on 23 December all the ships consisting of about twenty warships and merchant vessels, put to sea in a gale.

During the three-day passage to Palermo it blew harder than Nelson ever remembered. The royal visitors and their suite, for whom he and his officers had sacrificed their sleeping quarters, proved poor sailors. The King's Confessor fell out of his bunk and fractured his arm, the Duchess of Castelcicala cut her head on the admiral's sideboard, little Prince Alberto had convulsions; the others lay about helplessly listening to the shrieking of the wind and groaning of the seams, and waited for the end. Sir William Hamilton was discovered in his cabin clutching two loaded pistols. In answer to inquiries he said he did not wish to die with the guggle, guggle, guggle of salt water in his throat, and when he felt the ship sinking would shoot himself. Only his wife rose splendidly to the occasion, attending the Queen and her children, who had been deserted by their servants, by day and night.

On Christmas Day, 1798, Prince Alberto, 'having eat a hearty breakfast,' was seized with another convulsion: Lady Hamilton nursed him until evening, when he died in her arms. Early the next morning the *Vanguard* came to anchor in Palermo.

*   *   *

During the first four months of 1799 Nelson remained inactive at Palermo. These were not happy times. Firstly he was in poor health. The head wound he had received at the Nile, the effects of which never completely left him, brought on fits of irritability and depression and at times made him quite blind. 'There is no true happiness in this life,' he told St Vincent, 'and in my present state I could quit it with a smile'; and to Lady Parker he wrote: 'You who remember me always laughing and gay would hardly believe the change'. Secondly his relationship with Lady Hamilton was passing from friendship into intimacy, and he was suffering what Mahan calls 'the disquieting struggle between his passion and his conscience, which had not yet been silenced'. Week after week he languished at the dissolute Neapolitan Court when duty, as he knew only too well, demanded him elsewhere. Lastly, among his captains now scattered throughout the Mediterranean, all was not well.

His first problem was the appointment of Captain Sir Sidney Smith, of the *Tigre*, to the command of a squadron in the Levant. This talented young officer had already had a brilliant and adventurous career. In 1788 he entered the Swedish Navy, and for his bravery in the war against Russia was knighted. On the outbreak of the French War he was acting as a volunteer in the Turkish Navy. To join the British flag as soon as possible, he purchased a small boat at his own expense, and having manned it with what English seamen he could find, sailed to join Lord Hood's fleet at Toulon. He arrived in time to be present at the evacuation, and with Captain Miller blew up the arsenal and French shipping. In 1795 he was appointed to the *Diamond* frigate, and after a series of brilliant and successful attacks on enemy Atlantic ports, was captured in the mouth of the Seine while trying to tow out a French lugger. The French, who had come to fear his exploits, refused to exchange him on parole, and he was taken as a prisoner to the Tower of the Temple in Paris. For two years he smuggled home valuable reports of enemy intelligence; and after a number of daring but abortive attempts to escape, he succeeded in reaching England.

Smith's appointment to the Levant was rather peculiar: for as well as his naval commission from the Admiralty, he bore credentials from the Foreign Office appointing him Joint Plenipotentiary to Turkey with his brother Spencer Smith, as Resident Minister. The Cabinet had taken this unusual step in view of Smith's experience of the Levant and the importance of Anglo-Turkish relations. But his terms of reference were so ambiguously worded that St Vincent and Nelson both got the impression (not in fact true) that he was to act independently of them. Some doubt must have occurred to Smith himself, and a courteous letter to Nelson on his arrival might have avoided the unpleasantness that followed. But tact was not Smith's strong point. He was arrogant, overbearing and self-willed. During his stay at Gibraltar St Vincent 'experienced a trace of the presumptuous character of this young man'; and on arrival at Malta Smith wrote airily to Hamilton that he was leaving that night for Alexandria, where he hoped to meet Captain Hood, 'who naturally falls under my orders as being my junior'.

Nelson's reactions to this letter was explosive. That any

captain – and especially a captain unknown to him – should dare to assume authority over any of his beloved band was insulting enough; but that the Admiralty should sanction such a step was intolerable. He had recently assured St Vincent that he would not leave the command without his approval. Now he wrote asking to be relieved immediately: '*I do feel, for I am a man*, that it is impossible for me to serve in these seas with the Squadron under a junior Officer: – could I have thought it! – and from Earl Spencer! Never, never was I so astonished as your letter made me. As soon as I can get hold of Troubridge, I shall send him to Egypt to endeavour to destroy the Ships in Alexandria. If it can be done, Troubridge will do it. The Swedish Knight writes Sir William Hamilton that he shall go to Egypt, and take Captain Hood and his Squadron under his command. The Knight forgets the respect due to his superior Officer: he has no orders from you to take my Ships away from my command; but it is all of a piece. Is it to be borne? Pray grant me your permission to retire, and I hope the *Vanguard* will be allowed to convey me and my friends Sir William and Lady Hamilton to England.'

Troubridge reached Palermo from Leghorn in early January. Nelson had awaited his arrival with impatience, for he was one of the few people with whom he could discuss the situation; but he found Troubridge in almost as demented a frame of mind as himself.

When Nelson was writing the Nile despatches he had purposely omitted mentioning the accident to the *Culloden*, lest Troubridge be excluded from the honours. Realizing later it was impossible to keep it secret, he wrote openly to St Vincent: 'He commanded a Division equally with Sir James Saumarez by my order of June; and I should feel distressed if any honour is granted to one that is not granted to the other'. And there followed a glowing testimonial to his abilities: 'I have experienced the ability and activity of his mind and body; it was Troubridge that equipped the squadron so soon at Syracuse – it was he that exerted himself for me after the Action – it was Troubridge who saved the *Culloden* when none that I know in the Service would have attempted it – it was Troubridge whom I left as myself at Naples to watch movements – he is, as a friend and an officer, a *non-pareil*'.

What Nelson feared came to pass. Before leaving Naples he heard from Spencer that it was intended to give medals to the captains, and promotion to the first lieutenants of all ships engaged. He took this to mean (as it did) that the *Culloden* was not to be included. 'I hope and believe that the word "engaged" is not intended to exclude the *Culloden*,' he wrote frenziedly, 'the merit of that ship and her gallant captain are too well known to benefit by anything I could say. Her misfortune was great in getting aground while her more fortunate companions were in the full tide of happiness. No! I am confident that my good Lord Spencer will never add misery to misfortune.' He ended on a note of unabashed favouritism: 'Indeed no person has a right to know that the *Culloden* was not as warmly engaged as any ship in the squadron. Captain Troubridge on shore is superior to captains afloat.' And to St Vincent he wrote: 'For heaven's sake, for my sake, if it is so, get it altered'.

At this time St Vincent and Nelson were both fighting for Troubridge's services. St Vincent had written to Spencer that he wanted Troubridge – 'who I consider as the greatest man in his walk that the English Navy ever produced' – as his first captain. Nelson, hearing of the request, implored St Vincent to let him remain. 'I am not surprised that you wish him near you, but I trust you will not take him from me. I very well know he is my superior, and I so often want his advice and assistance.' Troubridge could not have been ignorant of all this, yet it did little to comfort him. Nor was he made any happier by the news that his first lieutenant had *as a special favour* been promoted, for it clearly showed that Spencer *had* intended to exclude the *Culloden*; and as there was no mention of the medal he presumed he was not to have it. He now became obsessed with a notion that his conduct had merited the Admiralty's disapproval; and a hitherto unpublished letter to Saumarez written after leaving for Egypt, shows both his true feelings at the time and friendly regard for the man who he knew had every cause to regard him with jealousy and suspicion.

Dear Sir James,

I find my accident at Aboukir has blasted my character at the Admiralty. I am sure I felt sufficient without their adding such marked disapprobation of my conduct. Time may possibly wear it off, but at present I am truly miserable as Lord Spencer has, I am told, accepted the *Culloden* in everything, which I believe is all they could do without trying me by a Court Martial. When I am better acquainted with their Lordships' disposition towards me, I shall probably apply for one if they are not beforehand with me in ordering it.

As I bore no share in the glory of the day and at present labour under disgrace at Charing Cross, I must beg to withdraw my name from your happy Egyptian Club, for my feelings are so deeply wounded, it would always freshen my memory of the unpleasant situation of the *Culloden* on that ever memorable day. Tho' I do not believe any one officer or man in the fleet casts the least slur on me, still some one must have poisoned their Lordships' minds against me, and I clearly see that without something fortunate happens to me, I shall not have my Flag if I live to get to the top of the List.

I trust you will see, my good friend, the propriety of my request. I take the liberty of addressing you as the first proposer of the Club. I would write to each member singly but I have not spirits. This has given me such a cheque I believe I shall never hold my head up again. Lord St Vincent has been so good as to promote my first Lieutenant which has relieved me a little, as my Sins being visited on them was an additional grief to me. God bless you . . .'

The unhappy states of mind of two of his best officers caused St Vincent much pain, and on 13 February, he wrote to Spencer from Gibraltar: '. . . I am much more affected by the discontents of Lord Nelson and Captain Troubridge: the former continuing seemingly determined upon his relinquishing his command and returning to England, and the latter in such a state of despondency from the slight he has received which he terms an indelible disgrace, that I really am put to my wits' end how to act.'

With Troubridge's arrival in Egypt, officially to organize an attack on enemy shipping at Alexandria, in reality to frustrate any designs Sidney Smith might have on Hood and Hallowell, the situation for both men eased. Troubridge's mission took up all his energy and he later heard that Lord Spencer had been 'expressly authorized by His Majesty' to present him with the Nile medal. Nelson also adopted a calmer frame of mind. With Troubridge as senior officer in Egyptian waters he felt confident that Smith would soon find his proper place; and a friendly letter from St Vincent assured him he had not been unreasonable in his views. For the moment he said no more about leaving the command.

CHAPTER 9

But there were things to worry about elsewhere. The situation at Malta was not satisfactory. By the turn of the year the French had lost all their strongholds except Valetta, and it seemed that this too must soon fall. Ball wrote to Nelson that he anticipated 'a speedy and successful conclusion,' and Nelson told St Vincent: 'Captain Ball has, at this moment, I hope, finished with Malta'. But these hopes were not realized. A vigorous attack on Valetta failed owing to treachery; and the siege continued.

On the face of it, Nelson's and Ball's optimism was justified. The French garrison numbered no more than 3500 officers and men, of which nearly a quarter were in hospital with venereal disease, scurvy and fever. Their rations were four ounces of salt meat three days a week, two ounces of beans and an ounce of oil the other four, a pound and a half of bread daily, a quart of wine every ten days, and a glass of brandy every five.

But Nelson and Ball had underestimated their staying powers which, under Vaubois's leadership, were remarkable; nor could they have reckoned on the weather which Ball described as 'the worst the inhabitants say they have had these thirty years'. Despite this a body of well-led troops should have been able to carry Valetta. Nelson himself, with the crews of two or three ships of the line, might have done wonders. 'The sight of your flag would rejoice us all,' Ball told him, 'and do infinite good.' But to these and other pleas Nelson was deaf: 'I am so tied by their Sicilian Majesties that I cannot move'. And so the French proved an equal match for the ill-equipped, half-starving Maltese.

Just how pitiable was the condition of the Maltese only Ball knew. For a start they had no proper government. The King of Naples had assumed sovereignty of the island in the autumn of 1798: the crazy Czar of Russia, who had been made Grand Master of the Order of St John, was also interested, and so was the British Government; but none seemed inclined to shoulder responsibility for the inhabitants. 'I must beg leave to point out to your Lordship,' wrote Ball to Nelson, 'that four thousand Maltese soldiers have been serving more than five months without pay or clothing, who are now so ragged as to make it impossible to do duty much longer.' George Elliot in the *Goliath* recorded there were always between 140 and 200 Maltese serving on board as supernumeraries. 'They seldom remained above a few weeks, for when they were well fed, they returned to the shore blockade, and plenty of their half-starved countrymen were ready to come in their place.' They had practically no powder and very few muskets: an outbreak of malignant fever spread to the *Alexander* and caused the deaths of several men. 'My mind has suffered considerably,' wrote Ball, 'at beholding so much misery without the power of alleviating it.'

Soon Ball found himself assuming the duties of civilian Governor ashore, and at the insistence of the Maltese, presiding at their council meetings. With Nelson's permission he turned over the *Alexander* to his first lieutenant for days at a time, while he toured villages and outposts, helping and advising.

THOMAS HARDY
From the portrait by Evans painted in 1834, showing the full-dress uniform of a rear-admiral. Hardy is wearing the Ribbon and Star of a Knight Grand Cross of the Bath, and the Medal of Trafalgar.

ALEXANDER BALL

From the portrait by Pickersgill, painted between 1804 and 1809, showing the full-dress uniform of a rear-admiral. Decorations are the Order of St. Ferdinand and Merit, and the Medal of the Nile. The scene in the background represents the entrance to Grand Harbour, Malta.

This was a job which suited him admirably; he was able to use his powerful faculties to the full and relate them to problems which required immediate action. 'My friend Ball,' Nelson told St Vincent, 'is adored and deservedly by all ranks.' When in January it had seemed as though the French garrison would capitulate, the Maltese implored Ball to stay as Governor until the end of the war: the same thought had occurred to Nelson who, fearful of dissensions between the British, Russian and Neapolitan Governments, had urged Ball's claims on all three. Ball accepted the suggestion whole-heartedly; but he trusted it would not interfere with his career. All his letters to Nelson are full of gratitude: 'Your Lordship has made me the happiest fellow in the world'. And to Lady Hamilton with whom he kept up a warm correspondence ('I cannot help loving you and esteeming you very much'), he wrote: 'I would rather be Lord Nelson than any Duke or indeed any man in England, and you may guess how proud I am in having such a friend'.

Nelson's correspondence was now greater than ever before. 'If you get six lines,' he told his brother, 'it is as much as you can expect, for I have more writing than two hands could well get through.' In addition to despatches to 'Petersburg, Constantinople, the Consul at Symrna, Egypt, the Turkish and Russian Admirals, Trieste, Vienna, Tuscany, Minórca, Earl St Vincent and Lord Spencer,' there was also 'the business of sixteen sail of the line' – routine correspondence with his captains about administration and discipline. From Alexandria Hallowell wrote of the poor state of the *Swiftsure*. 'Our seams are so open that in rainy weather the people cannot sleep dry in their hammocks. Our boilers are so bad that we can scarcely make shift to dress the provisions.' The *Goliath* was not much better. 'Captain Foley,' wrote Ball, 'says his ship is leaky, she makes thirteen inches of water an hour.' Foley was also having trouble with his officers. His chaplain had asked permission to return to England to settle his private affairs; his surgeon, Dr Wood, had died of the Maltese fever; his first lieutenant, Mr Wilks, had applied to be retired: 'He is so impregnated with the venereal disease as to make it necessary for him to undergo a

severe mercurial discipline before he can possibly be delivered
from his miserable state.' Hood, whose brother Captain
Alexander Hood had been killed in action in the *Mars*, requested permission to go home to settle his estate. Louis, lying
off Leghorn for the protection of the Grand Duke of Tuscany
and his family, was experiencing the same troubles with the
northern Italians as Troubridge had with the Neapolitans.
'Such an unaccountable slackness among all ranks of people in
this country is beyond description, and I really wonder that
some spirit does not start up among them – but the idea of a
Frenchman staggers them all.'

An added responsibility for Nelson was the Portugese
squadron, commanded by English ex-merchant navy captains.
'I never expect any real service from that squadron,' Nelson
told St Vincent. 'The Marquis de Niza has certainly every good
disposition to act well, but he is completely ignorant of sea
affairs. All their commanders are commodores, and it is
ridiculous to hear them talk of their rank and of the impossibility
of serving under any of my brave and good captains.' At
Naples Troubridge had given them an order to proceed to sea.
'Some are doing it,' he had reported to Nelson, 'and some are
thinking about it.' At Alexandria de Niza offered Hood anything he needed. 'On my mentioning water,' wrote Hood,
'there was instantly a difficulty, and therefore I thought it
better not to embarrass him and declined it.' 'The Portugese
squadron,' concluded Nelson, 'are totally useless.'

During these difficult times there was one person on whom
Nelson could wholeheartedly depend. This was the rock-like
Hardy, who was proving the best flag-captain he had had.
Miller and Berry had discharged their duties admirably, but
both were too much individualists to be wholly satisfactory.
Miller had other interests besides his work, such as sketching
and painting: Berry was a fighter rather than an administrator.
Hardy gave himself entirely to the job in hand. Soon after
joining he found the general standard of seamanship very poor.
On giving an order to take in a reef in the main topsail, and
finding half the crew ignorant of the duty, he took off his

cocked hat and buckles, ran up aloft and laid out on the yard
himself. This made a great impression on Nelson and the ship's
company. So did the speed with which he refitted the *Vanguard*
at Naples. Nelson saw no chance of sailing for Malta in under
six weeks: Hardy reported himself ready in three. On the
officers too Hardy exerted a firm and just discipline. Not
finding the midshipmen as alert as he wished and inclined to
walk the deck with hands in their pockets, he ordered the tailor
to sew up the pockets (an affront, it is said, for which the
future Admiral Jocelyn Percy never forgave him). 'Hardy,'
Nelson told St Vincent, 'was bred in the old school and I can
assure you that I have never been better satisfied with the real
good discipline of a ship than the *Vanguard*'s.'

Yet it was on Nelson personally that Hardy had the most
marked influence. 'How is it,' Nelson once said to him, 'that
you and I never disagree, while my other captains never let me
do a thing without at first resisting?' 'It is, Sir,' replied Hardy
bluntly, 'from my being always first lieutenant when you like to
be captain, and flag-captain when you have a fancy for being
admiral.' Hardy worshipped Nelson, not with Troubridge's
emotionalism nor Ball's outspoken fervour, but with a quiet
and constant devotion. Nelson's friendship with Troubridge
was always uneasy: Troubridge laid bare his mind to Nelson and
gave him both praise and criticism: Hardy, who allowed nobody
to penetrate his thoughts, offered him neither. Between the
two men an intense personal admiration grew up. Each respected
the other for those qualities – the flashing brilliance of the one,
the imperturbability of the other – which the other lacked.

Nelson's relationship with Lady Hamilton eventually destroyed his friendship with Troubridge. To Hardy it was no
matter for friction: he did not approve of it any more than
Troubridge, but it was a part of the Admiral's private life and
no concern of his. But where it affected discipline he acted
unflinchingly. A boat's crew, having misbehaved themselves,
asked Lady Hamilton to use her influence in getting them off
punishment. She spoke to Hardy, who 'said very little and
rather gave her to understand she had been successful'. The

next morning he gave the offenders a dozen lashes for misbehaviour, and another dozen for applying to Lady Hamilton; and he told her that would be the standard punishment for anyone else for whom she interceded. To this Nelson made no protest.

On 17 March 1799, Troubridge returned to Palermo, with Hood in the *Zealous* and Hallowell in the *Swiftsure*. The attack on Alexandria had not been successful and Troubridge remained moody and depressed. 'My ill-luck still sticks to me in these seas,' he wrote to Nelson before his arrival. 'I was in hopes I should have wiped off the stain at the Admiralty.' He had handed over the command to Sidney Smith, leaving the *Theseus* and *Lion* under his orders; this disposition suited Nelson, for Smith was a personal friend of Miller, and Captain Dixon of the *Lion* was not one of Nelson's original band.

Nelson's attitude towards Sidney Smith had clarified. He would deal with him in his own way. 'Whilst you do me the honour in giving me the command of the detached squadron,' he told St Vincent, 'I *will be* Commander of it and suffer no, not the smallest interference of any captain, however great his interest may be': An early letter to Nelson from Smith had borne the pompous superscription: '*Chevalier Grand Croix de L'ordre Royal et Militaire de L'Épée de Suède, Ministre Plenipotentiare de sa Majesté Brittanique près la Porte Ottomane et Chef de son Escadre dans les Mers du Levant.*' In a typically direct reply Nelson showed Smith clearly where he stood.

'Your situation as Joint-Minister at the Porte makes it absolutely necessary that I shall know who writes to me – therefore I must direct you, whenever you have Ministerial affairs to communicate, that it is done jointly with your respectable brother, and not mix Naval business with the other; for what may be very proper language for a Representative of Majesty, may be very subversive of that discipline of respect from the different ranks in our service. A Representative may dictate to an Admiral – a Captain of a Man-of-War would be censured for the same thing.'

Troubridge, Hood and Hallowell did not stay long at

Palermo, for their services were wanted elsewhere. On 31 March, Nelson ordered Troubridge to take the *Zealous*, *Swiftsure* and *Minotaur* (just joined from Leghorn) and seize the islands in the Bay of Naples 'in order to prevent the French forces from getting any supplies of corn or other articles by sea'. Nelson was in hopes Naples would soon be restored to its rightful owners. The French could spare only a small garrison and the city was being governed by the 'Parthenopeian Republic' – Neapolitan officials with Jacobin tendencies who had accepted office from fear of anarchy. Cardinal Ruffo, who had landed from Palermo in his native Calabria with seven stalwart men, was now marching towards the capital with 17,000 peasants.

The expedition was immediately successful. Troubridge and his squadron arrived in the bay on the night of 2 April. He sent Hallowell to Procida and Hood to Ischia with wide powers: if all Jacobins and traitors were handed over, private property would be respected. The two officers went ashore the next morning, and by twelve o'clock terms had been agreed. That afternoon Troubridge was writing to Nelson: 'All the Ponza Islands have the Neapolitan flag flying. Your Lordship never beheld such loyalty: the people are perfectly mad with joy and asking for their beloved Monarch.'

Troubridge's next task was to bring Jacobins and traitors to justice. This proved a long business, for many had gone into hiding. 'It frequently happens in the rounds at night,' he told Nelson. 'If, when challenged *Che Viva*, they answer *La Republica*, they are shot; and the Republicans do the same if the answer is *Il Re*. This makes it dangerous to move after dark.' But the local inhabitants proved willing collaborators, and the zeal with which they ferreted the traitors from their hiding-places was matched by Troubridge's ferocious treatment of them. 'I have a villain by name Francesco Boneore on board,' he wrote, 'who commanded the castle of Ischia. The moment we took possession of the castle the mob tore this vagabond's coat with the Tricoloured Cape and Cap of Liberty Button to pieces, and he had the impudence then to put on His Sicilian

Majesty's regimentals again. I tore his epaulet off, took his cockade out and obliged him to throw them overboard. I then *Honoured* him with irons.' Another suspected traitor refused to give an account of himself: Troubridge put him through the motions of hanging, saying that if he could not make the rascal *speak* he would make him *squeak*. A parcel arrived from the shore was found to contain the head of a traitor; with it was a note from a Mr J. M. Vitella, who had done the deed. Troubridge endorsed the note: 'A jolly fellow. T. Troubridge,' and sent it to Nelson, with apologies, 'the weather being very hot,' for not also forwarding the head. Nelson approved. 'Send me word some proper heads are taken off. This alone will comfort me.'

Among the traitors sent on board were a party of priests over whom Troubridge had no jurisdiction. He sent to Palermo for a judge, whom Nelson despatched in the *Minerve*. A week later Troubridge wrote to Nelson: 'The judge appeared to me to be the poorest creature I ever saw, frightened out of his senses, and talks of it being necessary to have a Bishop degrade the priests before he can execute them. I told him to hang them first and if he did not think the degradation of hanging sufficient, I would piss on their d–d Jacobin carcases. I recommended him to Punish the Principal Traitors the moment he passed sentence, no Mass no Confession, but immediate death. Hell was the proper place for them.'

By the end of April most of the traitors had been rounded up. There was so many against whom 'only murmurs' had been proved that Troubridge decided to remit sentence of death. He and Hallowell marched to the main square in full-dress uniform, accompanied by troops and marines. 'The men were all drawn up and the Prisoners with their eyes bound and all the ceremony gone through except firing when I directed the pardon to be read. One of them was almost gone before it was finished. I trust it will have a good effect.' Troubridge's exertions had left him exhausted. He ended a letter to Nelson abruptly: 'I am really very ill. I must go to bed. This treachery fairly does me up.' He was also distressed by the lack of food

168

for the inhabitants, many of whom were half starving. Most of his frantic appeals for money and corn remained, like Ball's, unanswered; and he wrote bitterly to Nelson: 'I can no longer make promises in the King and Queen's name when they appear to be so little interested for their loyal subjects'.

At the beginning of May reports reached Troubridge that the French were beginning to evacuate Naples, 'robbing and plundering every person and shop as they go.' 'If we could but muster a few thousand soldiers,' he wrote to Nelson, 'what a glorious massacre we should have.' He sent Hood to Salerno, and Hallowell and Louis to Castellamare, and soon both towns were flying the King's colours. More traitors were sent on board the *Zealous*, and had much the same effect on Hood as Troubridge: 'I have more than twenty infernal Jacobins. I never saw such an infernal set of vagabonds and rascals in my life. They tell me so many lies we cannot believe a word they say.' Having no judge, Hood advised the local people to dispose of them themselves, 'but none of them have the spirit to take my advice except Schipari who has not troubled me with a single Jacobin. He despatches them soon.' Louis at Castellamare found the *Minotaur* besieged by émigrés. 'What can be done with them?' he asked Troubridge. 'Pray let me know, it will be out of character to fill the ships with all that may present themselves.'

With the capture of Salerno and Castellamare the road to Naples lay open. Reports of the evacuation of the French were confirmed, although the Neapolitan Jacobins were pressing them to remain. 'They begin,' said Troubridge, 'to shake in their shoes.' Cardinal Ruffo and his army were nearing the capital and it seemed to be only a matter of days before the Royalists re-entered the city; 'Troubridge tells me,' wrote Nelson, 'he thinks his next letter will be from Naples'. The situation at Malta had also improved, and on the same day Nelson told Spencer: 'I am in great hopes the garrison will surrender to the meritorious and indefatigable Ball'. But before either of these events could happen, something occurred which instantly altered the situation. Troubridge and Ball received word to join Nelson immediately with all sail of the line. A French fleet was again at large in the Mediterranean.

* * *

Soon after hearing of the disaster of the Nile, the French Directory decided to reinforce or re-embark their forces stranded in Egypt and Malta. To do this it was necessary to raise the blockades of Alexandria and Valetta, and this meant sending into the Mediterranean a fleet so large that the British would have to concentrate all their forces to meet it. There were at Brest about twenty-five ships of the line: these were not enough to match St Vincent's total force of thirty-five ships, but by joining with the Spaniards at Cadiz the French hoped to assemble a combined fleet superior to it.

The expedition began to prepare in December, 1798, under the direction of Vice-Admiral Bruix, French Minister of Marine, but owing to the difficulties of assembling equipment along a coast closely watched by British cruisers, was not ready to sail until mid-April. By this time its activities had become known to the British Cabinet, who thought that it was destined against Ireland – a belief the French encouraged by publishing false reports in the Paris newspapers. Spencer accordingly instructed Lord Bridport, blockading Brest with sixteen sail of the line, that if the French Fleet put to sea and eluded him, he was to fall back on Cape Clear.

On 20 April 1799, Bridport sent the *Anson*, Captain Philip Durham, to reconnoitre Brest Roads, and he reported fourteen sail of the line preparing for sea. At 5 p.m. on the 24th, Sir James Saumarez, commanding the advanced squadron in the *Caesar*, reported the enemy moving. The weather during the next two days was foggy so that Bridport was obliged to keep clear of the coast. This was Bruix's opportunity, and on the night of the 25th he put to sea with twenty-five sail of the line. They were spotted next morning by the *Nymphe* frigate, which hastened to rejoin the Commander-in-Chief. Bridport, following his instructions, made sail northwards towards the Irish coast. Any doubts as to the enemy's destination were dispelled by the capture of the French cutter *Rebecca* bearing despatches for Ireland – a French ruse which proved wholly successful. He also sent word by express packet to St Vincent at Gibraltar, to Lord Keith (who because of St Vincent's health had recently gone out as his second-in-command) at Cadiz; and by the *Dolly* cutter to England.

The *Dolly* reached Plymouth Sound late on the night of the 29th, and Admiral Sir Thomas Pasley, the Port-Admiral, summoned all captains on board his flag-ship, the *Cambridge*. 'The utmost activity,' said the Naval Chronicle, 'pervaded every department. The women were all sent on shore at 2 o'clock a.m. The officers visited all the houses at North Corner and called out of their beds all the seamen and marines on shore at liberty. At 3 a.m. they were sent off in boats in high spirits on hearing the French Fleet was out: cheering and huzzaing till they got on board their respective ships.'

Among the ships in the harbour was the *Bellona*. She had only recently been commissioned and not yet completed fitting-out: when the *Dolly* arrived she had neither guns nor powder on board. Her crew worked all night and by daylight, when the signal 'Enemy's Fleet at Sea' was seen flying at the Telegraph Post on Maker Heights, Sir Thomas Thompson reported ready to proceed. 'An astonishing proof of the activity of British seamen,' commented the Naval Chronicle. (The exertions however proved too great for Mr Monday, Surgeon's Mate, who in a fit of despondency cut his throat so dreadfully that he expired. 'Verdict: lunacy.') Pasley sent Thompson personal congratulations: 'No officer deserves a better ship's company', and to Spencer he wrote: 'The activity of Sir Thomas Thompson upon this occasion does him great credit.'

The Plymouth squadron did not sail immediately, for doubts as to the destination of the French Fleet had now arisen. The despatches taken in the *Rebecca* proved suspicious and Bridport off Cape Clear reported he had sighted nothing. At a Cabinet meeting on 3 May Admiral Young agreed with Pitt and Dundas that the French had probably gone to the Mediterranean, and that some reinforcements should be sent to St

Vincent. Rear-Admiral Whitshed was ordered to hoist his flag in the *Queen Charlotte* at Portsmouth, proceed to Plymouth to collect the squadron lying there, and sail for the Mediterranean. The Board's intentions were also sent to Admiral Pasley at Plymouth, and the Admiralty messenger, Mr Winchester, covered the 210 miles from London on horseback in under twenty-three hours. On 6 May the Plymouth correspondent of the Naval Chronicle was writing: 'Arrived at 2 p.m. off the Sound and lay to, the *Queen Charlotte*, 110, Rear-Admiral Whitshed, Captain Irwin. She made a signal for several ships in Cawsand Bay and fired a gun, on which the following men-of-war got under weigh and joined her at 7 o'clock p.m. – *Bellona* 74, *Captain* 74, *Defiance* 74, *Repulse* 64, *Phoenix* 38, *Ethalion* 38. At 8 p.m. the whole stood down Channel.'

The French Fleet meanwhile were pressing on south. On 4 May Bruix came abreast of Cadiz. A strong westerly wind was blowing into the harbour, and this and the presence of Keith's squadron at the entrance prevented the Spanish Fleet from leaving. Not wishing to risk action in such weather, Bruix continued on his course. Next day St Vincent at Gibraltar watched him pass through the Straits, and at once sent for Keith. Keith arrived on the 9th and on the 12th the two Admirals with sixteen sail of the line followed Bruix into the Mediterranean. Keith's departure from Cadiz opened the door to the Spanish Fleet, which put to sea on the 14th, and passed through the Straits on the 17th. Rear-Admiral Whitshed's squadron was only two days' sailing behind. 'We have just arrived at Gibraltar,' wrote Midshipman Anderson of the *Bellona* to his father on the 19th, 'and hear that the French Fleet has gone to Egypt, the English after them and the Spaniards after them. And we are going after them. I am very happy with Sir Thomas.'

But Anderson was wrong in supposing the French were going direct to Egypt. On 14 May Bruix brought his fleet into Toulon, and a week later the Spaniards entered Cartagena. On the same day St Vincent and Keith reached Port Mahon in

Minorca, where they were reinforced by four sail under Rear-Admiral Duckworth, whose ships had captured the island the previous November. On 26 May St Vincent heard of the arrival of the Spanish fleet at Cartagena and cruised between that port and Toulon to prevent them joining the French. On the 30th he learnt that Bruix had put to sea again two days earlier eastward-bound, and he detached Duckworth with the *Leviathan, Foudroyant, Northumberland* and *Majestic* to reinforce Nelson, then lying at Palermo with ten sail of the line (*Vanguard, Culloden, Zealous, Swiftsure, Minotaur, Lion, Audacious* and three Portugese 74s; Ball and Foley from Malta had not yet joined). Duckworth's departure reduced St Vincent's fleet to sixteen sail, but four hours later the balance was restored by the arrival of the squadron under Whitshed.

On reaching Palermo Duckworth handed over the *Foudroyant* to Nelson, who had always intended her for his flag, and on 8 June he and Hardy transferred from the *Vanguard*. Nelson was in a happier frame of mind than for some time. Surrounded by his trusted band and with the prospects of leading them once more against the enemy, his ailments had suddenly left him. 'I have our dear Troubridge for our assistant,' he wrote to St Vincent, 'in everything we are brothers. Hood and Hallowell are as active and good as ever: not that I mean to say any are otherwise: but you know these are men of resources. If the two fleets join, I am ready, and with some of my ships in as high order as ever went to sea.'

But one piece of news brought by Duckworth depressed him. This was that St Vincent's health was now so bad that he intended to strike his flag and return home. Nelson's debt to St Vincent was enormous. The glories of the Nile belonged, as he well knew, as much to St Vincent as himself. The Admiral had rid the Fleet of apathy and corruption and restored it to a fighting brilliance unrivalled since the days of Elizabeth. 'I am a living example of your goodness,' Nelson told him after the Nile, 'for such a select band as you gave me never can, I fear, be equalled.' And in their personal relations St Vincent, by trusting Nelson implicitly, by understanding and tolerating his varying whims and humours, had won Nelson's lasting respect.

There was no word as to St Vincent's successor, but Nelson feared it would be Keith. He had no grudge against Keith personally, but he regarded him as he had regarded Hotham – a commonplace officer, lacking flair himself and unable to appreciate it in others; also he felt – not unreasonably – that his long experience in the Mediterranean might have fitted him for the command himself. On behalf of his captains and himself he implored St Vincent to remain:

'My dear Lord, We have a report that you are going home. This distresses us most exceedingly and myself in particular; so much so that I have serious thoughts of returning, if that event should take place. But for the sake of our Country, do not quit us at this serious moment. I wish not to detract from the merit of whoever may be your successor; but it must take a length of time, which I hope the war will not give, to be in any manner a St Vincent. We look up to you, as we have always found you as to our Father, under whose fostering care we have been led to fame. If my dear Lord, I have any weight in your friendship, let me entreat you to rouse the sleeping lion. Give not up a particle of your authority to any one; be again our St Vincent, and we shall be happy.'

But by the time St Vincent received this he had struck his flag, given over the command to Keith, and embarked for home.

* * *

Nelson's squadron now numbered fourteen sail. He remained at Palermo a week, without receiving any fresh news of the enemy. On 12 June Ferdinand told him that the Royalist troops under Cardinal Ruffo were about to enter Naples and besought him, in view of the civil strife likely to ensue, to go there to keep order. Nelson agreed, and having embarked the Hereditary Prince and 1700 Sicilian troops, put to sea with the squadron. He had hardly cleared the bay when the *Bellerophon* and *Powerful* were seen approaching from the northwards.

These were further reinforcements from Keith, who sent word that the French had at last been sighted steering to the eastward, and their destination might be Naples or Sicily.

At this news Nelson put back to Palermo, disembarked the troops, and proceeded with the squadron to cruise off Marittimo. He was angry with Keith for not having sent a larger reinforcement. To St Vincent he expressed his regrets 'that his Lordship could not have sent me a force fit to meet the enemy,' and to Keith he wrote tartly: 'The French force being twenty-two sail of the line, four of which are first-rates, the force with me being only sixteen sail of the line, not one of which was oɪ three decks, three being Portugese and one of the English being a 64, I had no choice left but to return to Palermo'. This injured tone was quite unjustified, for by sending Nelson two sail Keith had reduced his own force to nineteen – a number which, when Ball and Foley joined, would be only one more than Nelson's.

On 20 June Nelson heard that the Admiralty had despatched a powerful reinforcement of twenty sail from the Channel Fleet. Four of these ships, under the command of Admiral Gardner and including the *Caesar*, had broken off at Lisbon to escort home the Nile prizes, but the remaining sixteen under Collingwood, now a rear-admiral, were approaching Port Mahon. Having sighted nothing himself, and satisfied that with this force Keith would be unlikely to call on him, Nelson decided to resume his plan of going to Naples. Foley and Ball joined him on the 18th, and on the 21st the squadron reached Palermo. Remaining only long enough to embark Sir William and Lady Hamilton and receive authority from Ferdinand to act as his representative in all matters, Nelson sailed again northwards.

Soon after leaving harbour Nelson received a despatch from Captain Foote (Fremantle's successor in the *Seahorse*), whom Troubridge had left as senior officer at Naples, that he and Cardinal Ruffo had agreed on a treaty of capitulation with the Neapolitan insurgents contained in the sea-forts of Ovo and Nuovo. The insurgents were to be allowed to march out of the forts with colours flying and embark in transports for Toulon; the French garrison at St Elmo were not included in the arrangement, but their commander was to ratify the treaty before it was carried out. On arrival at Naples Nelson observed flags of truce flying from the *Seahorse* and the two forts, and learnt that Ruffo and Foote had put their signatures to the treaty the day before. He at once denounced it as 'infamous,' and since its terms had not been executed, hoisted a signal annulling it. Ruffo came on board the *Foudroyant* and implored Nelson to rescind his decision. There was a heated argument, but Nelson was adamant; the only terms he would consider were unconditional surrender, and for this he had the written authority of Sir John Acton, the Prime Minister. Faced by Nelson's eighteen warships, moored against the arrival of the French in close line-of-battle across the bay, the insurgents had no option but comply. They marched out of the forts and embarked in the transports which they hoped would take them to Toulon, but which anchored instead under the guns of the fleet. Here they lived in appalling conditions for several weeks, at the end of which many were put to death.

During the next few days other rebels were rounded up, among them Commodore Caracciolo, senior flag-officer of the Neapolitan Navy, who was found hiding in a ditch inland, disguised as a peasant. He was accused among other crimes of firing on his late flag-ship, the *Minerva*, off Procida and causing the deaths of several loyal seamen. He was brought on board the *Foudroyant* in the early morning of 29 June, bound hand and foot, by Ruffo's irregulars. Hardy, shocked by his appearance, which another eye-witness described as 'pale, with a long beard, half dead, and with downcast eyes,' ordered his bonds to be removed, showed him to a vacant cabin and offered him refreshment. An hour later Nelson convened a court martial of Neapolitan officers to try Caracciolo for treachery. The trial began at ten o'clock under the presidency of Count Thurn, Captain of the *Minerva*, and by the afternoon Caracciolo was found guilty. Despite a plea from the prisoner, supported by Count Thurn and Sir William Hamilton, for twenty-four hours to prepare his soul, Nelson ordered the sentence to be carried out at once; and at 5 p.m. Caracciolo was run up the *Minerva*'s yard-arm by his own seamen.

Nelson's conduct in annulling the armistice and his treatment of Caracciolo have been the subject of controversy ever since. Many have maintained he was within his rights, others that he assumed a responsibility to which he was not entitled and that his conduct is the only blemish on an otherwise honourable career.

That his proceedings against the insurgents were legal there seems no doubt; he had the verbal authority of Ferdinand to act for him and the written authority of his Prime Minister to enforce unconditional surrender, the terms of the capitulation had not been carried out, and as a principal he had every right to annul them. And yet how much better if he had not done so. Ruffo, whom he denounced as 'a worthless fool,' was a man of some vision. As a native of the country he had far more cause than Nelson to nurture hatred and revenge, yet he saw the advantages of an amnesty. 'If we do not make them believe that we are completely persuaded that it was necessity, error, the force of the enemy and not treason, that occasioned the rebellion, we play into the hands of our enemy and cut off the way to reconciliation.' It was all very well to talk of loyalty, but to whom, as Caracciolo pointed out in his trial, did one owe loyalty, when the King – the symbol of Government – and his entire Court had fled overseas? Foote too had put his name to the treaty because in the absence of other instructions he presumed Ruffo was the representative of the King. In any event he had pledged British honour. Nelson, by annulling the treaty, had broken the pledge. As a British admiral he was expected to be detached and impartial; instead he showed that very partisanship he so often deplored in others.

It was the same with Caracciolo. The Neapolitan Navy was under Nelson's orders, so his right to court-martial him could hardly be questioned. But, as Mahan points out, there was no need for the fearful speed with which the business was carried out. Summary punishment might be necessary and fitting for a mutineer of St Vincent's fleet, but not for the flag-officer of a foreign navy.

The root cause of the trouble was Lady Hamilton. Nelson's relationship with her and her friendship with the King and Queen had led him to attach an importance to the Court of Naples disproportionate to the rest of his command; and during the long months at Palermo, when he had voluntarily relinquished 'active' service (the only kind that suited him), he had conceived a hatred for the French and their supporters which was almost unbalanced.

The only enemy stronghold now holding out in Naples was the fortified castle of St Elmo. Nelson told Troubridge to take 1000 variously assorted Russian, Swiss, Albanian and Calabrian troops, as well as seamen and marines from the fleet, and begin operations against it. Ball acted as second-in-command until Nelson ordered him to return to Malta, when his place was taken by Hallowell. Although the castle was manned by only a few hundred Frenchmen, it lay on the summit of a steep hill and was almost impregnable: the Russian Commander said it could not be taken in less than three months and that by an army several thousands strong. Under Troubridge, 'who,' said Nelson, 'placed his battery, as he would his ship, alongside the enemy,' it soon capitulated. 'Troubridge took the strong castle of St Elmo in ten days,' wrote Sir William Hamilton, 'a regular engineer would have been six weeks making his approaches.' And Nelson wrote to Spencer: 'I presume to recommend Captain Troubridge for some mark of His Majesty's favour: it was supposing you, my dear Lord, ignorant of his merits was I to say more than that he is a first-rate General'.

The Neapolitan Kingdom was now clear of French troops except for two small garrisons at Gaeta on the sea-coast and Capua, twenty miles inland. Nelson despatched Troubridge and Hallowell with 1000 seamen and marines to march against Capua. Then came word from Keith that Bruix's fleet (which for the past month he had been chasing up and down the Riviera) had reached Cartagena; he was going in pursuit of it and he ordered Nelson to take 'all or the greatest part of the force under your Lordship's orders' to the protection of Minorca. Although Nelson knew Keith's fleet numbered thirty-one sail of the line, while that of the combined fleet was forty, he refused to obey, justifying his action in a curt reply: 'As I believe the safety of the Kingdom of Naples depends at the present moment on my detaining the squadron, I have no scruple in deciding that it is better to save the Kingdom of Naples and risk Minorca than to risk the Kingdom of Naples and save Minorca'. Three days later he received a more peremptory demand from Keith for the whole or greater part of his force, which he answered by sending Duckworth and four sail, or one quarter of the ships under his command.

Nelson's refusal to comply with Keith's orders are further instances of his contempt for a man whom he regarded as his inferior, and his infatuation with the affairs of the Kingdom of Naples. In justifying himself to Keith he showed that very limitation of vision he had condemned in Hotham, four years earlier. The real issue at stake was neither Minorca nor Naples, but the British Fleet. If Keith had engaged the enemy and been defeated owing to lack of reinforcements, Nelson's career would have been ended; as it was he received a severe reprimand from the Admiralty. Fortunately for him the combined fleets left Cartagena on 24 June, outward bound. They entered Cadiz on 11 July and sailed again on the 21st. Keith passed the Rock on the 30th in pursuit. But he was too late. On 15 August his frigates entered Brest Roads to find that Bruix, after a round cruise of three and a half months in which he had effected nothing, had brought the combined fleets to anchor twenty-four hours before.

Amid all these unsatisfactory proceedings there occurred one happy event. On 16 June 1799, Admiral Gardner detached the *Caesar* into the Tagus to bring out the Nile prizes. It must have been a proud moment for Saumarez when he made his reappearance with the five ships, which eight months earlier he had brought into harbour as battered and leaking wrecks, now splendidly refitted and commissioned under the British flag. Three weeks later, on a rainy morning with the wind blowing gently from the south-west, the squadron and their prizes entered Plymouth Sound. A great crowd had gathered to welcome them, among them the ever vigilant correspondent of the *Naval Chronicle*:

'This morning, per signal, the French prizes passed up harbour. The bands of the Marine Corps, the Royal Cornwall, and First Wilts were posted on the headlands playing "Rule Britannia," "God Save the King," and "Britons Strike Home," accompanied by nine hearty cheers from hundreds of spectators assembled on the joyful occasion. Each ship, as she passed, returned the cheers: the men-of-war through which the prizes passed, manned ship and cheered also.'

Bruix and Keith had returned to harbour without loss or glory. But five more ships had been added to the roll of the Royal Navy.

CHAPTER 10

On Keith's departure from the Mediterranean, Nelson was left as Commander-in-Chief – an appointment confirmed by the Admiralty, subject to Keith's return 'or some other your superior officer'.

His first task was to complete the evacuation of the French from the Neapolitan dominions. Troubridge arrived back from Capua at the end of July, having accepted its surrender from General Giradon and also arranged terms of capitulation for Gaeta. Nelson sent Louis to Gaeta with a copy of the terms, which stipulated the garrison should be delivered up two hours after the *Minotaur*'s arrival. The Commander at Gaeta, not having signed the terms himself, asked time to consider them, which Louis granted. Nelson, still hating all Jacobins and with Foote's conduct fresh in his memory, was indignant. 'I am hurt and surprised that the capitulation has not been complied with. I have not read your enclosed paper. You will execute my orders or attack it. The fellow ought to be kicked for his impudence. You will instantly take possession of the gates and fortress. I had reason to expect that it had been done long ago.' The capitulation, in fact, was effected a few hours after the *Minotaur*'s arrival. Louis, who had acted in the best of faith, was much put out. 'I can only say,' he replied, 'that I defy any man existing to exert himself more than I have done both in mind and body upon this piece of service. I did what I thought right and was in hopes it would have been approved of.' So unexpected was the rebuke that he did not forget it; as late as 7 November he was complaining that 'the severe lines from your Lordship were such as to hurt my feelings very much'. This was the first occasion on which Nelson's bitterness led him to write so bluntly to one of his captains: unfortunately it was not the last.

The Kingdom of Naples was now clear of French troops, and Ferdinand, who had arrived on board the *Foudroyant* after the surrender of St Elmo, was expected to return to his Palace. But civil strife was still raging in the capital, and under the dreaded Giunto people were being sent to the block daily. Having re-established a government, Ferdinand told Nelson he wished to return to Sicily.

The *Foudroyant* sailed for Palermo on 5 August. Nelson left in the Bay the *Culloden, Minotaur, Goliath, Swiftsure* and *Audacious*: Hood had gone to join Duckworth's squadron at Minorca: Ball with the *Alexander* and *Lion* was blockading Malta. Nelson appointed Troubridge Senior Officer, Coast of Italy, and to bolster up his morale granted him a broad pendant – a happy event for Troubridge, capped soon after by a baronetcy for his services in retaking Naples.

During August Nelson remained at Palermo, Troubridge with his squadron in the Bay of Naples. It was a month of intense heat and freak weather. Many of the Court had bilious attacks. Troubridge reported that with the temperature at ninety degrees, there was a fall of hail, 'the largest I ever saw, many as big as Pigeon's Eggs.' At Naples the appalling massacres continued. 'To-day,' Troubridge wrote on 20 August, 'departed this life, Princes, Dukes, Commoners and Ladies to the amount of Eleven, some by the Axe, others by the halter. I sincerely hope they will soon finish on a great scale and then pass an act of oblivion. Death is a trifle to the prisons.' He begged Nelson to induce the King to return. 'His Majesty's obstinacy in not coming here may be serious. The money spent by the Court at Palermo gives much discontent, 50,000 people unemployed, Trade discouraged, Manufacturers but few and them not encouraged. What can be expected?' Nelson agreed, but told Troubridge it was useless. 'I am afraid our preaching is spending our breath for no purpose . . . Nothing will move him.'

All French forces had now been cleared from the west coast of Italy except for the garrisons at Civita Vecchia and Rome. Nelson ordered Troubridge to take the *Culloden*, *Minotaur*, *Swiftsure* and *Mutine* to reduce them. Troubridge did the business his own way. He sent Louis and Hallowell ahead with a flag of truce to Belair, the garrison commander at Civita Vecchia, to say that Russian troops of Field-Marshal Suvarov were marching into the Roman State, 'and I think it necessary to apprise you that all prisoners-of-war taken by the Russians are invariably sent to Siberia'. This had the desired effect. Louis, anxious not to repeat his mistake at Gaeta, effected an immediate capitulation. Troubridge forwarded a copy of the terms to Nelson, with apologies for its illegibility ('Mr Harryman is the only person I have to write French and Italian: he frequently mixes the three languages so together that he cannot read it'). The departure of the *Swiftsure* to reinforce Duckworth greatly reduced the number of seamen ashore, a handicap of which the French took full advantage. 'These notorious thieves tease and thieve so much,' Troubridge wrote, 'that I am really and truly in a very severe fever. They now begin to be a little more civil as I gave two of their officers a D—d good beating and promised the rest the same if they were impertinent.'

Belair also offered to treat for the garrison at Rome. Louis went there and in accepting its surrender fulfilled a strange prophecy. After Nelson's arrival at Naples from the Nile, an Irish priest, Father M'Cormick, told him that one day he would take Rome with his ships. Nelson said this was impossible as Rome was several miles inland. The priest replied that notwithstanding it would happen. When Nelson heard that Louis had rowed up the Tiber in his barge and hoisted English colours on Castle St Angelo, he was so struck that he recommended Father M'Cormick to the Pope.

The taking of Rome and Civita Vecchia marks the end of Nelson's great period of Mediterranean glory. He remained on the station another eight months, but this was a period of decline and fall: they were probably the most unhappy months of his life.

*   *   *

The first distressing event was the gradual dispersal of the captains. In August came news of the tragic death of Miller. The *Theseus* and *Tigre* were lying off Acre, where Sidney Smith was conducting a heroic stand against Bonaparte's Egyptian Army. 'Captain Miller,' Smith wrote to St Vincent, 'had long been in the habit of collecting such of the enemy's shells as fell in the town without bursting, and of sending them back to the enemy better prepared and with evident effect: he had a deposit on board the *Theseus* ready for service when by an accident for which nobody can account, the whole took fire and exploded at short intervals.' The after part of the ship was wrecked: thirty-five men were killed and forty-five wounded. Nelson was greatly upset. To Davison, the prize-agent for the Nile, he wrote: 'Poor dear Miller is dead, and so will be your friend Nelson; but until death he will wear your medal that was intended for Miller'. And during the next two years he joined with his captains in planning a memorial to 'my much-lamented friend'.

The next three officers to go were Hood, Foley and Hallowell. Hallowell remained on the station for some time, but with Duckworth's departure to Cadiz, did not fall again under Nelson's orders. Hood and Foley stayed at Gibraltar a few weeks, then, as the *Goliath* and *Zealous* were in need of a refit and Hood had received permission to go home to settle his brother's estate, they sailed for England. Before leaving, Hood sent Nelson a letter which expressed the feelings of them all: 'I shall ever feel your friendship towards me with gratitude from the bottom of my heart, and it will ever give me the greatest happiness to serve under your command whenever the state of the *Zealous* will admit of her being once more in service'. But although Foley and Hallowell were to serve under Nelson again, Hood had saluted his flag for the last time.

The next officer to go, and the one whose loss Nelson felt most, was Hardy. It was always understood his appointment was temporary and that as soon as Berry had recovered he should resume his old place. But Berry's illness had lasted longer than he expected. On 4 June, the sixty-second birthday of the King, on which he inspected 10,000 militiamen in Hyde Park, Berry wrote to Nelson: 'Everybody is in high bustle to-day save your humble servant who is by no means equal to embark into the show of Hyde Park or the elegant assembly of the drawing-room'. But he added: 'The hopes of soon recovering and being able to embark give me fresh spirits'. A month later, when the ex-Viceroy of Corsica was appointed Ambassador at Vienna, he wrote he 'could on no account let Lord Minto escape without saying a word to you': he was still 'on a vegetable diet,' but intended to apply for a passage soon. His application was successful and he sailed from England in the *Bulldog*, rejoining Nelson on 15 October.

Nelson liked Berry well enough, but must have regarded his return with some misgivings. During Berry's absence of more than a year, Hardy had shown what a really high standard a ship's company could attain under a first-rate officer. It is significant that although Berry wrote several letters to Nelson during his convalescence in London, there is no record between January and October, 1799, of Nelson having written to him. Possibly one reason for silence was Berry's friendly relationship with Lady Nelson, which Nelson must have found embarrassing; but it is also possible he could no longer say with truth that he looked forward to Berry 'commanding the *Foudroyant* for the flag'.

Nelson endeavoured to keep Hardy on the station. The *Princess Charlotte* being temporarily without a captain, he appointed him to the command. 'My friend Hardy,' he told Spencer, 'will make a man-of-war of her very soon and I make it my earnest request that if Captain Stephenson is not sent out to her, Captain Hardy may be allowed to remain in her.' But the new captain had already left England and arrived a few weeks later. 'Poor Hardy,' Nelson told Ball, 'consequently turned adrift.' There were no other vacancies, so Nelson ordered Hardy to England with his despatches. 'I am very sorry that Captain Hardy is unemployed,' Ball wrote to him, 'but trust he will soon be afloat again. He is too valuable an officer to remain long on shore.' And Troubridge, who at this time was more in the habit of censuring than praising his fellow-captains, told Nelson: 'I am really sorry for Hardy, a zealous, hard and good officer'.

Following on the departure of St Vincent, the loss of the better part of his captains was to Nelson a great grief. The structure of his professional life had suddenly crumbled. There would be other Commanders-in-Chief and other captains; but the freedom of action which St Vincent had given to him and which he had given to his captains, would not be repeated. The squadron with which he had set out on his long chase of Bonaparte had, for discipline and fighting efficiency, never been equalled. 'Our ships are very healthy,' said Nelson, 'and I have no doubt from the constant attention of the captains will always be kept so.' And Troubridge wrote: 'If discipline is once suffered to relax, I wish to be on shore. Tho' poor, I would sooner give up my commission than hold my ship as the captains of the Channel Fleet do, the men not half so comfortable as ours.' Miss Knight wrote of the esteem in which they were held ashore: 'Many of our captains, to my knowledge, did not spare their own purses that their men might be supplied with such wine and food as were required for the preservation of their health. It is no less worthy to remark that I cannot recall to mind a single scandalous story relating to any of our officers serving in that gay and fascinating latitude.' Ferdinand expressed gratitude for the retaking of Naples by giving Troubridge, Ball, Hood, Hallowell, Hardy and Louis a diamond box containing his portrait and the specially-created 'Order of St Ferdinand and Merit'. His wife Queen Charlotte called them 'those excellent captains, the pupils of our hero, saviour and friend Nelson'.

*   *   *

With the clearing of the French from the sea-coast of Italy, the only remaining 'active' spheres of operations were the Levant and Malta. At Acre Sidney Smith had done wonders. With only two ships of the line and a few thousand ill-equipped Turks he defied for over two months the Army of Egypt. Then Bonaparte, with half his army killed or incapacitated by disease, raised the siege and turned southwards. British sea-power had won another battle; without the warships which fed supplies to the garrison Acre would have been impossible to defend. 'If it had not been for you English,' Bonaparte said afterwards, 'I should have been Emperor of the East. But wherever there is water to float a ship we are sure to find you in the way.' Nelson was stirred by Smith's conduct. Petty differences did not prevent him from giving praise where it was due, and wholeheartedly. 'The immense fatigue you had in defending Acre has never been exceeded, and the bravery shown by you and your brave companions is such as to merit every encomium which all the civilized world can bestow. Be assured, my dear Sir Sidney, of my perfect esteem and regard and do not let anyone persuade you to the contrary. But my character is that I will not suffer the smallest tittle of my command to be taken from me: but with pleasure I give way to my friends, among whom I beg you will allow me to consider you.'

The operations in the Levant were too distant for Nelson to influence. But Malta, nearer at hand, was another matter.

The continued siege maddened him. He was, he confessed, 'in desperation' about it.

On returning to the blockade Ball learnt the French had not received any fresh supplies and were now in a wretched condition. 'They have nearly eaten all the dogs, cats, horses and mules in the garrisons.' They had not surrendered before because of the discipline of Vaubois. 'He has shown himself full of resources. He has placed spies in every company to give him early notice of any intention to mutiny that he may crush it in the bud, and he has had the art to make the soldiers believe that the arms of the French Republic are victorious and that Naples is still in their possession.' What distressed Ball more was the continued misery of the Maltese. 'I pay and feed weekly 2500 armed peasants, besides supporting 1000 poor and distressed families.' He begged Nelson 'to apply to the Ambassadors of those sovereigns who guarantee the government of this island to contribute their proportion for its support'. He even appealed to Lady Hamilton: 'I most earnestly solicit your influence with Her Sicilian Majesty to assist the Maltese. If your Ladyship knew half their sufferings, I am sure you would be their warm advocate.'

Ball later told Coleridge that this period at Malta was the most trying of his life. His affection for the Maltese was returned a hundredfold. 'They became incapable of acting in concert,' said Coleridge, 'without his immediate influence; and it was remarkable with what child-like helplessness they were in the habit of applying to him even in their private concerns.'

Despite his worries, Ball's reports remained calm and considered, and his love and admiration for Nelson shine through all his letters. Ferdinand had just made Nelson Duke of Bronte in Sicily, and the pleasure with which Ball addresses him as 'Your Grace' is evident. 'I hope all will end well,' Ball wrote to Sir William Hamilton, 'I am the only person who does not despond. I am as sanguine as I was in the Nile business and feel a presage that His Grace's auspicious flag will bear us happily through all our difficulties.' And he sent Lady Hamilton a present of 'a beautiful ass' which he hoped would exercise her into health.

Nelson now determined to make an all-out effort to win Malta. He knew that nothing could be done without troops. Russian troops were expected, but owing to the whims of the Czar their arrival was uncertain. But there were English troops garrisoning Minorca, and early in October Nelson sailed for Port Mahon to ask General Erskine for a detachment. The General demanded so many conditions as to make agreement impossible. Nelson, 'almost broken-hearted,' returned to Palermo, where he continued supplications by letter. Troubridge meanwhile, having arrived at Palermo from Civita Vecchia and found Nelson gone, sailed for Minorca after him. By the time he reached the island Nelson had left for Palermo, but Troubridge met General Fox, Erskine's successor. Fox gave permission for 1500 troops garrisoning Messina under General Graham, to go to Malta, and on 25 November Troubridge arrived at Palermo with the news. Fearful that Fox might change his mind, Nelson shifted his flag to a transport and before Troubridge had time to anchor ordered him to sail with the *Culloden* and *Foudroyant* to Messina.

Troubridge and Berry embarked troops and sailed for Malta. They reached the island on the morning of 15 December, and in entering the harbour the *Culloden* was damaged by grounding. ('I run on a rock in the middle of the Channel,' said Troubridge, 'the vagabonds who made it ought to be hung.') The troops were landed, and gave much satisfaction to Ball. 'I feel particularly obliged to Sir Thomas for his very cordial co-operation. Brigadier-General Graham is equally attentive, his Regiments behave in a manner entirely to their credit.'

But the wretched plight of the Maltese continued, and now it was Troubridge's turn to beg Nelson for money and supplies. His forceful, angry letters make interesting contrast to Ball's. 'I find,' he wrote to Nelson a week after his arrival, 'there is an order in Sicily against corn being exported. If the Sicilian Government throws the same impediment in my way as they did before, by trying to starve people, I must give up fretting and fagging to no purpose.' Four days later he wrote: 'I have little left in the *Culloden* and hourly expect the General will say, if the supplies are stopped from Sicily, take me and my soldiers off. I cannot leave *them* to be starved tho' I shall have the painful task of leaving the inhabitants to their fate. I beseach your Lordship, press them for a *Yes* or *No*, the crys of hunger are now too great to admit of the common evasive answer usually given by the Sicilian Government.' On New Year's Eve he wrote: 'Many happy returns of the day to you. I never spent so miserable a one. I am not *very tender-hearted* but really the distress here would, if you could see it, move a Neopolitan.' Finally on 5 January, 1800, having in desperation seized some corn-ships at Girgentio, he wrote: 'I have this day saved 30,000 people from dying but with this day my ability ceases. As the King of Naples or rather the Queen and her party are bent on starving us, I see no alternative but to leave these poor unhappy people to starve without our being witness to their distress. I curse the day I ever served the King of Naples. We have characters to lose, my Lord: these people have none. Do not suffer their infamous conduct to fall on us.'

Troubridge's angry criticisms were not altogether fair. Ferdinand was rich and might have given more, but that he had given more than his share nobody could deny. The British and Russian Governments, which had promised to bear equal expenses, had not contributed a penny. 'I will never ask his Sicilian Majesty for another ounce,' Nelson told Troubridge, 'till our part is fulfilled.'

By the New Year Nelson realized that the troops under General Graham would not be sufficient to carry Valetta. Furthermore he learnt that the Russian troops which had arrived at Messina had suddenly been withdrawn by the Czar. This news was depressing, but worse was to follow. Keith had returned to the Mediterranean as Commander-in-Chief.

*   *   *

Having commanded the station officially for the past six months, virtually for the past eighteen, Nelson had supposed he would not be superseded. But the Admiralty no longer had the same faith in him. Since leaving Naples he had – apart from the short trip to Mahon – remained at Palermo, at times suffering the indignity of hoisting his flag in a transport. His attachment to Lady Hamilton had become public news and was being discussed openly in London drawing-rooms. Fantastic stories were circulating of how the pair stayed up at supper-parties and the gambling-tables far into the night. 'They say here,' wrote his friend, Admiral Goodall from South Audley Street, 'you are Rinaldo in the arms of Armida and that it requires the firmness of an Ubaldo and his brother knight to draw you from the Enchantress.'

To Ball and Troubridge the affair was particularly distressing. 'I am quite concerned,' Ball wrote to Saumarez, 'at the many severe paragraphs which have been put in the newspapers respecting him and Lady Hamilton.' ('I am convinced,' he added loyally, 'there has not been anything improper between them.') He and Troubridge tried to change Nelson's habits, making his health an excuse for voicing their opinions. 'I feel infinite concern that Your Grace has a complaint in the eye,' wrote Ball. 'I am afraid Sir William's late hours do not agree with it. I shall lay the fault to her Ladyship, because if she were to go to bed early, Sir William would soon follow.' Troubridge wrote from the heart: 'I see by your Lordship's last letter your eyes are bad. I pray, I beseech, I intreat you not to keep such horrid hours, you will destroy your constitution. Lady Hamilton is accustomed to it for years, but I saw the bad effects of it in her the other day, she could not keep her eyes open, yawning and uncomfortable all day.' A week later he wrote: 'If you knew what your friends feel for you, I am sure you would cut all the nocturnal partys, the gambling of the people at Palermo is publicly talked of everywhere. I beseech your Lordship leave off. Lady H's character will suffer, nothing can prevent people from talking, a Gambling Woman in the eyes of an Englishman is lost.'

Ball and Troubridge also wrote to Lady Hamilton: 'Be assured,' Troubridge told her, 'that I have not written from any impertinent interference but from a wish to warn you of the ideas that were going about, which you could not hear of, as no person can be indifferent to the construction put on things which may appear to your Ladyship innocent and, I make no doubt, done with the best intention – still your enemies will and do give things a different colouring. You may not know that you have many enemies, I therefore risk your displeasure by telling you.' In reply Lady Hamilton promised Ball and Troubridge she would gamble no more. But the damage had been done.

Keith's reappearance in the Mediterranean was a cruel blow to Nelson and a matter for bitter comment among the captains. His failure to bring Bruix to action had aroused the contempt of the whole Fleet. After he had passed the Straits, Ball wrote to Nelson: 'They begin to talk loud at Gibraltar at the combined fleets having run about in such a manner with impunity. I hope to God Ld. K will stop all their mouths by destroying the enemy's fleet, but the prejudice of all the captains against him is such as will make it very difficult to do away.' From Mahon Troubridge wrote: 'This undetermined method of acting convinces me he is no great thing and *a true Scot*'. In England, Sam Hood wrote: 'I wish Lord Nelson had been given the command; things, I think, would have gone altogether more to our advantage'.

When Keith arrived, Louis wrote from Mahon, where he had gone to refit: 'I see My Lord Keith is out among us after all. Should any arrangement take place, I hope your Lordship will not leave me out, as I really offer myself to follow your fortune during the war. This comes from my heart and soul. I am not fond of new faces.' Troubridge and Ball expressed themselves similarly. 'We of the Nile,' commented Nelson bitterly to Troubridge, 'are not equal to Keith in his estimation and ought to think it an honour to serve under such a clever man.' And Captain Blackwood of the *Penelope* frigate recently arrived on the station, an officer unknown to Nelson, wrote that he was proceeding to Leghorn by way of Palermo 'as I did not wish to fall in with Lord Keith, who would most probably have changed the good orders your Lordship gave me'.

Keith's return resulted in an astonishing piece of good fortune for Nelson. On arrival at Genoa he ordered Nelson to join him. Nelson could not refuse, but went in bitter mood. 'I cannot command,' he wrote to Lady Hamilton, 'and now only obey.' He joined Keith at Leghorn and sailed with him back to Palermo to embark Neapolitan troops for the siege of Malta. The squadron remained at Palermo a week during which Keith saw what he afterwards described as 'a scene of fulsome vanity and absurdity': then they pushed on for Malta.

Off Malta Keith received a report that a French squadron had been sighted near the west coast of Sicily. He took station in his flag-ship off the harbour entrance, and detached Nelson with the *Audacious* and *Northumberland* to chase to windward. Nelson pushed westwards in dirty weather for three days. On the morning of 18 February he sighted the *Alexander* (under the command of her first lieutenant) and *Success* frigates in chase of several French ships, among them a ship of the line. This was the *Généreux*, wearing the flag of Rear-Admiral Perrée, who had sailed from Toulon to bring supplies and reinforcements to Valetta. The *Success* closed the *Généreux* and fired several broadsides, one of which killed Admiral Perrée. The *Foudroyant* came up and fired a single broadside. The captain of the *Généreux* returned it and then, having no further stomach for the fight, struck his colours.

It must have been a proud moment for Berry to see the English flag hoisted in the ship to which, eighteen months earlier, he and Thompson had surrendered. Nelson was, as Ball put it, 'a heaven-born Admiral.' For over a year he had not been near Malta, and now on his first visit he had captured one of the two ships that had escaped from the Nile. 'Twelve out of thirteen,' he wrote to Lady Hamilton that evening, 'only the *Guillaume Tell* remaining.'

On Nelson's return to Malta, Keith ordered him to take over the blockade while he himself went to Genoa. But Nelson had practically decided that his Mediterranean service was at an end and while it lasted nothing would keep him from Lady

Hamilton. 'My state of health is such,' he told Keith, 'that it is impossible I can longer remain here. Without some rest I am gone. I must therefore, whenever I find the service will admit of it, request your permission to go to my friends at Palermo for a few weeks and leave the command here to Commodore Troubridge.' Nelson's health was bad, but never before had he allowed it to interfere with his duty. Ball and Troubridge, who knew his real motives, implored him to remain. 'Remember, my Lord,' wrote Troubridge, 'the prospects are rather good at present of reducing this place and that *William Tell, Diane* and *Justice* are the only three ships left from the Nile Fleet. I beseech you to hear the entreaties of a sincere friend and do not go to Sicily for the present.' And Ball wrote to Lady Hamilton: 'I do not think a short stay here will hurt his health, particularly as his ship is at anchor and his mind not harassed. Troubridge and I are extremely anxious that the French ships and the French garrison of Valetta shall surrender to him. I would not urge it if I were not ultimately convinced it would add both to his honour and happiness.'

But to these pleas Nelson was deaf. Included in Keith's instructions was an order to discontinue Palermo as a fleet base and substitute Syracuse or Messina instead. This was too pointed a comment to escape Nelson, and on 4 March he wrote to Lady Hamilton: 'My health is in such a state and to say the truth an uneasy mind at being taught my lesson like a schoolboy that my determination is made to leave Malta on the 15th morning of this month, or the first moment the wind comes favourable'. He left even earlier – on the 10th – and at Palermo once more hoisted his flag in a transport. He sent back the *Foudroyant* to the blockade with orders to rejoin him in a fortnight, 'by which time,' he told Keith, 'I hope some decisive turn will take place in my complaint'.

Before leaving for Malta Berry said to Miss Knight: 'I think we shall take a prize'.

*   *   *

At the beginning of 1800 Troubridge's health and balance of

mind once more deteriorated. The immediate cause was the prolonged misery of the Maltese which he was unable to alleviate. For this Troubridge laid the entire blame on the Neapolitan Court, against which he had conceived a hatred as unbalanced as Nelson's detestation of Jacobins. A further worry was the befriending of that Court by the man he loved above all others. Finally, in February, 1800, he became seriously ill with jaundice and fever.

Behind these causes there lay one deeper. In their private relationships Troubridge and Nelson were gradually drifting apart. The long convivial evenings when, as in the *Captain* and *Agamemnon*, the two had sat discussing plans and tactics far into the night, had ceased to exist. 'I wish, I wish, I was at your elbow,' Troubridge wrote. But Nelson did not want him there. This, the emotional side of his life, was now filled by Lady Hamilton.

Nelson's relationships with Troubridge and Lady Hamilton were by their natures too intimate and contradictory to reconcile. Further, because there was now a side of Nelson's life about which he could not longer be intimate with Troubridge (and of which he knew Troubridge disapproved), he ceased to be intimate on any. When he realized the gulf opening between them he was genuinely distressed. He did not want to forfeit the friendship but he was in the grip of forces beyond his control, and powerless to prevent it. When Troubridge at the height of his illness was unable to write for several days, Nelson sent a fractious note accusing him of ingratitude. The effect was catastrophic. 'It has really so unhinged me that I am quite unmanned and crying. I would sooner forfeit my life, my everything, than be deemed ungrateful to an officer and friend, I feel it so much. Pray, pray, acquit me for I really do not merit it. There is not a man on earth I love, honour and esteem more than your Lordship.'

A friendly letter from Nelson brought some comfort, but it could not alter Troubridge's general state of mind. From now on his letters become one long catalogue of complaints, criticisms and abuse. Nelson tried to soothe him. 'You know, my dear friend, that I highly approve and admire your public conduct; but for you to fret yourself to death because you believe that all the world are not so honest as yourself is useless – and makes all people sorry to see you torment yourself.' But it was without effect. Troubridge had become jealous of the woman whose affections had supplanted his, and worse, jealous of brother officers who, he imagined, were now sharing with Nelson the intimacy he had once enjoyed.

The sneaking tell-tale comments which enter Troubridge's correspondence at this time do not make pleasant reading. 'I think Rear-Admiral Duckworth has been corresponding with the Admiralty beyond what a junior admiral in my opinion ought,' he wrote from Mahon. Before leaving for Malta he told Louis he had no wish to go there. Louis repeated this to de Niza, and de Niza, who was waiting to be relieved, to Ball. 'I am perfectly aware,' Ball told Nelson, 'that Your Grace's marked goodness to me has created much envy at which I am not surprised, but your Grace knows that I have ever rendered justice to the abilities of Sir Thomas Troubridge. I took the liberty last year of expressing to you the satisfaction I should have in seeing him with the command of the blockade here . . . I therefore trust he no longer feels sore at my having this command.' Next Troubridge turned on Captain Dixon of the *Lion:* 'Went to Syracuse without orders a considerable time since and not returned. I fear his head is deranged. If it was not for his family, I should certainly bring him to a court martial.' Finally he turned on Nelson's flag-captain. 'Sir Edward Berry is gone off giving improper receipts signed only by the Purser's steward and blending sugar and slops in one receipt, tho' every boy in the service knows they are distinct offices. If a captain is above looking to see the receipts are regular, he should go to his wife.' Another letter explained his real motives. 'Leave the *Foudroyant* out and hoist your flag in the *Culloden*. Everything shall be done to make it comfortable and pleasing to you: a month will do all. If you comply with my request, I shall be happy as I shall then be convinced I have not forfeited your friendship.'

Distasteful as these aspersions were, there was some truth in them. Since Berry's return the good order of the *Foudroyant* had lapsed. 'The Ship,' said Midshipman Parsons, 'was not in a high state of discipline.' An incident which illustrates the difference between Berry and Hardy had occurred during Keith's short visit to Palermo. At a ball given by the King the *Foudroyant*'s midshipmen in their cups charged the Royal foot-guards. There was a scuffle and one midshipman was wounded. 'For this notable and ill-timed feat,' said Parsons, 'Lord Nelson stopped our leave for six months.' Berry took the punishment as a slur on his authority, and informed Nelson that he also would remain on board until further orders. Nelson took up his pen to soothe another captain. 'You shall rally, you shall be well,' he told Berry, 'young men will be young men and we must make allowances. If you expect to find anything like perfection in this world you will be mistaken: therefore do not think of little nonsenses too much. Let all pass over and come and dine here. As you are ready to execute my orders, take this of coming to this house as a positive and lawful one.' With Hardy as captain the incident might still have happened, but Nelson would probably have let Hardy give the punishment himself; nor is it easy to imagine Hardy sulking in his cabin and refusing to come on shore.

A further proof of Berry's instability is supplied by Midshipman Parsons in his account of events after the *Foudroyant* had left Nelson at Palermo. The ship reached Malta on the afternoon of 29 March, 1800, and anchored in the Marsa Sirocco. There were also in the harbour the *Lion*, Captain Dixon, the *Culloden*, still unseaworthy owing to the damage to her bottom, the *Alexander*, and the *Penelope* frigate, Captain Blackwood.

Late that night, it being very dark and windy, the harbour was suddenly illuminated by rockets, blue lights and false fires. This was the prearranged signal from an officer Troubridge had placed ashore that French ships were putting to sea. According to Parsons its effect on Berry was rather different.

'The ship was put in battle order and the crew impatiently waited the order of our Captain who, deficient in general knowledge of the French language, had acquired a phrase that from its rarity, was deeply impressed on his mind and influenced his conduct. He said the French were practising a *ruse de guerre* and remaining fast at anchor. The frequent flashes and roar of heavy artillery caused a disposition in the minds of our officers to doubt the correctness of their gallant commander's judgment; and a message delivered from the *Minorca* that the commodore had sent him to say that the *Guillaume Tell* was going large on the starboard tack closely followed and fired into by the *Penelope* frigate; and that we being the only ship in the squadron able to cope with such a monster were ordered to bring her to close action instanter.

'The *ruse de guerre* haunting the mind of our captain, prevented immediate obedience; and things remained in the same state of quietude until broken by a shot from the *Port Mahon* being athwart our stern, and, "Oh, the *Foudroyant* ahoy," from a hoarse powerful voice compelled the attention of our chief. "I am ordered by Captain Manly Dixon to express his great surprise at the inactivity of the flagship of Lord Nelson. It is his most positive orders that the *Foudroyant* cut from her anchor and bring the *Guillaume Tell* to close action without losing a moment's time. Nor am I to leave you, Sir, until all your sails are set in pursuit of the flying enemy with whom Captain Blackwood is in close and interesting conversation." This gentle intimation dispersed the idea engendered by the *ruse de guerre* and the *Foudroyant* was crowded with all sail that could bring her into the conference of Captain Blackwood and Admiral Decrès . . .'

The *Foudroyant* had lost valuable time, and when she cleared the harbour the *Guillaume Tell* and *Penelope* were far out to sea. Blackwood had the advantage of the wind and tacked to and fro across the enemy's stern. 'I became only casually exposed to his stern-chasers,' he wrote, 'whilst he suffered much from our broadsides.' This was a repetition of Fremantle's treatment of the *Ça Ira*. Decrès could have borne up and brought his own broadsides to bear, but this would have enabled the *Lion*, already in sight astern, to catch up. Blackwood hung on to the

Guillaume Tell through the night and by dawn had brought down her main and mizen-masts. The *Lion* now ranged up and at 5 a.m. came to close action. After half an hour she was so damaged that she became unmanageable and dropped astern.

The *Guillaume Tell* would now probably have escaped but for the arrival of Berry bearing a full spread of canvas. 'Here again,' said Parsons, 'our noble captain's imaginative turn hoodwinked his judgment. "Youngster," he said to me, "tell the officers of the main and lower decks to remain prepared but not to fire without my orders as I think the *Guillaume Tell* has struck at the sight of us!" ' The shambles of the enemy may have led Berry to suppose he was incapable of further action – but this was far from so. In reply to his hail to surrender, Decrès brandished a sword over his head and fired a musket. Berry had not furled his sails in anticipation of the enemy striking, and as the *Foudroyant* swept past, the enemy poured in a broadside which 'almost unrigged her'. It took Berry several minutes to wear round and his next attempt to engage was no happier than the first; so accurate was the *Guillaume Tell's* fire that half the *Foudroyant's* masts were carried away and she fell astern. While she was repairing the damage, the *Lion* and *Penelope*, both severely disabled, carried on a desultory fire. Then Berry ranged up again. Whatever he lacked in judgment he made up for in bravery; and such was his zeal to get at close quarters that he almost rammed the enemy. After a few more broadsides, the *Guillaume Tell*, now totally dismasted and having suffered frightful casualties, hauled down her flag.

The *Guillaume Tell* had fought a most gallant battle. She had taken on and very nearly beaten three British ships, two of which were her equal in size. 'A more heroic defence,' says James, comparing it with that of the *Leander*, 'is not to be found among the records of naval actions.' The hero of the hour was not Berry nor Dixon (who, as Troubridge was only too ready to point out, had displayed poor seamanship), but Blackwood of the *Penelope*. 'I have not language to express the high sense of obligation I feel myself under to Captain Blackwood,' Dixon wrote to Nelson, and Decrès in his report to the French Admiralty gave Blackwood the credit for his surrender. Nelson warmed to the news. With his genius for recognizing uncommon character, he wrote to Blackwood with typical extravagance: 'Is there a sympathy which ties men together in the bonds of friendship with hardly a personal knowledge of each other? If so, which I believe, it was so to you. Your conduct and character on the late glorious occasion stamps your fame beyond the reach of envy. It was like yourself, it was like the *Penelope*. Thank and say every kind thing for me to your brave officers and men.'

The *Lion* and *Foudroyant* were too damaged to take charge of the prize ('our once excellent cabin,' Berry told Hamilton, 'is now a hurricane house'), and the *Penelope* had the honour of towing the *Guillaume Tell* into Syracuse. A few days later the squadron, refitted with jury-masts, sailed to Palermo. Ferdinand and the Court came down to the harbour to welcome them. 'Our well-squared yards,' said Parsons, 'were covered by sailors in their long-quartered shoes, check shirts, blue jackets and trousers white as driven snow, with queues hanging down their backs, while three bold and active boys climbed the royal masts and sat on the trucks apparently much at ease.' That night there was a ball on board, attended by the Royal Family. Decrès was present, and in reply to a toast to his health told Nelson that to Captain Blackwood alone was he indebted for the capture of his ship. He then kissed Blackwood warmly on both cheeks. 'We all perceived,' said Midshipman Parsons, 'by the heightened colour that Captain Blackwood would willingly have dispensed with the fraternal hug.'

Upon this scene of rejoicing there entered one unhappy note. From Troubridge, left alone at Malta, sick and in his own words 'really soured with the world,' there came a series of frenzied letters threatening to bring Dixon and Berry to court martial. And he enclosed a report of proceedings which, for sheer frightfulness, he had not yet equalled: 'Four of the English deserters are taken in *Guillaume Tell*, two dead of their wounds: the other two are here, one with both legs off and the other has lost his arm. A Court Martial is ordered: if they will but live Monday, they will be tried and meet their deserts immediately. We shot and hung a Maltese for carrying in two fowls and to-morrow I hope will be a gala day for the old lady who I have long been wishing to hang, that carried in intelligence. She swore she was with child, and possibly she will try some stout fellow: even then it will be good policy to destroy the *breed.*'

With the capture of the *Guillaume Tell* the last of the French Nile Fleet had been taken. Her captors had only one regret. 'Need I tell you,' Berry wrote to Hamilton, 'it was for the presence of him who first led me to glory.' Even Decrès told Blackwood that 'he was much hurt his Lordship was not in the *Foudroyant*'. But Nelson had no such wish, or if he did was eager to refute it. 'I thank God I was not present,' he told Keith, 'for it would finish me could I have taken a sprig of these brave men's laurels; they are, and I glory in them, my darling children, served in my school, and all of us caught our professional zeal and fire from the great and good Earl St Vincent.' He had now decided his Mediterranean service was at an end. 'Thus, owing to my brave friends,' he wrote to the Secretary of the Admiralty, 'is the entire destruction of the French Mediterranean Fleet to be attributed, and my orders from the great Earl of St Vincent fulfilled. My task is done, my health is finished, and probably my retreat for ever fixed unless another French Fleet should be placed for me to look after.' To Spencer he wrote more frankly. 'Lord Keith sending me nothing, I have not of course a free communication. I have wrote to him for permission to return to England where you will see a broken-hearted man.' Another reason for return was the arrival at Palermo of Arthur Paget to relieve Sir William Hamilton as Ambassador. Nelson and the Hamiltons planned to travel to England together, 'but whether by water or land depends on the will of Lord Keith'.

Keith, despite his disapproval of Nelson's conduct and Nelson's contemptuous attitude to his orders, treated his application with surprising generosity. 'I am very sorry, my dear Nelson, for the contents of your letter, and I hope you will not be obliged to go. Strictly speaking I ought to write to the Admiralty before I let a flag-officer go off the station; particularly as I am directed to send you, if you like it, to Egypt: but when a man's health is concerned, there is an end to all, and I will send you the first frigate I can lay hold of.'

During his remaining two months on the station, Nelson saw the last of his captains slip away. Ball, still valiantly trying to reduce Valetta (which he did not accomplish until the autumn) was, as military governor ashore, no longer directly under his orders. Louis left him when a fire destroyed the *Queen Charlotte* and Keith shifted his flag to the *Minotaur*. Finally Troubridge received orders to take the leaking *Culloden* home and become St Vincent's flag-captain in the Channel Fleet. On the eve of Troubridge's departure, Ball wrote to Nelson: 'He is, I think, dangerously ill. He has some humour in his blood which is fixing in his hand, and he has a cough which so affects his lungs that he spits blood. Instead of going on active service he requires immediate repose and a strict regimen.'

When his captains heard he was leaving they expressed their sorrow in no small terms. Keith's chilly disapproval and the strictures of Lord Spencer, now beginning to be heard for the first time, could not alter the feelings of those who knew and loved him. 'General Graham,' complained Ball to a friend at Malta, 'gives in to Lord Keith's prejudices, as he relates and repeats whatever is against our friends at Palermo. He does not do it to me, knowing my friendship revolts at it . . .' 'It is impossible,' he concluded, 'that any person can feel more pure regard for him than I do, for I have seen him in the hour of danger and difficulties and I never can forget his great and immortal traits.' Blackwood wrote to Lady Hamilton, with whom he had become warm friends ('in thunder, in lightning or in rain, I will bind myself to do whatever you desire'): 'My greatest regret is that we are so soon to lose a valuable friend, under whom we should never fail to succeed'. Louis, complaining of his 'flag at the fore,' spoke of his misery at parting and desire to serve Nelson wherever he might go.

Troubridge wished he could have carried the party home. Berry, last to take his farewell, wrote: 'I do not like even the smallest idea of leaving you – tho' for only a short time'. But perhaps the greatest tribute came from his own barge's crew.

'My Lord,

It is with extreme grief that we find you are about to leave us. We have been along with you (though not in the same ship) in every Engagement your Lordship has been in, both by Sea and Land; and most humbly beg of your Lordship to permit us to go to England as your Boats' crew, in any Ship or Vessel, or in any way that may seem most pleasing to your Lordship.

My Lord, pardon the rude style of Seamen who are but little acquainted with writing, and believe us to be, my Lord, Your most humble and obedient servants,

Barge's Crew of the *Foudroyant*.'

On 14 June Nelson arrived at Leghorn with the *Foudroyant* and *Alexander* which, against Keith's orders, he had taken from the blockade of Naples to convey the Queen of Naples and her suite on their journey to Vienna. The same day Bonaparte, who at the end of 1799 had slipped back to France with Admiral Ganteaume in the frigate *Muiron*, completely routed the Austrian Army at the battle of Marengo. A month later Nelson struck his flag, and accompanied by the Queen of Naples, Sir William and Lady Hamilton, Miss Knight and a vast quantity of baggage which included Hallowell's coffin, set out overland on the first stage of his journey home.

PART IV

Champion of the North

CHAPTER 11

During the two years that Nelson was in the Mediterranean, life for Betsey and Fremantle had undergone many changes. Soon after the return of Betsey's parents from Italy in 1798 they decided that life in London was too expensive and to live in the country. They found what they wanted in Buckinghamshire, 'about two miles from the turnpike road in the village Swanburn, very agreeably situated on a hill. There is three little fields with the house and a good kitchen garden.' The price was 1000 guineas, but Fremantle offered 900, and on the day after the Nile this was accepted.

Here they lived for the next two years, during which Betsey lost both her parents. Her father, whose health had been 'quite ruined with the *millions* of medicines he has always taken,' died in October, 1798, and a year later her mother followed him. But the cycle of nature went on. In June, 1799, a year after the birth of Thomas, Emma was born. Eleven months later Charles appeared. 'I think him a pretty child,' said Betsey, 'but Fremantle calls him an ugly dog.'

The pair took a full part in the life of the village, and Fremantle found himself acting as local squire. 'A riot having taken place at Drayton occasioned by the people of the canal,' he was sent for to restore order. 'Twenty-six of them are taken and are to be sent to Aylesbury jail to-morrow.' On Swanbourne feast-day Fremantle was called on to do the honours.

He and Betsey gave the prize for the girls' smock-race, but 'few girls ran for the smock as they pretended to be shy'. However, 'the ass and poney race and men trying to catch a hen with their teeth was the most amusing part of the whole'.

They made several trips to London; there were dances where they saw the Prince of Wales and Mrs Fitzherbert, and musical evenings at Mrs Villars' in North Audley Street and at Lady Palmerston's, where Betsey 'heard Miss Anguish, who has a delightful voice'. At the opera they were disappointed not to hear Banti ('she was brought to bed in the middle of the day'), but Betsey thought the new Ballet Taglioni very pretty. Fremantle sat for his portrait to Pellegrini, and Betsey's verdict was 'excessively like and very well done'. They received a visit from Foley, who had paid off the *Goliath* and was on his way to commission the *Elephant*: Betsey found her old suitor 'very stupid'.

For Christmas, 1799, they went to the Buckinghams at Stowe, taking Thomas, who was Lord Buckingham's god-child: 'he was taken a great deal of notice of and much admired'. On the night of their arrival there was a dinner-party of thirty: the next day 'three hundred poor people dined here on the remains of last night's supper'. There was Mass every day, 'as three priests are now in the house'. Lord George, the Bucking-hams' elder son, on his eleventh birthday 'gave a supper to the poor children and a shilling apiece; there was eighty of them, the servants danced'.

By the beginning of 1800 Fremantle's health had quite recovered. Buckingham asked Spencer for employment for him, and in an interview with the First Lord in May, Fremantle was told he was to be given a ship of the line. The appointment did not come through immediately, and during the spring and early summer he remained at Swanbourne. This was a year of intense heat. 'We have charming weather and the cornfields look beautiful,' wrote Betsey on 2 August. 'The price of bread and wheat falls very much and there is plenty of it.' But just before the harvest was due to be gathered there was a series of terrible rainstorms. The effect was catastrophic. The price of wheat soared and there were riots everywhere. 'The poor people', wrote Betsey, 'are truly starving.'

On 21 August Fremantle was appointed to the *Ganges*, 74, at Portsmouth. Betsey was 'quite miserable at his going,' but flattered he had been given such a good ship. Fremantle took as midshipman one Hutchings, the son of a Swanbourne farmer, in the hope of raising volunteers for the ship. But he was not successful. 'Although I talked to the overseers of the parishes and the boys themselves,' he told Buckingham, 'I could not persuade any of them to go nor did any of the overseers dare to urge them on the subject.' Such was the horror with which most Englishmen regarded life in their Navy.

On 24 August Fremantle left Swanbourne, and that night Betsey wrote in her diary: 'I feel quite at a loss and wretched alone – poor little Tom distressed me many a time in the course of the day enquiring when his papa would come home again'. Two days later Fremantle sent his first letter. 'My ship is quite perfect and I have every reason to be perfectly satisfied with her and my appointment.' The *Ville de Paris* was also in the harbour. She was flying St Vincent's flag, and Troubridge, who had only returned to England three weeks earlier, had arrived on board as Captain of the Fleet.

*   *   *

On his return from the Mediterranean in the autumn of 1799 St Vincent, aged sixty-five and still in poor health, had retired to his country house at Rochetts in Essex, not intending to serve again. But the indiscipline of the Channel Fleet, which had never properly recovered from the mutiny of 1797, at length led Spencer to call on the only officer capable of restoring it to order.

St Vincent hoisted his flag in the *Ville de Paris* in March, 1800, and took command of forty sail of the line, having Admiral Sir Alan Gardiner as his second-in-command, Rear-Admirals Collingwood, Whitshed, Berkeley and Cotton as junior flag-officers, and among his captains Foley in the *Elephant*, Saumarez in the *Caesar* and Thompson in the *Bellona*. Captain Grey was flag-captain of the *Ville de Paris*, the post of Captain of the Fleet being left open until Troubridge's return.

When Nelson heard of St Vincent's appointment he wrote: 'My heart rejoices to hear you are so well recovered and that there are hopes of your being employed in the Home Fleet, when our gentlemen will not find it so necessary as it has been to go into harbour to be refitted; but you will have a Herculean labour to make them what you had brought the Mediterranean Fleet to'. These were prophetic words. To the captains of the Channel Fleet St Vincent's appointment was not popular. Under Bridport they had enjoyed a lax discipline which they did not wish to see changed. 'May the discipline of the Mediterranean Fleet never be introduced into the Channel Fleet,' was the toast given by one captain at a dinner-party before St Vincent's arrival. It was a vain hope. On his first morning in the *Ville de Paris* the Admiral called for his secretary: 'Mr. Tucker, bring me the Mediterranean order-books'.

As a start St Vincent set about improving the men's health. This was specially necessary, for whereas Bridport had stationed the Fleet several leagues off Brest, with frigates occasionally scouting the Roads, he intended to keep them 'well in with Ushant with an easterly wind,' and to place an advanced squadron of five ships close in to the Black Rocks. Under Bridport the health of the men had been shamefully neglected by the ships' surgeons. St Vincent gave his opinion of them in a typical letter to the Medical Board: 'The moment they obtain a diploma, they think themselves above the most ordinary and useful parts of their duty, play on the flute and at backgammon the whole day and make their journals from Cullen and other medical authors which give them a reputation with your Board without the smallest title to it'. With the assistance of Dr Baird he issued a series of orders for the well-being of the men. Hog-sties were to be done away with and sick-bays built in their place: bedding was to be regularly aired: lower decks were to be dry-scrubbed with holystone to keep out the damp;

men with coughs were to wear flannel next to the skin: lemon juice and sugar was to be issued as the standard anti-scorbutic.

The next task was to improve the discipline. 'I could relate such atrocious proceedings in some of the ships,' he told Nepean, the Secretary of the Admiralty, 'that would make your hair stand on end.' The real evil lay, as it had in the Mediterranean Fleet, not with the men but the officers, and in particular the captains. 'You cannot conceive,' he told Spencer, 'how few men are qualified to command ships of the line as they ought to be.' In another letter he wrote: 'A captain commanding a squadron in this department has no authority, the captains having lived together "Hail fellow, well met", and there having been neither discipline nor subordination in the squadron. No service can be carried on with energy unless there is distinction of rank in the commanding officer.'

One thing to which St Vincent particularly objected was the captains communicating with the Admiralty without reference to him. 'If your Lordship,' he wrote bluntly to Spencer, 'does not put an extinguisher upon the gossiping correspondence carried on between your Neptunes at the Board and the officers of every description in the squadron, neither I nor any other person who may be thought fitter for the purpose, can command it.' And to Nepean he wrote: 'A hint to your clerks will remedy what I will not tolerate'.

He next turned to the captains themselves. One of the worst grievances of the men was that the officers were allowed leave in harbour but they were not. The marines of the *Bellona* sent a petition to the Admiralty (remarkable in that they all signed their names with an X): 'We have been on Board between three and four years and We Earnestly Intreat Your Lordship to take into consideration Our Earnest Request, to have some time allowed us on shore'. This could not be granted, but some equality could be reached by forbidding the officers to sleep on shore. In another memorandum he ordered all captains to mount twenty-four hours' guard at Brixham watering-place to prevent desertion – a measure which meant, among other discomforts, sleeping on the bare ground with only a sail-cloth as protection.

At sea he was equally authoritative. Under Bridport the captains had been in the habit of turning in for the night irrespective of manoeuvres. This, like everything else that happened, came to St Vincent's notice. 'The Commander-in-Chief,' came an order, 'cannot suppose it possible that any captain of a ship under his command is off the quarter-deck or poop when any movement of the ship is made, night or day.' He had his own methods of enforcing it. One cold, wet night the order was given for the Fleet to tack in succession. Mr Tucker went down to the Admiral's cabin to tell him the manoeuvre was about to be made. The cabin was empty but St Vincent's clothes were on his chair. Search was made but without result. Captain Grey ordered the alarm not to be given until the ship had gone round. Mr Tucker, who had gone on another search, found the Admiral standing at the far end of his stern gallery, wearing his flannel dressing-gown and cocked hat. 'Hush, sir, hush, hush!' said St Vincent. 'I want to see how the evolution is performed in such a night of weather; and whether Jemmy (*Captain Vashon of the* Neptune *next astern*) is on deck.' There was silence, broken at last by a hoarse cry from astern: 'Are you all ready forward there?' 'Ay,' said St Vincent, 'that will do,' and returned satisfied to his cabin.

St Vincent's measure caused much disgruntlement, and even Spencer thought he was acting too harshly. But the Admiral remained firm: 'I have great deference for your judgment,' he told him, 'but the *suaviter in modo* will not do here. I have tried it in vain'. Collingwood wrote home: 'I see disgust growing round me very fast. Instead of softening the rigours of a service which must from its nature be attended with many anxieties, painful watchings and deprivation of everything like comfort, a contrary system is pursued.' The forbidding of sleeping on shore was particularly resented, as the wives of many captains were living in Plymouth. One gave the toast: 'May the next glass of wine choke the wretch'. Several captains protested. To one St Vincent instructed Tucker to say that if he could not put up with separation in war-time, 'it would be very unwise and unjust for him to delay for one day his intention of retiring'. To another, who asked for an inquiry to clear his character, he replied: 'You are a young man and rather over-hasty in applying for an investigation. The mere sound of Court Martial has the same pestilential effects as a suspicion of female chastity.'

Several captains objected to the guard-mounting at Brixham. The reply again was that his captains might think or do, write or say what they chose, but while he commanded the Channel Fleet he was determined they should do their duty. 'There was a kind of tacit engagement,' St Vincent told his friend Lloyd, 'that any interference of mine with the interior economy of the respective ships of the squadron should be resisted.' 'But,' he assured Spencer, 'I will not be deterred from doing my duty by the ill-humour of individuals. *I will be obeyed.*'

These strictures did not apply to those captains whom long experience had taught him to trust; and his letters to Spencer emphasize the wish for more. 'Pray let me have all who served with zeal and attachment with me in the Mediterranean, instead of the old women some of them in the shape of young men I am burthened with.' Among the former was Sir Thomas Thompson; and Midshipman Anderson wrote that, when the Fleet was suddenly ordered to sail on a report of the enemy being out, Thompson told the hands they must go to sea without their pay. 'They answered they were always ready and willing.' The report proving false, the *Bellona* returned to harbour. 'Sir Thomas again called the people to muster aft,' said Anderson, 'to read an order that he received from the Earl, mentioning what great compensation it was to him to see that the officers and ship's company under Sir Thomas should behave with such extraordinary activity, and that we were a pattern to the whole Fleet.'

Saumarez also had a happy ship. 'I enjoy the satisfaction,' he told his wife, 'of having a very quiet and well-disposed ship's company who are kept orderly and, I flatter myself, well regulated, without exercising severity or rigour.' St Vincent had appointed him to command the advanced squadron off the Black Rocks. This was the most responsible post in the Fleet, requiring great courage, endurance and seamanship. (The sailors called the place New Siberia, St Vincent by a pleasantry of his own, The Elysian Lake.) 'I repose such unbounded confidence in your zeal and judgment,' he wrote to Saumarez, 'that I sleep as soundly as if I had the key of Brest in my possession.' These were not fulsome words, for St Vincent's opinion of Saumarez had softened. One evening in the *Ville de Paris*, Saumarez told the Admiral he was much disappointed at not being given a baronetcy after the Nile: Lord Spencer, he said, had led him to think that it would be granted. St Vincent heard the request sympathetically and wrote to Spencer 'to request you will bring it about if possible, as nothing can gratify me more than the officers who have so signalized themselves under my auspices should be rewarded'.

To Foley also St Vincent gave his support. When Collingwood was inspecting the *Elephant* he remarked that he never saw fewer seamen among the seamen, or poorer landsmen among the landsmen. Foley protested to St Vincent and St Vincent forwarded his letter to the Admiralty. The Board replied that Foley had completely misrepresented Collingwood's remarks, and instructed St Vincent to warn him to be more correct in future. Foley again protested to St Vincent, and the Admiral supported him with all the weight of his authority. 'Captain Foley,' he told Spencer, 'than whom a more honourable man and zealous officer does not exist, is so much wounded by the rebuke I was directed to convey to him that I have been under the greatest apprehension lest he should resign his comission.' To Nepean he wrote, 'If Vice-Admiral Young is permitted to mix so much gall in your ink, every officer of spirit and distinction will be driven out of the service; and if the monstrous letter which was written to me in consequence of Captain Foley's just representation is not done away with, you will soon have a captain to name for the *Elephant*; and the next impertinance I receive will make room for Sir Hyde Parker.' Such an attitude was not to be ignored. Collingwood wrote an amended report to the Admiralty and Foley received a soothing letter from Spencer. Three weeks later St Vincent wrote to Nepean in calmer mood: 'When you are better acquainted with Captain Foley, you will esteem him as we all do; for under a heavy look lies a sound and excellent understanding, great temper and pleasant wit: to his own family he is a most kind and generous benefactor and in all private transactions perfectly chaste and correct.'

By the end of August conditions had so far improved that Fremantle, a week after joining the *Ganges*, was writing to Buckingham: 'Nothing can be more gratifying to me than the accounts I hear of the state and discipline of the Fleet. I feel as much confidence and there seems as much respect and obedience in every ship as at any period of my service.' But the old Admiral, with higher standards, would only commit himself to say: 'This fleet, which when I came to it was at the lowest ebb of wretched and miserable discipline, is now above mediocrity'.

* * *

The *Ville de Paris*, with Troubridge as Captain of the Fleet, sailed from Spithead for Torbay in September, 1800, followed soon after by the *Ganges*.

Troubridge had again recovered his health, but was still distraught at the breach of friendship with Nelson. On arrival at Plymouth he heard that Nelson was to hoist his flag in the Channel Fleet. 'If you put into Plymouth,' he wrote, 'my house is ready for your reception if you will do me that honour. My girls will do all to please.' He presumed that the *San Josef*, 120, would be Nelson's ship. 'I take the liberty of recommending for your Captain, Hardy. He is a seaman and will act different to B——. I really was ashamed and astonished to see B—— sitting still and your Lordship going out to carry on the duty. Pardon me for what I have taken the liberty of saying. I know you saw it in the same light as I did, tho' you did not set him in order.' He had received a letter from Nelson who had persuaded the Neapolitan Government to grant him a pension of £500 a year. Two months earlier when Lady Hamilton had offered to intercede for him, he had sent her a curt refusal. Now he wrote: 'I beg your Lordship to accept the acknowledgements of a grateful heart'.

All now seemed well between Nelson and Troubridge. But the day that Troubridge wrote this reply he received another letter from Nelson again complaining that he had not heard from him, again accusing him of ingratitude. The effect was much as before. 'Your letter has given me much uneasiness. How for a moment could your Lordship think me neglectful to an officer and friend I esteem so much and to whom I feel so weighty obligations. Among all my numerous faults be assured, my Lord, ingratitude is not one, and being accused by one I so much honour and esteem really and truly hurts me much.' A month later he was explaining his letters had been delayed because, not knowing how Nelson was returning, he had directed them to the Post Office at Portsmouth. 'When your Lordship had read my letter I am sure you can find no difficulty of acquitting me of ungrateful behaviour.'

But Troubridge now had other things to occupy him. 'Seven-eighths of the captains who compose this fleet,' St Vincent wrote to the Commissioner of Plymouth Dockyard, 'subtracting from the number those who served long under me in the Mediterranean, are practising every subterfuge to get into harbour for the winter. I am at my wits' end to compose orders to meet every shift, evasion and neglect of duty.' Troubridge soon found them out for himself. 'Government would save much if these old women captains could be put safe on shore, it is what they are always expressing a wish for. I could give you a long list of these old ladies who have forgot everything they ever knew.' The corrupt administration of the dockyard particularly angered him. At the hospital he was unable to find the surgeon, Dr Ball. 'The sick must be shamefully neglected if he is so late every day. I found the bags of turnips thrown down in the middle of the dirt and exposed to the wet. The hospital walls are still very damp and the Fires of Coal do not burn well.' Troubridge's zeal sometimes led to his undoing.

Over some trifle he admitted to Nepean: 'I am naturally of such a cursed irritable disposition that I had worked myself into a fever and should probably, if things had taken an unfavourable turn, have committed some rash act, for I had felt I had acted for the sole good of my country'. St Vincent summed up the character of his Captain of the Fleet nicely. 'Troubridge's patience is almost exhausted and he exclaims most feelingly against the degeneracy of our profession. It serves however as a spur to his labours, and he is finding resources to meet every occasion.'

The terrific strain imposed by St Vincent's vigorous discipline was beginning to tell on ships and crews. 'Sir James Saumarez will never complain,' he wrote to the First Lord in September, 'but I am told he is as thin as a shotten[1] red herring.' The truth was, as St Vincent wrote to Pasley: 'Everyone appears tired of the war'. On all sides, at sea and at home, where the corn-fields lay flattened and the poor were starving, there was a longing for peace. Overtures for an armistice which Bonaparte was making in Paris led many to believe that it might happen. 'I form very sanguine hopes,' Saumarez wrote to his wife, 'that peace will shortly extend its blessed influence over these countries, and that I shall have the satisfaction to enjoy without interruption the sweets of domestic comfort.' Collingwood wrote: 'Every officer and man in the Fleet is impatient for release from a situation which daily becomes more irksome to all. Would to God this war were happily concluded!' Thompson told the *Bellona*'s ship company that the French would soon be forced to make peace. 'At the word "Peace,"' wrote Midshipman Anderson, 'the men were so infatuated that they instantly gave Sir Thomas three cheers on the Quarter-deck.' But for the moment these hopes were not to be fulfilled.

On 30 October St Vincent, having received permission from Spencer to spend the winter at Torre Abbey because of his health, struck his flag in the *Ville de Paris*, and hoisted it in the *Bellona* at Torbay. Sir Hyde Parker assumed command of the Fleet at sea.

1. Spawned.

213

Troubridge, having heard of Nelson's impending arrival in England, obtained leave to go to London to meet him. Hardy, with the same intentions, had already been waiting some time.

* * *

Since his arrival home at the end of 1799 Hardy had not been happy. In London he had called on Lord Spencer, 'who was very polite,' he wrote to Nelson, 'but has not hinted anything about a ship'. He remained in London in the hope of getting employment, but without success. Nelson's Egyptian Club sword was delivered to him from the armourer's and he gave it to Mr Davison for transmission to the *Foudroyant*. Like Berry, Hardy made friends with Nelson's family. Lady Nelson complained pathetically that the Admiral's letters were written 'quite out of spirits,' and Hardy loyally assured her that it was because of 'the tiresome people' he had to deal with.

At the end of July Hardy, having heard no more about a ship or Nelson's arrival, left London ('No man would remain here for pleasure that could exist on bread and water in the country') for Dorset. He stayed at Portisham until he had definite news Nelson was nearing home, and at the beginning of October returned to London, taking lodgings at 9, Duke Street, 'within half a dozen Dores of Lady Nelson'.

On 6 November it was known that Nelson had arrived at Yarmouth. Two days later Hardy was writing to Manfield: 'Notwithstanding all the newspapers, his Lordship is not arrived in town and when he will God only knows. His Father has lost all patience, her Ladyship bears up very well, but I much fear she also will despond. Should he not arrive to-morrow, I shall set out for Yarmouth, *as I know too well the cause of his not coming*. Sir Thomas Troubridge waits to-day for his arrival but sets off this evening for Torbay. He thinks my going to Yarmouth advisable.' Troubridge, he added, had spoken to Lord Spencer about a ship, 'and done everything in his power to serve me.'

On 9 November Nelson, accompanied by the Hamiltons

and Miss Knight, arrived in London at the height of one of the worst thunderstorms for years, and met his wife and father in the hall of Nerot's Hotel. This was the end of a leisurely journey across the continent during which he had feasted and idled at the principal European Courts. He had seemed to enjoy it, and remained oblivious of the criticism aroused by his open admiration of Lady Hamilton. 'She leads him about like a keeper with a bear,' wrote Lady Minto from Vienna, and at Dresden a Mrs St George observed: 'Lady Hamilton takes possession of him and he is a willing captive, the most submissive and devoted I have ever seen'. Yet his profession was never far from his mind, and to anyone who showed interest he opened his heart. 'He speaks in the highest terms of all the captains he had with him off the coast of Egypt,' wrote Lady Minto, adding that 'without knowing the men he had to trust to, he would not have hazarded the attack.' Her nephew Fitzmaurice quoted Nelson as saying: 'If I had taken a fleet of the same force from Spithead, I would sooner have thought of flying than attacking the French in their positions; but I knew my captains, nor could I say which distinguished itself most'. Miss Knight wrote to Berry: 'He seems affected whenever he speaks of *you*, and often sighs out "Where is the *Foudroyant*?" '

Nelson's first letter on reaching England was to the Secretary of the Admiralty. 'I beg you will acquaint their Lordships,' he wrote from Yarmouth, 'of my arrival here this day, and that my health being perfectly established, it is my wish to serve immediately; and I trust that my necessary journey by land from the Mediterranean will not be considered to be a moment out of active service.' On the night of his arrival in London he called on Spencer, who told him that he was to hoist his flag in the *San Josef* as soon as she was commissioned.

There could be no question as to who would be Nelson's flag-captain. It did not require Troubridge's comments on Berry to tell Nelson that Hardy was the better man for the post. And yet it must have been a difficult decision, for Hardy's appointment to the *Vanguard* had been only temporary, and a letter from Berry, bringing home the *Princess Charlotte* with

215

Keith's despatches had expressed the hope of serving with Nelson again. Nelson avoided an embarrassing situation by telling Berry: 'You know how I am fixed with Hardy who could not get a ship'; but Spencer had promised 'that if the *Princess Charlotte* is good, you have a fair chance for her'. Troubridge or Saumarez would probably have taken this as a slur on their characters, but Berry was not the man to nurture resentment for long; and he wrote at once to Hardy congratulating him.

Troubridge postponed his return to Torbay, and he and Hardy saw much of Nelson in London. Nelson took Hardy to dinner at the Guildhall, and invited him to his box at the Opera for a performance of *The Mouth of the Nile*. It was an incongruous party consisting of Nelson, between his wife and Lady Hamilton in the front row, and Hardy, Sir William Hamilton, and Nelson's father behind. Both Hardy and Troubridge realized that, as they had feared, Nelson's relationship with Lady Hamilton was not something that could be shaken off with the dust of Sicily, and that soon he must come to a decision about the future. Troubridge took aside Miss Knight and told her that what could be condoned at Palermo was looked on differently in London, and that if she continued to associate with the party her character must suffer; whereupon Miss Knight, 'greatly embarrassed,' took refuge in the house of Mrs Nepean.

His leave at an end, Troubridge returned to Torbay; and at 3 a.m. on the morning of 14 November Hardy took his seat in the Mercury Coach for Dorchester. Remaining only long enough to see his family and settle his affairs, he continued on his way to Plymouth.

For the rest of the year Hardy was paying off the *Namur*, 98, and transferring her ship's company to the *San Josef*, preparatory to Nelson's arrival. In November the *San Josef* was moved into the New Dock where she was coppered and crowned with a light figurehead of St Joseph. (It was interesting, the *Naval Chronicle* remarked, that when the Spanish Admiral, Don Gravina, was visiting Plymouth in 1791, he was asked if this was not the largest dock he ever saw. He replied that it was, but it would not hold the *San Josef*, one of the first-class of Spanish men-of-war.) Hardy was happy in his new job and working again in a familiar atmosphere. 'Do tell the girls at Possum,' he wrote to his friend Manfield, 'I will not trouble them to get Mince Meat for me as my acquaintances here are so numerous I never dine at home.' However, he presented a Dorset leg of mutton to Admiral Pasley, 'and the old Baronet was very much pleased'.

Nelson meanwhile was undergoing the greatest personal crisis of his life. For some time he had hoped to reconcile his relationships with his wife and Lady Hamilton, not realizing it was impossible. The first sign of the collapse of his marriage (which had never existed except in name) occurred when he accompanied the Hamiltons to Fonthill for Christmas, leaving his wife and father in London. In London he had been acclaimed wherever he went and his presence at the theatre was enough to crowd the house. But society looked on the affair rather differently. At Court the King asked Nelson after his health and then, without waiting for a reply, turned and talked to a general 'in great good humour'. ('It could not be,' remarked Collingwood acidly, 'about *his* successes.') Lady Spencer, who had written him a glowing letter after the Nile, showed marked coolness, 'for which,' Nelson told Davison, 'she never had any just cause'. Even Betsey admitted she had no patience with Nelson, 'at his age and such a cripple to play the fool with Lady Hamilton'.

On 1 January 1801, Nelson was made vice-admiral, the rank he held until his death. On the 13th, after an angry scene with Lady Nelson in which she told him he must choose between herself and Lady Hamilton, he parted with her for the last time and set out for Plymouth. At Honiton he inquired for Mrs Westcott, the mother of the only captain killed at the Nile. He found her, 'poor thing, except for Government and Lloyd's, in very low circumstances. The brother is a tailor, but had they been chimney-sweeps it was my duty to show respect.' Mrs Westcott confided that she had not received her son's Nile medal: Nelson, with typical generosity, gave her his own. The same evening he visited St Vincent at Torre Abbey. The two had not met since Nelson's departure into the Mediterranean with Ball and Saumarez nearly three years earlier, and St Vincent found him much changed. 'Poor man!' he wrote Nepean, 'he is devoured with vanity, weakness and folly, was strung with ribbons, medals, etc., and yet pretended that he wished to avoid the honours and ceremonies he everywhere met with upon the road.'

On 17 January Nelson reached Plymouth and his flag, blue at the fore, was hoisted in the *San Josef* and 'cheered by the whole Fleet'.

         *   *   *

Nelson's efforts to prepare the *San Josef* for sea were hampered by various social functions. Four days after his arrival he retraced his steps to Exeter to receive the freedom of the City; and on return to Plymouth was obliged to repeat the ceremony there. Some events he refused to attend. On 19 January, the Queen's birthday, he and several captains dined at Admiral Pasley's. The party went on to a ball at the Long Room, but Nelson retired to bed. Next day he called on Troubridge's sister, who had been keeping house for her brother since his wife's death. ('Respect for him,' Nelson told Lady Hamilton, 'and his having prepared his house for me, made it proper.') From Miss Troubridge – 'about fifty-five, pitted with the small-pox, and deafer by far than Sir Thomas T.' – he learnt that he had given great offence by not attending the ball. 'But,' he assured St Vincent, 'my promise is solemnly made not to go to an Assembly till a Peace.'

On 31 January Hardy reported the *San Josef* ready for sea, and Nelson sailed to the fleet-anchorage at Torbay. During his two weeks there, he saw much of Troubridge. When the *Ville de Paris* was ordered to sea, Troubridge lived on board the *San Josef* as his guest. This was the last occasion on which the two old friends met for any time, and Troubridge did all he could to please. At dinner there were the usual toasts. 'Troubridge always says,' Nelson wrote to Lady Hamilton, 'now comes the fourth and old toast – all our friends, the King, success to the Fleet, and though last, not least Lady Hamilton.' Whether Troubridge, in a final effort to win back Nelson's friendship, said anything so unlikely, or whether Nelson invented it to please Lady Hamilton, it is impossible to say. But other captains were sincere in their inquiries. Hardy, Fremantle and Gould sent remembrances: Darby, spotting in the Admiral's cabin a picture of Lady Hamilton which Hardy on his own responsibility had had framed, asked Nelson 'to say everything which is kind and that he wishes he could see you instead of the picture'.

Troubridge had allowed Nelson's incoming letters to be addressed to his office at Brixham ('which will give them to me,' Nelson told Lady Hamilton, 'four hours sooner'). Little did he realize the passionate nature of their contents nor that at the end of January Lady Hamilton, in such secrecy that only her mother knew of it, had given birth to Nelson's daughter, Horatia. Joyful as this news was, it did not prevent the lovers from being consumed with jealousy. Nelson heard a report that Emma 'had hit the Prince of Wales' fancy,' and knowing his reputation, became tortured that she would succumb to him. 'Don't let him touch, nor sit next you; if he comes, get up. God strike him blind if he looks at you – this is high treason and you may get me hanged by revealing it. Oh God, that I were! . . . Does Sir William want you to be a whore to the rascal? . . . Oh God! Oh God. keep my senses!' Nor were Lady Hamilton's letters free from recrimination. 'Troubridge is gone to bed,' wrote Nelson one night, 'and I am alone with all your letters except the cruel one. That is burnt and I have cut out all the scolding words and have read them forty times over, and if you were to see how much better and prettier they read, I am sure you would never write another scolding word to me.'

Another matter which concerned Nelson was Miller's monument. The organizing of it had been left to Berry, who told Nelson he thought £200 would be a fitting subscription and that Flaxman had agreed to do the work. ('I can only repeat,' Berry told Flaxman, 'that we do not mean to be shabby.') Nelson approved, and if no one else subscribed he would be answerable for the whole sum. But he thought the captains of St Vincent should also share, and in that case less than £500 would not be proper. He asked Berry to tell him the proposed inscription. 'We must take care not to say too much or too little. The language must be plain as if flowing from the heart of one of us sailors who have fought with him.'

Berry wrote to St Vincent, who agreed to the captains of the 14 February subscribing. 'Truly happy I am,' Berry told Troubridge, 'to hear you and Lord St Vincent approve of the monument for our late dear coadjutor Miller – a man whom we knew and there was but one opinion of him. £500 will by no means be too much if the captains of the 14th February subscribe and those of Sir Sidney Smith; and my opinion is they ought to have that honour, but none but brother officers; and I would not even allow Davison to subscribe but that you will be a better judge of. Sir James [Saumarez] and Sir Thomas Thompson are the only subscribers I know of, though no doubt can be entertained of all hands, *nem con*.' Berry wrote to the Dean of St Paul's who agreed to the monument being placed in the cathedral. 'I want to get the precise date and a few other documents and then we can form an inscription. Of course our aim *must be* simplicity. Truth needs no ornaments: Miller requires none, himself was all.'

Early in February Nelson heard that Pitt's Government had come to loggerheads with the King over Catholic emancipation, and resigned. Addington, the Speaker of the House, had agreed to form a new ministry. St Vincent was to succeed Spencer at the Admiralty and take Troubridge as one of the naval lords. 'I am sorry Mr Pitt is out,' Nelson wrote to Lady Hamilton. 'I think him the greatest Minister this country has ever had and the honestest man.' Nor did Troubridge's appointment please him. 'Our friend Troubridge is to be a Lord of the Admiralty, and I have a sharp eye and almost think I see it. No, poor fellow, I hope I do him injustice; he cannot surely forget my kindness to him.' This tone was strangely prophetic.

But Nelson now had greater things to think about. War was looming in the Baltic and Sir Hyde Parker, who had handed over the Channel Fleet to Sir Henry Harvey, was collecting a great fleet at Yarmouth. Nelson was ordered to transfer with Hardy from the *San Josef* to the *St George*, 98, 'as Lord Spencer says I must go forth as the Champion of England in the North'. On 17 February he received orders to proceed to Spithead, preparatory to joining Hyde Parker as second-in-command.

The *San Josef*, with Troubridge on board as passenger, came to anchor at Spithead on the morning of 21 February. Troubridge set off for London at once. 'When I gave him a letter for you,' wrote Nelson to Lady Hamilton, 'it rushed into my mind that in ten hours he would see you. A flood of tears followed – it was too much for me to bear.' However, he obtained three days' leave to visit London and see for the first time his baby daughter. On 22 February Betsey wrote that her husband was 'coming into Portsmouth with some other ships from the Channel Fleet. But their stay will be so short that I do not think it is worth while for me to go to meet Fremantle.' Ten days later, still at Swanbourne where there was 'much distress and misery,' she wrote: 'Fremantle has been obliged to take eighty men of the 49th Regiment on board, and they are going on some grand expedition.' The same day Nelson, having embarked Lieutenant-Colonel Stewart and six hundred men in the *St George*, sailed for the Downs. Thompson in the *Bellona* and Fremantle in the *Ganges* followed and a week later Rear-Admiral Graves in the *Defiance* and Foley in the *Elephant*.

St Vincent and Troubridge meanwhile were installing themselves at the Admiralty. Saumarez, promoted to rear-admiral on 1 January, had returned to the advanced squadron at the Black Rocks. Hood was in the *Venerable*, 74, with the main fleet off Brest, and Berry was refitting the *Princess Charlotte* at Woolwich. Both wrote congratulating Nelson on his appointment. Nelson told Hood in reply, 'I am glad you have quitted that d—d *Courageux*; she would have drowned you in chase of an Enemy's Squadron': and to Berry he wrote from Yarmouth: 'Why won't you come here for a day and look at us?' Louis, Hallowell, Blackwood and Ball continued under Keith in the Mediterranean.

CHAPTER 12

Since his return to Paris after the victory of Marengo, Bonaparte, now First Consul of France, had not been idle. The preposterous terms he had offered to England in the summer of 1800 had been rejected. The stumbling-block to his plans was the British Fleet, which had frustrated all previous attempts at foreign aggression, not excluding a landing in England. To destroy the Fleet was impossible, but there were other means to bring the country to her knees. From the Baltic States – Russia, Sweden and Denmark – England obtained some of her most vital imports; grain for the growing industrial population, timber and hemp for her ships.

During the American War the Baltic States had combined to claim immunity against the traditional right of warring nations to inspect neutral cargoes for contraband; the flag of their protecting warships, they said, was sufficient guarantee. At the time England, weak at sea, could only protest. Now Bonaparte informed Sweden and Denmark that he proposed waiving his own right of search. It was a clever move, and the result exactly as he hoped. The Danish Government reasoned that, if one of the two great warring nations could do without search, so should the other. On 25 July the Danish frigate *Freya*, Captain Krabbe, was escorting a small convoy through the Channel when the *Nemesis* frigate bore up, and Captain Baker demanded to search. Captain Krabbe refused. A boat was sent away from the *Nemesis* and on approaching the convoy was fired into by the *Freya*. The *Nemesis* returned the fire and several seamen were killed and wounded on both sides.

This time Britain was able to enforce her claims. Lord

Whitworth, backed by a powerful naval squadron, went to Copenhagen and extracted from the Danish Government an admission of liability to search and a promise not to convoy their shipping in future.

The danger seemed to have been averted. But Britain had not reckoned with the First Consul. Bonaparte had not extended the waiving of right of search to Russia because Russia was still technically his enemy. But of all the Baltic States she was by far the most influential. He knew of the Czar's anger at the defeat of his Austrian allies and his subsequent refusal to send troops to Malta; and for months past he had been courting him. When a batch of Russian troops was captured in Holland, he sent them home in new uniforms. Then as a supreme gesture he offered to hand over Malta to the Czar, providing the garrison held out. In September, 1800, Malta fell, not to Vaubois but Ball, and although the Czar was Grand Master of the Order of St John, he was not consulted about the island's future. This news, following on Marengo, was irritating enough; the capture of the *Freya* and the appearance of Dickson's squadron in the Baltic enraged him. He saw his ally England bent on plunging Europe into war, and Bonaparte as the champion of liberty. On 7 November he placed an embargo on all British ships in Russian ports, amounting to about two hundred sail. A few escaped, but others were burnt and their crews marched in chains into the interior. By December he had persuaded Sweden, Denmark and Prussia to join him in a revived Armed Neutrality of the North. They agreed to resist by force attempts to search their shipping; and to back their claims they had over a hundred sail of the line. Bonaparte's schemes had worked to perfection.

This was a critical moment for England. Austria was on the point of making peace, the Kingdom of the two Sicilies had concluded an armistice forbidding British warships to enter her ports, and the French had reoccupied Northern Italy and Leghorn. The International situation was worse than before the Battle of the Nile. Except for Portugal, England had not an ally in the world.

But she still had her Navy. It had saved her in the past and now it was to save her again. Pitt, in the last few weeks of office, acted swiftly. On 14 January 1801, while Nelson was bumping along the coast road to Plymouth, the Cabinet ordered the seizure of all ships of the Baltic powers at sea and in harbour. A fortnight later orders went out for a fleet to assemble at Yarmouth.

The command of the Fleet was given to Hyde Parker, chiefly because St Vincent had advised Spencer that he was 'the only man to face them'. This was not the view of Nelson who had experienced his half-heartedness in the Riviera in 1795, nor of many other officers. Parker, aged sixty-two, had just married a girl of nineteen, described by St Vincent as 'batter pudding,' and his thoughts were more on a ball she was giving than the proposed expedition: Nelson also found him 'a little nervous about dark nights and fields of ice'. His flagship, the *London*, did not reach Yarmouth until 10 March and eighteen hours later he had not shifted his flag. 'This is the rate we Baltic gents go at,' complained Nelson to Troubridge. 'How nice it must be laying abed with a young wife to a damned raw cold wind.'

Besides Nelson's irritation at the delay in sailing – for he knew that every hour enabled the enemy to grow stronger – he found Parker had no intention of taking him into his confidence. 'When I receive a message both by Hardy and Murray,' he wrote to Troubridge, 'there can be no reason why I may not tell it. "Tell Lord Nelson that the present composition of the van is not my arrangement." I had placed Foley and Fremantle instead of a 64 and 50, but Sir H. run his pen through them and placed them as they stand. When I said, "Sir H., will two 64's and a 50 do well together?" his answer was, "Well, put the *Zealous* between them." You may *make* your comments. I *feel* mine.'

Parker's treatment of his second-in-command did not pass unnoticed. Colonel Stewart told Nelson it had aroused much anger, and Vice-Admiral Dickson said that all were scandalized at his gross neglect. But for Nelson there was one compensation – the captains who were serving under him, and especially his old friends. 'It is not that I care what support I may have as far as relates to *myself*,' he told Troubridge, 'but the glorious support I am to *have*, marks me.' Foley and Thompson he knew he could depend on. Hardy's worth showed itself 'every day and hour'. Captain Murray of the *Edgar*, who had fought in the *Colossus* at St Vincent, 'I have no doubt will support me'. Fremantle wrote to Betsey: 'Nelson is just the same man I ever knew him, and show me every attention and kindness possible'.

Troubridge received Nelson's letters sympathetically, though he begged him not to write in the same vein to St Vincent. Nelson told him: 'I give you 10,000 thanks for your kind letters. Every letter of yours is in the *fire* and ever shall, for no good but much harm might arise from their falling into improper hands.' As a result of his repeated requests, orders arrived for the Fleet to sail immediately. Nelson was delighted. 'The ball for Friday night knocked up,' he wrote to Troubridge, 'by your and the Earl's unpoliteness to send gentlemen to sea instead of dancing with nice white gloves.'

The next day Hyde Parker hoisted the signal to weigh, and with twenty sail of the line formed into three divisions under himself, Nelson and Graves, set course to the eastward. The object of the expedition was to bring to an end the armed neutrality of the North. Parker's instructions were to proceed to Copenhagen, and land Mr Vansittart of the Foreign Office, who would try to obtain a peaceful settlement. If this was unsuccessful he was to attack firstly Copenhagen, and then the Russian Fleet at Reval. The Admiralty, appreciating some problems could only be decided on the spot, instructed Parker 'to govern yourself under the different circumstances to the best of your judgment and discretion'. Possibly for this reason Parker did not communicate his intentions to the Fleet. Five days after leaving Yarmouth Fremantle was writing to Betsey that he still had no knowledge of their destination.

The passage across the North Sea was made in bitter weather. Every evening the Fleet anchored for the night. 'It took us nearly an hour at daybreak,' wrote George Elliot (now a lieutenant of the *St George*), 'to shovel down the snow from our tops and yards before we could weigh.' Many officers and men recently returned from the Mediterranean found it difficult to acclimatize themselves. Elliot said the weather was very trying to his skin and feelings, Fremantle that his ship's company were hacking from morning to night with coughs.

On 19 March the Fleet was off the Skaw, the northernmost tip of Denmark. Two hundred miles ahead lay the island of Zealand, on the east side of which is Copenhagen. Beyond Zealand is the Baltic, which can be reached either by the Sound, a narrow channel separating the east cost of Zealand from Sweden, or by the Great Belt, which divides the west coast of Zealand from Denmark. There was a fair wind blowing, and Nelson was for pushing on to Copenhagen at once. He called on Hyde Parker and 'ground out something,' but found the Admiral cautious and undecided. The next day Parker sent away Mr Vansittart in the *Blanche* frigate to Copenhagen, and sailed with the Fleet towards Zealand.

On 23 March the Fleet anchored off Elsinore, the location of Shakespeare's Hamlet, in the north of Zealand. Vansittart arrived in the *Blanche* and reported his terms had been rejected. Parker called a council. 'Now we are sure of fighting,' Nelson wrote to Lady Hamilton, 'I am sent for. When it was a joke I was kept in the background.'

The officer who steered Nelson's boat to the *London* wrote that at the council the heads appeared very gloomy. The officers of the *Blanche* reported the Copenhagen defences much stronger than supposed. Nelson's first proposal was to bypass Copenhagen and make for Reval: Russia was the trunk of the confederation and if that was hewed down the branches would fall with it. Parker disagreed: even if an attack on the Russian Fleet was successful, casualties would occur and there would still be a hostile fleet in the rear. Nelson conceded the point but affirmed that Copenhagen should be attacked immediately: what was to be avoided at all costs was a junction of the enemy fleets. He then questioned the officers of the *Blanche* as to the

JAMES, BARON DE SAUMAREZ

From the mezzotint by Say after the painting by Phillips, showing
the full-dress uniform of a rear-admiral. Decorations are the
Ribbon and Star of a Knight of the Bath, and the Medals of St.
Vincent and the Nile. The scene in the background represents the
action off Algeciras.

THOMAS THOMPSON
From the miniature by Engleheart, showing undress uniform of a
captain of over three years' seniority. The medal is that of the Nile.

state of the enemy's defences – a method he called 'bringing people to the post'. Satisfied their positions were not impregnable, he returned to the *St George* and wrote a brilliant memorandum. 'The more I have reflected the more I am confirmed that not a moment should be lost in attacking the enemy: they will every day and hour be stronger: we never shall be so good a match for them as at this moment.' His conclusion was typical: 'The measure may be thought bold, but I am of opinion the boldest measures are the safest'.

Nelson's plan, put forward with his customary enthusiasm and clarity, succeeded in carrying the council; and Hyde Parker hoisted the signal to proceed by the Great Belt. The decision was not unanimous. 'Lord Nelson is quite sanguine,' Fremantle wrote to Betsey, 'but as you may well imagine there is a great diversity of opinion.' Captain Domett, the Captain of the Fleet, urged postponement of the attack. Admiral Graves feared they would be 'playing a losing game, attacking stone walls'. Captain Murray wrote to Troubridge (whose son Tom was a midshipman in the *Edgar*): 'I see no prospect of success, and am of opinion that if we once get into the Roads, we shall be very glad to get back again; for some of our ships must be disabled and I fear cannot do theirs any harm. However, I hear we are to go in *neck* or *nothing*.'

The Fleet had proceeded a short way towards the Great Belt when, owing to navigational difficulties, Parker decided after all to go by the Sound. He refused to commit his ships to the dangers of the narrow channel until he had heard whether the Governor of Elsinore would allow them to pass. The Governor replied that as he did not know their intentions he would open fire. Parker had committed himself too far to withdraw, and taking this to be a declaration of war, announced his intention of pushing through. These negotiations and the waiting for a fair wind caused another three days' delay. Nelson was almost beside himself, and even Fremantle wrote: 'I think if we had had the good fortune to have undertaken this business a week ago we should have more probability of succeeding. I should say the Danes are exceedingly alarmed but delay gives them courage and they will by degrees make Copenhagen so strong that it may resist the attack of our fleet.'

On 29 March Nelson shifted his flag to the *Elephant*, of lighter draught than the *St George*, and on the 30th the Fleet proceeded in single column through the Sound. Nelson's division led, Parker's was in the centre, and Graves's brought up the rear. The ships were fired on by the Danish batteries, but by hugging the Swedish coast they kept out of range. At midday the Fleet came to anchor five miles north of Copenhagen.

Attack having been agreed, Parker, Nelson, Graves, Fremantle and other senior officers embarked in the *Amazon* frigate, Captain Riou, to reconnoitre the enemy defences. The Danes had removed all buoys marking the channels, and that night the masters and pilots laid others. Next morning Nelson made another survey of the defences, and then there was a final council of war. Many officers, awed by the strength of the enemy, urged abandoning the attack. But Nelson was determined on it and put forward his proposed plan.

The main enemy defences consisted of some twenty armed hulks, stretched in single column from north to south along the sea-front of the town. Flanking them at the northern end was a formidable strongworks on piles called the Three Crowns Battery. Opposite the hulks was a large shoal called the Middle Ground: its western side was separated from the hulks by a passage called the King's Channel, and its eastern side from the island of Saltholm by another passage called the Outer Channel. There were, therefore, two methods of approaching the enemy: either by proceeding into the King's Channel from the north, or by passing down the Outer Channel to the end of the Middle Ground and turning into the King's Channel from the south. Both methods had their disadvantages: the first, which meant passing the Three Crowns Battery, Nelson called 'taking the bull by the horns'; the second, which he favoured, depended for its success on a change of wind from north to south. Nelson proposed that he should lead the main attack with ten sail of the line, while Parker with the remaining ten approached the Three Crowns Battery from the north.

Hyde Parker accepted the plan, and generously gave Nelson twelve ships instead of ten. These were the *Elephant*, Nelson and Captain Foley; *Defiance*, Graves and Captain Retallick; *Edgar*, Captain Murray; *Monarch*, Captain Mosse; *Bellona*, Captain Sir Thomas Thompson; *Ganges*, Captain Fremantle; *Russell*, Captain Cuming; *Agamemnon*, Captain Fancourt; *Ardent*, Captain Bertie; *Polyphemus*, Captain Lawford; *Glatton*, Captain Bligh; *Isis*, Captain Walker; and there was to be a squadron of five frigates under Captain Riou in the *Amazon*. Hardy was to transfer temporarily to the *Elephant* as a volunteer.

On the morning of 1 April Parker, Nelson and Graves made a final inspection of the defences in the *Amazon*. Then at one o'clock Nelson hoisted the signal for Riou to take station at the head of the line and for the squadron to follow him down the Outer Channel. 'The shout with which it was received throughout the division,' wrote Colonel Stewart, 'was heard at a considerable distance.'

* * *

One of the heroes of Copenhagen was Captain Edward Riou. He served under Nelson for only a few days, yet made a lasting impression on him. Colonel Stewart wrote that Nelson was much struck by the *Amazon*'s discipline and seamanship, and Nelson himself called Riou 'that good man and excellent officer'. One person who knew Riou well was Byam Martin, who has left a striking portrait. 'A pleasing gloom hung over his manly countenance unlike anything I have ever witnessed in any other person. His eye was peculiarly striking, beaming with intelligence . . . There was a pensiveness of look and reserve in his manner which sometimes made strangers regard him as cold and repulsive, but this first impression was soon removed and all who knew him loved him. There was an innate modesty in the man which made him utterly unconscious of the admiration with which he was regarded by all classes'.

In 1789 Riou had an extraordinary adventure as lieutenant in command of the *Guardian* frigate. The ship left England in

August with a cargo of plants, livestock and machinery, also a number of convicts, for the settlement at Botany Bay in New South Wales. She reached Capetown on 24 November and sailed again to the eastwards. On Christmas Eve, in a dense fog, she collided with an iceberg, and began to settle. Next morning the crew demanded the boats, and Riou allowed those who wanted to abandon ship. Four boats got away, heavily laden, leaving on board Riou, the boatswain, the carpenter, a midshipman and about twenty men. Riou divided them into watches for pumping, and by superhuman efforts they gradually checked the leak. Two weeks later they seemed to have made little headway, some of the crew had ulcers and scurvy, others broke into the spirit room and became drunk and mutinous: Riou broke his arm in striking one of them and so could take sights only in the greatest pain. But he kept the men at it, and on 21 February his brilliant seamanship was rewarded by the sight of land. 'Thank God!' he wrote, 'it was the Cape of Good Hope. The ship had been running right for it.'

One of the four boats had also reached land: and in England the crew's report of the loss of the *Guardian* had been accepted. The news of her arrival at Capetown astonished everyone, and Lord Howe and others paid tribute to Riou's leadership. The King said, 'It is one of the finest proofs of exalted courage and humanity ever shown'. Riou was promoted immediately to commander and soon after to Post-rank.

*   *   *

Nelson's squadron, superbly led by the *Amazon*, came to anchor south of the Middle Ground a little after eight in the evening. As the *Elephant*'s cable ran away Nelson called out: 'I will fight them the moment I have a fair wind'. He sat down to dinner with Graves, Foley, Hardy, Fremantle, Riou and others. Colonel Stewart wrote that Nelson was in the highest spirits and drank to a leading wind and to the success of the ensuing day. After dinner the captains returned to their ships except Riou, whom Nelson took with Foley into the after cabin to prepare the orders for the attack. Hardy embarked in a small boat and took soundings round the hulks as far as the leading ship. He returned on board at eleven o'clock and reported deep water up to the enemy's line. Nelson was then lying in his cot on the deck of the after cabin, dictating orders. At one o'clock the orders were completed and sent to the forward cabin, where half a dozen clerks were waiting to copy them. Reports began coming down from the officer of the watch that the wind was shifting to the southward. This news, almost too good to be true, prevented Nelson from sleeping. With each fresh report he called out to the clerks to hasten. At six o'clock, by which time he had dressed and breakfasted, the clerks had finished. At seven the signal was made for all captains; at eight the masters and pilots came on board, and Mr Briarly of the *Bellona* (master of the *Audacious* at the Nile) volunteered to lead the line. They then returned to their ships and at nine-thirty, the wind having veered round to the south, Nelson hoisted the signal to weigh.

The orders for attack were quite simple. Unlike the Nile, where little could be foreseen and much was left to the initiative of individual captains, each ship had precise instructions. The *Edgar, Ardent, Glatton, Isis* and *Agamemnon* were to anchor opposite the first nine enemy hulks: the others in the order *Bellona, Elephant, Ganges, Monarch, Defiance, Russell, Polyphemus,* were to engage the remaining eleven hulks and the Three Crowns Battery: the leading ship, the *Bellona,* was to anchor abreast the tenth hulk, and the rearmost one, the *Polyphemus,* opposite the Three Crowns Battery, so that the order of battle would be the order of sailing reversed. Riou's frigates were to hold themselves ready for whatever service might arise.

The action opened disastrously. Nelson's old ship, the *Agamemnon,* had anchored too far up the Outer Channel the night before and was unable to weather the Middle Ground. Next the masters of the *Bellona* and *Russell,* not trusting Hardy's soundings, ran their ships ashore on the south-western corner of the Middle Ground. Nelson's force, already too slender for certain victory, was reduced by one quarter.

The remaining nine ships slowly approached the enemy's

line. The scene was vividly remembered by Midshipman Millard of the *Monarch*: 'Our minds were deeply impressed with awe, and not a word was spoken throughout the ship but by the pilot and helmsmen; and their communications, being chanted very much in the same manner as the responses in our cathedral service and repeated at intervals, added very much to the solemnity'. At ten o'clock the *Edgar*, leading the van, anchored opposite her opponent. At ten-thirty the southern division was engaging the enemy and an hour later the action was general. The grounding of the *Agamemnon*, *Bellona* and *Russell* had left a gap in the British line opposite the dreaded Three Crowns Battery. Hyde Parker could not engage it, for the same wind which enabled Nelson to attack prevented his division from bearing up. Riou, seeing what had happened and without waiting for orders, proceeded with his squadron to take up the vacant position.

For the next three hours both sides engaged in what Rear-Admiral Graves called 'the hottest action that has happened this war'. Casualties, especially on the hulks, mounted even quicker than at the Nile. Before the *Ganges* anchored, Fremantle's master was killed and his pilot wounded, and he conned the ship into position himself. Early on Captain Mosse of the *Monarch* was killed. 'His card of instructions was in his left hand,' said Midshipman Millard, 'and his right hand was raised to his mouth with the speaking-trumpet. He was laid in the sternwalk and a flag thrown over him.' The *Monarch* suffered terrible casualties: when Millard went down to the main deck he found 'not a single man standing the whole way from the mainmast forward.' In the *Edgar* Captain Murray lost his first, second and fifth lieutenants. The *Bellona* and *Russell* were engaging the enemy from the sandbank when an unlucky shot carried away Thompson's left leg. The bursting of several of the *Bellona*'s guns caused nearly eighty casualties, among them Midshipman Anderson, hit on the knee. Nelson was in his element, cool, detached, his spirit splendidly matching the hour. He and Colonel Stewart were walking the deck when a shot hit the mainmast and the splinters fell round them. 'It is

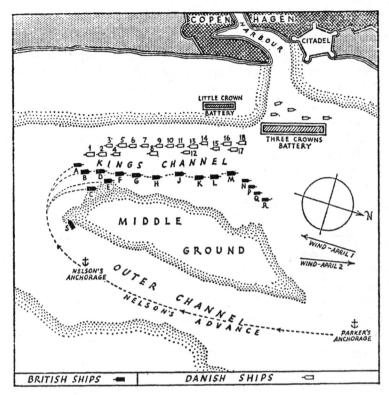

THE BATTLE OF COPENHAGEN

	British Ships	Guns		Danish Ships	Guns	Result
A	DESIRÉE	36	1	PROVESTEEN	56	taken and burnt
B	POLYPHEMUS	64	2	VALKYRIEN	52	,, ,, ,,
C	RUSSELL	74	3	NYBORG	20	escaped—then sunk
D	ISIS	50	4	RENDSBORG	20	taken and burnt
E	BELLONA	74	5	JUTLAND	54	,, ,, ,,
F	EDGAR	74	6	SVOERDFISKEN	34	,, ,, ,,
G	ARDENT	64	7	KRONBORG	22	,, ,, ,,
H	GLATTON	50	8	DANNEBROG	64	caught fire—blew up
J	ELEPHANT	74	9	HAJEN	30	taken and burnt
K	GANGES	74	10	ELVEN	18	escaped
L	MONARCH	74	11	FLOTILLA OF GERNER	34	escaped
M	DEFIANCE	74	12	AGGERSHUUS	20	escaped—then sunk
N	AMAZON	38	13	ZEELAND	74	taken and burnt
P	BLANCHE	36	14	CHARLOTTE AMELIA	26	,, ,, , ,,
Q	ALCMENE	32	15	SOHESTEN	26	,, ,, ,,
R	DART	18	16	HOLSTEIN	64	taken and added to the Navy
S	AGAMEMNON	64	17	INFODSTRETTEN	64	taken and burnt
			18	HJOELPEREN	30	escaped

warm work,' said Nelson, 'and this day may be the last for any of us.' Then, stopping short, he exclaimed with emotion: 'But mark you, I would not be elsewhere for thousands'.

At about twelve-thirty Sir Hyde Parker, observing the *Agamemnon*, *Russell* and *Bellona* aground, and the enemy resistance stronger than expected, discussed with his two captains whether to hoist the recall. Captain Domett, (whom George Elliot called 'as old and more nervous than Sir Hyde,') was for doing it; but Captain Otway suggested going to the *Elephant* to see if it was necessary. Parker agreed, but before Otway reached the *Elephant*, Domett persuaded the Admiral to hoist the signal. Graves, being nearer to Parker than Nelson, was the first to see it. 'Oh Jesus!' he exclaimed. As a flag-officer he was bound to repeat it, but hoisted it forward of the mast where Nelson could not see it; and he kept his own signal for close action flying.

Soon after, the *Elephant*'s signal lieutenant read Parker's signal and reported it to the Admiral. Knowing the critical stage the battle had reached and that a withdrawal at that moment would mean defeat, Nelson replied: 'Mr Langford, I told you to look out on the Danish Commodore, and let me know when he surrendered. Keep your eyes fixed on him.' On his next turn round the deck the conscientious Langford asked whether he should repeat the signal. 'No,' replied Nelson, 'acknowledge it.' Langford did so and Nelson then asked whether his own signal for close action was still flying. Langford said it was. 'Mind you keep it so,' said Nelson, and then, turning to Colonel Stewart: 'Do you know what's flying on board the Commander-in-Chief? No. 39!' Stewart asked what it meant. 'Why, to leave off action,' said Nelson. 'Leave off action!' he repeated. 'Now, damn me, if I do.' He put the telescope to his blind eye and trained it on the flag-ship. 'You know, Foley,' he said, 'I have only one eye. I have a right to be blind sometimes. I really do not see the signal.'

For one officer the signal had disastrous results. Captain Riou, valiantly drawing the fire of the Three Crowns Battery with his frigates, saw the signal when it was hoisted, but since the rest of the Fleet continued fighting, took no action. Then Graves repeated it; and although the place where he hoisted it obscured it from Nelson, Riou could not miss it; nor in the smoke of battle could Riou see that Graves's signal for close action was still flying. Regretfully he gave the order to withdraw, exclaiming, 'What will Nelson think of us?' As the frigates turned away, the batteries, unhampered by their fire, poured in several broadsides. Several men near Riou were killed. 'Come then, my boys,' he cried, 'let us all die together.' Hardly had he said this when a raking shot cut him in two.

By two o'clock the enemy's defences were on the point of collapse. Several hulks had already struck, among them the Danish Commodore's flag-ship which, with 270 killed and wounded out of a crew of 336, was ablaze from stem to stern and drifting out of the line. Others had their flags shot away but remained in action. Nelson, thinking they too had struck, was angry at what he supposed a violation of the rules of warfare. This and the critical state of his own ships led him to send ashore a flag of truce that unless the enemy broke off action he would set fire to the prizes 'without having the power of saving the brave Danes who defended them'. While waiting for a reply, he summoned Captains Bligh and Fremantle of the ships astern and ahead of him and thanked them publicly on the quarter-deck for their support. He then proposed to move the less-damaged ships against the section of the enemy's line still firing. Foley and Fremantle said the navigational difficulties were too great and dissuaded him; as it turned out, it was well they did.

Nelson was deciding what next to do when General Lindholm representing the Crown Prince, arrived on board to ask the purpose of the truce. Nelson replied that it was humanity, and to allow the Danish prisoners and wounded to be removed from the prizes: for any other matters he referred Lindholm to Hyde Parker. Lindholm went away in a boat to the *London*, but before he reached her the Crown Prince gave orders for the cease fire. Nelson signalled the *Glatton*, *Elephant*, *Ganges*, *Defiance* and *Monarch* to weigh in succession clear of the enemy line.

But these ships were so unmanageable that all except the *Glatton* ran ashore on the Middle Ground. 'Luckily we had to contend with an enemy much beaten,' wrote Fremantle, 'and who did not take advantage of our situation: otherwise all those ships must have been lost.' For Nelson the action had ended not a moment too soon.

* * *

Copenhagen was the bloodiest battle in which Nelson fought. 'I have been in a hundred and five engagements,' he wrote, 'and to-day is the most terrible of them all.' The British casualties were just under 1000 killed and wounded, the enemy's, according to a Danish officer, over 3000 in killed alone. Colonel Stewart described the carnage in the hulks as dreadful, Fremantle as exceeding anything he had ever heard of – 'the Nile ships are not to be compared to the massacre on board them'. The prizes, said Midshipman Asperne, were perfect sieves, 'there not being hardly a single plank in any of them but what has at least ten shot-holes in it'.

Copenhagen also was the only battle in which Nelson came near to defeat. At St Vincent, the Nile and Trafalgar the issue, once action had started, was never in doubt: the only question was, how great the victory? But at Copenhagen, for one critical hour, the battle might have gone either way.

The events that led to victory were similar to those of the Nile. St Vincent's master-hand, which so contributed to the defeat of Brueys, was also partly responsible for Copenhagen. The captains he had sent into the Mediterranean in the summer of 1798 – 'the *élite* of the Navy of England' – were all graduates of his school: of the twelve ships with which Nelson passed down the Outer Channel on the night of 1 April, half had experienced the same training in the ill-disciplined Channel Fleet. And the same sense of cohesion among officers and men, of being the instrument of Nelson's will, which at the Nile had turned victory into conquest, succeeded at Copenhagen in averting defeat. If Graves and Riou had obeyed immediately the signal to withdraw, defeat would have been unavoidable. Under any other admiral they probably would have obeyed. But Riou's dying words: 'What will Nelson think of us?' epitomized the feelings of everyone in the Fleet. Courage and seamanship Nelson took for granted: what won Copenhagen for him and in the last analysis all his battles, was his unshakable and infectious will to win.

On the night of the battle Nelson returned to the *St George* with Fremantle, and at 3 a.m. he dictated to Fremantle his report of proceedings. He was back in the *Elephant* for breakfast and later in the day went ashore with Hardy to dine with the Crown Prince and discuss terms for an armistice. Many officers were despondent about his chances of success: now that the first flush of victory was over they were asking what it had gained. 'I fear we shall not have much to boast of,' wrote Admiral Graves, 'when it is known what our ships suffered and the little impression we made on their Navy.' And Murray told Troubridge: 'It is a bad business and we had better not have made the attack. What will be thought of it in England, I don't know.'

But these officers had not reckoned with Nelson. When he arrived with Hardy at the waterfront he found a strong guard assembled to protect them from the mob, which the Crown Prince had feared might attack them. But the people of Copenhagen, with their trade brought to a standstill, wanted peace; and their reception was the opposite to that expected. 'He was hailed with cheers by the multitude,' Fremantle wrote to Buckingham, 'and "*Viva* Nelson" resounded until he got to the Palace, much to the annoyance, I believe, of His Royal Highness and his ministers.' Hardy wrote that the welcome reminded him of the ceremony at Guildhall 'when we went to Lord Mare's show'.

The Crown Prince opened the interview by asking Nelson's purpose in coming to the Baltic. Nelson replied with his usual directness: 'To crush a most formidable and unprovoked Coalition against Great Britain'. The conversation continued in this fashion for two hours. 'I will venture to say,' said Hardy, 'His Royal Highness never had so much plain trooth spoken to him in his life.' By the end of the interview nothing had been decided. The Crown Prince was in a dilemma. He could not remain in the Coalition without courting further hostilities from Britain, and he could not withdraw without displeasing Russia. Negotiations continued while the British ships refitted in preparation for a second bombardment. On 9 April the Crown Prince heard that the Czar had been assassinated. The mainspring of the Coalition being removed, he was now able to come to terms. It was agreed that hostilities should cease for fourteen weeks, during which Denmark would suspend her part in the Coalition, open her ports to the British Fleet and leave her ships unarmed. Nelson took Foley and Fremantle to complete the negotiations, and they were ratified and signed in the *London*.

Nelson's skill as a diplomatist won him even higher praise than his conduct of the battle. 'The more I see of His Lordship,' wrote Hardy, 'the more I admire his great character; for I think on this occasion his political management *was if possible* greater than his bravery.' When Ball heard the news in the far-off Mediterranean he wrote: 'This last brilliant occasion has proved to the world that you possess the abilities of a statesman as well as the qualities of a great hero'. And St Vincent wrote from the Admiralty: 'Your Lordship's whole conduct from your first appointment to this hour is the subject of our constant admiration. It does not become me to make comparisons: all agree there is but one Nelson.'

On the day after the armistice, Fremantle told Betsey he had been performing 'as disagreeable a piece of duty as I think ever occurred in my service'. This was the transferring of the wounded Thompson from the *Bellona* to the *Isis* in which he was to go home. 'Figure to yourself,' wrote Fremantle, 'the removal of a poor man whose leg is just amputated, from the side of one ship; and having hauled him up the side of another, his agonies were great.' It reminded him, he said, of what he had suffered at Santa Cruz, 'and the never-ceasing attention you showed me'. Nelson wrote Thompson a letter, recently discovered by Thompson's descendants. 'I have been so much taken up with the business of the armistice and together with the weather and my very indifferent state of health that I have absolutely been unable to come to see you, but I rejoice to hear such very good accounts. Patience, my dear fellow, is a virtue. (I know it, yet I never possessed it in my life, yet I can admire it in others.) I will assuredly see you before we part.'

Thompson reached Yarmouth in the *Isis* on 25 April. He was in great pain and very much depressed. 'I am lain down, having patiently to wait my cure or dissolution, as it shall please God. I am now totally disabled and my career is run through only at the age of thirty-five.' There was a comforting letter from St Vincent: 'Nothing will be wanting on my part to console and compensate you,' and suggesting a memorial for a pension. Another friendly correspondent was a Mr Brook-Watson, who had also lost a leg. 'Long experience which I do not lament, has taught me that no machine will answer your purpose so effectually as the simple hick-leg.' The fitting of it was difficult and he advised Thompson not to try any other machine until he had met him. The interview must have been satisfactory, for by June Brook-Watson was sending instructions for the first fitting: 'The Bees-wax plaister is to be put on the bare knee and a large stocking drawn over it which will keep it in its place and most effectually prevent the part from chaffing. When the plaister shall become bare of wax, a fresh one must be employed, but one a month will answer. It must be taken off on going to bed.'

In July Thompson learnt that his memorial was successful and he was to be given a pension of £500 a year. His days of active service were over, but by August he had recovered sufficiently to take command of the Royal Yacht, the *Mary*.

* * *

The ratification of the armistice enabled Hyde Parker to go to Reval to settle affairs with the Russians; and all the Fleet except the *St George* and *Agamemnon* entered the Outer Channel. Fremantle in the *Ganges* led: the ship was drawing 22 feet, and the depth of water was nowhere more than 27. 'We just touched ground once,' he wrote, 'but never stopped.' Several other ships grounded but all got through, and that night Parker anchored the Fleet in Kioge Bay, south of Copenhagen.

Three days later Nelson was about to follow them: he had transferred the *St George*'s guns to an American merchant-ship to lighten her, but the wind became foul and prevented him from moving. At six in the evening he received a message from Hyde Parker that the Swedish Fleet was at sea and he was going after them. Fearful of missing an action, Nelson embarked in a boat with Mr Briarly (who was going to pilot the *St George* through the Outer Channel). 'All I had ever seen or heard of him,' wrote Mr Briarly, 'could not half so clearly prove to me the singular and unbounded zeal of this truly great man.' Such was Nelson's haste that he did not wait for his boat-cloak. The night was very cold and Mr Briarly offered him his. 'No, I am not cold,' answered Nelson, 'my anxiety for my country will keep me warm.' In reply to a question as to whether the Fleet had sailed, he said: 'If they are, we shall follow them to Carlscrona in the boat, by God!' At midnight, after a six-hour pull without food or drink, they reached the *Elephant* and Nelson asked the astonished Foley if he might once more trespass on his hospitality.

The Fleet sailed next morning, but as usual Parker was in no hurry: on the 19th Hardy caught up in the *St George* and Nelson rejoined his flag-ship. By the time they arrived off Carlscrona the Swedish Fleet was back in its anchorage. Two days later Parker heard from Count Pahlen, the Russian Foreign Minister, that the Russian Fleet had orders to abstain from hostilities. Nelson was for pushing on to Reval at once, and while the Russian Fleet was vulnerable, pressing home terms for a favourable armistice ('A fleet of British men-of-war are the best negotiators in Europe'). But Parker, satisfied with Pahlen's assurances, returned with the Fleet to Kioge.

For Nelson an important anniversary was coming round. On 24 April he wrote to Foley: 'Sunday the 26th being the birthday of our Guardian Angel, Santa Emma, whose prayers I can answer were offered to the throne of heaven both at the

Nile and on the 2nd for our success, and it is my firm belief that they had much more influence than any ever offered by a heathen goddess or any other saint ever made by the best Pope, so it is our duty to express our gratitude where due. Therefore I have to request that as her kindness was spread over you as well as all other of our Mediterranean friends now in the fleet, that you will be on board the *St George* on Sunday at about 3 o'clock.' Fremantle received a briefer summons. 'If you don't come here on Sunday to celebrate the Birthday of Santa Emma, damn me if I ever forgive you.' Other captains received similar invitations, and on the 26th twenty-four guests, including Admirals Parker and Graves, pledged Santa Emma in a bumper of champagne.

One guest had to leave rather hurriedly. Hyde Parker was beginning to doubt Pahlen's word, and he ordered Fremantle to sail in the *Lynx* lugger to St Petersburg with despatches. Fremantle arrived on 7 May, was 'exceedingly well received' by Count Pahlen, and delivered the despatches. While waiting for a reply, he did some sightseeing; the Winter Palace, the Hermitage, the Palace of Prince Potemkin, and the Palace at Orienbaum where the Czar was strangled. 'To relate to you all the modes he had found out to torment and tyrannize over his subjects,' he wrote to Betsey, 'will fill a folio volume; and I am only surprised to think he was suffered to live so long.' The new Emperor, he said, had the reputation of being a mild, tractable young man, 'but with not sufficient firmness of character to govern Russia as his grandmother did.' Fremantle received a reply to the despatches, and returned to the Fleet. His visit had been friendly and it was evident the Russians were not bent on hostilities; but nothing had been said about giving up the English merchant-ships and their crews.

At Kioge Bay Fremantle found that Hyde Parker had been ordered home and Nelson appointed to succeed him. This was a bitter blow to Parker who had not asked to be relieved, and to Nelson who had received permission to go home for his health and was on the point of embarking for England. Opinion as to Parker's conduct varied. Captain Murray wrote to Troubridge:

'I have much to say to you about our manoeuvres here but will not make *paper speak*. When we meet we will talk it over, but I must say that I think if Lord Nelson had commanded this fleet, all the Swedish Fleet that was out would have been in our possession. I don't know, of course, Sir H.P.'s orders, therefore it is not fair to judge, but certainly we have not been active.' Some officers, including Fremantle, were angry at Parker's dismissal, and it was left to Nelson to sum up his conduct fairly. 'They are not Sir Hyde Parker's real friends who wish for an inquiry. His friends in the Fleet wish everything to be forgot, for we all respect and love Sir Hyde; but the dearer his friends, the more uneasy they have been at his *idleness*, for that is the truth – no criminality.'

For Nelson himself, sick and wishing only to return to Lady Hamilton, the appointment was not pleasing. He had been placed junior to an admiral who had proved himself incompetent, won the battle and the peace for him, and now there was nothing more to do, told that he was to succeed him. Troubridge, still trying to please, sent congratulations which were coldly received. 'Sir Thomas Troubridge,' Nelson wrote to Lady Hamilton, 'has the nonsense to say, now I was a Commander-in-Chief, I must be pleased. Does he take me for a greater fool than I am?'

As soon as Parker had departed, Nelson, in contrast to Parker's cautious methods, proceeded to Reval to settle things with the Russians. On arrival at sunset, he sent ashore to ask why the Governor had not returned his salute. Such was his name that a higher authority came on board to explain that it was intended to return the salute at daylight: he brought with him the Governor whom George Elliot found in the bottom of the boat 'in chains, hand and feet, and he not knowing whether his head was to be cut off'.

Nelson's vigorous measures procured release of the English merchant-ships, and brought to an end the Armed Neutrality of the North. Operations in the Baltic were over.

Nelson asked to be relieved. 'Send for us all home,' he wrote to Troubridge, 'at all events for your old and faithful friend.'

SAMUEL HOOD

From the mezzotint by Clint after the portrait by Hoppner painted probably in 1807, showing full-dress uniform of a captain of over three years' seniority. The decorations are the Ribbon and Star of a Knight of the Bath, the Order of St. Ferdinand and Merit, and the Medal of the Nile. The background scene represents Hood's frigate action of 1806.

THOMAS LOUIS

From the mezzotint by Daniell after the portrait by Livesay, showing full-dress uniform of a rear-admiral. The decorations are the Order of St. Ferdinand and Merit, the Order of Maria Theresa, and the Medal of the Nile.

During the remaining few weeks he found the service increasingly irksome. Although he kept the Fleet in the highest state of discipline and good health, his mind was elsewhere and, as usual when deprived of active service, his nervous ailments returned. 'With him,' wrote Colonel Stewart, 'mind and health invariably sympathized.' He complained of a swelling of the heart, and of a consumptive cough brought on by the Baltic climate. 'What he felt most,' said George Elliot, 'was the want of morning freshness in the air. It was the same dry stuffy feeling at four in the morning as at eight at night.'

His never failing comfort, as always, was the support of his captains. 'All the fleet are so truly kind to me,' he wrote to Ball, 'that I should be a wretch not to cheer up. Foley has put me under a regimen of milk at four in the morning. Murray has given me lozenges and all have proved their desire to keep my mind easy, for I hear of no complaints or other wishes than to have me with them. Hardy is as good as ever . . .' And Murray wrote to Troubridge: 'What we should have done or shall do without him, I know not. The more I see of him, the more I admire him.'

Only rarely Nelson sat down to a meal alone. Colonel Stewart wrote that he rose every morning about four o'clock, and by eight had despatched the business of the Fleet. He breakfasted at five, a meal to which he usually asked the officers of the middle watch. 'A midshipman or two were always of the party,' wrote Colonel Stewart, 'at table with them he would enter into their boyish jokes and be the most youthful of the party.' To dinner he invited the captains and ships' officers in rotation. Captain Murray brought young Tom Troubridge over, and described the visit in a letter to the boy's father. 'Tom and I dined with His Lordship on Sunday. He gave Tom a cake but says I shall spoil him by keeping him to mess with me. (I say, *No*; he would learn *trash* by being in a cockpit so young and will be as good a sailor by eating in the cabin as by eating below.) He says Tom is too polite by half and "my lords" him too much, and tells him *you* were never so polite.'

On 12 June Nelson learnt that his request for recall had been answered. 'To find a proper successor,' St Vincent had told him, 'is no easy task; for I never saw the man in our profession, excepting yourself and Troubridge, who possessed the magic art of infusing the same spirit into others.' However Admiral Pole had agreed to fill the post and was on his way to the Baltic.

There remained one duty for Nelson to perform; the knighting of Admiral Graves, who had been awarded the Order of the Bath in the King's birthday honours. It was a happy occasion for Nelson, for in the same list Saumarez and Ball had been made baronets. Nelson left the arrangements to his flag-captain. 'Hardy,' he told Lady Hamilton, 'has trimmed out the quarter-deck in his usual style of elegance.' A chair, draped with the Union flag, was placed on the skylight gratings: above it was the Royal Standard. Either side of the quarter-deck was a guard of honour of marines and soldiers of the Rifle Corps: at the after end stood the captains of the Fleet in full-dress uniform.

At the appointed hour Nelson came up the quarter-deck fore ladder, followed by Captain Parker bearing the sword given to Nelson by the Nile captains, and by his secretary carrying on a satin cushion the emblems of the Order of the Bath. The three made their reverences to the throne and took up position in front of it, facing aft. Captain Parker read the citation, after which Admiral Graves, supported by Captains Hardy and Retallick (Graves's flag-captain in the *Defiance*), advanced from the after end of the quarter-deck and was introduced to the throne. 'The Rear-Admiral then kneeled down, and Lord Nelson, in the name of His Majesty, laid the sword on the shoulders of the Rear-Admiral; the Knight Elect then rose and, bending his body a little forward, Lord Nelson, with the assistance of Captains Hardy and Retallick, put the Riband over the new Knight's right shoulder and placed the Star on his left breast.' The preparative signal was hauled down and the Fleet fired a salute of twenty-one guns. The procession retired the way it had come, Sir Thomas Graves leading: the Royal Standard was furled and the troops beat the retreat.

Two days later Admiral Pole arrived, and Nelson prepared to return home. 'His resignation,' said Colonel Stewart, 'was attended with infinite regret to the whole Fleet, and there was a complete depression of spirits.' Before leaving, Nelson issued a general memorandum:

'Lord Nelson cannot allow himself to leave the Fleet without expressing to the Admirals, Captains, Officers and Men how sensibly he has felt, and does feel, all their kindness to him, and also how nobly and honourably they have supported him in the hour of Battle, and the readiness which they have shown to maintain the honour of their King and Country on many occasions which have offered . . .

The Vice-Admiral assures them that he will not fail to represent to the Lords Commissioners of the Admiralty their highly praiseworthy conduct; and if it pleases God that the Vice-Admiral recover his health, he will feel proud, on some future day, to go with them in pursuit of further glory, and to assist in making the name of our King and Country beloved and respected by all the world.'

On 19 June Nelson embarked in the *Kite* brig for England. About the same time the Plymouth correspondent of the *Naval Chronicle* was writing that Rear-Admiral Sir James Saumarez, Bart, had sailed from Cawsand Bay with five ships of the line on a secret service: they were victualled and stored for five months, and their orders were not to be opened until they had arrived in a particular latitude.

CHAPTER 13

The black clouds on which the people of Britain had looked at the beginning of 1801 were everywhere lifting. Nelson had struck the first blow at Copenhagen: hard upon it came good news from the Mediterranean.

In the autumn of 1800 Lord Keith and General Sir Ralph Abercromby had assembled a large naval and military force at Gibraltar to attack the Spanish Fleet in Cadiz. The operation was abandoned because of bad weather, and it was decided to divert it to Egypt to overthrow the French Army of the East.

Among Keith's captains were Hallowell, in the *Swiftsure*, flying the flag of Sir Richard Bickerton, second-in-command, Louis in the *Minotaur*, and Blackwood in the *Penelope*. All were delighted at the prospect of the expedition, for the French had been gradually re-establishing themselves in their old Mediterranean footholds. 'This country has been so dull since you left it,' Louis wrote to Lady Hamilton, 'nothing but misfortunes and misery have taken place, and I am sorry to say the French with all their villainy have taken possession.'

In December 1800, the expedition reached Malta, now under British occupation. Since Vaubois's surrender in September, Ball's position had become increasingly difficult. General Pigot, in command of the occupation forces, had shown him scant respect. He had refused to allow him to sign the Articles of Capitulation or hoist the colours of the Order of St John, forbidden him a guard and placed him in rank below the Town-Major. It was a delicate situation, for whereas Pigot was heartily disliked by the Maltese whom he treated as a conquered people, and by his own officers, Ball was adored by both. Yet he kept his dignity. 'I continue giving the General every aid,' he wrote to Nelson, 'and do not allow his insults to affect the public operation.'

Pigot's behaviour eventually came to the ears of Dundas, who sharply reprimanded him. This eased Ball's position until the arrival of Abercromby who, jealous of Maltese admiration for Ball, ordered him to return to the *Alexander*. But the Bishop of Malta, who, in Ball's words, 'at the head of the clergy and all the corporate bodies, waited on him to express their gratitude to me and solicit that I might not be removed; which Sir Ralph found was the effect of real attachment, and as he risked losing the island by removing me, he requested me to remain some time longer'. Later Abercromby recommended Ball for employment elsewhere, and soon after Ball, 'truly disgusted,' resumed command of the *Alexander*.

News of the arrival of Keith and Abercromby at Malta was not long in reaching Bonaparte; and guessing their intentions, he sent orders to Rear-Admiral Ganteaume at Brest to sail with reinforcements to Egypt.

Ganteaume's squadron of seven sail, with Rear-Admiral Linois as second-in-command, left Brest on 23 January 1801. On 9 February, they passed the Straits, and the *Success* frigate, Captain Shuldham Peard, sailed in pursuit. News of the enemy also reached Rear-Admiral Sir John Borlase Warren who with six sail was blockading Cadiz: twenty-four hours later he followed the *Success* into the Mediterranean.

The *Success* kept the enemy in sight for four days but on the 13th, owing to a sudden change of wind, she was captured. Learning that Keith and Abercromby had already left Malta for Egypt, Ganteaume altered course for Toulon. Warren meanwhile had reached Minorca and having been joined by Ball in the *Alexander* and another 74, he sailed for Toulon to blockade Ganteaume in the roads. On hearing this Bonaparte ordered Ganteaume to sail again: if he found it impossible to enter Alexandria he was to land his troops on the coast.

Ganteaume made several attempts to break out, and finally got away on 27 April. But he was too late. Abercromby had landed his troops near the scene of Nelson's victory at Aboukir, defeated the French at his first pitched battle, and was now advancing on Alexandria.

Unaware of this Ganteaume arrived at Leghorn in mid-May. Because of sickness in the squadron he ordered Rear-Admiral Linois to take three ships – the *Indomptable*, *Formidable* and *Dessaix* – back to Toulon, while he continued with the other four. He reached a position on the African coast two hundred miles west of Alexandria on 7 June, and learning of the British presence in Egypt, sailed to Derna to land the troops. He was frustrated first by the spirited defence of the inhabitants, then by the appearance of enemy frigates; and without waiting for

247

two of his storeships (subsequently captured by the frigates), he crowded sail from the coast.

At the beginning of June Keith had despatched from Aboukir a convoy of light transports and cartels under Captain Hallowell in the *Swiftsure*. On 22 June off Cape Derna, Hallowell heard that Ganteaume's squadron was in the vicinity, and left the convoy to reinforce Warren at Malta. At 3.30 a.m. on the morning of the 24th Hallowell sighted the enemy squadron hull down to leeward, and altered course to escape. But the French had sighted him simultaneously and turned in pursuit. The *Swiftsure* was in need of refit and they began to gain. By two in the afternoon the *Indivisible* (Ganteaume's flag-ship) and *Dix-Août* had approached to within gunshot. Hallowell bore away in the hope of disabling the other two ships and making his escape to leeward. They tacked and frustrated him. At 3 p.m. a general action began and continued until 4.30 p.m. when the *Swiftsure* found herself surrounded by all four of the enemy. Her sails and rigging had been cut to pieces and she was incapable of further manoeuvring. Seeing that escape was impossible, and in order to avoid further bloodshed, Hallowell hauled down his colours.

Hallowell and his officers went on board the *Indivisible*, and the *Swiftsure* was taken in tow: so badly was she damaged that despite the exertions of all Ganteaume's artificers it was six days before she could be put under sail. Ganteaume's treatment of the *Swiftsure*'s officers was in striking contrast to that of M. le Joille towards those of the *Leander*. 'I feel it a duty I owe to Admiral Ganteaume,' Hallowell wrote to Keith, 'to mention the handsome manner in which we have all been treated by the officers of his squadron, and by him in particular: the strictest orders have been issued to preserve the property of every individual and he has done everything in his power to render the situation of the officers and men as comfortable as possible.'

Ganteaume reached Toulon on 22 July, and Hallowell was released on parole. But before this Bonaparte had received news of a second defeat of his Army of the East. Outside

Alexandria the British had routed a French force of 10,000 men. Abercromby had fallen in the battle but his successor, General Hely-Hutchinson, was on the march for Cairo.

Bonaparte resolved to make a last desperate attempt to win back Egypt. He had recently purchased six Spanish ships at Cadiz for an attack on Portugal, and these were fitting out under Rear-Admiral Dumanoir le Pelley: there were also in the port six Spanish ships under Vice-Admiral Moreno. The only other available ships were the three which Ganteaume had sent back from Leghorn. Bonaparte proposed that these should sail for Cadiz under Rear-Admiral Linois and join the twelve ships there. Entry into Cadiz presented no difficulties, for since Warren's departure the approaches had remained unguarded. The whole force would sail to Italy, embark as many troops as possible, then descend on Egypt in Hely-Hutchinson's rear.

It was a feasible enough plan, and with Keith's fleet at the far end of the Mediterranean might have succeeded. But Bonaparte had not reckoned with St Vincent. As soon as the old Admiral heard of the preparations at Cadiz, he ordered a squadron under Sir James Saumarez to assemble at Plymouth: so the enemy should not get wind of its intentions, its destination was kept secret. 'Sir James Saumarez,' St Vincent wrote to the Governor of Gibraltar, 'will, I trust, be able to counteract whatever plan of operations may be in contemplation at Cadiz.'

His foresight was swiftly rewarded. Linois sailed from Toulon on 25 June with the *Formidable, Indomptable* and *Dessaix*, reaching the entrance to the Straits on 1 July. Gibraltar Bay was empty of British ships, but he captured the brig *Speedy* at sea and from Captain Lord Cochrane learnt that Saumarez's squadron had arrived off Cadiz three days before. Not wishing to risk battle against so superior a force, Linois anchored his ships under the guns of Algeciras on the west side of Gibraltar Bay. Next day Saumarez heard of his arrival, and having been joined by Sam Hood in the *Venerable* from Ferrol, threw out a signal for the *Caesar, Pompée, Spencer, Hannibal* and *Audacious* to proceed with despatch to Gibraltar and to prepare for battle.

Linois had no doubts of remaining long unmolested. 'Recollecting the desperate attacks of the English at Alexandria and Copenhagen,' wrote an officer in his squadron, 'we would not but expect that their squadron would come and attack.' The Bay of Algeciras was open to the sea and afforded little protection, apart from rocks and shoals near the shore. He drew up his ships parallel and as close to the town as possible, in order from north to south *Formidable, Dessaix, Indomptable,* and waited for the enemy.

At 7 o'clock on the morning of 6 July Miss Sarah Fyers, daughter of the officer commanding the Royal Artillery at Gibraltar, was interrupted at breakfast by her father, who had just seen a squadron of English ships rounding Cabrita Point from the westward. She ran outside and saw for herself Saumarez's squadron, the *Venerable* leading, standing in close order of battle in line ahead. 'It certainly was a sight,' she wrote, 'to see those magnificent ships with their white sails shining in the sun and following each other at intervals.' She went down to a vantage-point near the pluviometer and found it already thronged with people. 'Every soul seemed to have congregated on the line wall or on the heights, and the murmur of so many voices came to us like the sound of the sea-waves.' The squadron cleared the point and turned to the northwards. With the help of glasses Miss Fyers saw crowds of women and children running up the steep hill behind Algeciras 'to get out of the way of shot and shell.'

On board the British ships the officers and men waited for battle. The day before Saumarez had mustered the ship's company of the *Caesar* for God's blessing. His flag-captain, Brenton, described the scene as deeply impressive. 'The crew were all dressed in white: and being arranged according to their respective divisions on the quarter-deck, with the band and the marines on the poop, and the admiral and the officers under the poop awning, an effect was produced highly animating, solemn and appropriate.' Sam Hood came on board the *Caesar* for a conference, and in view of his local knowledge agreed to lead the squadron into battle. In the abilities of his captains Saumarez had absolute faith: Hood, and Darby of the *Spencer*, had fought with him at the Nile; Shuldham Peard of the *Audacious* (appointed on his release after the capture of the *Success*) had served with him under St Vincent; Stirling of the *Pompée* and Ferris of the *Hannibal* were experienced officers. The prospect of action did not have on Saumarez the quickening feverish effect it did on Nelson; instead he remained in his flag-captain's words, 'as usual, calm, cheerful and collected'.

By eight-thirty the leading British ships had approached to within gunshot of the enemy. There was little wind and the *Venerable* was suddenly becalmed. Captain Stirling in the *Pompée* passed her, and proceeded to take up Hood's position abreast Linois's flag-ship, the *Formidable*. He discharged two broadsides into the *Indomptable* and *Dessaix* as he went by. A shot from the second broadside crashed into the cabin of the *Hannibal*, disturbing her captain and Lord Cochrane, who were still at breakfast. The *Audacious* and *Venerable* anchored abreast the *Dessaix* and *Indomptable* respectively. The remaining British ships, baffled by light winds, did not get up till forty minutes later. The *Caesar* took station between the *Pompée* and *Audacious* and on the *Dessaix*'s starboard bow. The *Hannibal* and *Spencer* were prevented by lack of wind from joining the line and formed a second outer line, the *Spencer* anchoring on the *Audacious*'s starboard bow and the *Hannibal* on the *Caesar*'s.

For the next hour the two sides engaged in what a Spanish eye-witness called 'a most obstinate and bloody action'. By the end of it the French ships were so badly damaged that Brenton proposed sending a flag of truce to demand surrender. But at this moment a breeze sprang up and Linois ordered his ships to cut their cables and run closer inshore. Saumarez signalled his ships to follow them.

Linois's squadron, being now in shallower water, were afforded much greater protection; but for Saumarez the manoeuvre was disastrous. As soon as the *Pompée* had cut her cable the wind swung her round so that her head faced the enemy; and she was raked by the *Formidable* without being able to bring her own guns to bear. She fought gallantly for some time, but having become unmanageable was towed out of action by the squadron's boats.

To the *Hannibal* a worse disaster occurred. Not realizing the enemy ships were on the point of beaching, Captain Ferris took his ship so close to the *Formidable* that she grounded. Efforts by the squadron's boats to get her off were unsuccessful, and having suffered heavy casualties, she struck her colours. She was boarded by officers from the *Formidable* who, having no spare colours of their own, hoisted the English colours upside down. Unknown to them, this was the signal in the British Navy for 'Ship in distress and need of assistance.' It was seen by the gun-boat *Calpe* which, loaded with artificers from Gibraltar Dockyard, was cruising in the vicinity. She proceeded alongside the *Hannibal* and disembarked the artificers, who were immediately made prisoner.

The remaining four British ships were still endeavouring to work up. But the wind again dropped, and now there was a danger of drifting on the rocks and shoals. At half past one, having fought for nearly four hours, Saumarez broke off action; and leaving the *Hannibal* to the enemy, retired with his squadron to Gibraltar.

The damage to the enemy was considerable: their masts and rigging were badly cut up, their casualties of 800 killed and wounded double those of the British. All the same, the British had lost one ship and the French none. Brenton wrote that on arrival at Gibraltar Saumarez retired to his cabin 'with a deep sense of the responsibility he had incurred'. Always fearful of censure, he searched for justification of conduct which no one thought of questioning. 'I should be miserable,' he wrote to his wife, 'had I to reproach myself for having undertaken the enterprise on light grounds, or with having failed in the planning and execution; but on the contrary it is admitted by every one to have been most judicious. It is therefore only in the result that I have been unfortunate. I have been too much employed to reflect on the light in which the business may be viewed in England: but conscious of having done my duty to the utmost of my exertions, I shall be indifferent to the rest.'

Orders went out for all ships to be repaired immediately and for the wounded to be admitted to the hospital. Learning of the appalling condition of the *Hannibal's* wounded, that their belongings had been plundered and that they had been taken to a disused stable without water or surgical attendance, Saumarez asked Linois to send them to Gibraltar. Linois replied he could do nothing without consulting the Marine at Paris, but he returned Captain Ferris and Lord Cochrane. Saumarez ordered Ferris to England with his despatches, and according to Brenton their parting was deeply moving. 'Tell the Admiralty, Sir,' said Saumarez, 'that I feel convinced I shall soon have an opportunity of attacking the enemy again and that they may depend on my availing myself of it.'

These words were soon fulfilled. Knowing it would only be a matter of time before Saumarez was again ready to attack, Linois sent an express to Massaredo at Cadiz for a squadron to escort his ships there. Massaredo ordered Vice-Admiral Moreno to prepare for sea the *Real Carlos*, 112, *Hermenegildo*, 112, *San Fernando*, 96, *Argonauta*, 80, and *San Augustin*, 74, together with the French *St Antoine*, 74. These ships sailed from Cadiz on the morning of 9 July, observed by Captain Keats in the *Superb*, 74, who proceeded southwards ahead of them. That afternoon Saumarez sighted the *Superb* rounding Cabrita Point flying the signal 'Enemy at Sea'; and a little later the Spanish squadron came to anchor in Algeciras Bay.

Saumarez now gave orders for his ships to be prepared for sea as soon as possible. The *Pompée* was too badly damaged to be completed in time and her crew were dispersed among the other ships. The *Caesar* was also very unseaworthy, but Brenton promised to have her ready in time. The exertions of the ships' companies to prepare again for battle were the admiration of all at Gibraltar. Brenton wrote that, although many men were ashore for gunpowder and other stores, there was not a single case of desertion or drunkenness. The crew of the *Caesar* volunteered to work all night, and were only dissuaded when Brenton told them that they would be unfit for battle. Several of the wounded in the hospital escaped and hid themselves in their ships.

On the morning of 12 July the enemy was observed preparing for sea. The British ships were refitting up to the last moment. When Saumarez hoisted the signal to weigh, the *Caesar* was still taking in ammunition. At noon the enemy proceeded seawards and at half past one began rounding Cabrita Point. At half past two the *Caesar* warped from the mole: her band was playing 'Come, cheer up, my lads, 'tis to glory we steer,' and a band on the shore answered with 'Britons, strike home'. The line wall was again crowded with spectators. Miss Fyers was at her old station near the pluviometer: she wrote that she could see nothing but human heads, and that when the *Caesar* left 'a shout arose from the assembled multitude such as I never heard before or since'.

The responsibility which Saumarez had taken was considerable. As Brenton points out, the enemy force was twice his own with treble the gun-power: six of their ships were fresh from harbour while all his, except the *Superb*, had been roughly handled in battle. 'Our Chief had counted the cost,' said Brenton, 'and made up his mind to the enterprise. His intention was to throw his whole force upon whatever part of the enemy's line he might be able to reach; depending upon the talents of his captains and the discipline of his ships to make up for the disparity of force, especially in a night action.'

By 8 p.m. the enemy had rounded Cabrita Point. They were sailing in two divisions in line abreast, the *Indomptable*, *Formidable*, and *Dessaix* ahead, and the five Spanish ships and *St Antoine* in the rear. The British squadron in line ahead, led by the *Caesar* and *Venerable*, followed some miles astern. Because of their damage they were not able to gain much, and Saumarez hailed Keats in the *Superb* to go on ahead and attack the enemy ship nearest the Spanish shore. The *Superb* put on a full spread of canvas, quickly passed the *Caesar* and *Venerable*, and was soon out of sight in the darkness.

At about eleven-twenty Dr Outram, the *Superb*'s surgeon, was walking the deck with his captain when a large vessel was reported close on the larboard bow. This was the huge *Real Carlos* of 112 guns. Keats took the *Superb* to within three hundred yards without being seen and poured in several rapid broadsides. At the third broadside the Spanish ship caught fire; whereupon Keats broke off the action and went in chase of the *St Antoine*, reported on the starboard bow.

On board the *Real Carlos* Keats's broadsides caused complete confusion. The Spaniards had not imagined they would be attacked, and when the *Superb* opened fire the captain and officers were at the supper-table. Immediately the crew began firing in all directions. Several shots struck the *Hermenegildo*, which immediately took her consort for an enemy. What one Spanish eye-witness described as 'a very smart engagement' then commenced between these ships. Saumarez, coming up fast in the *Caesar*, gripped Brenton's arm and exclaimed: 'My God, Sir, look there! The day is ours'. The *Hermenegildo* had run on board the *Real Carlos* and also caught fire. 'A more magnificent scene never presented itself,' said Brenton, 'than two ships of such immense magnitude as the Spanish first-rates on board of each other in flames, with a fresh gale, the sea running high and their sails in the utmost confusion.'

Soon after midnight the flames reached the magazines, first of the *Real Carlos* and then the *Hermenegildo*, and both ships blew up with tremendous explosions, taking to the bottom nearly 2000 men. Dr Outram, watching from the deck of the *Superb*, described the spectacle as 'sublime and appalling'. The deep red glare spreading over sky and sea, the roar of the flames and the shrieks of the despairing Spaniards would, he said, never be effaced from his memory. Saumarez, who had seen *L'Orient* blow up at the Nile, wrote: 'So awful a scene I have never yet witnessed'. Miss Fyers at Gibraltar recorded that the flames illuminated the southern end of the Rock, and that officers on duty could see to read by the light.

The rest of Saumarez's squadron were still pursuing the flying enemy. Keats came up with the *St Antoine*, and after an hour's action capped a brilliant night's work by bringing her to surrender. At dawn the *Venerable*, close inshore, found herself near the *Formidable* which had dropped astern. Action was joined at five-fifteen and continued until six-forty-five when the *Venerable*, having lost her main-mast, ran aground. Because of the wind Saumarez was not able to give support, but he sent Brenton with a message to Hood to burn his ship rather than surrender. Brenton found Hood sitting on a gun on the quarter-deck, 'cheerfully waiting for the assistance he knew the Admiral would send'. Hood told Brenton: 'Tell Sir James I hope it is not yet so bad with the old *Venerable*. I hope to get her off soon. These rascals shall not have her.' Soon a wind sprang up which enabled the *Thames* frigate to tow the *Venerable* clear. The *Formidable*, having suffered much damage, followed her consorts into Cadiz. Satisfied that nothing more could be done, Saumarez collected his scattered squadron and returned to Gibraltar.

* * *

Lieutenant Philip Dumaresq, Saumarez's first lieutenant and near relation, landed with the despatches at Mount's Bay, Cornwall on 30 July 1801, and set out for London. At the Admiralty he was warmly received by St Vincent, who squeezed his hand and exclaimed rapturously: 'I knew it, I knew it. I knew the man. I knew what he could do. It is the most daring thing that has been done this war. It is the first thing. I knew it would be so.' He made out Dumaresq's commission for commander, and sent him on to the Prime Minister. To Saumarez he wrote: 'The astonishing efforts made to refit the crippled ships at Gibraltar Mole surpasses everything of the kind within my experience, and the final success in making so great an impression on the very superior force of the enemy crowns the whole'.

The news quickly spread and brought fresh rejoicing among people who had hardly left off celebrating the victories at Copenhagen and in Egypt. Nelson was overjoyed and again showed how little he let personal animosity affect professional admiration. 'Again and again I rejoice with you at Sir James Saumarez,' he wrote to St Vincent. 'No small degree of merit

must attach itself to your Lordship for nicking the time of
sending out the squadron.' ('Your effusions upon the subject
of Sir James,' St Vincent replied, 'are natural to your good
heart, equally void of jealousy and suspicion.') At Plymouth
the mail-coach arrived from London decorated with the Royal
and Union Standards and the words SAUMAREZ and
VICTORY emblazoned on a blue background. Someone
wrote a poem in the *Naval Chronicle* beginning: 'Victorious
Saumarez for thee, We wake the strings to songs of praise'.
Little James Saumarez wrote that in Guernsey the Governor
had drawn up all the troops to fire a *feu de joie*: 'Uncle John
had all the colours you had taken hung upon the outside of
Grandpapa's house which made a great shew'. The general
feeling was summed up by Saumarez's sister-in-law: 'You are
now the theme of every conversation, the toast of every table,
the hero of every woman, and the boast of every Englishman.'

As at the Nile and Copenhagen, the effects of the victory were
more important than the victory itself. Not only were Bonaparte's schemes for relieving Egypt finally overthrown, but his
relations with Spain with which he was negotiating for an
attack on Portugal, were seriously damaged. The enemy
casualties were over 3000 killed and wounded – not far short
of those at Copenhagen and the Nile – and of these two-thirds
were Spaniards, including many women and children of the
nobility who were taking passage to Cadiz. Their deaths caused
much anger at Madrid. 'We have almost daily accounts from
Cadiz,' Saumarez wrote to his wife, 'describing the disagreements between the French and Spaniards as most serious.' On
20 July, eight days after Saumarez' victory, peace was formally
concluded between Spain and Portugal; and the Spanish
Government informed Bonaparte they wished to terminate as
soon as possible 'an alliance which has become irksome to the
Court of Madrid'.

*   *   *

After the Nile Saumarez had been upset by the omission of his name from the despatches. Two similar incidents occurred to upset him after Algeciras.

The first concerned the sending of reinforcements from England. In his letter of congratulation St Vincent informed Saumarez that in view of the importance of the Cadiz station it was to be separated from Lord Keith: a squadron under Vice-Admiral Pole in the *St George* was on its way to join him: St Vincent regretted that Saumarez's seniority prevented him having the command.

Sensitive as ever, Saumarez took the appointment as a slur on his abilities and wrote to St Vincent to protest. The admiral was not pleased. 'I cannot sufficiently express my surprise at the contents of your public and private letters,' he replied, and begged to point out that Saumarez was now second-in-command, whereas under Keith he had been fourth. Nepean wrote in stronger terms. 'Their Lordships,' he wrote, 'cannot consider you a competent judge of the extent of the force which may be proper for them to appropriate. They cannot but disapprove of your having made this complaint and hope that on cooler reflection you will see the impropriety of prescribing to their Lordships the line of conduct they should pursue.' Troubridge's private letter was more friendly but even he admitted, 'the Chief is much hurt'.

The other matter was the question of honours. On 2 September Saumarez wrote to his brother Richard that the praises from the Admiralty could not have been greater if he had taken thirty line-of-battle ships. 'Is it not surprising that they should cease there and not a syllable said on promotion for the first lieutenant or anything intended for myself? I still expect that a peerage will be confirmed and, on the meeting of a Parliament, the grant of a pension. It makes me fear that my services will be disregarded in the same manner as I experienced after the Nile.'

In mid-September Saumarez heard he was to be made Knight of the Bath. The choice of a suitable honour had been difficult. He had already been granted a baronetcy, and short of a peerage, the Order of the Bath was the only one possible.

The Government probably reasoned that Algeciras in no way compared with Camperdown and the Nile, for which Duncan and Nelson had been made peers. On the other hand, it did seem unfair to put Saumarez on a par with Graves who, with much lesser responsibilities, had been made a Knight of the Bath for Copenhagen.

Saumarez was bitterly disappointed. He wrote again to St Vincent, 'forcibly and in a manner that I think he will consider the red riband but a poor reward'. To Troubridge too he wrote, 'shuddering at the thought of being taxed with ingratitude' – a strange reversal of roles. St Vincent, exasperated, replied firmly that the red riband was the most he could expect; and to the Prime Minister he wrote: 'What shall I say upon Sir James Saumarez his expectations which are worked up to a pitch beyond all comparison?'

For Saumarez the last straw was cancellation of his appointments of the squadron's officers to the *St Antoine*, and word that no further promotion of officers (a subject on which Captains Ferris and Hood had also written with feeling) could be expected. To his brother he gave full vent to his feelings. 'The conduct of Lord St Vincent has been scandalous, and what Mr Tucker points out only proves to me he is the tool of his Lordship. Lord St Vincent has proved to me he has no claims from me. I shall soon resume my calm and forbearance, but I have been deeply affected by the conduct of the Admiralty towards me.'

Vice-Admiral Pole took over command at the beginning of September. Saumarez, anxious to escape from a situation now thoroughly disagreeable, asked permission to go home. This too was refused. His spirits revived in November at the occasion of his knighting by General O'Hara, a ceremony attended by the whole Gibraltar garrison; but for the rest of the year he continued on the station, thoroughly disgruntled and unhappy.

PART V

Against Invasion

CHAPTER 14

In the summer of 1801 Bonaparte's plans were everywhere crumbling. Nelson's victory at Copenhagen had reopened the Baltic to British trade; the French Army of the East had been finally defeated at Cairo; Saumarez's victory had prevented the invasion of Portugal and seriously damaged French relations with Spain.

The First Consul knew he would soon be forced to make peace; and he wanted peace as a breathing-space in which to hatch new plans. But he knew that England also wanted peace, and to obtain the best terms he must show he was ready to go on fighting. So he drew his last card – the threatened invasion of England. Orders went out for all flat-bottomed craft to proceed to Boulogne and other Channel ports, and for troops released from Austria by the Treaty of Lunéville to assemble on the heights of the Pas de Calais: at the same time he put out feelers for peace.

'His only object,' wrote Thiers, 'was to give England clearly to understand what was intended, i.e. a direct invasion, upon the success of which he would not hesitate to risk his life, his glory and his fortune; that if he did not succeed in obtaining reasonable concessions from the British Cabinet, his resolution was taken.'

In England the effect was as he hoped. On 21 July the Horse Guards issued a warning that invasion was imminent and suspended all leave. Lord Cornwallis was appointed to the Eastern Command, 'as there are grounds to believe,' wrote the Duke of York, 'that the French mean to invade this country.' On 22 July, 5000 volunteers paraded in Hyde Park; and in villages along the south coast meetings were held to discuss local defence.

At such a moment it was inconceivable the services of Nelson would be ignored. He had arrived back in England on 1 July, tired and far from well and looking forward to some weeks of domestic peace. Three weeks later he was appointed to 'a squadron on a particular service' – the defence of the south coast from Beachy Head to Orfordness. Disappointment at having to shorten his leave was palliated by messages from the Prime Minister and First Lord that only his presence in the Channel could quiet the public mind.

The thirty ships of his command were mostly frigates and gunboats (for the Channel Fleet was still keeping watch over Brest), and their captains were unknown to him. With only two officers was he at all intimate: Sam Sutton who had fought in the *Alcmene* under Riou at Copenhagen and then relieved him in the *Amazon*, in which Nelson now hoisted his flag; and young Captain Edward Parker whom Nelson had also brought from the Baltic, and in whose bravery and good-ness he realized some of the disappointed hopes for his step-son. Of his Mediterranean captains only Hardy and Berry were near him. Hardy had told Manfield that much as he liked the *St George* he did not wish to serve any admiral but Nelson: he left the ship when Pole went to join Saumarez, and was appointed to the *Isis* frigate in the Downs. He saw Nelson occasionally, as did Berry who, having paid off the *Princess Charlotte*, was given the *Ruby*, 64, on the North Sea Station adjoining Nelson's command. 'I have desired twenty marines to be sent to you as you are short of complement,' Nelson wrote to him; 'and whatever I can do to make your *Ruby* comfortable you are sure I shall be happy in doing.'

Twice Nelson carried the war into enemy territory by making attacks on the French gunboats at Boulogne. These were not altogether successful, but convinced him the invasion was an empty threat. 'The craft which I have seen,' he wrote, 'I do not think it possible to row to England; and sail they cannot.' His health was still bad and he was finding the prolonged separation 'from all I hold dear' unbearable. 'Nothing to be done on the great scale,' he wrote to St Vincent, 'the services on this coast are not necessary for the personal exertions of a Vice-Admiral.' This was true, but St Vincent replied: 'The public mind is so much tranquillized by your being at your post that it is extremely desirable that you should continue there: in this opinion all His Majesty's servants, with Sir Thomas Troubridge, agree'.

St Vincent mentioned Troubridge in the hope that Nelson, however unreasonable he might think the Admiralty, would respect the views of his oldest friend. But it had the reverse effect. Nelson, knowing Troubridge's opinion of Lady Hamilton, saw a plot to keep him from her. On 13 August he told her his fears: 'It is not my fault I cannot get up to London to see you. I believe it is all the plan of Troubridge; I have wrote both him and the Earl my mind.' Suspicion hardened into belief and soon hardly a letter to Lady Hamilton passed without some bitter comment. 'As for Troubridge,' he wrote on 17 August, 'never send a letter through him. I shall never write to him again until his letters are done away.' Next day: 'You ask me what Troubridge wrote? There was not a syllable about you in it.' On the 24th he assured her that whatever Troubridge might say he had no friends out of her house, and on the 31st there was a scathing reference to 'one of my *lords and masters* Troubridge'.

The tragedy of this breach is that it need never have happened. It was caused on the one hand by Nelson's tortured mind which ascribed to the Admiralty motives which were not there, and on the other by Troubridge's lack of feeling and imagination. In all his relationships, both with superiors and subordinates, Nelson demanded warmth and affection: when these were reciprocated, as with Lord Hood, St Vincent and most of his captains, he was at ease; when they were lacking,

as with Hotham and Keith and Saumarez, he was not. Nelson
was a fighter, not an administrator, and the formal voice of
authority irritated him. It was a double misfortune that the
authority to which he was now responsible was partly vested
in the man who had once been his subordinate and intimate
friend. If Troubridge had understood this, if he had continued
to speak with the freedom of the past, all might have been well.
But the mantle of authority had fairly wrapped him round: he
was a Lord of the Admiralty and he could not forget it. (Nor,
to do him justice, was he unmindful of the reception his efforts
to please had met with in the past.) His attempts to retain
Nelson's friendship without touching the intimacy they had
once enjoyed, aroused Nelson's bitter anger. In one letter he
hoped Nelson was getting walks on shore, in another he en-
joined him to wear flannel next the skin. 'He is, I suppose,'
said Nelson, 'laughing at me.'

Early in September, 1801, the Hamiltons paid Nelson a
fortnight's visit at Deal. Emma's presence temporarily cheered
him, but with her departure depression and ill-health returned.
'I came on board,' he wrote after leaving her, 'but no Emma.
No, no, my heart will break. I am in silent distraction. My
dearest wife, how can I bear our separation. Good God, what a
change. I am so low that I cannot hold up my head.' His
distress was increased by the death of his 'dear son' Parker
who had been wounded in one of the Boulogne attacks and
been lingering between life and death ever since. He was chief
mourner at the funeral for which he had paid all expenses, and
several eye-witnesses observed him in tears. 'I fear his loss
has made a wound in my heart which time will scarcely heal,'
he told St Vincent, and to Dr Baird he wrote: 'He was my
child, for I found him in distress'.

At the end of September another attack on Boulogne was
cancelled as the negotiations for peace were concluding. On
4 October word reached England that the preliminary articles
had been signed in Paris. The terms were not advantageous,
but people had been wishing for peace so long that they did not
care. In London the mob seized the French representative's

carriage and pulled it through cheering crowds to Downing Street. At Plymouth, in a heavy downpour of rain, a great bonfire was lit on the Hoe, consisting of 800 barrels of pitch 60 feet high and 240 feet in circumference: the ships in harbour lit their toplights and threw up rockets and blue flares. At Devonport, 5000 soldiers from the Plymouth Blues, Julian's Rangers, Dock Association, Langmead's Volunteers and Seobill's Artillery, all wearing laurels in their cockades, fired off 220 pieces of cannon. 'It was the grandest spectacle,' said the *Naval Chronicle*, 'ever witnessed in the West of England.' Lieutenant Nicholson, sent in to Brest by Admiral Cornwallis, was entertained to dinner by Admirals Villaret and Don Gravina and taken on a round of theatres. At Oreston the press-gang of Lieutenant John Newton ('forty-one years a lieutenant in the Royal Navy'), which in nine years had raised 3000 men, was paid off among scenes of wild enthusiasm. 'No words,' wrote Betsey, 'can describe the universal joy.'

But there was one man not sharing it. When Nelson heard the news he wrote to the Admiralty to be relieved. The reply was that he was to fly his flag for some time longer. He submitted grudgingly, 'for I do not wish to quarrel with the *very great folks* at the Admiralty at the last moment'. He remained shut up in his cabin in the *Amazon* for another week, cold and miserable. Then he heard that hostilities were to cease officially from the 22nd. Whatever the reason of the Admiralty for detaining him before, they had none now; and he wrote again for permission to come ashore. The reply, this time from Troubridge, was that he was not to think of leaving his station until the 22nd when he would be granted ten days' leave: but he was to fly his flag until the peace treaty was ratified.

Nelson's frustration and anger could hardly contain themselves. If he had ever had doubts as to the Admiralty's motives, they were finally dispelled: St Vincent and Troubridge were deliberately keeping him from Lady Hamilton. 'I am become a cypher,' he wrote to her, 'and he [Troubridge] has gained a victory over Nelson's spirit. I am kept here for what he may be able to tell: I cannot.' Hardy proved a sympathetic listener.

'The Admiralty,' he wrote to Manfield, 'seem determined to oppose him in everything he wishes. Troubridge, like a true politician, forsakes his old friend (who has procured him all the honour he has got) and sticks by the man who is likely to push him forward hereafter.' From Hardy, who seldom ventured an opinion on anyone and had much to thank Troubridge for, these were harsh words. Messages of sympathy from Nelson's friends ('there are many Troubridges in this world,' wrote Sir William Hamilton, 'but Nelsons are rare') brought no comfort. On 16 October he released his pent-up feelings to Lady Hamilton in the most bitter letter he ever wrote:

'My dearest friend,

To-morrow week all is over – no thanks to Sir Thomas. I believe the fault is all his, and he ought to have recollected that I got him the medal of the Nile. Who upheld him when he would have sunk under grief and mortification? Who placed him in such a situation in the Kingdom of Naples that he got by my public letters *Titles, the Colonelcy of Marines, Diamond Boxes* from the King of Naples, 1000 ounces in money for no expenses that I know of? Who got him £500 a year from the King of Naples? and however much he may abuse him, his pension will be regularly paid. Who brought his character into notice? Look at my public letters. *Nelson,* that Nelson that he now *Lords* it over. So much for gratitude. I forgive him, but my God I shall never forget it. He enjoys shewing his power over me. Never mind; altogether it will shorten my days. Poor Captain Somerville has been begging me to intercede with the Admiralty again; but I have been so *rebuffed* that my spirits are gone, and the *great* Troubridge has what we call *cowed* the spirits of Nelson; but I shall never forget it. . . .'

So ended a friendship of twenty-eight years. Six days later Nelson left his command to take up permanent residence with Sir William and Lady Hamilton at the house which she had bought for him at Merton, Surrey.

*   *   *

The unhappy weeks Nelson had spent on the south coast, Betsey had passed at Portsmouth in lighter vein. Troubridge had warned her of Fremantle's return from the Baltic and at the beginning of August she set out from Swanbourne with Tommy. She met Fremantle at Portsmouth 'in the street,' and was delighted that after a year's absence Tommy recognized his father.

While the *Ganges* was being refitted Fremantle joined Betsey in the social life of the port. There was entertaining on board ships in the harbour, and Betsey met many old friends, including Lord Garlies and George Elliot, neither of whom she had seen since *Britannia* days: Elliot, then a boy of thirteen, was now 'so much grown that I could not have known him'. The *Elephant* was in harbour, and they took Foley on several expeditions. A visit to Carisbrooke Castle was marred for Betsey by letting herself be driven in a gig by Foley 'who, *en passant*, is not the best of coachmen'. He redeemed himself when they went by boat to Fareham for dinner and got stuck on the mud on the way back. 'The tide falling fast, we were on the point of remaining there all night had it not been for Captain Foley's exertions who, in the dread of remaining in that disagreeable situation, took possession of one of the oars and we got off.'

By September repairs to the *Ganges* and *Elephant* were completed and they sailed to join the Channel Fleet. Betsey returned to Swanbourne. With the news of peace she expected Fremantle home, and was distressed to hear that the *Ganges* and *Elephant* had been detached to the West Indies on a special mission. ('How angry Foley and Fremantle will be,' commented Nelson.) Fremantle told Buckingham what had happened and his patron asked St Vincent to recall the *Ganges*. Such was his authority that St Vincent acceded; he wrote also to Duckworth at the Leeward Islands for the return of Foley. The *Elephant* and *Ganges* reached Spithead in January, 1802. The West Indian climate had affected the health of both officers: the wound in Fremantle's arm had broken out afresh and Foley was suffering from a complaint of the eyes.

Having paid off their ships they went on leave, Fremantle to Swanbourne, Foley to his home at Ridgeway in Wales.

The conclusion of operations in Egypt released many ships of the Mediterranean Fleet. Hood arrived at Spithead on 28 September 1801 to pay off the *Venerable*. ('Sir James Saumarez had been particularly attentive to me,' he wrote to Bridport, 'and I must ever feel his friendship for his very handsome statement of my conduct.') The disposal of his officers worried him, especially Midshipmen Harrison and Rundle ('the former the mother is in a fair way of spoiling by sending him money and clothes without my knowledge'), and he had to sit on a court martial on Sir William Parker. He finally got away in November and went down to the West country to visit Lord Bridport.

Next to arrive was Hallowell who, after his release by Ganteaume, had been court-martialled for the loss of the *Swiftsure* and honourably acquitted. He was followed by Ball and Louis, who reached England in December.

One officer who did not return was Saumarez. His repeated requests to be relieved were all turned down, and when Vice-Admiral Pole was recalled in December he again assumed command of the Cadiz station. He was at Gibraltar in February 1802, when the Governor, General O'Hara, died, and he despatched Blackwood in the *Penelope* to England with the news. The King appointed his son, the Duke of Kent, to fill O'Hara's place, and it was arranged that Hardy should carry him out in the *Isis*. Hardy waited on the Duke at Windsor and a week later embarked him and 'twelve waggon-loads of trunks and cases' at Falmouth. At Gibraltar the Duke was received by Saumarez: Hardy was rewarded for his trouble with a present of a soup tureen.

In May Saumarez superintended the evacuation of Minorca, which under the peace treaty was being handed over to Spain. St Vincent then offered him the peacetime command of the station, but he refused, and at the end of June was at last given permission to return home. The *Caesar* reached Spithead on 23 July, where according to the *Naval Chronicle*, 'she was

received as an old friend returned to port after a long absence.'
Saumarez was joined by his wife and went to Guernsey on leave.

Before paying off their ships, Louis and Blackwood sat on
two interesting courts martial, not unconnected with each
other.

In 1797 one of the most terrible mutinies in the British Navy
had occurred on board the frigate *Hermione* in the Spanish
Main. While the crew were reefing the topsails her tyrannical
commander, Captain Pigot, called out that he would flog the
last man down. In their efforts to reach the rigging two men
missed their hold and fell to their deaths on the deck. When this
was reported, Pigot replied: 'Throw the lubbers overboard'.
Next day the crew, oppressed by a commission of unbridled
cruelty, broke into open mutiny. They murdered the captain,
four lieutenants, the purser, surgeon, boatswain and a midshipman of fourteen; and having taken possession of the ship
carried her into the Spanish port of La Guira.

The Spaniards fitted out the *Hermione* under their own flag
and employed her at sea for the next two years. In September,
1799, Hyde Parker, then commanding at Jamaica, heard of
her arrival at Puerto-Cabello and ordered Captain Edward
Hamilton in the frigate *Surprise* to cut her out of the harbour.
This Captain Hamilton did in one of the most brilliant attacks
of its kind, and the *Hermione* was restored to the Royal Navy.

On arrival at La Guira the mutineers had been paid a
ransom by the Spanish authorities and discharged. Most were
subsequently captured by British ships and, after court martial,
executed. But in March, 1802, John Jones, an ex-steward of the
Hermione, and not concerned in the mutiny, recognized in
Portsmouth Dockyard David Forrester, one of the worst of the
mutineers. Forrester was secured and taken to the guard-
house, where he was visited by the Port-Admiral, Admiral
Holloway. He admitted he had been instrumental in killing
Captain Pigot and the lieutenant of marines. Holloway asked
if he had been easy in his conscience since. Forrester replied
that he had, as he had had orders from the captain of the fore-
castle, and if he had not obeyed them would have been killed

himself. 'Supposing,' said Holloway, 'I was to ask you to kill one of these soldiers standing here, would you do it?' 'Yes,' replied Forrester, 'if I thought you would kill me if I refused.'

A court martial was convened and Blackwood, just arrived in the *Penelope*, was appointed to sit on it. For the defence it was said that Forrester had served in the captain's boat of the *Bittern* for five years and behaved very well. But the evidence for the prosecution was damning. John Jones testified that on the day of the mutiny he saw Forrester coming out of the captain's cabin and that Forrester had said: 'I have just launched your bloody master overboard, and he said to me as I was launching him overboard: "Oh, David Forrester, are you against me too?" "Yes, you bloody rascal," I replied.' Forrester was sentenced to death and executed on board the *Gladiator*.

Louis's court martial was to try the officer who had re-captured the *Hermione* from Puerto-Cabello – Captain Sir Edward Hamilton. On leaving his ship one morning Sir Edward had given orders to the gunner to clean the quarter-deck guns and carronades. Finding on return this had not been done, he ordered the gunner and his crew to be seized up, that is lashed hands and feet to the rigging some way above the deck. For many years this was a standard form of punishment, but recently it had been made illegal. It was a bitterly cold day and the gunner, who was a very old man, called to the ship's surgeon that unless he were brought down he would faint. He was not brought down until the middle of the afternoon and on reaching the deck did faint. He applied as he was entitled to, for a court martial; and Sir Edward Hamilton was found guilty and dismissed the Navy. Later, owing to his record of service, St Vincent reinstated him and he rose to the rank of rear-admiral.

These stories are tributaries in the main stream of events; but they show that the humanity of Nelson's captains was not universal.

* * *

The Peace of Amiens (ratified in March, 1802) lasted from the early winter of 1801 until the summer of 1803. During this time most of the captains were living on half pay (12s a day) with their families in the country.

A week after arriving at Merton, Nelson took his seat in the House of Lords and seconded St Vincent in a motion thanking Sir James Saumarez on his victory. His speech, which was rather long and full of naval technicalities, was not kindly received: when he apologized to their Lordships for intruding on their time, there was a chorus of 'Hear, hear'. This ungracious gesture cut Nelson to the quick. The speech, he wrote to Sutton, was bad enough but well-meant – 'anything better than ingratitude'.

He made several trips to London, sometimes to fulfil public engagements, occasionally to accompany Sir William Hamilton to Literary Association meetings, more often to see his daughter Horatia, with whom he would play for hours. Once he found himself with Hyde Parker, Troubridge and Lords Minto, Hood and Hotham on the witness bench of the Old Bailey. A captain Macnamara of the Royal Navy, whom he had known at Bastia, had been riding in Hyde Park when his Newfoundland dog became involved in a scuffle with that of Colonel Montgomery, described by Eugenia Wynne as 'a handsome young man'. A duel between the masters had followed, fatal to Colonel Montgomery; and Captain Macnamara was arrested for manslaughter. The distinguished witnesses testified that the accused was not of a vindictive nature and he was acquitted.

But for most of the time Nelson remained at Merton. Here lay his real interests. In congenial surroundings and the company of the woman he loved, he regained his health and composure. 'He has been *very, very* happy since he arrived,' wrote Lady Hamilton. He took a great interest in his small estate and was frequently to be seen with old Tom Cribb, his head gardener, discussing plans for improving it; and the villagers, with whom he traded instead of ordering from London, soon became his friends.

But there was still much correspondence: letters to Sam Sutton about the disposal of the officers and his effects in the

Amazon, others from old friends asking for help in finding places for relatives or friends. These met with little success. On taking office St Vincent had declared he would fill vacant offices with the most efficient men he could find, 'and pay no regard to the recommendations of any person whatever'. This was a radical change of policy, for friends of the aristocracy and serving officers had always had precedence. But St Vincent persevered, continuing to reject every application sent to him, including those from all the princes of the blood.

Nelson saw the matter differently. Still smarting from the Admiralty's treatment of him on the south coast, he took the rejection of his recommendations as a personal snub. St Vincent assured him a just distribution of the patronage was very difficult: 'I have nothing for it but to act upon the defensive, as Your Lordship will be compelled to do whenever you are placed in the situation I at present fill'. To this Nelson was blind. 'I have not a scrap of interest, I assure you,' he complained to those who asked for his help; and to Berry he wrote bitterly: 'The time was, the present Lords did not think the Admiralty infallible in their judgment'.

Another matter which worried him was honours for Copenhagen. He had been given a viscountcy (a 'clever man' at Tenby suggested his motto should be *'Honor Est a Nilo'* – an anagram of Horatio Nelson), and Graves had been knighted; but no rewards had been given to the captains, officers and men. Nelson understood from St Vincent that the Government did not wish to offend Denmark by issuing medals during the war, but that as soon as it was over they would be granted. On 19 November the City of London voted its thanks to the forces which had captured Egypt. This showed that the omission of a vote of thanks for Copenhagen had been deliberate. Nelson wrote to the Lord Mayor to protest, sending copies of his letter to St Vincent and Addington. St Vincent replied that, far from encouraging the issue of medals, he had always been rigorously opposed to it. Nelson, who considered Copenhagen his greatest victory, was 'thunderstruck': he told St Vincent he had never doubted medals would be granted and had assured his captains that they could depend on receiving them. 'Either Lord St Vincent or myself,' he wrote to Davison, 'are liars.'

Despite this set-back Nelson continued to press for medals. 'You may judge my feelings,' he told Sutton, 'but I am fixed never to abandon the fair fame of my companions in danger.' But he was not successful. Disgusted, he wrote to Foley that he would never wear his other medals until those for Copenhagen were granted. When the City of London passed a motion thanking him for his services on the south coast, he asked them to withdraw it: in September he refused an invitation to dine with the Corporation and in November with the Lord Mayor. 'Never,' he wrote angrily, 'till the City of London thinks justly of the merits of my brave companions on the 2nd April, can I, their Commander, receive any attention from the City of London.' It was this devotion to their interests that made Nelson so loved by all who served him. In 1804 he again petitioned a new Board of Admiralty without success; and after his death his captains, led by Foley, continued to press for recognition. But no medals were issued, and it was not until 1838 – thirty-seven years after the battle – that the only surviving captain (John Lawford of the *Polyphemus*) was made a Knight of the Bath.

Many people think that Nelson's captains viewed his relationship with Lady Hamilton with disapproval. Apart from Troubridge and Hardy, there is no evidence for it. Foley, Fremantle, Hood, Hallowell, Ball, Louis, Murray, Domett and Sutton all accepted Lady Hamilton's hospitality. Not even Hardy's disapproval prevented him calling when he could. 'I stole three hours to-day to go to Merton,' he told Manfield on the eve of his departure with the Duke of Kent, 'her Ladyship was quite angry that I could not stay longer.' Ball, always a devoted admirer of Lady Hamilton, paid several visits. In June, 1802, he was made governor of Malta. Before leaving he wrote to Nelson regretting he could not have paid a final visit and sending his love to his 'dear sister Emma'.

On one occasion Ball, Hood and Lieutenant Layman (who

had fought at Copenhagen in the *Isis*) stayed at Merton together. After tea Nelson was engaged with Hood in a heated discussion over some small matter, and Layman remarked to Ball what an extraordinary character he was, little in little things, but by far the greatest man in great things he ever saw. Ball agreed and told Layman why the portrait promised to his Nile captains had never been painted. When the squadron arrived at Naples an artist was commissioned for the work and invited the captains to breakfast. Some time afterwards the captains observed that the artist had not begun, and deputed Ball to ask when he intended to. 'Never,' replied the artist. 'There is such a mixture of humility and ambition in Lord Nelson's countenance that I dare not risk the attempt.'

There is no evidence of Louis, Berry or Thompson having visited Merton at this time; but there is equally no evidence of their leaving their country estates. Louis had bought a house at Cadewell, near Newton Abbot, in Devon; Berry remained in his native Norfolk, and Thompson had settled down at Hartsbourne Manor, in Hertfordshire. Louis, almost as fanatical an admirer of Lady Hamilton as Ball, wrote to her and Nelson regularly.

The two other captains who never visited Merton were Saumarez and Troubridge. Saumarez was not a personal friend, and Nelson probably would not have welcomed a call, but Troubridge's absence hurt him deeply: he still craved for the friendship he had done so much to destroy. 'I thank you,' he wrote to Murray, 'for taking the trouble of driving seven miles to make me a visit; for could you believe it, there are those who I thought were my firm friends, some of near thirty years standing, who have never taken that trouble.' Again, when writing to Troubridge about Miller's monument, he ended: 'The spirit of liberality seems to be declining; but when I forget an old and dear friend may I cease to be . . . Your affectionate Nelson and Bronte.'

In July and August, 1802, Merton requiring some repairs, Nelson and the Hamiltons journeyed to Sir William's estates in Pembrokeshire. It was a triumphal tour and wherever

Nelson went he was received enthusiastically. (The only exception was Blenheim, where the party was cold-shouldered by the Duke of Marlborough who, having been recently cuckolded himself, had no wish to be associated with further scandal.) At Oxford Nelson and Sir William received the degree of Doctor of Civil Law in full convocation. At Ross the party embarked in a boat on the Wye and were cheered by hundreds of spectators on the bank: at Merthyr Tydfil Nelson's presence caused 'a delirium of joy'.

At Milford Haven Foley joined the party. The week before he had married Lady Lucy Fitzgerald, daughter of the Duchess of Leinster, whose sister, the beautiful Lady Sarah Napier, had nearly married George III. Foley had bought the estate of Abermarlais Park near Llandovery, but while it was being prepared was honeymooning at his old home of Ridgeway, owned by his elder brother. An invitation to Nelson and the Hamiltons to stay had been hotly contested by Mrs Foley, who did not relish the prospect of entertaining Emma; but the two brothers overruled her and the invitation was accepted. On the night of their arrival the avenue and house were illuminated with all the lanterns and candles the village of Haverfordwest could supply. After dinner Foley's little niece, aged six, came down to dessert: fears at the sight of a one-armed, one-eyed admiral were dispersed by him hoisting her on to his knee and dropping grapes, one by one, into her mouth.

The party continued their triumphal progress through Pembroke, Swansea, Hereford, Birmingham and Warwick, and arrived back at Merton on 5 September; here Nelson remained until called to sea nine months later. The tour had been a great personal success: he had been overwhelmed by the spontaneous enthusiasm he had met everywhere. In far-off Malta Ball followed the newspaper accounts with avid interest. 'I think his Lordship and Sir William must have been almost overpowered by such a load of caresses and kindnesses,' he wrote to Lady Hamilton, 'as for your Ladyship I believe you could *hip hip hip* your Nelson when every other power was exhausted.'

The Fremantles remained at Swanbourne where Betsey continued to produce children with clockwork regularity. In May, 1802, she gave birth to her third son, Henry, at whose christening Hyde Parker was chief godparent: eleven months later she produced a second daughter. A succession of incompetent cooks was followed by one who suited admirably but refused to stay without a kitchen-maid and exorbitant wages. 'Servants,' commented Betsey, 'are great torments.'

Fremantle took a vigorous part in the Aylesbury elections, and at the last moment offered himself as a candidate. Three days before polling-day he was 'in the fidgetts' about the result. But he was not successful in defeating Mr Dupré and Mr Bent who, according to Betsey, were spending a great deal of money in shameful bribery. He also bought a farm and seventy acres, and with this and the election and occasional fox-hunting, he was 'pretty well occupied'. Eugenia visited them from time to time and sometimes they went to London. At dinner at Hyde Parker's Betsey met Lady Lucy Foley. 'Very plain indeed,' was the verdict on her old suitor's wife, 'but seems affable and agreeable in her manners.'

Three officers who did not enjoy the comforts of home for long were Hallowell, Hood and Hardy. In the summer of 1802 Hallowell was appointed Commodore, West Coast of Africa, flying his broad pendant in the *Argo*, 44. In November Hood sailed for the West Indies in the *Blenheim* to become Commissioner at Trinidad. Hardy heard a rumour that Troubridge was going to hoist a broad pendant in his *Isis* and take up the East Indies command. He hoped not. 'Tho' a particular friend of mine,' he told Manfield, 'I do not think we should make it out so well together in the same ship, as he is extremely hasty on duty.' However on return from Gibraltar orders came for the *Isis* to be paid off. In London Hardy dined with Troubridge and St Vincent, who promised him another ship, saw Lady Nelson with whom he kept up a warm friendship, and after calling at Merton went to Dorset on leave.

He was not left idle long. On 11 July he was appointed to the *Amphion* frigate at Portsmouth, and wrote to Manfield: 'You

275

see my friend Tom Troubridge has not forgotten me'. His first duty was to carry to Lisbon the new British Ambassador, Lord Robert Fitzgerald, and his family and staff. After two days sailing in perfect weather Hardy was obliged to put into Portland, 'as Lady Robert could not stand the fatigues of the sea any longer; and how she is to get to Lisbon God only knows'. She was not the only one to suffer. 'Out of a wife, eight children, as many female servants, a secretary and six men servants, his Lordship had not a soul to put the children to bed and dress them this morning, but two women belonging to the ship. However he bears it with the most Christian forti- tude.' The passage to Lisbon could hardly have been worse: it took the *Isis* thirty-one days to get there, and only eight to get back.

St Vincent and Troubridge were hard at work at the Admiralty. Having spent the past seven years improving the fleets, St Vincent now set about rectifying the abuses which were rotting the Navy's civil departments. His standard letter of thanks for congratulations on his appointment had been: 'The decay of discipline and of every other good principle in the Navy is much to be deplored and every nerve I possess shall be exerted to restore it to its pristine vigour'. The unjust system of patronage had been the least of the evils. A task which called for stronger measures was what Byam Martin called 'the cleansing of the Augean stables of the fearful corruption prevailing in the dockyards'.

That there was some jobbing and petty dishonesty among the contractors was common knowledge: but the extent of it was not realized until the Board toured Plymouth, Portsmouth and Chatham in the summer of 1802. They found no proper accounts kept of income and expenditure, artificers paid twice over for the same work, others paid for work they had never done, infrequent mustering of men and stock, officers openly appro- priating stores for their own use. Even St Vincent's eyes were opened. 'I am sorry to tell you,' he wrote to Nepean, 'that Chatham Dockyard appears by what we have seen to-day a viler sink of corruption than my imagination ever formed.

Portsmouth was bad enough but this beggars all description.'

So great were the abuses and so many people engaged in them that St Vincent proposed a parliamentary commission to investigate the dockyards and report its findings to the House of Commons. The proposal was somewhat novel and the Cabinet rejected it ('mutinied' was St Vincent's word). He told them if they continued refusal he would resign his office and cease to sit in the House of Lords. He won his way and the commission was appointed. It made in all twelve reports, as a result of which the system of jobbing and contracting came to an end, and the dockyards were brought under Admiralty control. Of all the measures taken by St Vincent for the good of the Navy this was one of the greatest.

In all this Troubridge was at St Vincent's right hand. As might be expected, the corruption of the dockyards enraged him. 'You talk of my violence of language,' said St Vincent to a friend. 'Why, I am a mere lamb compared to Troubridge.' The appalling disclosures at Chatham made St Vincent fear that someone in the Commons would rise up to ask on what grounds the inquiry had been made. 'In this event,' he told Tucker, 'I hope Sir T. Troubridge will be guarded should a sudden impulse make him start up to reply, and that he will not show too much warmth.'

On another occasion Troubridge's temper nearly led to his undoing. Mr Giles, St Vincent's coachmaker, who was the first to discover the schemes of the traitor, Colonel Despard, took Troubridge one night to a roof through which they observed him and his associates plotting. 'So absolutely uncontrollable was Sir Thomas's animosity and rage,' says St Vincent's biographer, 'that it required the utmost effort to keep him from darting in to arrest them at once.' Giles's attempts to restrain Troubridge created a noise which Troubridge, because of deafness, did not hear, but which the traitors did, and they drew their pistols and searched. But they were not successful and a subdued but still angry Troubridge allowed himself to be led down to the ground and escorted back to the Admiralty.

CHAPTER 15

During the peaceful months of 1802 and 1803, while England's sea-captains were enjoying their first domestic happiness for years, Europe was again moving towards war. Napoleon (he now used his first name only) had thought peace with England would give him a free hand on the Continent. But he had misunderstood his enemy. With each new act of aggression and breach of trust, opinion in England hardened against him and when he pressed for the evacuation of Malta in accordance with the peace treaty, the government refused point-blank: the island was the first stepping-stone for an attack on the East (which Napoleon was planning) and the guarantees promised for its independence had not been forthcoming.

Napoleon sent for Whitworth, the British Ambassador, and ranted for two hours. But it was without effect. Any beliefs the British may have had in the First Consul's good faith were dispelled by news of hostile preparations in the Channel ports and of French commercial agents making plans of English harbours. The general view was that, if war was inevitable, the sooner it was started the better.

For Napoleon war was also inevitable, but he wanted time to prepare for it. The obstinate attitude of the British had caught him off guard. Soon after the preliminaries had been signed he had sent a fleet of twenty-eight sail under Admirals Villaret, Ganteaume and Linois, together with five Spanish sail under Don Gravina, the whole carrying an army of 21,000 men, to seize the island of San Domingo from the independent Negro leader, Toussaint L'Ouverture. The expedition was a failure. Although defeated, L'Ouverture's men inflicted terrible casualties on the French, which were later increased by fever. Napoleon's fleet was still in West Indian waters, and before starting hostilities against the greatest naval power in the world he wanted them home.

But the British were in no mood for delaying. A series of proposals and counter-proposals came to nothing, and on 7 May 1803, Whitworth was told that unless his terms were accepted within thirty-six hours he was to ask for his passports. They were not accepted and on 12 May he returned home. Four days later England declared war.

The Navy was not as ready as it might have been. For once events had proved St Vincent wrong. The old Admiral, with the rest of the Cabinet, had believed there would be no war. Side by side with his great work of cleansing the dockyards (and partly as a result of it) he had been effecting drastic economies: since the Peace, the Sea-Fencibles had been disbanded, 40,000 seamen had been paid off, and the line-of-battle ships reduced by half.

Six weeks of negotiations gave the Navy some opportunity to rearm. In March orders went out for 10,000 seamen to be raised immediately. From Portsmouth the *Amphion* sailed on impress service to Cork: other ships went to Welsh and southern English ports. Troubridge's son-in-law, Captain Richardson of the *Juno* (Hood's old ship) dropped down to St Helen's to pick up men from the homeward-bound trade. Ashore the press-gangs roamed the waterfronts day and night, and such was their reputation that people returning to Gosport could obtain a boat only with difficulty. At Plymouth the gangs boarded colliers and fishing vessels in the harbour and raided the gin-shops ashore. One evening they picked up 400 seamen and landsmen, another they seized a party of unfortunate holiday-makers. From the Royal Marine depot at Stonehouse twelve recruiting parties marched out to find men 'in different parts of England and Scotland'.

Next, from their country retreats, the admirals and captains were summoned to their ships. On the day war was declared Cornwallis sailed with ten battleships for the station off Brest. Lord Keith was ordered to collect a fleet at Plymouth. At Portsmouth Admiral Gardner was appointed Commander-in-Chief: Admiral Holloway returned as Port-Admiral and was received with a hearty peal on the bells.

Nelson's old captains were not long in finding employment. Saumarez, having received the freedom of the City of London and a pension of £1200 a year, was appointed Commander-in-Chief the Nore with his flag in the *Zealand*; his flag-captain, Captain Mitchell, had risen from the lower deck. Later, when invasion again threatened, Saumarez was made Commander-in-Chief of the Channel Islands with his flag in the *Grampus*, 50, and headquarters in his native Guernsey. Blackwood, always a frigate captain, was given command of the *Euryalus*, 36, and Louis was appointed to the *Conqueror*, 74. 'I think her a very fine ship indeed and equal to *Minotaur*,' he wrote to Nelson, adding: 'Pray command me if I can serve in any shape whatever, youngsters or anything else.'

For Nelson the war came at a useful moment. On 4 April Sir William Hamilton died in London, attended to the last by his wife and Nelson. Hardy posed to Manfield the question on everybody's lips: 'How her Ladyship will manage to live with the Hero of the Nile now, I am at a loss to know, at least in an honourable way', and even Nelson admitted to Berry: 'All London is interested'.

The problem was shelved by current events. It had always been understood that if war came Nelson should have the command in the Mediterranean. The *Victory* was to be his ship and Sam Sutton was to fit her out: Hardy, still in the *Amphion*, was to change with Sutton when she was ready. In March Berry had written Nelson a pathetic letter from Norfolk: 'I can no longer resist again offering myself as a candidate to serve with you, either temporary or permanent'. Their long years of comradeship prevented Nelson from refusing point-blank. 'You know how happy I should be to have you in any fleet I command,' he replied, 'particularly on the day of battle: I should be sure of being well supported.' He advised Berry to use his own judgment in asking for employment, but felt he would have no difficulty; although with Troubridge at the Admiralty he must have known how small the chances were.

As a Commander-in-Chief Nelson was entitled to a First Captain, or Captain of the Fleet. Foley was then living in

London, and Nelson called at his house in Manchester Square and offered him the post. But Foley's health was still bad and he had to refuse. 'Lord Nelson,' wrote his wife, 'expressed his regret in a manner so strong and so affecting as to have made a very great impression on my memory.' Nelson then offered the post to Captain Murray who had fought in the *Edgar* at Copenhagen. At first Murray also refused, saying that captains of the fleet often came to disagreements with their admirals, and his admiration for Nelson was such that he would rather not risk it. Nelson replied that if there were disagreements he would talk to him not as his captain but as his friend; and Murray joined the *Victory*.

There were the usual requests from fellow officers for berths for midshipmen, and to nearly all Nelson acceded. Whatever the policy of the Admiralty, he looked on relations of brother officers as 'legacies to the service'. To Foley, who asked him to take the orphaned son of a younger brother, he replied: 'I only desire that you will charge yourself in reminding me of your nephew. In whatever station I may be, I should be most ungrateful if I could for a moment forget your public support of me in the day of the Baltic, or your private friendship which I esteemed most highly.' To Thompson, who had a young *élève*, he wrote: 'Send the boy with a line to Sam Sutton'. Berry spoke of a Forster relation and said he would see the Admiralty folks at Baghdad before asking them: he too joined the *Victory*.

One officer who received a last-minute appointment was George Elliot. He was staying with his father's secretary, Colonel Drinkwater, at Brentford, but had gone to London for a ball at Lord Keith's. There at midnight an Admiralty messenger delivered a note from St Vincent that if he was at Portsmouth by daylight he could embark in the *Victory* to take command of the *Termagant* sloop in the Mediterranean. ('It was an invariable rule with St Vincent,' commented Elliot, 'to do things at the last possible and most inconvenient moment.') He ran home to his father's lodgings in Arlington Street, laid hold of some of his clothes (Lord Minto was still sitting in the Lords) and instructed a post-chaise to drive 'like fury' to Portsmouth. He arrived there at eight o'clock and found the *Victory* still in harbour.

Nelson, who had arrived two days before, was less pleased at the delay. He had found the *Victory* 'in a happy state of confusion,' and his opinion of Sutton was 'a good man but not so active as Hardy'. As usual he was champing to get to his post. To one who had spoken of his sailing he remarked: 'I cannot before tomorrow and that's an age'.

On the evening of Elliot's arrival (which he spent having sets of uniform hastily made up at the local tailors), another passenger arrived – his uncle, Hugh Elliot. He also had received a last-minute appointment – to relieve Arthur Paget in Sir William Hamilton's old post at Naples; and he was accompanied by his brother, Lord Minto, who had come to see him and his son off and say good-bye to Nelson.

On Friday, 20 May, Nelson embarked in a shower of rain; and that afternoon the *Victory*, with Sutton still in command, set sail out of harbour, accompanied by Hardy in the *Amphion*: as Cornwallis had discretion to retain the *Victory* off Ushant, the two captains were not to exchange until reaching the Mediterranean. Before leaving, Nelson scribbled Lady Hamilton a farewell note. 'The boat is on shore and five minutes sets me afloat. I can only pray that the great God of Heaven may bless and preserve you and that we may meet again in peace and true happiness. I have no fears.'

*   *   *

One officer who did not apply for employment immediately was Fremantle. He wanted his old ship, the *Ganges*, and in June when he heard she was at Portsmouth he went to London to see the First Lord. Two weeks later his appointment was gazetted. Fremantle's manservant, David, volunteered to accompany him to sea, but it was agreed that the groom James, who according to Betsey had once been on that element and never wished to encounter it again, should remain at Swanbourne.

As the day of parting drew nearer Fremantle's enthusiasm waned. 'He really goes to sea quite *à contre coeur*,' wrote Betsey, 'as he was now so comfortably settled here.' At dinner on the eve of his departure he was so upset he began to cry and had to leave the room. Ten days later Betsey, with her sister, Justina, and the children, joined Fremantle at Portsmouth. She remained there a month, entering in her diary her usual caustic comments: 'Nurse ill and obliged to go to bed where she was soon terrified at being attacked by a regiment of Bugs'. 'Dined at the Commissioners: A Haunch of Venison so stinking we could scarcely sit at table.' 'Walking home poor Justina received such a hard pinch from a sailor, she was quite frightened.' She went with Fremantle on a tour of Haslar Naval Hospital, and thought the building, with its 2100 beds, very clean and comfortable. 'I went through one of the wards and tho' there was but one man in bed, it struck me as a melancholy sight.'

On 25 September Fremantle, who had expected to stay at Portsmouth some time, received orders to take the *Ganges* to sea. 'These sudden orders have upset all our schemes,' wrote Betsey dejectedly. After a farewell dinner, at which she satisfied herself that Fremantle's cabin was 'very comfortable and nice,' she returned on shore 'stupid with disappointment.' Fremantle dropped down to St Helen's, and with a fair wind sailed to join Cornwallis off Brest.

Nelson meanwhile was pressing south in the *Amphion*. He had left the *Victory* to look for Cornwallis, with a note that, if the Admiral did not need the ship, to send her on as soon as possible. On 3 June Nelson sighted the Rock of Gibraltar for the first time since his pursuit of Brueys five years before, and having been joined by the *Maidstone* frigate passed through the Straits into familiar waters. On 11 June he sent away Hugh Elliot in the *Maidstone* for Naples, and on the 15th saluted the flag of his old captain, the Governor of Malta. Lady Ball entertained the Admiral to tea. Ball wrote to Lady Hamilton that he thought Nelson had never looked better: Nelson thought Ball well but a little melancholy.

From Malta Nelson sailed for Toulon. On 25 June he came abreast of Naples and the sight of Vesuvius and the roofs of the houses shining in the sunshine overwhelmed him with memories. '*Dear* Naples,' he wrote to Lady Hamilton, 'if it is what it was.' Ten days later a strange squadron was sighted: it was Sir Richard Bickerton with the nucleus of the Mediterranean Fleet; the *Gibraltar*, 80, *Triumph, Belleisle, Superb, Renown, Donegal, Kent*, 74s, *Agincourt* and *Monmouth*, 64s.

The captain of the *Superb* was still Richard Keats, the hero of Saumarez's victory. Nelson had not served with him but knew of his reputation. As a lieutenant in the *Prince George* Keats had been chosen, with Foley, to supervise the instruction of the young Duke of Clarence. He made an instant impression on Nelson. But his health was not good and Nelson ordered him to Naples on fourteen days' convalescence. 'Give me leave,' he wrote to Hugh Elliot, 'to introduce Captain Keats to your particular notice. I esteem his *person* alone as equal to *one* French 74.'

Nelson told Elliot that his nephew had taken command of the *Termagant* and asked him to send back by Keats 'some little matters – tea, sugar and a few hams – acceptable to young housekeepers'. George Elliot was in a bad way, for his predecessor in the *Termagant*, an old Scot of sixty, had been so angry at being superseded by a boy of eighteen that he had refused to sell his livestock or cutlery. 'The Scot's name was Fife,' wrote Elliot, 'but he was better known as *Old Music*, though he was certainly very much out of tune.' Several captains came to Elliot's assistance. Hardy gave him a boat canteen, Captain Gore some table-cloths, Captains Donnelly and Moubray pots and pans and chairs. 'I soon found myself set up,' wrote Elliot, 'and able to ask *two* officers to dine when I had anything to give them to eat.'

With his new fleet Nelson proceeded towards Toulon. He waited only for the coming of the *Victory*. 'Although Captain Hardy's kind attention cannot be excelled,' wrote Nelson's secretary to Lady Hamilton, 'yet the comfort of a large ship in this climate is so desirable that we are all wonderfully anxious to fall in with her.' She arrived at last on 30 July and Nelson, Hardy and the staff transferred from the *Amphion*.

In the great ship which had worn the flags of Keppel, Kempenfelt, Howe, Hood and St Vincent, and which before long Nelson himself was to immortalize, he took up his station off Toulon. The last watch had begun.

*　　*　　*

To the casual reader the years 1803–5 are singularly devoid of naval interest. No fleet actions took place: no grand expeditions were launched. And yet they were two of the most important years in England's naval history; for her seamen the most arduous.

For Napoleon was surrounded. When Nelson took his station in the *Victory* off Toulon he completed the last link in a chain which stretched from the Texel to the north coast of Italy. Inside this chain Napoleon was impotent. He had the greatest army in the world and he was powerless to use it. Without sea-power his schemes of aggression were set at nothing.

There remained, as he saw it, but one thing to do – disregard the perimeter and strike at the centre, attack England itself. It was true that half his fleet were still making their way back from the West Indies to Rochefort, Ferrol and other Atlantic ports, but he did not intend to use them. He had accepted the supremacy of British sea-power and he proposed to ignore it.

This time invasion was to be no mere threat. Men were sent into the forests to cut down trees, and orders went out to all seaport and river towns of northern France to hasten the construction of flat-bottomed boats. In addition to the Grand Army, the Dutch were to provide 16,000 troops, and 200 barges, the Swiss 30,000 troops. Napoleon intended that by the autumn 150,000 men would be ready to embark in 2000 barges. They would sail on a foggy night in three groups and land in southern England: he would lead the expedition in the aptly named *Prince de Galle*. The impotence of his own ships would be to his advantage, for they would keep the British fleet immobilized off Brest. By the time Cornwallis arrived in the Channel, London would be sacked and among the ruins he would be accepting the country's surrender. The Grand Army was to destroy British sea-power.

In England the news of the project was at first received sceptically: there had been scares of this sort before. But as the great armament grew and rumours, magnified a hundredfold, filtered into London, the seriousness of the danger was appreciated. 'I begin to be half alarmed at the attempt to invade this country,' wrote Betsey, 'these horrid French are such desperate wretches.' Another correspondent wrote that the topic of invasion had superseded every other from conversation. Yet the mood of England was more anger than fear. Napoleon was beginning to be hated as never before; and no one doubted that if he and his soldiers came, they would be driven into the sea. 'I trust, my dear Fremantle, in God and English valour,' wrote Nelson from Toulon, 'we are enough in England if true to ourselves.'

This Shakespearian cry summed up the feeling everywhere. When preparations for resistance were made, the whole country answered the call. 'Everybody here is a soldier,' wrote Eugenia Wynne at Burton, 'whether they like it or not.' On the whole they did. In answer to a request for volunteers 300,000 men came forward, among them Cabinet Ministers, poets and peers. There were no weapons to give them except pikes, and with these they drilled enthusiastically all over the countryside. As far north as the Lake District and the lowlands of Scotland, Wordsworth and Scott sweated on route marches over their native hills. Even the children became infected: from her bedroom at Swanbourne Betsey watched seventeen Winslow boys, wearing paper caps and armed with sticks, march down the village street. All over the country great beacons were built to give warnings of the first landings: along the Channel coast a chain of Martello towers were erected as a first line of defence.

But as those who wielded the weapon of British sea-power knew, England's defence lay elsewhere. They knew – although they could not convince their countrymen – that the navigational difficulties of Napoleon's schemes were impossible to overcome and that without a supporting battle-fleet his project must fail. When Admiral Montagu captured two invasion craft in the Downs he thought them so contemptible they must be a feint. To a group of nervous fellow peers St Vincent replied caustically: 'I do not say they cannot come, my Lords, I only say they cannot come by sea' (true in 1804 and again in 1940). The safety of the realm lay where it had always lain, not in pikes or beacons of Martello towers, but in the wooden walls, in the victors of St Vincent, the Nile and Copenhagen; in Keith and Louis off the Texel, Saumarez and Blackwood in the Channel, Cornwallis and Collingwood off Brest, Fremantle at Ferrol, Nelson, Hardy, Murray and Keats in the Mediterranean. It was, in Mahan's immortal words, those far distant, storm-beaten ships, on which the Grand Army never looked, that stood between it and the dominion of the world.

*   *   *

Although by the New Year of 1804 Napoleon's naval advisers had reached the same conclusions, he never gave up hope or relaxed preparations. As late as the autumn of 1804 Foley was writing to Nelson: 'We are more than ever threatened with invasion'. During these long months the chain that surrounded France was never broken. '*Les Anglais*,' wrote the Naval Prefect at Brest despairingly, '*sont constamment sur nos côtes.*' The strain on ships and crews, aggravated by St Vincent's economies, was terrific; and only men of the calibre of Nelson and Cornwallis could have withstood them.

Their object – to keep their fleets at sea – was the same, but their problems were different. Cornwallis was within a day's sailing of England and had some of his wants supplied. Such visits were few and brief, for he was determined never to relax the watch. Against the merciless buffeting of the seas, bitter weather and lack of fresh food there were no remedies. 'Our ships are so worn down,' wrote the second Secretary of the Admiralty, 'that they are like post-horses during a general election.' When Collingwood arrived in harbour after a spell off Brest, he found the *Venerable* rotten to the core. 'We have been sailing for the last six months with only a sheet of copper between us and eternity.' The crews, in one captain's words, were 'worked to death'; and with salt beef, maggoty biscuits and stagnant water as their diet, it was impossible to check disease. Sir Robert Calder's crew became so infected with ulcers that he landed the worst on an island in Berehaven Bay to be cured by milk, vegetables, 'and the smell of earth'. The ship's company of the *Ganges* went down with a raging inflammation of the eyes: Fremantle stayed in his cabin for four days, his head swathed in bandages and a night-cap. Such ailments were the rule rather than the exception.

Nelson's chief problem was to keep his 'crazy' ships seaworthy: refitting was impossible, as his slender force of ten sail never exceeded that of the French in Toulon, and the nearest dockyards at Malta and Gibraltar were over seven hundred miles away. Nor, St Vincent told him, could he expect reinforcements. The health of the Fleet, although constantly on his mind, presented fewer difficulties, for the Mediterranean provided plenty of fruit and vegetables. More important was to keep the men contented, for being so far from home, they felt in danger of being forgotten. It was a very real danger, as Nelson knew. When the City of London voted its thanks to the blockading fleets, they mentioned Cornwallis's flag-officers by name but omitted Nelson's. In reply to Nelson's protest the Lord Mayor said he did not know who Nelson's flag-officers were. In order to combat the effects of stagnation, of what Nelson called 'allowing the sameness of prospect to satiate the mind,' he kept the Fleet on the move. Sometimes they visited the Maddalena Islands between Sardinia and Corsica, sometimes they looked in at Villefranche, Barcelona or Rosas. The results were all that Nelson hoped. In December, 1804, eighteen months after taking the command, he wrote to the Admiralty: 'The Fleet is in perfect good health and good humour, unequalled by anything which has ever come within my knowledge, and equal to the most active service which the times may call for'.

The strain of the blockade fell most heavily on the captains. Such luxuries as they enjoyed were small compensation for the responsibilities of their ships and health of their men. Often in rough weather they remained on deck all night, and days went by without their taking off their clothes. They snatched at any trivial pastime to occupy their minds. One captain grew mustard and cress on the quarter-deck, another kept a small aviary. Fremantle took to brewing spruce beer and smoking 'segars': in desperation for reading material he embarked on *Family Secrets*, a book of pornography thrust upon him by the purser: this sufficed until a parcel of Shakespeare and Cobbett arrived from Betsey. Their thoughts were divided equally between their ships and their homes. 'On the quarter-deck I am the captain,' wrote Codrington, 'in my cabin I am the husband and father with a full sense of the blessing of being so.' Nelson told Lady Hamilton that his only thoughts were of her and the French Fleet.

Their greatest comfort was letters. 'Pray tell me all you can think about our family,' wrote Collingwood, 'and about the beauties of your domain – the oaks, the woodland and the verdant meads.' Codrington told his wife that all her little chit-chat, however ridiculous in other eyes, was entertaining to him. For their part the captains found letter-writing difficult for, as Fremantle put it, the 'very sad sameness' made all days like one. 'It would be little to tell you,' said Codrington, 'that yesterday we wore ship and the day before we tacked ship, although any difficulties attending those simple acts might require all our skill and exertion.' Their letters, like their wives', were full of trivia. Fremantle spoke of his need for tooth-paste, of the goat that fell down the hatchway and deprived him of milk for his tea, of the dishonesty of his servant David, of his cook who knew nothing but roast and boiled.

Any deviation from routine was an opportunity for a long letter. When the *Ganges* visited Gibraltar for a refit, Fremantle drew up a journal of where he had dined, how he had spent the evening and his observations on the company; at Ferrol he described a dinner-party ashore where his fellow guests included the captains of the French ships he was blockading. But such visits were rare, and mostly the captains suffered what Collingwood called 'unremitting hard service, giving up everything that is pleasurable to the soul or soothing to the mind, and engaging in a constant contest with the elements'.

Only the knowledge that in their hands the safety of their country lay made such service tolerable.

* * *

Apart from Murray (recently promoted rear-admiral) and Hardy who, Nelson said, were everything he could wish or desire, his captains were unknown to him. 'I am with perfect strangers,' he wrote soon after joining, 'although I believe very good men.' Except for Keats he did not attain the same intimacy with them as his companions of the Nile. But on all he exercised the same healing influence, making them feel they belonged to an envied and exclusive brotherhood. He abhorred formal councils of war, preferring to take them into his confidence by walks on the quarter-deck or in the easy conversation of the dinner-table. His trust, as always, was implicit. 'I can assure you, Sir,' he wrote to a Spanish nobleman, 'that the word of every captain of a British man-of-war is equal, not only to mine, but to that of any person in Europe, however elevated his rank.'

There are many instances of his extraordinary tact and consideration. Keats complained that Murray was deliberately withholding a supply of hammocks of which his men were in need. Any other admiral would have sent Keats a sharp rebuke. But Nelson explained in the gentlest terms that there were not the hammocks to spare. 'The situation of First Captain is certainly a very unthankful office, if there is a deficiency of stores he must displease the whole fleet . . . I wish, my dear Keats, you would turn this in your mind and relieve Admiral Murray of the uneasiness your conversation has given him.' When Captain Layman was placed at the bottom of the list of commanders for running the *Raven* brig on the rocks, Nelson pleaded with the First Lord to rescind the sentence. 'I own myself one of those who do not fear the shore, for hardly any great things are done in a small ship by a man that is; therefore I make very great allowances for him. Nor do I regret the loss of the *Raven* compared to the value of Captain Layman's services which are a national loss.' This was the Nelson touch and its effect was magic. 'The admirals and captains,' wrote his secretary, 'are all wonderfully attached to him and as contented as men can be. Those that had been a long time in the country before we arrived and were anxious to get home have forgot that entirely.'

Officers were not slow to repay such consideration. Towards the end of 1804 the Admiralty again separated the Cadiz from the Mediterranean station, and gave the command of it to Vice-Admiral Sir John Orde. This was the officer who had complained to St Vincent at Nelson's being given command of the Nile Squadron in preference to himself, and as a result had been sent home. The appointment was a cruel blow to Nelson, for it robbed him of his main source of prize-money; nor was the situation eased by Orde taking over Nelson's frigates when they passed the Straits and sending them elsewhere.

Determined to get important despatches to Lisbon, Nelson sent for Captain Parker of the *Amazon*, one of his best frigate-captains and a nephew of St Vincent. He ordered him to sail direct for Lisbon and, contrary to Orde's instructions, to avoid meeting his fleet. 'Here are your orders,' he said. 'I have not signed them because Sir John Orde is my senior officer; but if it should come to a court martial, Hardy can swear to my handwriting and you shall not be broke. And remember, Parker, if you cannot weather that fellow, I shall think you have not a drop of your old uncle's blood in your veins.'

When Parker cleared the Straits there was a full moon shining, and he was sighted by one of Orde's look-out frigates, the *Eurydice*. She closed the *Amazon* to order her to join Orde's flag. Her captain went on board and turned out to be young William Hoste. 'Captain Hoste,' said Parker, 'I believe you owe all your advancement in the service to my uncle, Lord St Vincent, and to Lord Nelson. I am avoiding Sir John Orde's squadron by desire of Lord Nelson. You know his handwriting. Do you think it would be better if you were not to meet the *Amazon* this night?' Hoste, after a little reflection, left the ship without showing Parker his orders. Parker continued on his way and arrived with the despatches at Lisbon.

With most of his old captains Nelson kept in close touch. Ball was his most frequent correspondent, and to some extent filled the place vacated by Troubridge. During Nelson's first months on the station their relationship was uneasy. Ball was no longer Nelson's subordinate but, in another sphere, his equal, a situation which Nelson resented. 'He is, I assure you, a great man,' he wrote to Lady Hamilton, 'and on many occasions appears to forget he was a seaman. He is bit with the dignity of the *Corps Diplomatique*.' Here was an echo of Nelson's criticisms of Troubridge at the Admiralty. But Ball's advice was too valuable to lose, and once Nelson had swallowed his pride they resumed their friendship. It grew as the months went on and soon hardly a week passed without Nelson confiding his thoughts or asking for advice. 'I do most earnestly desire that you will say anything to me that you please,' he wrote. 'I can never take it amiss.'

Ball's appointment was ideal. The Maltese adored him: this was the first time within memory they had been treated as a free people. Ball's private secretary during 1804 was the poet Coleridge, who wrote of the esteem in which Ball was held. 'Whenever he appeared in Valetta the passengers on each side through the whole length of the street stopped and remained uncovered until he had passed.' Coleridge often accompanied Ball on rides round the countryside, and he tells how groups of women and children fell into rank behind them, singing a song composed in Ball's honour; and how in every cottage, however poor and distant, they were sure to find two crude paintings – one of the Virgin and Child, the other of the Governor.

With other old captains Nelson also kept in touch. 'I received a most friendly letter from Lord Nelson a few days ago,' Fremantle told Betsey, 'of course it contains nothing new, but is a proof of his attachment.' Foley wrote occasionally from

Abermarlais and begged to introduce Dr Gillespie, the new Physician to the Fleet. Berry continued his pathetic appeals for employment, but Nelson assured him (truthfully enough) that he had no interest at the Admiralty. 'It is vexing to be unemployed at such a moment,' he wrote, 'but it is useless to fret oneself to death when the folks aloft don't care a pin about it.'

Only with Troubridge did Nelson cease to correspond. There are records of a few letters, but all concern the administration of the Fleet. It seems their friendship had finally dissolved and neither wished to renew it: entreaties and recriminations were at an end.

Troubridge's star was on the decline. In the spring of 1804 he was promoted rear-admiral; but a month later Addington's ministry fell and the Board of Admiralty resigned. Pitt became Prime Minister and Lord Melville First Lord. St Vincent's and Troubridge's reign had not been popular. A few officers, it is true, were grateful for services rendered: Fremantle told Betsey, whenever she heard Troubridge was out, to call on Miss Troubridge 'and express the sentiments I entertain of his kindness and attention'. Others like Berry and Louis who had suffered from their rudeness and obstinacy felt differently. Nelson received the news calmly but not without bitterness. 'I am sure that nine-tenths of those who now abuse the Earl and Troubridge,' he wrote to Lady Hamilton, 'were and would be again their most abject flatterers were they again in office. For myself I feel above them in every way and they are below my abuse of them. Now no longer in power I care nothing about them, and now they can do no harm to anyone, I shall no longer abuse them.' This was a far cry from the spirit of 1798.

When Troubridge heard that Addington was supporting Pitt's ministry he became, it is said, 'devoured with rage and chagrin.' This, and a belief that a ministry opposed to him would never give him employment, prevented him asking for it. He remained at home for several months, during which, it seems, he became taken with Betsey's sister Harriet.

But in thinking the new Board had no use for his services

Troubridge had misjudged Melville's character. In the autumn of 1804 the First Lord remarked to several officers at dinner that he was surprised, even hurt, that Troubridge had not asked for employment. A few days later Troubridge called at the Admiralty. He was shown up to the First Lord who to his great surprise gave him a friendly reception. Melville said he would be pleased to appoint him to whatever station he chose: the East Indies Command was to be divided and he suggested one of them; and he could name his own ship. Troubridge accepted the offer and asked for the *Blenheim*. In March, 1805, he hoisted his flag in her and sailed for the East Indies, never to return.

Towards the end of Nelson's Mediterranean Command, two of his old captains, Hallowell and Louis, served with him again.

Hallowell was in the *Argo* on the African coast when in 1802 he heard of Napoleon's expedition to San Domingo. Fearing it might lead to the reopening of hostilities, he sailed to Barbados on his own initiative to support Sam Hood. On the outbreak of war he helped Hood recapture St Lucia and Tobago: his friendly advice, Hood told the Admiralty, had been invaluable. Hallowell returned to England with Hood's despatches.

His next mission was rather peculiar. The Arab Chief, Elfi Bey, who had been sheltering in England, had persuaded the British Government that if he were to return to Egypt, he could influence the Arabs against French aggression. His real object, as Hallowell found out after embarking him, was to obtain power for himself. Going through the Mediterranean Hallowell asked him whether, if the French landed, the English could be sure of his support. 'To this he answered with great warmth,' Hallowell told Nelson, 'that if *any* enemy was to attempt to land, he would devour the flesh from their bones, and enforced his expressions by taking hold of his hand between his teeth saying, "*Thus* would I treat them".' Hardly had Hallowell landed his passengers at Aboukir when he was approached by two rival chiefs, Osman and Ibrahim Bey, who were out for Elfi's blood. 'I think,' Hallowell wrote to St

Vincent, 'that he stands a fair chance of being assassinated.'

On his return down the Mediterranean Hallowell called in at the Fleet off Toulon, bringing Nelson a present of wine. 'You will never be a rich man,' Nelson told him, 'if you keep on giving away.' He took presents for Lady Hamilton and promised Nelson to visit her at Merton. 'His spirit is certainly more independent than almost any man's I know,' Nelson told her, 'but I believe he is attached to me.'

In England Hallowell paid off the *Argo* and commissioned Sidney Smith's old ship, the *Tigre*. Her quarter-deck, said the *Naval Chronicle*, would be very brilliant, as Hallowell was taking many young gentlemen of rank, among them a son of Lord Spencer. In this ship Hallowell sailed again for the Mediterranean, rejoining Nelson in September, 1804.

Louis spent the winter of 1803-4 under Collingwood off the Black Rocks. On St George's Day, 1804, he was promoted rear-admiral and appointed to the North Sea Squadron under Keith. He remained in the Channel and North Sea during the whole of 1804; but he had never liked Keith and begged Nelson for an opportunity to join him. 'Whenever you write,' he told Lady Hamilton, 'say how much I regret not being with him.' At the end of 1804 Nelson's junior flag-officer, Rear-Admiral Campbell, was invalided home, and Nelson asked the Admiralty to send Louis in his place. Louis arrived in the Fleet early in 1805, hoisting his flag in the *Canopus* (the captured *Franklin*), commanded by Jane Austen's brother. 'The arrival of Admiral Louis,' wrote Nelson, 'will enable me to get a little rest.'

CHAPTER 16

But there was to be little rest for Nelson from now on. For Napoleon had at last recognized what his naval advisers had been pressing for months – that only with the support of his Fleet could the invasion of England succeed.

He first tentatively accepted the idea in the summer of 1804, when he ordered La Touche Tréville at Toulon to break out into the Atlantic, release the squadrons at Cadiz and Rochefort, and having by-passed Cornwallis off Brest, to appear in the Channel with sixteen sail. La Touche Tréville sailed, but sighted Nelson's advanced frigates and returned to harbour. Soon after he died of heart failure, caused, the French papers said, by climbing the signal tower at Sepet to look at the British Fleet. ('I always pronounced that would be his death,' Nelson told Ball.) His successor was Villeneuve, the officer who had escaped from Aboukir with the remnants of Brueys's fleet.

As the months passed Napoleon's conceptions grew: an isolated expedition was useless: if he were to use his fleets at all he must use them, like everything else, on the grand scale. The return of the West Indian expedition had brought his capital ships up to eighty: to these he proposed to add the Fleet of Spain. Secret negotiations with his old ally bore fruit in September when Pitt, hearing that French troops were marching across Spain to man their ships at Ferrol, decided to force Spain's hand. A squadron of frigates was ordered to intercept a Spanish treasure-fleet returning from South America. The Spaniards gave flight and their flag-ship blew up, carrying to the bottom the Captain-General of Peru and his wife and family. On 12 December 1804, Spain declared war.

Napoleon was now ready to put his huge schemes into execution, to mobilize the whole of his own and the Spanish Fleet for the single purpose of crushing England. The Brest, Toulon and Rochefort squadrons commanded by Ganteaume, Villeneuve and Missiessy, together with what Spanish ships were available at Cadiz and Cartagena, were to break their blockades simultaneously and sail for the West Indies. They were to destroy as much British trade as possible, to draw the British battle-fleet after them; then, having formed a junction of fifty sail of the line, they were to double back to Europe, enter the unguarded Channel and rendezvous with Napoleon at Boulogne.

From the start the scheme misfired. Napoleon had ordered Ganteaume to sail only if he could avoid giving battle, for it was essential his fleets should arrive in the Channel intact. But Ganteaume could not break Cornwallis's iron ring. 'Out again every morning and in again about a couple of hours,' wrote Midshipman Coleridge. 'I'm sure we were always ready to give them a bout.' Villeneuve got away in January, 1805. Nelson spent a hectic six weeks searching for him up and down the Mediterranean, reliving the agonizing doubts of his pursuit of Brueys, only to find that a Gulf of Lyons gale had obliged his enemy to return to harbour. The one squadron to get clear away was Missiessy's. He reached the West Indies and did some damage which caused a slump in the City; then, hearing of Villeneuve's failure, made for home.

Napoleon was furious with Villeneuve. 'What is to be done,' he declared, 'with admirals who allow their spirits to sink, and resolve to be beaten at the first damage they suffer? The great evil of our Navy is that the men who command it are unused to the risks of command.' Another evil he might have mentioned was that, after months of inactivity, spars and rigging were rotten, and crews half-trained, seasick and mutinous. Nelson, whose fleet had not seen a dockyard for twenty months, was equally contemptuous; 'Bonaparte has often made the boast that our Fleet would be worn out by keeping the sea; but he now finds, I fancy, that his Fleet suffers more in a night than ours in a year.'

Not knowing that Missiessy was returning from the West Indies, and hoping that Ganteaume might get clear, Napoleon ordered Villeneuve to sail again. The French Admiral left Toulon on 30 March with eleven sail of the line. Off Cartagena he signalled the Spanish ships there to join him; they replied they had not completed their ammunition and asked him to wait. But haunted by the thought of Nelson, Villeneuve pushed on for the Straits. On 9 April he came abreast of Cadiz: Orde, covering the approaches with a much smaller force, retired northwards. Having been joined by one French and five Spanish ships under Gravina, Villeneuve disappeared into the Atlantic.

Nelson was lying with his fleet at Palmas in Sardinia when he heard of Villeneuve's escape. During the past months his health had again deteriorated and he had the Admiralty's permission to return home. Now all such thoughts left him. He had one single dominant idea: to seek out the enemy and bring them to battle, whatever they were and however long it took him. 'I am in truth half dead,' he wrote to Ball, 'but what man can do to find them out shall be done.'

Having no knowledge of the enemy's destination and believing it might be Egypt, he spread the Fleet between Sardinia and Africa to bar their passage to the eastward. 'I shall neither go to the eastward of Sicily or to the westward of Sardinia,' he told Hugh Elliot, 'until I hear something positive.' It was the right decision, but for one who knew the suffering of inaction an agonizing one. He remained in this area a week. On 16 April Hallowell joined from Palermo with news that a big troop convoy – Pitt's secret expedition which was to co-operate with the Russians in the Mediterranean – had just left England. Nelson concluded that this was Villeneuve's object and that he must have gone westwards. But he could not act on surmise and not until a week later did he learn that Villeneuve had passed the Straits. News of the junction with Gravina made him think the expedition was destined against England; and subject to information at Gibraltar, he proposed to take his Fleet to the Channel. 'I trust this plan will meet with their Lordships' approbation,' he told the Admiralty, 'and I have the pleasure to say that I shall bring with me eleven as fine ships of war, as ably commanded and in as perfect order and in health, as ever went to sea.'

After two weeks' battling against foul winds, Nelson sighted the Rock of Gibraltar. 'O, French Fleet, French Fleet,' he wrote to a friend, 'if I can but once get up with you, I'll make you pay dearly for all you made me suffer.' He watered and provisioned at Tetuan, and after a brief stop at Gibraltar came to anchor in Lagos Bay. Here he received information which at once altered his opinion. Vessels lately arrived from England reported no enemy movements in the Bay or Channel; and Rear-Admiral Campbell of the Portugese Navy (who had warned Jervis of the Spaniards' approach at St Vincent) reported that he had seen the combined fleets steering to the westward with his own eyes. On 9 May 1805, Nelson came to his great decision. 'My lot is cast and I am going to the West Indies.'

The next morning the Fleet weighed and sailed. They consisted of the *Victory*, Vice-Admiral Nelson, Rear-Admiral Murray, Captain Hardy; *Canopus*, Rear-Admiral Louis, Captain Austen; *Superb*, Captain Keats; *Spencer*, Captain Stopford; *Donegal*, Captain Malcolm; *Tigre*, Captain Hallowell; *Leviathan*, Captain Bayntun; *Belleisle*, Captain Hargood; *Conqueror*, Captain Pellew; *Swiftsure*, Captain Robinson; and the frigates *Decade*, *Active* and *Amazon*. Rear-Admiral Bickerton in the *Royal Sovereign* was left to guard the Mediterranean.

The passage across the Atlantic was uneventful. Now that he felt certain he was on the enemy's track Nelson became calmer in mind. During the long months in the Mediterranean he had thought out the tactics he proposed to employ. He summed them up in a lucid memorandum – the well-tried formula of concentrating on a portion of the enemy's line and annihilating it in detail – and circulated it to his captains. Consideration for them, as always, was uppermost. When the *Superb*, badly in need of a refit, began retarding the speed of the Fleet, he sent a soothing message to Keats. 'I am fearful that you may think the *Superb* does not go as fast as I could wish. However that may be, I would have you be assured that I know and feel the *Superb* does all which is possible for a ship to accomplish; and I desire that you will not fret upon the occasion.' This attitude was in striking contrast to the methods of the French: Napoleon had forbidden Villeneuve to tell his captains even where they were going.

The Lesser Antilles, to which Nelson was bound, consist of a group of islands about a thousand miles long, stretching from north to south in the order Barbuda, Antigua, Guadeloupe, Dominica, Martinique, St Lucia, St Vincent, Grenada, Tobago and Trinidad: Barbados lies about one hundred miles to the eastwards of St Lucia. Most of the islands were in British possession, but Guadeloupe and Martinique were French.

Nelson arrived at Barbados on 4 June, where he found Rear-Admiral Cochrane and two ships which had been sent after Missiessy on his escape from Rochefort. From Cochrane and General Myers, Governor of the Leeward Islands, he learnt that a message had been received from General Brereton at St Lucia that the combined fleets had been sighted steering to the southward a week before. 'There is not a doubt in any of the admirals' or generals' mind,' wrote Nelson, 'but that Tobago and Trinidad are the enemy's objectives.' This was contrary to his own opinion, which was that Villeneuve had made for the safety of Martinique; but in the face of such positive information he could only submit, and having embarked two thousand troops sailed with the Fleet to the southwards. 'I resisted the opinion of General Brereton's information,' he wrote, 'till it would have been the height of presumption to have carried my beliefs further.'

Yet Nelson, with his extraordinary instincts, was right. Villeneuve had arrived at Martinique on 13 May and remained in the vicinity ever since. A thousand of his men had died of fever and another thousand were sick; and having heard that Missiessy had returned to France and with no news of Ganteaume he dared not undertake any large-scale operations. His only success was the capture of 'His Majesty's Sloop' Diamond Rock, an island pinnacle off Martinique which had been fortified by Sam Hood two years before. On 4 June Rear-Admiral Magon joined him with two battleships from France and instructions to wait for Ganteaume for another five weeks: if Ganteaume did not arrive he was to return to France, release the squadrons at Ferrol and appear in the Channel with thirty-three sail of the line; in the meantime he was to capture what British islands he could. Villeneuve accordingly sailed for Guadeloupe to embark troops for an attack on Barbuda.

Nelson meanwhile had arrived at Trinidad, found the roadstead empty and sailed northwards. On 9 June he received his first accurate information – that the enemy had been sighted off Dominica three days before. He was almost in despair. Had it not been for General Brereton's 'damned intelligence,' he said, he would have met Villeneuve where Rodney had defeated de Grasse twenty-five years earlier. He pushed northwards as fast as possible, but now it was too late. Villeneuve, on his way to Barbuda, had captured off Antigua a convoy of sugar-ships from which he learnt of Nelson's arrival. This was enough for him, and abandoning all his projects he crowded sail into the Atlantic. Nelson heard this at Antigua four days later. Fearful that Villeneuve might fall on British shipping in the Bay, he despatched the brig *Curieux* to England with news of his departure; then, after only a week's stay in the West Indies, he sailed after him.

The long return passage was as uneventful as the outward one. Not knowing Villeneuve's destination, Nelson steered for the Straits: it was still possible the enemy were bound for Egypt, and the protection of the Mediterranean was his first commitment. After the excitement of the last weeks, depression again settled in. 'Midnight,' he wrote in his diary on 21 June, 'nearly calm. Saw three planks which I think came from the French Fleet. Very miserable which is very foolish.' The responsibility for what he had done was his, but his disappointment he could share with his captains. Whenever the weather was fine he invited them to dine. 'I shall always be truly glad to see you,' he wrote to Keats; and to Captain Malcolm, 'I can give you little, for I got nothing except some trifles at Barbados; but accept the little I can offer you.' Such thoughtfulness had its own reward. 'We are all half-starved and otherwise inconvenienced by being so long away from a port,' wrote Captain Stopford, 'but our full recompense is – we are with Nelson.'

On 18 July Nelson sighted Cape Spartel, and a little later the squadron under Collingwood (who had relieved Orde) keeping watch at Cadiz. The frigates which he had sent on ahead rejoined him. 'No French Fleet,' he wrote, 'nor any information about them.'

Nor could there have been any: for unknown to Nelson Villeneuve was still labouring across the Atlantic. Unknown to him too the great weapon of British sea-power was coming into full operation. On 19 June, nine hundred miles north-east of Antigua, Captain Bettesworth in the *Curieux* sighted Villeneuve's fleet. Waiting only long enough to note their numbers and course, he pressed on his way. He reached Plymouth on 7 July, and late the following night was in London. Melville was no longer First Lord, for the Commissioners investigating the dockyards had revealed a misappropriation of funds at a time many years before, when he was on the Navy Board. His successor was Admiral Charles Middleton, Lord Barham, eighty years old but with his faculties intact and in the line of great naval administrators. He had gone to bed when Captain Bettesworth arrived and his staff did not wake him until the morning (for which he roundly cursed them). Then, while shaving, he made his dispositions. If Villeneuve was making for Cadiz or the Straits he would be met by Nelson and Collingwood, if for Brest by Cornwallis. But if he was heading for Rochefort or Ferrol neither of the blockading squadrons would be strong enough to meet him alone. He would therefore unite these squadrons under Admiral Calder and order him to take station one hundred miles west of Finisterre. Within four hours of this decision Admiralty messengers were on their way to Portsmouth and Plymouth.

On 12 July the orders reached Admiral Stirling at Rochefort. On the 15th his five battleships joined Calder's ten, and they sailed for their station. There, on 22 July, two days after Nelson had landed at Gibraltar (the first time he had set foot on shore for two years), they encountered the combined fleets. Barham's plans had worked to perfection. Here was the opportunity which Nelson had been seeking for three months of putting an end to Napoleon's schemes and destroying French naval power for a generation. But Calder was not of the stuff of Nelson. The battle, like the Glorious First of June, was indecisive. Calder broke off the action after capturing two Spanish ships and made no attempt to re-engage. 'I could not hope to succeed without receiving great damage,' he wrote; 'I had no friendly port to go to, and had the Ferrol and Rochefort squadrons come out, I must have fallen an easy prey.' Villeneuve, thankful for such a release, made sail for home.

Nelson heard of Bettesworth's arrival on 25 July, and sailed to the northward. But he was too late. The wind was against him and by the time he reached the latitude of Finisterre, Villeneuve and Gravina were in Ferrol. On 15 August he came into the Channel Fleet off Brest. Calder and Stirling had joined the day before so that Cornwallis now had under him thirty-six sail of the line. Such was the miracle of British sea-power. All the threads had been drawn together: England's Navy was concentrated at the time and place most necessary for her defence.

Nelson remained in the Fleet only two hours, for orders were waiting for him to proceed with the battered *Superb* to England. The only officer to communicate with him was Fremantle, now in command of the *Neptune*, 98: he sent over a bundle of the latest newspapers by his servant, who reported on return that Nelson looked 'very ill'. Then, having sent Louis thanks for his squadron's support, Nelson made sail up Channel.

On the way to Spithead Keats and Nelson discussed the contents of Fremantle's newspapers. All expressed anger at Calder's failure, and suggested that if Nelson had been in command it would have been a different story. But this was not Nelson's view. 'Who can, my dear Fremantle,' he wrote, 'command all the success which our country may wish? We have fought together and therefore well know what it is. I have had the best disposed fleet of friends, but who can say what will be the event of a Battle? and it most sincerely grieves me that in any of the papers it should be insinuated that Lord Nelson could have done better.'

On 18 August the *Victory* and *Superb* came to anchor at

Spithead. The next evening Nelson set out in the rain, for the last time, for Merton and London.

* * *

The ignorance of Englishmen as to sea affairs had been reflected during the past three months in the country's changing moods. First it was anger: people were shocked at the apparent ease with which the enemy moved in and out of port. 'Their idea is,' wrote Collingwood, 'that we are like sentinels standing at a door who must see and may interrupt all who attempt to go into it.' As the weeks passed without news of Nelson or the combined fleets they became afraid; and they blamed Nelson for his failure to find Villeneuve just as they had his failure to find Brueys. 'The cry is stirring up fast against him,' wrote Admiral Radstock to his son in the *Victory*, 'and the loss of Jamaica would sink all his past services into oblivion.' Then came the news of the pursuit across the Atlantic, Nelson's saving of the West Indies, and the return of the combined fleets to harbour.

The relief was enormous. Nelson's enterprise captured the public imagination like nothing before. At Portsmouth crowds thronged the ramparts and greeted his barge with prolonged huzzas. In London he was welcomed 'almost as a conqueror,' and could not go into the street without being surrounded by a mob. 'It is really quite affecting,' wrote Lord Minto, 'to see the wonder and admiration and love and respect of the whole world.'

Nelson took a more sober view. 'I am now set up as a conjuror,' he told Keats, 'and God knows they will soon find out I am far from one.' His mind was already on the future. On his first morning in London he called on the old First Lord, who, he confessed, was almost an entire stranger. Barham had been always sceptical of Nelson's reputation, but a half-hour's interview altered his opinion; and it was arranged that Nelson should return to the Mediterranean as soon as he and the *Victory* were ready.

Nelson divided the last ten days of August between Merton

and London. It was a time of bustle rather than repose, for he had many engagements to fill, his house was full of relations and there was a constant stream of visitors, among them the Duke of Clarence and his once difficult subordinate Sir Sidney Smith. But all the time he was thinking of when he would be called and of the tactics he would adopt when finally he fell in with the French Fleet. Captain Keats stopped at Merton after paying off the *Superb*, and to him, pacing the strip of grass he called the quarter-deck, Nelson outlined his tentative plan of attack.

The established system of conducting a sea-fight was for both fleets to converge from parallel lines, and for each ship to grapple with her opposite in the line. The disadvantage of this method, said Nelson, was that no day was long enough to obtain a decisive result. He would therefore form his fleet into three divisions. One would be kept in reserve to be employed by the admiral commanding it as circumstances required. With the other two divisions in line abreast, he would launch his attack at right angles to the enemy's line. He hoped to break the line at about a third of the way from the vanship: the van and rear would be immobilized, the centre crushed: it was the embodiment of his favourite dictum: 'Only numbers can annihilate'. 'What do you think of it?' he asked Keats, and then before Keats could reply, he exclaimed: 'I'll tell you what I think of it. I think it will surprise and confound the enemy. They won't know what I am about. It will bring forward a pell-mell battle, and that is what I want.'

The call came sooner than Nelson expected. When Napoleon heard of Villenueve's return to Ferrol he was waiting with his army at Boulogne. Furious at his failure, he ordered him to sail again. On 13 August Villeneuve left Ferrol with an augmented fleet of twenty-nine sail of the line. News of his departure reached England soon after Nelson's arrival and people again became uneasy. But Villeneuve did not get far. His ships were rotten, the crews seasick and mutinous, and he knew that he could not reach the Channel without fighting Cornwallis. On 15 August he abandoned the enterprise and fled for Cadiz.

Collingwood guarding the approaches with three sail retired southwards; then having sent for Calder and Bickerton and despatched the *Euryalus* to England, he resumed his watch.

The *Euryalus* made a five-day passage to Lymington, and on the evening of 1 September Captain Blackwood set out in a post-chaise for London. At five the next morning he reached Merton and found Nelson already up and dressed. There was no need to explain his arrival. 'I am sure you bring me news of the French and Spanish Fleets,' said Nelson, 'and I think I shall yet have to beat them.' Blackwood went on to London where the news soon spread. 'Thank God, thank God, a thousand and a thousand times,' wrote Lord Radstock to Nelson, 'that these Jack O'Lanterns are once more safely housed without having done that mischief which was so justly to be dreaded.' From the Channel greater news followed. Disgusted by the timidity of his admirals, Napoleon had given up his plans for invasion, broken camp, and marched southwards to face a new Russo-Austrian alliance which Pitt had once more brought into being. The Grand Army had bowed to British sea-power.

England was now ready to take the offensive. On the morning of Blackwood's arrival Nelson followed him to the Admiralty and saw the First Lord. He agreed to join the Fleet as soon as the *Victory* was ready. His command was to include the whole of the Mediterranean, Gibraltar, and the approaches to Cadiz.

At the end of the interview Barham picked up a copy of the Navy List and asked Nelson to choose his captains. 'Choose yourself, my Lord,' replied Nelson, 'the same spirit actuates the whole profession. You cannot choose wrong.' But Barham insisted. With his vast experience he knew, as St Vincent had known in 1798, and Nelson himself knew, the importance of dependable subordinates. 'Have no scruples, Lord Nelson, there is my secretary. Give your orders to him and rely on it that they shall be implicitly obeyed.'

Most of the captains of Nelson's choice were already with the Fleet. But there was one he could help. Two days before he had received another letter from Berry with the postmark Edinburgh. Two changes at the Admiralty had led Berry to hope for employment, but all his requests had been turned down. The consequence, he said, was disgust on his part and a resolve to apply no more; and he had taken his wife on a tour of the Lake District and Highlands. 'A man's standing in the Service,' he wrote bitterly; 'and his reputation – and who has not that reputation that served with you – all goes for nought. I know Your Lordship will do what you can.' Such an appeal was not to be resisted.

There was some doubt as to Hardy's ability to serve. The long months at sea had brought on severe rheumatism, and on arrival at Portsmouth he was very ill. However a week's convalescence in Dorset (during which he had a long audience with the King on his last visit to Weymouth) restored him to health; and on the day after Blackwood's arrival he returned to Portsmouth. Admiral Murray was no longer available as he was executor for his father-in-law's estate; Nelson, feeling he could find no adequate substitute, left the post vacant.

Nelson's last ten days in England are among the most romantic of his life. In his own time it was not Trafalgar that stamped his fame but the years of endurance that led to it. The chase to the West Indies had established the country's faith in him as never before; and when people heard that he was going out once more, nothing could restrain them. Messages of goodwill poured in from all over England. From Wales and Guernsey, Foley and Saumarez sent congratulations: Sam Sutton called in person at Merton: Admiral Murray waited for him at Portsmouth. In London Lords Hood and Radstock sent messages they would shake his hand at any place, day and hour he cared to name. The Prince of Wales, just back from Stowe where he had been a fellow guest with Betsey, summoned him to Carlton House to say goodbye. Pitt, at his last interview, accompanied him to the door of Downing Street. 'I do not think,' said Nelson proudly, 'he would have done so much for a prince of the blood.'

Lord Minto said that Nelson's reception on his arrival was

307

beyond anything in a play or a poem. So, too, was his departure. It is impossible to read the story of the last weeks of his life without feeling that it was part of a predestined pattern.

Nelson's genius was composed of many parts. There was his devotion to duty, his singleness of mind, his courage, his humanity, his humility, his pride; but greater than all of these was his surrender to his destiny. What makes his story one of the great natural tragedies of all time is his certainty of approaching death and conquest of the spirit over it. During these last days the thought of return hardly entered his head. Before leaving London he called on the upholsterers who were storing Hallowell's coffin and told them, lightheartedly enough, that he might soon need it. On the night of his departure from Merton he prayed by the bedside of his daughter; then, before entering the coach, he wrote in his private diary.

'*Friday night*. At half past ten, drove from dear, dear Merton where I left all which I hold dear in this world to go to serve my King and Country. May the great God whom I adore, enable me to fulfil the expectations of my country; and if it is His good pleasure that I should return, my thanks will never cease being offered up to the throne of His mercy. If it is His good Providence to cut short my days upon earth, I bow with the greatest submission, relying that He will protect those so dear to me, that I may leave behind. Amen. Amen. Amen.'

He arrived at Portsmouth early the next morning and was met by Hardy. He despatched his business by noon and in the afternoon made his way to the bathing-machines where the *Victory*'s barge was awaiting him. The story of his final departure is told in Southey's famous words:

'A crowd collected in his train, pressing forward to obtain a sight of his face – many were in tears and many knelt down before him and blessed him as he passed. All men knew that his heart was as humane as it was fearless; that there was not in his nature the slightest alloy of selfishness or cupidity; but that with perfect and entire devotion he served his country with all his heart and with all his soul and with all his strength: and therefore they loved him as truly and fervently as he loved England.'

He embarked in the barge with Hardy, and the crowds thronged upon the parapet waved after him. He turned to Hardy and murmured: 'I had their huzzas before. Now I have their hearts.' It was what he had always wanted.

Next morning the *Victory* and *Euryalus* made sail out of harbour and set course for Cape Trafalgar.

* * *

During the past month Collingwood had been keeping watch off Cadiz. On 22 August he was joined by Bickerton and four sail from the Mediterranean, and a week later by eighteen sail under Calder, including the remnant of Nelson's Mediterranean Fleet. With this force he waited for Nelson's arrival.

Collingwood was not a popular officer. It is odd he should have been such a friend of Nelson, for no two men could have been less like. 'In the life of Lord Collingwood,' wrote George Elliot many years later, 'he is represented as the kindest-hearted and most considerate old man possible. I was many years in company with him and always considered him a selfish old bear. That he was a brave, stubborn, persevering and determined officer everyone acknowledged, but he had few, if any, friends and no admirers. In body and mind he was iron, and very cold iron.'

Collingwood's conduct of the Fleet was the very opposite to that of Nelson. The measures which he had condemned in St Vincent five years earlier he now practised himself. He seldom entertained, he discouraged intercourse between his captains, he allowed no neutral provision boats to enter the Fleet. His officers did not take to this kindly. They did not want society so much for its own sake as for what Codrington called 'that harmony so essential to a fleet destined to act well together *of binding the captains to their admiral*'. Calder, said Codrington, had no opportunity of entertaining his captains except by chance. 'A court martial on board his ship yesterday admitted us to as social a dinner as I was ever at. It was really a most animating sight; an admiral surrounded by twenty of his captains in social intercourse, showing a strong desire to support each other cordially and manfully in the event of battle.'

But such occasions were rare. The captains became disgruntled and their only consolation, said Fremantle, lay in the arrival of Nelson. 'I expect very soon to see your Lordship's handwriting at the bottom of my order,' Louis wrote, 'believe me it would be one of the first comforts I could name.' Codrington exclaimed in despair: 'For charity's sake, send us Lord Nelson, oh, ye men of power!'

He came at last on 28 September, and his coming was more wonderful than he or they had dreamed. 'Lord Nelson is arrived,' wrote Codrington, 'and a sort of general joy has been the consequence.' On his first two evenings all the admirals and captains dined in the *Victory*. 'The reception I met with on joining the Fleet,' he wrote, 'caused the sweetest sensation of my life. The officers who came on board to welcome my return forgot my rank as Commander-in-Chief in the enthusiasm with which they greeted me.' Fremantle told Betsey: 'The whole system here is so completely changed that it wears quite a different aspect'. Captain Duff of the *Mars*, an officer unknown to Nelson, wrote: 'He is so good and pleasant a man that we all like to do what he likes without any kind of orders. He is the pleasantest admiral I ever served under.'

For his Mediterranean captains Nelson had a special word. 'I was truly glad to see my old friends again,' he wrote to Louis, 'I have much to tell you.' Fremantle dined in the *Victory* with only Collingwood as his fellow guest; and Nelson gave him a letter from Harriet that Betsey had been safely delivered of her third daughter. Fremantle thought Hardy very ill – 'twenty years older than when I last saw him,' but well suited to his job: Nelson had 'grown fatter' and looked better than ever. 'I staid with him until eight at night – he would not let me leave him before. He desired me to come to him whenever I chose and to dine with him as often as convenient.'

Greetings over, Nelson made preparations for battle; for he

knew that the presence of so many ships in Cadiz would strain its resources to breaking-point and that soon Villeneuve must put to sea. He removed the Fleet from within sight of Cadiz to about fifty miles to the westward, so as to lure Villeneuve out and prevent his own ships from being driven into the Mediterranean by a westerly gale. He posted Blackwood in the *Euryalus* off the harbour approaches and kept communication with him by a chain of battleships. 'Let me know every movement,' he told him. 'I rely on you that we can't miss getting hold of them. Watch all points and all winds and weathers.'

Stocks of food and water were very low and Nelson ordered his ships to proceed to Gibraltar in rotation to re-provision. The first to go were Rear-Admiral Louis's squadron consisting of the *Canopus*, *Queen*, *Spencer*, *Tigre* and *Zealous*. Louis and Hallowell were heartbroken. 'You are sending us away, my Lord,' complained Louis, 'the enemy will come out and we shall have no share in the battle.' Nelson comforted him. 'The enemy will come out and we shall fight them; and I send you first to insure your being here to help beat them.' But Louis had spoken to Nelson for the last time.

On 9 October Nelson circulated his famous memorandum of attack – the final version of the plan he had outlined to Keats in the garden of Merton. He had already described it to the admirals and captains on the two nights after his arrival, and its effect had been magical. 'When I came to explain to them the Nelson touch,' he told Lady Hamilton, 'it was like an electric shock. Some shed tears, all approved. "It was new – it was singular – it was simple!" and from admirals downwards it was repeated, "It must succeed if ever they will allow us to get at them".'

The memorandum opened with the celebrated phrase: 'The order of sailing is to be the order of battle'. This was to save time, for every moment was precious. Then followed the plan of attack: two divisions to break the enemy's line at the centre, the third to support one of the other two. But it was not to be adhered to rigidly. 'Nothing is sure in a sea-fight beyond all others . . . In case signals can neither be seen nor perfectly understood, no captain can do very wrong if he places his ship alongside that of an enemy.' Here, in a few words, was what Nelson practised and encouraged all his life – flexibility in the interpretation of orders. It was what made him turn out of the line at St Vincent; it was what won him the Battle of the Nile; it was the great quality which stamped his conduct of the Fleet and was to be a pattern for it afterwards.

And during these last days Nelson worked for that other great ideal which had served him so well in the past – perfect cohesion of the Fleet, the 'binding of captains to their admirals.' 'I am not come forth to find difficulties,' he wrote to Ball, 'but to remove them.' Collingwood complained of his new flag-captain, Rotherham. 'We can, my dear Coll, have no little jealousies,' Nelson reminded him. 'In the presence of the enemy, all Englishmen should be as brothers.' Louis, on his way to Gibraltar, informed Nelson that Blackwood was not keeping his proper station. Blackwood wrote testily to Nelson refuting it. 'Do not, my dear Blackwood,' replied Nelson, 'be angry with anyone. It was only a laudable anxiety in Admiral Louis and nothing like complaining.' To Admiral Knight he wrote: 'In our several stations, my dear Admiral, we must all put our shoulders together, and make the great machine of the Fleet intrusted to our charge go on smoothly'.

In keeping with this attitude was his treatment of Sir Robert Calder. Public opinion against Calder had been stirring up fast: Nelson's brilliant pursuit to the West Indies had made Calder's failure seem all the more lamentable. ('We are all raving mad at Sir Robert Calder,' wrote one lady. 'I could have done better myself.') On joining the Fleet Nelson had the unpleasant duty of informing Calder of the Admiralty's disapprobation and that a court of inquiry had been ordered. Calder had been at sea ever since his action, and had little idea of the stir against him. 'Sir Robert has an ordeal to pass through,' Nelson told Collingwood, 'which he little expects.' Calder begged Nelson to be allowed to return home in his flag-ship, the *Prince of Wales*; and subject to the arrival of reinforcements, Nelson agreed. But with Louis's squadron at

Gibraltar, Nelson could hardly deprive the Fleet of a 90-gun ship. When Calder heard he was to go home in a frigate, he wrote to Nelson: 'The contents of your Lordship's letter have cut me to the soul. If I am to be turned out of my ship, after all that has passed, I have only to request I may be allowed to take my captain and such officers as I find necessary for the justification of my conduct as an officer, and that I may be permitted to go without a moment's loss of time. My heart is broken.' Nelson's humanity could not resist this appeal; and though Calder was no friend, he gave him permission to return in the *Prince of Wales*, thus depriving himself on the eve of battle of one of his most powerful ships. 'I may be thought wrong as an officer to disobey the orders of the Admiralty,' he wrote to Barham, 'but I trust that I shall be considered to have done right as a man, and to a brother officer in affliction – my heart could not stand it and so the thing must rest.'

Calder's departure reduced Nelson's force to twenty-eight sail, but the balance was partly restored by the arrival of Berry in the *Agamemnon*. Berry had had an exciting passage, having fallen foul of the Rochefort squadron the night before; and only superb seamanship had enabled him to escape. The *Agamemnon* was the ship in which, ten years earlier on the Riviera, Nelson had assumed command of his first detached squadron. It was a happy circumstance that she should arrive to take part in his last battle, commanded by her old first lieutenant and one of his most devoted admirers. The same day Nelson ordered William Hoste to transfer from the *Eurydice* to the *Amphion* in place of Sam Sutton, invalided home: Hoste was another old *Agamemnon* officer who had taken the Nile despatches to Naples in the *Mutine*. That day too the frigate *Aurora* passed the Fleet and Nelson spoke with her captain, George Elliot, Foley's signal midshipman in the *Goliath*. From Sir Thomas Thompson he received a letter and from Saumarez a present of some papers and a case of wine. ('I take it very kind of him,' he told Collingwood.)

Berry's reputation as a fighter was proverbial and his arrival caused a wave of optimism. 'Sir E. Berry is such a bearer of good fortune,' Blackwood wrote to Nelson, 'that I feel the enemy will make a bolt.' Nelson was more laconic. 'Here comes that fool Berry. Now we shall have a fight.' Six days later, at seven in the morning, the *Euryalus* was observed flying the long-awaited signal: 'The Enemy is coming out of port.'

CHAPTER 17

When Napoleon was breaking camp at Boulogne news reached him that Pitt's secret expedition had arrived at Malta, and that the Kingdom of the Two Sicilies were pressing for the evacuation of the French from Naples. He suddenly became aware of the danger that threatened his rear: England, Russia and Austria were combining in a gigantic plan to overthrow him. He at once turned his attention to the Continent. 'I shall invade Germany with 200,000 men,' he told Talleyrand, 'and shall not halt until I have reached Vienna.'

The fleets which had failed him in the Channel were to form a part of his schemes. They were to sail from Cadiz for the Mediterranean with the first favourable wind, pick up the Spanish squadron at Cartagena, and proceed to Naples to meet the British and Russian invasion.

Villeneuve received these orders at Cadiz on 28 September. He intended to sail immediately, but next day heard of Nelson's arrival and a rumour that he was going to attack the combined fleets in port. All the crews were put on harbour defence. Nothing having materialized by 8 October, Villeneuve called a council. It was agreed that with Nelson in the offing, the combined fleet could not hope to reach the Mediterranean unharmed, and that a more favourable opportunity, such as a gale which would scatter the British Fleet, should be awaited.

Soon after, two events occurred to change Villeneuve's mind. On 15 October he learnt that Admiral Rosily had arrived at Madrid on his way to relieve him; three days later that Louis's squadron had sailed from Gibraltar to the east-

CUTHBERT, BARON COLLINGWOOD

From the portrait by Howard, probably painted posthumously from an original, showing full-dress uniform of a rear-admiral. The decorations are the medals of the First of June, St. Vincent, and Trafalgar. The original appears to have been painted before Trafalgar, where Collingwood was a vice-admiral, and the Trafalgar Medal added afterwards.

THE EVE OF COPENHAGEN

From the artist's signed proof of a painting by Thomas Davidson.
The scene is the cabin of the *Elephant* on the evening of April 1st,

1801. Rear-Admiral Graves is standing on Nelson's right. The officer in the foreground having his glass filled is Riou. Also present were Hardy, Fremantle and Foley.

WILLIAM HOSTE
Portrait by an unidentified artist.

HENRY BLACKWOOD
From the portrait by Hoppner.

EDWARD RIOU
From the miniature by Shelley.

RICHARD KEATS
From the portrait by Jackson.

wards. He did not know that Nelson had been reinforced by single ships from England and imagined that his force was twenty-three sail as opposed to his thirty-three. Such a favourable moment might not come again and he resolved to clear his honour by a decisive victory. 'It would be too terrible for me,' he wrote, 'to lose an opportunity of showing I was worthy of a better fate.' On 18 October he wrote to Decrès: 'I shall put to sea tomorrow'.

When at nine-thirty next day Nelson received Blackwood's signal that the enemy were leaving harbour he was fifty miles out in the Atlantic. He hoisted the signals 'General Chase' and 'Prepare for Battle,' and stood with the Fleet towards the Straits. They continued under a press of canvas all day, but by one o'clock next morning when they reached the entrance to the Straits there was no sign of the enemy. Nor, as Nelson had hoped, was there any news of Louis.

Unknown to him the combined fleets had had great difficulty in leaving harbour and were only now clearing the coast: they were steering to the north-westwards so as to get a clear run through the Straits. Nelson heard this news at 7 a.m. and wore his fleet on to a parallel course. Visibility was poor and Blackwood did not have another opportunity of speaking to Nelson until the afternoon. 'The enemy,' he telegraphed, 'appears determined to push to the westwards.' 'That they shall not do,' wrote Nelson in his diary, 'if in the power of Nelson and Bronte to prevent them.' And he signalled to Blackwood: 'I rely on your keeping sight of the enemy'.

By 2 p.m. the combined fleets were well clear of the coast, and stood southwards for the Straits. Nelson continued on his northerly course, for he was afraid that if he showed himself too soon Villeneuve might bolt for Cadiz. Collingwood had come on board the day before, and urged him to attack at once. But Nelson was not the hot-blooded fighter he is sometimes represented: before every action he weighed the chances and made his dispositions accordingly. What he wanted was a full day's fighting, for only this could assure him the annihilating victory he had planned. To begin an action which might be broken off by darkness or by Villeneuve bolting for Cadiz would be worse than no action at all. Not until 8 p.m., when the combined fleets were to the eastwards of him, did he too turn south.

There was nothing to do now but maintain his distance and bearing from the enemy and alter the course of his Fleet as they altered theirs. He signalled his night instructions to Blackwood: 'If the enemy are standing to the southwards or towards the Straits burn two blue lights together every hour in order to make the greater blaze. If the enemy are standing to the westwards, three guns quick, every hour.' That evening he entertained a party of midshipmen to dinner. 'To-morrow,' he said to them, 'I will do that which will give you younger gentlemen something to talk and think about for the rest of your lives. But I shall not live to know about it myself.'

The two fleets steered southwards all night. At four in the morning the British Fleet again wore to the northwards. This was a preliminary to the attack and to cut off Villeneuve's line of retreat from Cadiz. Then at six-thirty Nelson hoisted the signal for his twenty-seven ships to form order of sailing in two columns (the third he discarded owing to lack of numbers), to steer eastwards towards the enemy fleet, and to prepare for battle.

Slowly the great ships took up their stations. In the weather column the *Victory* was followed by the *Téméraire, Neptune, Leviathan, Conqueror, Britannia, Agamemnon, Ajax, Orion, Minotaur* and *Spartiate*: a mile to the southward Collingwood's lee column formed up in the order *Royal Sovereign, Belleisle, Mars, Tonnant, Bellerophon, Colossus, Achilles, Revenge, Polyphemus, Swiftsure, Defence, Thunderer, Prince* and *Defiance*. Ten miles away on the eastern horizon, Villeneuve was standing to the southward with his thirty-three ships strung out in one single column. He watched Nelson's approach for about half an hour: then his nerve failed and he turned to the northward to bring Cadiz under his lee. By this manoeuvre Admiral Dumanoir Le Pelley in the *Formidable* led the van, Villeneuve in the *Bucentaure* and Admiral Cisneros in the *Santissima Trinidad* were in the centre, and Gravina in the *Principe de Asturias* commanded the rear. But Villeneuve was now too far to the southward to have any hopes of reaching Cadiz. Nelson swung his column a point or two to the northwards and signalled to Collingwood: 'I mean to attack the enemy's van and centre'.

Never did seamen prepare for action with more confidence in themselves and in the outcome. An officer in the *Belleisle* wrote that he was woken by the cheering of the crew, and that the delight on their faces exceeded anything he had ever witnessed. The first lieutenant of the *Ajax* found some of his men polishing the guns 'as if for an inspection,' and others dancing a hornpipe. 'All seemed deeply anxious to come to close quarters with the enemy.' During the morning the ships' companies were piped to dinner. The crew of the *Tonnant* sat down to bread and cheese and ale. 'Believe me,' said one of them, 'we ate and drank and were as cheerful as ever we were over a pot of beer.' The composure of the officers was also remarked on. An officer who spoke to Collingwood several times during the day was amazed that 'he did not show the slightest change from his ordinary manner'. His flag-captain, Rotherham, was asked to remove his cocked hat as it would make a mark for enemy sharpshooters. He replied he had always fought in a cocked hat and always would.

Yet no one doubted the gravity of what lay ahead. Many officers and men made their wills. A sailor in the *Revenge* heard one of his shipmates say: 'If one of Johnny Crapaud's shots knocks my head off, you will take all my effects; and if you are killed and I am not, why I will have all yours'. Nelson sent a last line to Lady Hamilton: Captains Blackwood and Duff wrote to their wives that they hoped to prove themselves worthy of them. Midshipman Aikenhead expressed his feelings to his family much as Midshipman Thorp had done before Santa Cruz: 'Should I, my dear parents, fall in defence of my King, let that thought console you. I feel not the least dread of my spirits. Accept, perhaps for the last time, your son's love.' Of these officers, only Blackwood was to survive the day.

In the *Victory* Nelson was making his own final preparations. He had sent for Blackwood early in the day and told him that he meant to keep him on board until the last minute, as he was going to 'bleed' the captains of the frigates. Blackwood asked if he might have the command of one of the two battleships whose captains had gone home as witnesses for Sir Robert Calder. Nelson refused him, saying it was their first lieutenants' 'birthrights'; but the mention of his unfortunate admiral struck a sympathetic chord. 'Hardy,' he said, 'what would poor Sir Robert Calder give to be with us now?'

Soon after Blackwood arrived Nelson took him and Hardy to his cabin to witness a last codicil to his will, in which he left Lady Hamilton and his daughter Horatia 'as a legacy to my King and country'. Then the two captains accompanied Nelson on an inspection of the mess-decks where the men of a dozen nations were waiting by their guns. Several times Nelson asked Blackwood how many prizes he thought they would take. Blackwood suggested fourteen would be 'a glorious result'. Nelson replied: 'I shall not be satisfied with anything less than twenty'.

Many of Nelson's officers were concerned about his safety, for which he showed his usual disregard. Hardy pointed out that his medals and orders would make him a conspicuous target for enemy riflemen. Nelson agreed, but said it was now too late to be shifting a coat. Blackwood urged him to move his flag to the *Euryalus* where it would be easier to conduct the battle. Nelson said that he would not hear of it and gave as his reason, 'the force of example'. The two captains then persuaded him to let the *Victory* drop back to third in the line, as it was essential that he should keep out of fire as long as possible. Blackwood went over to the *Téméraire* and *Neptune* to order them ahead. But Nelson made to attempt to shorten sail, and when the *Téméraire* crept up on his quarter he shouted over: 'I'll thank you, Captain Harvey, to keep in your proper station'. A few minutes later Fremantle received the same curt order.

A little after eleven o'clock Nelson retired to his cabin to

compose his farewell prayer, one of the most moving passages
ever written in the English language. With the opening lines he
sketched in, simply and fittingly, the background picture, the
fulfilment of his life's work. 'At daylight saw the enemy's
combined fleet from East to E.S.E. Bore away. Made the signal
for order of sailing and to prepare for battle.' This was the
overture: then, with a humility matched only by his transcendent courage, he gave himself up to his destiny. 'May the Great
God whom I worship grant to my country and for the benefit
of Europe in general, a great and glorious victory; and may no
misconduct in anyone tarnish it; and may humanity after
victory be the predominant feature in the British Fleet. For
myself individually I commit my life to Him who made me,
and may his blessing light upon my endeavours for serving
my country faithfully. To him I resign myself and the just
cause which is entrusted to me to defend. Amen. Amen.
Amen.'

Lieutenant Pasco, the flag-lieutenant, now entered the cabin
on some personal request. He found the admiral kneeling at
his desk in prayer, and withdrew. ('I could not at such a
moment disturb him with any grievances of mine.') Nelson
followed him to the poop. The wind had dropped almost
entirely, but a heavy swell was setting from the westward,
which heralded the approach of a storm. Fearful that after the
battle the Fleet would be driven on a lee shore, Nelson signalled
to prepare to anchor at the close of day.

It was at this moment, all preparations having been made,
that he asked Blackwood whether he did not think that one
more signal was wanting. After consultation with him and
Hardy he called to his flag-lieutenant: 'Mr Pasco, I wish to
say to the Fleet, "England confides that every man will do
his duty". You must be quick for I have one more signal to
make which is for close action.' Pasco asked if he might substitute 'expects' for 'confides' as the former was in the signal
book and the latter not. 'That will do,' replied Nelson, 'make
it directly.' Throughout the Fleet the signal was received with
bursts of cheering: on some the effect was described as 'truly

sublime': others, who missed the emotional content ('Do our duty?' cried one man. 'Why, of course we'll do our duty.'), were happy that their beloved admiral had remembered them.

The distance between the two fleets was now less than a mile. The scene, as one captain described it, was 'beautiful' and one which few ever forgot. The clouds had disappeared and the pale blue of the sky contrasted with the richer colour of the sea. The combined fleets, still standing to the northward with the wind on their larboard beam were strung out in one long crescent, the bulge towards the coast. Some of their ships were painted black, others black with red and yellow streaks. In the centre, shining in scarlet and white and with a huge, white figurehead of the Holy Trinity, towered the four-decked *Santissima Trinidad*, which in these waters had struck to Saumarez eight years earlier. The British Fleet had kept their formation of two columns, about a mile apart, with Collingwood's slightly in the lead: the figurehead of his ship was a full-length carving of George III, wearing the battle-dress of a Roman emperor and with the twin emblems of Fame and Fortune blowing golden trumpets on either side. As the great ships, with their black-and-yellow chequered hulls and carrying a full spread of canvas, glided through the water, they looked like a flock of huge, white birds. On board many of their bands were playing 'Britons, strike home,' and 'Rule, Britannia!'

The last twenty minutes were the most exacting of all. There is nothing more trying for a fighting man than to remain static under fire, having the means but not the sanction to reply to it. The enemy, being beam on to the British columns, were able to open fire first, and before long had begun to inflict casualties. The anxiety to return fire was very great, if only as a means of covering the ships in smoke; but the captains' orders were explicit and no one disobeyed them. Villeneuve, watching this slow relentless approach, animal-like in its stealth, was quite unnerved. 'Nothing but victory,' he murmured to his officers, 'can attend such gallant conduct.'

A little after noon Nelson watched Collingwood break the

enemy's line between the *Santa Ana* and the *Fougeux*. 'See how that noble fellow Collingwood carries his ship into action,' he cried. His own turn was about to come, and now it was time to say goodbye to the faithful Blackwood. 'I can do no more,' he said to him. 'We must trust to the Great Disposer of all events, and to the justice of our cause. I thank God for this great opportunity of doing my duty.' They shook hands at the front of the poop. 'I trust, my Lord,' said Blackwood, 'that on my return to the *Victory* I shall find your Lordship well and in the possession of twenty prizes.' Nelson's reply remained with him for the rest of his life: 'God bless you, Blackwood. I shall never speak to you again'.

During the last few hundred yards of her approach the *Victory* ran through a curtain of fire. Her steering-wheel was smashed, her sails and rigging cut to pieces: there were many casualties on the upper deck, including Nelson's secretary Mr Scott. As Nelson and Hardy were pacing the deck a splinter tore off the buckle of Hardy's shoe. 'This is too warm work to last long,' said Nelson. Then the moment came for breaking the enemy's line. Their ships were so close together that Hardy called out that he could not get through without running on board the *Bucentaure* or *Redoubtable*. 'I cannot help it,' replied Nelson. 'Go on board which you please.' The *Victory* crossed the wake of the *Bucentaure* and poured the whole of her larboard broadside into her stern, killing and wounding 400 men: then she ranged up alongside the *Redoubtable*. One by one the other ships followed her into action.

For the next three hours the battle raged with a ferocity that equalled Copenhagen. 'When the game began,' said a sailor of the *Royal Sovereign*, 'I wished myself at Warnborough with the plough; but when they had given us one duster, I bid fear kiss my bottom and set to in good earnest.' Midshipman Castle of the same ship told his family: 'It was glorious work. I think you would have liked to see me thump it into her quarters'. Many ships fought so closely that their guns touched the enemy hulls. After each salvo the crew of the *Victory* poured water on the sides of the *Redoubtable*, so as to prevent both ships from catching fire. Soon the smoke between decks became so thick the guns' crews could not see their neighbours. 'All that they knew,' said one seaman, 'was the crash of the shot smashing through the rending timbers, and then followed the hoarse bellowings of the captains of the guns as men were missed at the posts, calling out to the survivors, "Close up there, close up." ' The slaughter was terrible. With her first broadside the *Royal Sovereign* killed and wounded more than half the crew of the *Fougeux*. Of the *Redoubtable*'s ship's company of 600, 490 were killed and 81 wounded. Dr Scott, the chaplain of the *Victory*, described the cockpit as a butcher's shambles.

Stories of individual bravery were legion. Under the terrible fire of the British guns, the enemy ships began to drop out of action one by one, and orders were given for boarders. Captain Durham of the *Defiance* ordered Midshipman Jack Spratt to take possession of *L'Aigle*. All the *Defiance*'s boats were smashed, so Spratt placed a sword in his teeth and an axe in his belt and calling to the others to follow him, plunged into the sea. But the noise of the guns drowned his orders and he reached *L'Aigle*'s stern alone. He fought his way single-handed from the gunroom to the poop, killing and wounding several men, and although badly wounded himself, succeeded in holding the poop until the two ships touched and his comrades were able to jump over and relieve him. A seaman of the *Conqueror*, whose leg was amputated, said to the surgeon: 'Ah, Mr Beattie, I shall live now half as cheap as before: one pair of stockings will serve me twice as long'. In the *Tonnant* a splinter almost severed a gunner's toe from his foot. An officer urged him to go to the cockpit and have it dressed. 'No, sir, I am not the fellow to go below for a scratch', and taking out his knife he calmly cut his toe away. Captain Cooke of the *Bellerophon* was killed at almost the same moment as his lifelong friend, Captain Duff of the *Mars*. As he fell to the deck his quartermaster ran up to carry him below. 'No, let me lie quietly a minute,' said Cooke; a moment later he uttered his last words: 'Tell Cumby never to strike'.

At about the same moment Nelson fell, struck by a bullet

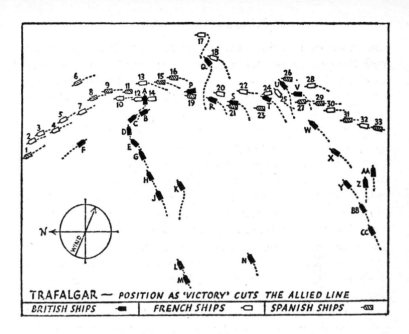

TRAFALGAR — POSITION AS 'VICTORY' CUTS THE ALLIED LINE

BRITISH SHIPS	FRENCH SHIPS	SPANISH SHIPS

British Ships	Guns	French Ships	Guns	Spanish Ships	Guns
A VICTORY	100	2 SCIPION (t.)	74	1 NEPTUNO (t.r.w.)	80
B TÉMÉRAIRE	98	3 INTRÉPIDE (t.b.)	74	6 RAYO (t.w.)	100
C NEPTUNE	98	4 FORMIDABLE (t.)	80	8 S. FRANCISCO DE ASIS (w.)	74
D LEVIATHAN	74	5 MONT BLANC (t.)	74		
E CONQUEROR	74	7 DUGUAY-TROUIN (t.)	74	9 S. AUGUSTIN (t.b.)	74
F AFRICA	64	10 HÉROS (e.)	74	11 ST'MA TRINIDAD (t.s.)	130
G BRITANNIA	100	12 BUCENTAURE (t.r.w.)	80	15 S. JUSTO (e.)	74
H AJAX	74	13 NEPTUNE (e.)	80	16 S. LEANDRO (e.)	64
J AGAMEMNON	64	14 REDOUTABLE (t.s.)	74	19 STA. ANA (t.r.)	112
K ORION	74	17 INDOMPTABLE (w.)	80	21 MONARCA (t.w.)	74
L MINOTAUR	74	18 FOUGUEUX (t.w.)	74	23 BAHAMA (t.w.)	74
M SPARTIATE	74	20 PLUTON (e.)	74	26 ARGONAUTA (t.s.)	80
N PRINCE	98	22 ALGÉSIRAS (t.r.)	74	27 MONTAÑÉS (e.)	74
P ROYAL SOVEREIGN	100	24 AIGLE (t.w.)	74	29 S. ILDEFONSO (t.)	74
Q BELLEISLE	74	25 SWIFTSURE (t.)	74	31 P. DE ASTURIAS (e.)	112
R MARS	74	28 ARGONAUTE (e.)	74	33 S. JUAN NEPOMUCENO (t.)	74
S TONNANT	80	30 ACHILLE (b.)	74		
T BELLEROPHON	74	32 BERWICK (t.w.)	74		
U COLOSSUS	74				
V ACHILLE	74				
W REVENGE	74				
X DEFIANCE	74				
Y DREADNOUGHT	98				
Z SWIFTSURE	74				
AA POLYPHEMUS	64	(b.)—Burnt		(t.)—taken	
BB THUNDERER	98	(e.)—escaped		(t.r.)—taken then retaken	
CC DEFENCE	74	(s.)—sunk		(w.)—wrecked	

from a sharpshooter in the *Redoubtable*'s rigging. Hardy ran up to help him. 'Hardy, I believe they have done for me at last,' he heard him say. 'I hope not, my Lord.' 'Yes,' came the sure reply, 'my backbone is shot through.'

* * *

Three marines raised him gently in their arms to carry him to the cockpit. He placed a handkerchief over his face so that the crew might not know what had happened. Although suffering greatly, his mind remained alert. Observing that the tiller's ropes which had been shot away had not yet been replaced, he called to a midshipman to tell Hardy of it.

At the entrance to the cockpit Dr Beatty, the surgeon, and Mr Burke, the purser, lifted Nelson from the arms of the marines. They stumbled, and Nelson asked who was carrying him. When told, he said: 'Ah, Mr Beatty, you can do nothing for me. I have but a short time to live. My backbone is shot through.'

Dr Beatty laid him against the ship's side, stripped him of his clothes and covered him with a white sheet. He examined the wound but could find no injury to the backbone. He asked Nelson what were his symptoms. Nelson replied that he felt a gush of blood in his breast every minute, and that he had no feeling in the lower part of his body. Beatty knew then that there could be no hope, but he kept the news from all except Hardy, Burke and Dr Scott.

For the next hour, surrounded by his wounded officers and men, and attended by the chaplain and purser, Nelson lay quietly in the *Victory*'s cockpit. From time to time sounds of cheering came to him from above. He asked what it signified and was told by Pasco who, also wounded, lay a little way from him, that another ship had struck. He began to get very hot and repeatedly asked to be fanned and for a drink of lemonade. Dr Scott and Mr Burke comforted him, saying that he would still live to bring home the news of a glorious victory. 'It is nonsense, Mr Burke, to suppose I can live,' he replied. 'My sufferings are great but they will soon be over.'

During this time Nelson called out frequently for Hardy, When he did not come his anxiety became very great. 'Will no one bring Hardy to me? He must be killed.' At length Mr Bulkeley, Hardy's assistant, arrived to say the captain could not leave the deck but would come down as soon as possible. He came at about half past two, and they shook hands. 'Well, Hardy,' said Nelson, 'how goes the battle? How goes the day with us?'

'Very well, my Lord. We have got twelve or fourteen of the enemy's ships in our possession.'

'I hope,' said Nelson, 'none of *our* ships have struck.'

'No, my Lord, there is no fear of that.'

Nelson then said: 'I am a dead man, Hardy. I am going fast. It will be all over with me soon. Come nearer to me.' Hardy bent down and Nelson whispered: 'Pray let my dear Lady Hamilton have my hair and all other things belonging to me.' After a few more minutes' conversation, Hardy again shook hands and returned to the deck.

Nelson now instructed Dr Beatty to attend to the other wounded as nothing further could be done for him. A few moments later he recalled Beatty to say that all power of motion and feeling below his breast had gone, 'and *you*,' he said emphatically, 'very well know I can live but a short time'. While Beatty re-examined him Nelson again exclaimed: 'You *know* I am gone'. In the face of such transcendent courage Beatty could hide the truth no longer. 'My lord, unhappily for our country, nothing can be done for you.' Overcome with emotion he turned aside. 'I know it,' said Nelson, 'I feel something rising in my breast which tells me I am gone.' Then he was heard to murmur several times: 'God be praised. I have done my duty.'

Hardy now made his second appearance, this time to congratulate Nelson on certain victory. Fourteen enemy ships had struck, possibly fifteen. 'That is well,' said Nelson, 'but I bargained for twenty.' Then, his mind still on his duty, he exclaimed emphatically: 'Anchor, Hardy, anchor!' Hardy said he supposed Admiral Collingwood would now take it on himself to direct affairs. 'Not while I live, I hope, Hardy,' cried Nelson, raising himself from the bed. 'No, do *you* anchor. For if I live I'll anchor.' Exhausted, he fell back. In calmer tones he told Hardy that he felt the end was now near. 'Don't throw me overboard, Hardy.' 'Oh, no,' replied Hardy, 'certainly not.' 'Then,' said Nelson, 'you know what to do.'

The moment had now come for Nelson to take farewell of Hardy. In recent years the famous scene of the admiral asking Hardy to kiss him has become, like other events of history, a subject more for laughter than tears. Some Englishmen indeed, not liking to believe their greatest admiral asked anything so effeminate, have created a legend that he said 'Kismet'.

And yet it was one of the most moving moments of Nelson's life. For of all his captains it was Hardy, in the last analysis, whom he loved most. His relationship with Troubridge and Ball had been more intimate, but less sure; for they had given him criticism as well as praise. The self-sufficient Hardy had offered neither; and Nelson had never dared to speak to him in the extravagant way he did to the others. To have asked Troubridge or Ball to kiss him would have been ridiculous and unnecessary; to ask Hardy was to demand something wholly alien to his nature. The captain knelt down and lightly kissed his forehead. Nothing could have been less fitting, nothing in the circumstance more right. 'Now I am satisfied,' said Nelson. 'Thank God, I have done my duty.'

And now came the final act of this strange drama. Hardy stood a moment looking down at the admiral. It may have occurred to him then that Nelson was thinking he had kissed him, not because he wanted to but because he could not refuse a dying man's request. Quietly he knelt down again and brushed his lips on the admiral's forehead. 'Who is that?' asked Nelson. 'It is Hardy,' replied the Captain. 'God bless you, Hardy,' said Nelson.

Hardy left the cockpit and returned to where the battle was raging on deck. Nelson's breathing now became very difficult. He asked his steward to turn him on his right side, and when this was done he said: 'I wish I had not left the deck, for I shall soon be gone'. To Dr Scott he said: 'Doctor, I have not been a *great* sinner,' and reminded him that he was leaving Lady Hamilton as a legacy to his King and country. His thirst increased and he asked repeatedly for drinks and to be fanned. His speech became more and more inarticulate. The last words he was heard to utter were: 'God and my country'. At thirty minutes past four he died.

CHAPTER 18

Nelson's great and glorious victory had been granted. Of the thirty-three ships of the combined fleet, eighteen were captured including Villeneuve's flag-ship, the *Bucentaure*, and the huge *Santissima Trinidad*, which struck to Fremantle. The four French van-ships under Dumanoir le Pelley escaped to the northwards; but a fortnight later they were brought to action off Cape Ortegal by Sir Richard Strachan, and all surrendered. The eleven remaining ships reached Cadiz, but never put to sea again. The British casualties of 1700 killed and wounded were less than a third of the enemy's; and they took some 20,000 prisoners. 'There never was,' Collingwood wrote to Thompson, 'so complete an annihilation of a fleet.'

The two enemy commanders-in-chief did not long survive Nelson. Villeneuve was taken prisoner on board the *Neptune*, where Fremantle found him 'very low'; then, when Blackwood was ordered home, he was shifted to the *Euryalus*. Villeneuve's conduct had earned him respect and sympathy, and when he went to live at Bishop's Waltham on parole, Pitt and Barham ordered that he was to be treated with every consideration. Blackwood, who had formed a high admiration of him, was shocked to find that he had been restricted 'the same as the lowest officers to whom country paroles are given, that is to a mile or so about the town on the turnpike road, and a fine of a guinea if out after five o'clock'. A word in the proper quarter put things to rights, but soon after Villeneuve was released on exchange. He never reached Paris. On the morning of 22 April 1806, he was found murdered in a hotel bedroom at Rennes. The criminal was not identified, but it was whispered that he was an agent of Napoleon.

Gravina's end was more noble. In the action he had been badly wounded in the arm. He refused to have it amputated and blood-poisoning set in. 'I am a dying man,' he said in March, 1806, 'but I hope and trust that I am going to join the greatest hero the world almost ever produced.' A few days later he was dead.

If Nelson had lived long enough to bring the Fleet to anchor, victory would have been complete. But Collingwood admitted that the thought had never occurred to him. He did not give the order until later in the evening when the gale was on them, by which time it was too late. The next four days were a nightmare for the Fleet. The storm raged unceasingly, they had no sight of sun, moon or stars, they were, in the words of one captain, 'fatigued beyond measure,' and the death of Nelson lay heavy upon them. Collingwood gave orders one moment and cancelled them the next. 'What he is doing, God knows!' commented Codrington, and Fremantle wrote: 'The poor man does not know his own mind five minutes together'. Many of the prizes were driven ashore and wrecked, others became unmanageable and were burnt. When the main body of the Fleet came to anchor south of Cadiz on 28 October, only four were left afloat.

The *Pickle* schooner, Lieutenant Laponetiere, left the Fleet on the 26th with Collingwood's despatches. Off the Scilly Isles she spoke to the *Superb*, outward bound to join the Fleet; her news was a cruel blow to Keats, who was hoping to arrive in time for the action, and was carrying letters from Lady Hamilton. The *Pickle* reached Falmouth on 4 November: Lieutenant Laponetiere set out in a post-chaise and arrived at the Admiralty at one o'clock on the morning of the 6th. He was shown up to the First Secretary, who was preparing for bed, and greeted him with the dramatic words: 'Sir, we have gained a great victory, but we have lost Lord Nelson'.

Everywhere the magnitude and significance of the victory was overshadowed by the death of Nelson. Lord Malmesbury wrote that he had never seen so little public joy. Even the mob were silent: 'What!' they cried, 'light up because our Nelson is killed!' Pitt, accustomed to being woken at all hours, was unable to get to sleep again, and rose at 3 a.m. for the day's work. Betsey learnt the news of the greatest naval victory since the Armada by the maid Nelly's 'ghastly appearance after breakfast'. The King was so upset he was unable to speak. 'I had not upon any occasion,' said his secretary, 'seen His Majesty more affected.' In many places people wept openly. At Naples Coleridge wrote that passers-by stopped to shake his hand because they had seen the tears on his cheek and guessed he must be English. At Castellamare George Elliot half-masted the *Aurora*'s colours and fired minute-guns. Until receiving a 'very proper rebuke for not saluting for the victory,' he had not thought to do otherwise.

Yet it was among Nelson's Fleet that his death was felt most deeply. 'All seemed to feel,' wrote one officer, 'not only that some great national calamity had befallen the land, but as if each individual had lost a friend and a leader.' A sailor in the *Royal Sovereign* wrote home: 'All the men in our ship are such soft toads, they have done nothing but blast their eyes and cry. Bless you! – chaps that fought like the devil sit down and cry like a wench.' Blackwood told his wife that he had never been so shocked or upset in his life and even the aloof Collingwood was moved to tears. Codrington wrote that Hallowell could hardly support himself. (Codrington had the captain of *L'Intrepide* on board as a prisoner, and Hallowell, in return for Ganteaume's kindness after the capture of the *Swiftsure* sent him a draft for £100 and a trunkful of clothes.) Keats and Louis wrote highly emotional letters to Lady Hamilton. Louis asked for some personal memento. 'I never made such a request before and never shall again, for no man can ever have the warmth of my heart and soul so strong and sincere.' Dr Scott summed up the feelings of them all. 'When I think, setting aside his heroism, what an affectionate fascinating little fellow

he was, how dignified and pure his mind, how kind and con-
descending his manners, I become stupid with grief for what I
have lost.'

The *Victory*, with Nelson's body preserved in a cask of spirits,
was towed by the *Neptune* to Gibraltar. After a short refit she
and the *Euryalus* sailed for England. At Portsmouth Hardy and
Blackwood discussed the codicil to Nelson's will which they
had witnessed, and agreed that it should be put before the
Government as soon as possible. They were both too busy to
visit Merton, but assured Lady Hamilton of their good intentions. 'Hardy may have spoken his mind on former occasions
more freely than you could have wished,' wrote Blackwood;
'but depend on it, the last words of our lamented friend will
influence his conduct.' And Hardy told her: 'It was ever our
Lord's last request to be kind to you, which I trust I shall never
forget'.

But despite Hardy and Blackwood's efforts, Nelson's dying
request was never answered; and after Trafalgar Lady Hamilton quickly fades from the scene. Ball, Louis and Hardy wrote
frequently, offering their help in any way; but she seldom
answered their letters. Never a woman with a sense of money,
she was soon in debt; and in 1815 she died in poverty at Calais.

Hardy remained at Portsmouth a week and then sailed for
the Nore. At Chatham Nelson's body was transferred to
Hallowell's coffin, which had been sent down from London. It
was placed on board the Commissioner's yacht, which proceeded slowly up river past ships with flags half-masted and to
the sound of minute-guns from batteries ashore. At Greenwich
the coffin was received by Lord Hood and taken to a private
apartment, preparatory to the lying-in-state.

The funeral was fixed for 9 January, and on the three days
preceding, Nelson's body lay on view to the public in the
Painted Hall. Hallowell's coffin had been enclosed in another
made by Mr France of Pall Mall, emblazoned with emblems
of his victories and described as 'the most superb ever seen in
Europe'. It was covered with a black velvet pall lined with
white satin, and erected on a platform six feet high. Above was

a great black canopy festooned with gold and surmounted with a golden wreath bearing the word TRAFALGAR. The chamber was lighted by candles placed on silver trays beside the coffin and by double rows of sconces round the walls. Ten banners on staves, bearing the quarterings of Nelson's arms, hung pendant towards the coffin. Ten mourners from the Lord Chamberlain's office, two on either side of the coffin, three on either side of the canopy, attended the body by day and night. Volunteers of the Greenwich and Deptford Associations kept the huge crowd continually on the move. During the three days' lying-in-state over 30,000 people passed through the chamber.

On 8 January the coffin was conveyed in a procession of State barges to the Admiralty. It lay overnight in the Captains' Room, watched by Dr Scott. Between three and four the next morning when it was still dark, crowds began assembling in the streets between the Admiralty and St Paul's, where Nelson was to be buried. At eight-thirty they heard the great bell of the cathedral tolling mournfully. With the coming of light – a clear crisp January day – troops took up their positions along the route. The principal mourners – the princes of the blood, representatives of the Lords and Commons, senior naval and military officers, officials of the College of Heralds and Nelson's relatives – assembled in Hyde Park, and then made their way by St James's Park and Constitution Hill to the Admiralty.

Here the coffin was brought out of the Admiralty Yard and placed in the funeral car, which had been modelled after the hull of the Victory. The figurehead represented Fame: above the stern was a poop lantern with the word VICTORY emblazoned in yellow letters. The sides were decorated with escutcheons; between them were scrolls bearing the names SAN JOSEF, L'ORIENT, TRINIDAD and BUCENTAURE. An ensign fluttered at half-mast.

At noon the huge procession formed up and started off. It was led by a body of cavalry, artillery and infantry from regiments quartered within a hundred miles of London, under the command of General Sir David Dundas. After them came forty-eight seamen of the *Victory* and forty-eight pensioners of Greenwich Hospital; officials of the College of Heralds; representatives of the City companies; two knights of the Bath (Sir Samuel Hood and Sir Thomas Trigge); members of the House of Commons; barons, viscounts, earls, marquises, dukes and princes. Then came the funeral car, closely followed by the Chief Mourner Admiral Sir Peter Parker (senior admiral in the Fleet), supported by Admirals Lord Hood and Radstock, and with Captain Blackwood as train-bearer. He was followed by six Assistant Mourners, Admirals Curtis, Pole, Hamilton, Caldwell, Bligh and Nugent, and by Captain Hardy bearing the Banner of Emblems. After them came Nelson's relatives, and several hundred naval and military officers brought up the rear. The procession was so long that these officers did not leave the Admiralty until after the troops under Dundas had reached St Paul's.

What impressed most onlookers was 'the awful silence,' broken only by the distant strains of the Dead March in Saul and the occasional sounding of minute-guns. 'It seemed,' wrote Lady Bessborough, 'one general impulse of respect beyond anything that could have been said or contrived.' As the funeral car passed along the Strand the rustle of people uncovering their heads could clearly be heard. Many people thought the numbers of soldiers excessive, and rested their eyes on Hardy and the 'dear forty-eight *Victory* men'. 'We had rather see them,' they said, 'than all the rest.'

At St Paul's twelve seamen of the *Victory* lifted the coffin from the car and carried it inside the western door. Here they were relieved by the principal pall-bearers, Admirals Orde, Whitshed, Harvey and Taylor. The procession moved slowly up the aisle, through shafts of golden sunlight streaming down from the high windows, past pews thronged with people who had been waiting patiently since seven in the morning, past the opening to the crypt under the dome and into the choir. The organ broke into the opening strains of 'I Know that My Redeemer Liveth'.

The service had begun at two o'clock. By the time it was over

332

darkness had fallen, and the cathedral was lit by rows of torches along the walls and by a huge octagonal lantern suspended under the dome. The bier, covered in black velvet and fringed with golden tassels, was placed in the choir to receive the coffin. The four admirals took their places alongside it. Six others – Domett, Drury, Douglas, Wells, Coffin and Aylmer – held a canopy above it: this was made of black velvet, supported by six small pillars and crowned with six plumes of black ostrich feathers: the valance was embroidered with emblems of Nelson's victories and his coat-of-arms, coronet and crest in gold.

The procession moved in inverse order from the choir to the opening to the crypt under the dome. Here the canopy was withdrawn and the pall removed. Clarenceux King of Arms placed Nelson's coronet on the coffin, and the Chief Mourner and relatives gathered round the opening. At thirty-three minutes past five o'clock Nelson's last remains were lowered into the crypt. Softly the choir began the last verse of the concluding anthem: 'His body is buried in peace'. And the chorus answered: 'But his name liveth for evermore'.

* * *

Trafalgar did not affect the immediate course of the war, which lasted for another ten years, but it made Napoleon's eventual defeat inevitable. 'It forced him,' wrote Fyffe, 'to impose his yoke upon *all* Europe or to abandon the hope of conquering Great Britain . . . It left England in such a position that no means remained to injure her but those which must result in the ultimate deliverance of the continent.' For two years after the battle Napoleon retained some hopes of defeating the British at sea. In 1807, at Tilsit, he concluded a secret treaty with the Emperor of Russia to revive the Armed Coalition of the North: one hundred and eighty ships of the Scandinavian Powers, mostly from Denmark, were to destroy England's fighting and mercantile fleets. This plan was forestalled by a powerful squadron under Lord Gambier which bombarded Copenhagen, accepted its surrender and returned to England with over seventy ships.

After this Napoleon adopted the Continental System. He declared the British Isles to be in a state of blockade and forbade British shipping to enter European ports. Fantastic as this policy sounds, it had some effect. By 1811 English factories had been forced to close down and warehouses were choked with unsold goods; and in 1812 Britain's insistence on her right of search led to war with America. But in the end it was France, not England that was defeated by the Continental System. Napoleon's refusal to grant concessions to Spain and Portugal brought about the Peninsular War. Other countries came to hate the French officials crowding their ports and resented the loss of trade with England as much as England herself. In 1812 Russia declared the blockade invalid, and six hundred British merchant-ships sailed into her ports. Three years later came Waterloo.

England's Navy had again triumphed. It had saved her from defeat by supplying her with the food on which her existence depended: it made ultimate victory certain by assuring her armies a free passage to the continent. 'If anyone wishes to know the history of this war,' said Wellington, 'I will tell them that it is our maritime superiority which gives me the power of maintaining my army while the enemy are unable to do so.' Even Napoleon, on the eve of being carried away to captivity, admitted ruefully: 'In all my plans I have always been thwarted by the British Fleet'.

The crucial years for England had been 1795 to 1805 – from Nelson's taking command of his first detached squadron on the Riviera to his death in the *Victory*. The main credit for naval successes in this period must be shared between two men – St Vincent and Nelson. St Vincent took command of the Fleet when, in his own words, it was 'at the lowest ebb of licentiousness and ill discipline,' and by his own ruthless methods shaped it into a weapon of dazzling power. This fleet was Nelson's inheritance. It is doubtful whether Nelson with all his genius could have done what St Vincent did in the last years of the eighteenth century: it is equally doubtful whether St Vincent could have made the same use of the

Fleet as Nelson. Each, in his different way, complemented the other.

Between St Vincent, Nelson and the main body of the Fleet stood the captains. It would be foolish to claim too much for them, or for that matter too little, for they were an integral part of the pattern. Great captains, as Tucker said, they assuredly were; but they owed much of their greatness to St Vincent and Nelson.

Those whom St Vincent called 'the *élite* of the Navy of England' became under Nelson's command 'the band of brothers'; and it was this above all that was the secret of their strength. What singles Nelson out from all other admirals was his profound respect for the individual. His captains were not instruments blindly to follow his orders, but men with hopes and wishes of their own. By taking them into his confidence at every opportunity, by explaining his intentions in detail, he so harnessed their minds to his that his will became the will of the Fleet. Lord Howe said the Battle of the Nile was singular in that every captain distinguished himself. Villeneuve echoed his words at Trafalgar: 'Every captain was a Nelson'.

Even so, something had to be left to chance. 'Nothing is sure in a sea-fight beyond all others. In case signals can neither be seen nor perfectly understood, no captain can do very wrong if he places his ship alongside that of an enemy.' General lines of conduct were laid down; within them captains were expected to act on their own. He not only gave them his trust but made them fully conscious of the responsibility of it; and their fear was not that of incurring his censure but of misinterpreting his intentions. The results were all he expected. 'His captains,' wrote the French historian Dupin, 'learnt in action to supply what had escaped his forethought, and in success to surpass even his hopes.'

The first results of their success were to bring the war to an end; but the long-term effects were far-reaching. For Trafalgar was the end of an epoch; it was the end of the sailing-ship era and the sailing-ship admiral, the end of the long series of eighteenth-century wars. It gave Britain a naval supremacy which remained unchallenged for over a hundred years. This supremacy was seldom abused. Nelson's successors sailed the world, charting its seas for the benefit of mankind, halting the aggressor, succouring the oppressed. Upon this supremacy and the peace which resulted from it, Britain consolidated her empire, laid the foundations of her trade, and gave to Europe a stability in which some of her greatest artists flourished. The nineteenth century was, for the most part, one of the most fruitful periods of European history. Its origins lay in the smoke of Aboukir and Copenhagen and Trafalgar. Its progenitors were Nelson and his Band of Brothers.

EPILOGUE

During the two years between Trafalgar and the adoption of the Continental System several French squadrons were active at sea; and the blockade of enemy ports was maintained. It was a galling service which the captains, under Collingwood's impersonal regime, felt keenly. 'It was formerly a pleasure to serve,' wrote Captain Bolton to Lady Hamilton; 'it is now become a toil.' Codrington described the Fleet as being 'hipped, dissatisfied and indifferent to the service'. An increase in captains' pay brought little comfort for, as Fremantle pointed out, it exactly covered the added income-tax. He was made president of a committee of three captains to administer a fund of £3,000 subscribed by the Fleet for a monument to Nelson. 'This you may publish,' he told Betsey, 'as I am not a little proud at being so, and at having in the first instance proposed the measure.' The monument was erected on the heights behind Portsmouth.

In December, 1805, two French squadrons under Admirals Willaumez and Leissegues broke out from Brest to attack British trade. Three British squadrons, under Sir Richard Strachan, Sir John Warren and Sir John Duckworth, sailed after them. After a brush with Willaumez's squadron Duckworth ran Leissegues to earth in the West Indies. Most of his captains were old Nelsonians: Captain Keats in the *Superb*, in which he was flying his own flag; Rear-Admiral Cochrane and Captain Morrison in the *Northumberland*, Rear-Admiral Louis and Captain Austen in the *Canopus*, Captain Stopford in the *Spencer*, Captain Sir Edward Berry in the *Agamemnon*, Captain Malcolm in the *Donegal*, Captain Pym in the *Atlas*. On 6 February 1806, these ships gained an overwhelming victory over Leissegues off San Domingo. Three of the enemy were captured, the other two destroyed and burnt.

On 25 September of the same year another French squadron of five large frigates broke out from Rochefort, also bound for the West Indies. They were met by a squadron of six of the line under Sam Hood, recently returned from Trinidad and flying his broad pendant in the *Centaur*. All but one of the enemy ships were captured. Hood was badly wounded in the arm, which was later amputated.

The following year saw Gambier at Copenhagen, and the beginning of the Continental System. From then until the end of the war no further major naval actions took place. In this year, their work as it were over, the first two of Nelson's captains died.

In 1805 Pellew and Troubridge suggested to the Admiralty that the two divisions of the East Indies Command be united. The Admiralty agreed: Pellew was ordered to absorb Troubridge's command into his own and Troubridge was appointed to the Cape. The *Blenheim* was very unseaworthy, having recently been aground in the Malacca Strait, and her captain urged Troubridge to delay sailing. But Troubridge, with his usual impatience, refused; and such was people's faith in him that many civilians embarked in the flag-ship as passengers. The *Blenheim* sailed from Madras on 12 January, 1807, with the *Java* and *Harrier* brigs in company. On 1 February they ran into a cyclone off Madagascar. The *Harrier* emerged alone. When last sighted the *Blenheim* and *Java* were flying signals of distress. Despite an extensive search carried out by Captain Thomas Troubridge, the admiral's son in the *Greyhound*, no trace of the ships was ever found. St Vincent was heartbroken. 'I shall never see Troubridge's like again,' he declared, 'I loved that invaluable man.'

Three months later Louis died. After the battle of San Domingo, for which he was made a baronet, he sailed with Duckworth for operations in the Dardanelles. Also in the squadron was the *Ajax*, commanded by Blackwood. On 14 February 1807, she caught fire, and sank: only 381 of her ship's company of 633 were saved, among them Blackwood. After the Dardanelles Louis was appointed to command the naval forces at Alexandria. Here on 16 May 1807, he died. His body was sent to Malta in the *Bittern*, given a military funeral by Ball, and buried near the grave of Sir Ralph Abercromby.

Ball, made a rear-admiral in 1805, died at Malta in 1809. He worked for the welfare of the Maltese up to the last – a policy which did not make him popular with the English ('who,' commented the *Naval Chronicle*, 'are too apt to despise foreigners'). But Maltese grief at his death was described as 'quite touching'. Public amusements were suspended for a week and public mourning ordered for a month. Ball was buried near Abercromby and Louis, and a mausoleum in the Lower Baracca erected to his memory.

Back in England Blackwood was court-martialled for the loss of the *Ajax* and honourably acquitted. He was offered the post of Pay Commissioner on the Navy Board, but, hoping for a West Indian governorship, refused. The governorship did not materialize and he was appointed to the *Warspite*, 74. He remained her captain for six years, serving in the North Sea squadron and Mediterranean and Channel Fleets; and in 1813 he was made Captain of the Fleet in the *Impregnable* for the visit of the allied sovereigns to London.

After the peace Blackwood was promoted to rear-admiral and made a baronet. In 1819 he was given a KCB and appointed to the East Indies command, where he rose to vice-admiral. His last appointment was as Commander-in-Chief, The Nore, from 1827–30. He died in 1832 at Ballyleidy in Ireland, the seat of his elder brother, Lord Dufferin.

Berry rested on his laurels. He had been in more battles than any other officer of the day, and was one of the few captains to hold medals for three general actions – the Nile, Trafalgar and San Domingo; he had taken part in the Glorious First of June and Cape St Vincent, as well as the defence of the *Leander* and the capture of the *Généreux* and *Guillaume Tell*. He was made a baronet in 1806. During the next nine years he commanded the *Barfleur* and the *Sceptre*, and, for the visit of the allied sovereigns, the *Royal Sovereign* yacht.

On 2 January 1815, many senior naval officers were rewarded for their war services by the newly-created Knight Grand Cross of the Bath and Knight Commander of the Bath. A rumour got about that these awards were to embody and supersede all others. Remembering the defence of the *Leander* seventeen years earlier, Berry wrote angrily to Thompson: 'As a Brother Companion in Arms, and having had Sharp Work together, I cannot help expressing to you my indignation at the idea of giving up the medals so honourably won by us. I consider them superior to a constellation of stars. . . . We must not be a rope of sand. Lord Nelson's motto should be uppermost in our thoughts: *Palmam qui meruit ferat*.'

In July, 1821, Berry was promoted to rear-admiral, but owing to ill-health he never hoisted his flag. His last years were marked by increasing debility and paralysis, and he died at Bath in 1831.

Thompson had lived quietly at Hartsbourne Manor since the Peace of Amiens. In 1806 he was made Comptroller of the Navy, and following the example of his predecessor applied for a baronetcy: this was gazetted on the same day as Berry's. In 1807 he was elected MP for Rochester and represented the borough until 1818. In 1809 he was promoted rear-admiral and in 1814 vice-admiral. In 1816 he was appointed Treasurer of the Royal Hospital at Greenwich and Director of the Chest in succession to Lord Hood. He was made GCB in 1822, and died at Hartsbourne in 1828.

Foley, still in poor health, remained at Abermarlais from 1805 to 1811, when he was promoted rear-admiral and appointed Commander-in-Chief, The Downs. The next year he was made vice-admiral. He returned to Abermarlais after the Peace and lived there for the next fifteen years. In 1820 he was made GCB on the vacancy caused by the death of Cornwallis, and in 1830 appointed Commander-in-Chief, Portsmouth. To Saumarez's congratulations he replied: 'Your friendly letter gave me much pleasure . . . I ever remember my station in Lord Nelson's line-of-battle and to have become your second in the instance brings all the matter fresh to memory.' In 1833 he died at Portsmouth and was buried in the garrison chapel in a coffin made from the planks of the *Elephant*. His wife's first cousin, Sir Charles Napier, the hero of Scinde and Meanee, was also buried in the chapel; and as a further coincidence their mutual ancestor, Charles II, had been married there to Catherine of Portugal.

Hallowell remained in the *Tigre* after Trafalgar, and in 1807 commanded the naval operations against the Turks at Alexandria. On 1 August 1811 – the thirteenth anniversary of the Nile – he was promoted rear-admiral and hoisted his flag in the *Malta*, 74, in the Mediterranean. After the peace he commanded the Irish station, and from 1821–4 was Vice-Admiral Commanding the Nore.

In 1828 Hallowell inherited the estate of Beddington Park, Surrey, from his cousin, Mrs Gee, together with a large sum of money. Mrs Gee had inherited it from her cousins the Carews, who had owned it since 1350, and a stipulation in the will was that Hallowell should change his name to Carew. On hearing of this unexpected windfall he is said to have remarked: 'Half as much twenty years ago would have been a blessing – but now I am old and crank'. In 1830 Hallowell was made full Admiral and next year given the GCB. He died at Beddington in 1834 and a monument was erected to his memory in the chapel: this consisted of a broken flag-staff and sword, crossed, with a wreath above bearing the word NILE.

After the action in which he lost his arm, Sam Hood sailed for England. On reaching Ryde the whole ship's company watched him lowered over the side. 'You would have really thought,' wrote an eye-witness, 'that every man in the ship was his brother.' Hood was nursed back to health by his wife (the daughter of Lord Seaforth, Governor of Barbados), and a month later was well enough to offer himself as a candidate in the General Election. He and Sheridan were returned for Westminster: they were chaired from the hustings at Covent Garden to the Thatched House Tavern in St James's Street in a huge procession led by 'constables, marrow-bones and cleavers,' two banners with the device 'The People's Choice' and 'Sacred to Female Patriotism,' effigies of Fox and Nelson, and a detachment of the *Centaur*'s seamen.

In 1807 Hood reassumed command of the *Centaur* and sailed with Gambier to Copenhagen. In October he was made rear-admiral and second-in-command to Saumarez in the Baltic Fleet. Here he won a brilliant action in the *Implacable* against the *Sevelode*, a Russian 74. In 1809 he was given a baronetcy, and for the next two years served in the Mediterranean Fleet with Fremantle, Hallowell and Blackwood. In 1812 he was promoted vice-admiral and appointed to the East Indies Command. He died of fever at Madras in 1816. A monument, 110 feet high, was erected to his memory at Butleigh, in Somerset.

Saumarez remained in the Channel Islands until 1806 when he became St Vincent's second-in-command in the Channel Fleet with the rank of vice-admiral. On St Vincent's retirement in 1807 he was offered the East Indies Command, but refused. In 1808 he accepted command of the Baltic Fleet and hoisted his flag in Nelson's *Victory*, which thirty years earlier he had joined as a lieutenant. For his services in the war against Russia and in the carrying out of delicate diplomatic negotiations Saumarez won much praise.

He returned to England in 1812, struck his flag, and retired from active service. He busied himself in the work of the Church in which he had always been interested, built a chapel on his estate in Guernsey and became president of several religious societies.

In 1814 various officers were given peerages for their war

services. Saumarez's rather pompous manner had never made him popular in high places and he was not among them, although Pellew, an officer junior to him, was. Once again Saumarez felt – again with some justification – that his services had been slighted. He continued to press his claims and in 1821 got the backing of Lord St Vincent. 'I feel very much for Sir James Saumarez,' St Vincent wrote. 'I have lost no opportunity of stating his high pretensions which in my judgment are very superior to any other upon the list of flag-officers.' But it was not for another ten years, when Saumarez's friend Grey succeeded Wellington as Prime Minister, that a barony was at last awarded him. Sixty-four officers of the Royal Navy Club gave Saumarez a celebration dinner and Hardy proposed his health. Saumarez disliked party politics and seldom visited the House of Lords: he only voted once (for the Reform Bill), and after Grey's retirement ceased attendance altogether.

But his sensibility lasted until the end of his life. When Keats died in 1834, he agreed to be one of the pall-bearers. For some reason he could not attend, and at a subsequent levee William IV, whose temper was never very steady and who was a friend of Keats, took him to task 'in strong language' in front of others. This reduced Saumarez to tears, and only a special audience at which the king accepted his explanation succeeded in calming him. Saumarez's last appointment was as Commander-in-Chief, Plymouth, from 1827 to 1830. In 1836 he died in Guernsey.

Fremantle remained in the Mediterranean until the autumn of 1806, when he came home for the General Election. Through the influence of the Grenvilles he was returned for Sandwich and appointed a Lord of the Admiralty. Betsey hardly had time to furnish their Admiralty apartments when the Government fell and Fremantle found himself unemployed. 'It is a pity Lord Grenville proposed the Catholic Bill,' wrote Betsey, 'for Pitt went out in the same cause.' They remained at Sanbourne for the next three years; Fremantle was made a baronet and given an honorary Doctorate of Law at Oxford. In 1810 he was promoted rear-admiral and hoisted his flag in the

Rodney, 74, in the Mediterranean Fleet under Sir Charles Cotton. 'Cotton is incapable of governing this Fleet,' Fremantle wrote to Betsey, 'jealous of Hood, led by his secretary – Hood is led by Hallowell who abuses Cotton publicly.' Betsey herself visited Scotland to see Eugenia who, after a stormy courtship, had married a Scottish laird, Robert Campbell, a relation of the Duke of Argyll.

Fremantle arrived home in 1814 in time for the visit of the allied sovereigns, and he and Betsey went to the ball at Burlington House:

'The Emperor of Russia with the Duke of Oldenburgh, King of Prussia and all arrived at ten o'clock. I was close to them when they first walked round the ballroom and saw them very plain. They afterwards mixed in the crowd and Alexander danced the whole evening and flirted with his partners . . . I stayed till seven o'clock in the morning and met almost everybody I knew in London. Fremantle got tired and went home an hour before me. Old Blücher is a delight.'

But the year which was such a glorious one for the nation ended sadly for Betsey; her sister Justina and her brother-in-law Robert Campbell both died.

In 1815 Fremantle was made KCB. ('The Order is quite spoilt by being divided into three classes,' wrote Betsey; 'Fremantle dreadfully annoyed at being placed in the second class.') On Napoleon's return to France he was made Commander-in-Chief, Channel Islands; but after Waterloo he was given the Mediterranean command. His headquarters were in Italy, and Betsey's diary is full of references to places and friends of twenty-five years earlier. In 1818 Fremantle was made GCB. On 19 December of the next year, without any warning, he died at Naples. It was a cruel blow to Betsey for it was here, twenty-two years earlier, they had been married; and for the first time in her life she missed writing her diary for ten days. There was a brilliant State funeral attended by the foreign ambassadors, the Duke of Leeds, Lords Spencer and Whitworth and all the English residents, in a procession of over sixty carriages. Betsey started her diary again on New Year's Day, 1820, and continued it without a break until her death in 1857.

It is perhaps fitting that the captain whom Nelson loved most should have survived him the longest.

In February, 1806, Hardy was made a baronet for his services at Trafalgar. Later that year, after being defeated in the election at Weymouth, he commissioned the *Triumph* and sailed with Sir Richard Strachan on his pursuit of Willaumez. From 1806 to 1809 the *Triumph* was based at Halifax, and Hardy married the daughter of his commander-in-chief, Sir George Berkeley. In 1809 he became flag-captain to Berkeley on the Lisbon station; and in 1812 he returned to Halifax in the *Ramillies* to take part in the American war.

He was back in England in time for the peace celebrations and in 1816 took part in a rather curious incident. Various malicious people had been libelling Hardy's wife, saying she had eloped with the Marquis of Abercorn. The *Morning Post* published the libels: Hardy sued them and was awarded £1000 damages. He suspected Lord Buckingham (who succeeded his father in 1813) as being the instigator of the trouble and accused him publicly. The result was a duel. Buckingham's second was Fremantle's brother William, Hardy's Lord March. Each contestant fired a shot; both missed.

After the Peace Hardy commanded the *Princess Augusta* yacht. In 1818 he hoisted his broad pendant in the *Superb*, and taking a son of Hallowell ('I have never forgotten,' he wrote to him, 'your kindness to me in former times'), sailed to command the South American Station. It was a difficult appointment for the War of Independence was raging, and Hardy had to exercise much tact. 'He was trusted everywhere,' wrote Captain Basil Hall, 'and enjoyed in a wonderful degree the confidence and esteem of all parties.'

Hardy returned to England in 1824, was made rear-admiral in 1825 and in 1826 hoisted his flag in the *Wellesley*. In 1830, on the personal recommendation of William IV, he became First Sea Lord. His predecessor was George Cockburn, his one-time captain in the *Meleager* and *Minerve*, who had taken Napoleon on his last journey to St Helena. One of Hardy's first duties was to give Cockburn his orders for the West Indies Command, a situation which, with his innate modesty, he found quite embarrassing. 'I cannot really believe I am First Sea Lord,' he said, 'the tables are so entirely turned.'

In 1831 Hardy was made GCB. The same year Lady Nelson died and Hardy, who had kept up his friendship with her, attended her funeral at Littleham, Devon. In 1834, on the death of Keats, he accepted the governorship of Greenwich Hospital, having promised the King that in the event of war he would take command of the Fleet. Hardy was a popular governor and carried out many reforms such as abolishing the red coats with yellow sleeves worn by pensioners who got drunk on Sundays. In 1836 the first railway was opened between Greenwich and London Bridge. Lady Hardy made up a party for the trip, but Hardy 'declined to go at any price, saying it was a needless risk to run'; and subsequent efforts to persuade him to travel by train proved equally unsuccessful. In 1837 Hardy was made vice-admiral. He died at Greenwich in 1839 and was buried in the hospital mausoleum: by his own request a favourite miniature of Nelson was placed in the coffin beside him. A monument was erected to his memory on the Dorset coast.

St Vincent outlived Nelson by eighteen years. After his retirement from the Channel Fleet in 1806 he never served again; but he spoke frequently in the House of Lords, and was a tireless letter-writer, setting down his thoughts and prejudices in his usual pungent language. His opinion of the new Orders of the Bath in 1815 was much the same as Berry's. He did not care, he said, whose names they put in the list, if only they had done him the favour of omitting his; and when he received a congratulatory letter he returned the envelope marked: 'Why persecutest thou me with GCB?'

Although his mind remained wonderfully active, his health began to fail, and in 1818 he went to live in the South of France. He took a villa near Hyères, on the coastline which in

1796 he had come to know so well. He visited Toulon dockyard, where he was received with enthusiasm and escorted round by Admiral Missiessy. His searching questions and keen interest caused much delight. 'I never spent,' he wrote to Berry, 'a more entertaining day.'

In 1819, his health partially recovered, he returned home. One of the first questions of his gardener was to ask permission to cut down an old oak. 'I command you to do no such thing,' replied the admiral, 'that tree and I have been long contemporaries: we have flourished together and together we will fall.' In 1821 he was made Admiral of the Fleet, the first officer (excluding the Duke of Clarence) ever to hold that rank. In 1823, having entered his ninetieth year, he died. He was attended by Dr Baird, his secretary Mr Tucker, and his old flag-captain, Sir George Grey.

* * *

Nelson's captains gave the Navy a great inheritance, and the Navy did not forget them.

Among Captain-class corvettes built in the Second World War were the *Berry*, *Blackwood*, *Foley* and *Hallowell*. The *Berry* and *Blackwood* were commissioned at Boston Navy Yard in 1943. The *Blackwood* was sunk by a U-boat in the English Channel in 1944, the *Berry* returned to the United States in 1946, the *Hallowell* served in the Royal Canadian Navy. The *Foley* was credited with having sunk at least one enemy submarine.

The *Saumarez*, *Hardy* and *Troubridge* were fleet destroyers. In December, 1943, the *Saumarez* was part of the destroyer screen escorting the battleship *Duke of York* in her action with the *Scharnhorst* off the North Cape. The destroyers attacked with torpedoes and scored three hits (including at least one from the *Saumarez*); these slowed up the *Scharnhorst*'s speed so that the *Duke of York* was able to catch up and sink her. In May, 1945, the *Saumarez* led a destroyer flotilla which attacked and sank the Japanese cruiser *Hagura* north of the Malacca Strait. In October, 1946, she and the destroyer *Volage* were damaged by mines in a channel north-east of Corfu – an incident which led to international repercussions.

There were two *Hardys* in the war. The first (the seventh ship of her name) led the destroyer attack at Narvik in 1940, for which her captain, Captain Warburton-Lee, was posthumously awarded the Victoria Cross: the ship was beached and became a total wreck. The second *Hardy* was commissioned in 1943 and in 1944 was sunk by a U-boat in the Arctic Sea.

The *Troubridge* was also commissioned in 1943, and served with the Mediterranean Fleet, where she took part in many minor actions. In 1944 she sailed for the Far East and in September, 1945, was present in Tokyo Bay at the proceedings which led to the conclusion of the Second World War.

After the war three Type 14 Frigates, the *Hardy, Blackwood* and *Murray* were built and commissioned but they have since all gone out of service, and at the present time no ship of the Royal Navy bears the name of any one of Nelson's captains.

ORIGINAL SOURCES

BRITISH MUSEUM
Nelson Papers. (Additional MSS. 34902-92)
Egerton Papers.
Thompson Papers.

NELSON MUSEUM, MONMOUTH
Llangattock Papers.

**PRIVATE PAPERS AND OTHER INFORMATION AT THE TIME OF THE
FIRST EDITION IN THE POSSESSION OF**
Major George Benson, DSO
Commander A. T. Blackwood, Royal Navy.
Mr A. J. Carter.
The Lord Cottesloe, CB.
Mr Montague Davenport.
Mr H. Foley.
The Hon. Dorothy Hood.
Dr H. B. Louis.
The Lady de Saumarez.
Lieutenant-Colonel Sir Thomas Thompson, Bart., MC.
Miss Joan Thorp.
Lieutenant-Colonel Sir St Vincent Troubridge, Bart., MBE.

PUBLISHED SOURCES

(*Dates are not necessarily those of first
publication but of the edition used by the
author*)

THE DICTIONARY OF NATIONAL BIO-
GRAPHY (and sources mentioned
therein)

THE NAVAL CHRONICLE (Various, esp.
Vols. 1–15)

THE MARINERS MIRROR (Var. esp. Vol.
21, 447 and 439. Vol. 16, 409. Vol.
15, 240. Vol. 8, 77)

THE HISTORICAL MANUSCRIPTS COM-
MISSION The Papers of J. B. Fortescue
at Dropmore. (See var. captains in
index)

THE NAVY RECORDS SOCIETY
Corbett, Julian S., *The Spencer Papers*.
(*Vols.* 1 and 2, 1913, 1914)
Corbett, Julian S., *Fighting Instructions*,
1530–1816. (1905)
Hamilton, Admiral Sir R. Vesey, and

Laughton, John Knox, *Recollections
of James Anthony Gardner*. (1906)
Hamilton, Admiral Sir R. Vesey, *The
Byam Martin Papers*. (*Three Vols.*
1902, 1898, 1900)
Jackson, Rear-Admiral T. Sturges,
Logs of the Great Sea-Fights. (*Two
Vols.* 1899, 1900)
Laughton, John Knox, *The Naval
Miscellany*. (*vols.* 1 and 2, 1901, 1910)
Laughton, Sir John Knox, *The Barham
Papers*. (*Vol.* 3, 1910)
Laughton, John Knox, and Sulivan,
J. Y. F., *Journal of Rear-Admiral
James*. (1896)
Leyland, John, *The Blockade of Brest*,
1803–1805. (*Two Vols.* 1898, 1901)
Markham, Sir Clements, *The Markham
Papers*. (1904)
Richmond, Rear-Admiral H. W., *The
Spencer Papers*. (*Vols.* 3 and 4, 1923,
1924)

Smith, David Bonner, *The St Vincent Papers*. (*Two Vols.* 1921, 1926)

Toogood, C. G., and Brassey, T. A., *Index to James's Naval History*. (1895)

Anon (Ed.), *The Naval Career of Sir William Hoste*. (1887)

Barrow, Sir John, Bart., *An Autobiographical Memoir*. (1847)

Beatty, William, *Authentic Narrative of the Death of Lord Nelson*. (1807)

Bevan, A. B. and Wolryche-Whitmore, H. B. (Eds.), *A Sailor of King George: The Journals of Captain Frederick Hoffman*. (1901)

Bourchier, Lady (Ed.), *Memoir of the Life of Admiral Sir Edward Codrington*. (*Vol.* 1, 1873)

Brenton, Captain E. P., *Life and Correspondence of John, Earl of St Vincent*. (*Two Vols.* 1838)

Broadley, A. M. and Bartelot, R. G., *Nelson's Hardy*. (1909)

Bryant, Arthur, *The Years of Endurance*. (1942)

Bryant, Arthur, *Years of Victory*. (1944)

Callender, Geoffrey, *The Naval Side of British History*. (1937)

Clarke, Rev. J. S. and M'Arthur, J., *The Life of Admiral Lord Nelson, KB*. (*Two Vols.* 1809)

Clowes, W. L. (and others), *The Royal Navy: A History*. (*Vols.* 4 and 5, 1899, 1900)

Coleridge, Samuel Taylor, *The Friend* (*The Third Landing-Place*). (1890)

Collingwood, G. L. Newnham, *A Selection from the Public and Private Correspondence of Vice-Admiral Lord Collingwood*. (1829)

Cornwallis-West, G., *The Life and Letters of Admiral Cornwallis*. (1927)

Dawson, W. R. (Ed.), *The Nelson Collection at Lloyds* (1932)

Desbrière, Edouard (trans. Eastwick), *The Trafalgar Campaign*. (*Two Vols.* 1933)

Dundonald, Earl of, *Autobiography of a Seaman*.) *Vol.* 1, 1860)

Edgcumbe, Richard (Ed.), *Diary of Frances, Lady Shelley*. (1912)

Elliot, Admiral The Hon. Sir George, *Memoir*. (*Privately Printed*. 1863)

Fitchett, W. H. *Nelson and His Captains*. (1902)

Fraser, Edward, *The Sailors Whom Nelson Led*. (1913)

Fremantle, Anne, *The Wynne Diaries*. (*Three Vols.* 1935, 1937, 1940)

Gatty, A., *Recollections of the Life of the Rev. A. J. Scott*. (1842)

Gordon, Pryse Lockhart, *Personal Memoirs*. (1830)

Gore, John, *Nelson's Hardy and His Wife*. (1935)

Hall, Captain Basil, *Fragments of Voyages and Travels*. (1846)

Herbert, J. B., *Life and Services of Admiral Sir T. Foley*. (*Privately Printed* 1884)

James, William, *The Naval History of Great Britain*. (*Vols.* 1–4, 1886)

Jeffrey, Reginald W. (Ed.), *Dyott's Diary*. (*Vol.* 1, 1907)

Knight, Cornelia, *Autobiography*. (*Two Vols.* 1861)

Laferia, A. V., *British Malta*. (*Vol.* 1, 1938)

Lewis, Michael, *The Navy of Britain*. (1948)

Long, W. H., *Naval Yarns*. (1899)

Lovell, Vice-Admiral W. S., *Personal Narrative of Events, 1799–1815*. (1879)

Luke, Sir Harry, *Malta*. (1949)

Mahan, Captain A. T., *The Influence of Sea Power upon The French Revolution and Empire*. (*Two Vols.* 1893)

Mahan, Captain A. T., *The Life of Nelson*. (1897)

Mahan, Captain A. T., *Types of Naval Officers*. (1902)

Markham, Admiral John, *A Naval Career During the Old War*. (1883)

Marshall, Lieutenant John, *Royal Naval Biography*. (*Two Vols.* 1923)

Masefield, John, *Sea Life in Nelson's Time*. (1905)

Minto, Nina Countess of, *Life and Letters of Sir Gilbert Elliot, First Earl of Minto*. (*Three Vols.* 1874)

Sources

Moorhouse, E. Hallam, *Nelson in England.* (1913)

Morrison, Alfred, *The Hamilton and Nelson Papers.* (*Two Vols. Privately Printed.* 1893)

Nicolas, Sir Harris, *Dispatches and Letters of Vice-Admiral Lord Viscount Nelson.* (*Seven Vols.* 1846)

Oman, Carola, *Nelson.* (1947)

Parsons, G. S., *Nelsonian Reminiscences: Leaves from Memory's Log.* (1905)

Pettigrew, Thomas, *Memoirs of the Life of Vice-Admiral Lord Viscount Nelson.* (*Two Vols.* 1849)

Phillimore, Rear-Admiral A., *Life of Admiral of the Fleet Sir William Parker.* (*Vol.* 1, 1876)

Rose, J. H., *The Life of Napoleon I.* (1935)

Ross, Sir John, *Memoirs and Correspondence of Admiral Lord de Saumarez.* (*Two Vols.* 1838)

Sichel, Walter, *Emma, Lady Hamilton.* (1905)

Smyth, Admiral W. H., *The Sailor's Word-Book.* (1867)

Southey, Robert, *The Life of Nelson.* (1922)

Stirling, A. M. W., *Pages and Portraits from the Past: The Private Papers of Admiral Sir William Hotham.* (*Two Vols.* 1919)

Tucker, J. S., *Memoirs of the Earl of St Vincent.* (*Two Vols.* 1844)

Woollcombe, G. D., *Sir Thomas Louis, Bart.* (*Privately Printed,* 1932: From the *Transactions of the Devonshire Association for the Advancement of Science, Literature and Art, Vol.* lxiv, pp. 249–56)

See also Douglas, Major-General Sir Howard, *Naval Gunnery* (Fremantle); Cottesloe, Lord, *Diary and Letters of Admiral Sir C. H. Fremantle, GCB* (Fremantle); Rutter, Owen (Ed.) *John Fryer of the Bounty* (Fremantle and Foley); Lee, Theophilus, *Memoirs* (Hallowell); *Beeton's Dictionary of Universal Information* (Ball); and various magazines and reviews, esp. *Gloucestershire Notes and Queries,* Vol. 1, 1881 (Ball); *Transactions of the Carmarthenshire Antiquarian Society,* Part 1 (Two unpublished letters from Nelson to Foley); *Blackwoods Magazine,* No. 1535, p. 190 (Hood and Midshipman Thorp); *Century Magazine,* Vol. 15, p. 20 (Troubridge); *Gentleman's Magazine* for 1828, p. 564 (Thompson); *Historical, Biographical, Literary and Scientific Magazine* for May, 1799 (Thompson); and the Nelson Papers in the *J. Pierpont Morgan Library,* New York City (Nelson to Hallowell).

INDEX

READ MORE IN PENGUIN

In every corner of the world, on every subject under the sun, Penguin represents quality and variety – the very best in publishing today.

For complete information about books available from Penguin – including Puffins, Penguin Classics and Arkana – and how to order them, write to us at the appropriate address below. Please note that for copyright reasons the selection of books varies from country to country.

In the United Kingdom: Please write to *Dept. EP, Penguin Books Ltd, Bath Road, Harmondsworth, West Drayton, Middlesex UB7 ODA*

In the United States: Please write to *Consumer Sales, Penguin Putnam Inc., P.O. Box 12289 Dept. B, Newark, New Jersey 07101-5289.* VISA and MasterCard holders call 1-800-788-6262 to order Penguin titles

In Canada: Please write to *Penguin Books Canada Ltd, 10 Alcorn Avenue, Suite 300, Toronto, Ontario M4V 3B2*

In Australia: Please write to *Penguin Books Australia Ltd, P.O. Box 257, Ringwood, Victoria 3134*

In New Zealand: Please write to *Penguin Books (NZ) Ltd, Private Bag 102902, North Shore Mail Centre, Auckland 10*

In India: Please write to *Penguin Books India Pvt Ltd, 11 Community Centre, Panchsheel Park, New Delhi 110017*

In the Netherlands: Please write to *Penguin Books Netherlands bv, Postbus 3507, NL-1001 AH Amsterdam*

In Germany: Please write to *Penguin Books Deutschland GmbH, Metzlerstrasse 26, 60594 Frankfurt am Main*

In Spain: Please write to *Penguin Books S. A., Bravo Murillo 19, 1° B, 28015 Madrid*

In Italy: Please write to *Penguin Italia s.r.l., Via Benedetto Croce 2, 20094 Corsico, Milano*

In France: Please write to *Penguin France, Le Carré Wilson, 62 rue Benjamin Baillaud, 31500 Toulouse*

In Japan: Please write to *Penguin Books Japan Ltd, Kaneko Building, 2-3-25 Koraku, Bunkyo-Ku, Tokyo 112*

In South Africa: Please write to *Penguin Books South Africa (Pty) Ltd, Private Bag X14, Parkview, 2122 Johannesburg*

INSPECTION COPY REQUESTS

Lecturers in the United Kingdom and Ireland wishing to apply for inspection copies of Classic Penguin titles for student group adoptions are invited to apply to:

Inspection Copy Department
Penguin Press Marketing
80 Strand
LONDON
WC2R 0RL

Fax: 020 7010 6701

E-mail: academic@penguin.co.uk

Inspection copies may also be requested via our website at:
www.penguinclassics.com

Please include in your request the author, title and the ISBN of the book(s) in which you are interested, the name of the course on which the books will be used and the expected student numbers.

It is essential that you include with your request your title, first name, surname, position, department name, college or university address, telephone and fax numbers and your e-mail address.

Lecturers outside the United Kingdom and Ireland should address their applications to their local Penguin office.

Inspection copies are supplied at the discretion of Penguin Books

READ MORE IN PENGUIN

PENGUIN CLASSIC BIOGRAPHY

 Highly readable and enjoyable biographies and autobiographies from leading biographers and autobiographers. The series provides a vital background to the increasing interest in history, historical subjects and people who mattered. The periods and subjects covered include the Roman Empire, Tudor England, the English Civil Wars, the Victorian Era, and characters as diverse Joan of Arc, Jane Austen, Robert Burns and George Melly. Essential reading for everyone interested in the great figures of the past.

Published or forthcoming:

E. F. Benson	**As We Were**
Ernle Bradford	**Cleopatra**
David Cecil	**A Portrait of Jane Austen**
Roger Fulford	**Royal Dukes**
Christopher Hibbert	**Charles I**
	The Making of Charles Dickens
Christopher Hill	**God's Englishman: Oliver Cromwell**
Marion Johnson	**The Borgias**
James Lees-Milne	**Earls of Creation**
Edward Lucie-Smith	**Joan of Arc**
Philip Magnus	**Gladstone**
John Masters	**Casanova**
Elizabeth Mavor	**The Ladies of Llangollen**
Ian McIntyre	**Robert Burns**
George Melly	**Owning Up: The Trilogy**
Raymond Postgate	**That Devil Wilkes**
Peter Quennell	**Byron: The Years of Fame**
Lytton Strachey	**Queen Victoria**
	Elizabeth and Essex
Gaius Suetonius	**Lives of the Twelve Caesars**
	translated by Robert Graves
Alan Villiers	**Captain Cook**

READ MORE IN PENGUIN

PENGUIN CLASSIC HISTORY

 Well written narrative history from leading historians such as Paul Kennedy, Alan Moorehead, J. B. Priestley, A. L. Rowse and G. M. Trevelyan. From the Ancient World to the decline of British naval mastery, from twelfth-century France to the Victorian Underworld, the series captures the great turning points in history and chronicles the lives of ordinary people at different times. Penguin Classic History will be enjoyed and valued by everyone who loves the past.

Published or forthcoming:

Leslie Alcock	**Arthur's Britain**
John Belchem/Richard Price	**A Dictionary of 19th-Century History**
Jeremy Black/Roy Porter	**A Dictionary of 18th-Century History**
Ernle Bradford	**The Mediterranean**
Anthony Burton	**Remains of a Revolution**
Robert Darnton	**The Great Cat Massacre**
Jean Froissart	**Froissart's Chronicles**
Johan Huizinga	**The Waning of the Middle Ages**
Aldous Huxley	**The Devils of Loudun**
Paul M. Kennedy	**The Rise and Fall of British Naval Mastery**
Margaret Wade Labarge	**Women in Medieval Life**
Alan Moorehead	**Fatal Impact**
Samuel Pepys	**Illustrated Pepys**
J. H. Plumb	**The First Four Georges**
J. B. Priestley	**The Edwardians**
Philippa Pullar	**Consuming Passions**
A. L. Rowse	**The Elizabethan Renaissance**
John Ruskin	**The Stones of Venice**
G. M. Trevelyan	**English Social History**
Philip Warner	**The Medieval Castle**
T. H. White	**The Age of Scandal**
Lawrence Wright	**Clean and Decent**
Hans Zinsser	**Rats, Lice and History**

READ MORE IN PENGUIN

PENGUIN CLASSIC MILITARY HISTORY

This series acknowledges the profound and enduring interest in military history, and the causes and consequences of human conflict. Penguin Classic Military History covers warfare from the earliest times to the age of electronics and encompasses subjects as diverse as classic examples of grand strategy and the precision tactics of Britain's crack SAS Regiment. The series will be enjoyed and valued by students of military history and all who hope to learn from the often disturbing lessons of the past.

Published or forthcoming:

Correlli Barnett	**Engage the Enemy More Closely**
	The Great War
David G. Chandler	**The Art of Warfare on Land**
	Marlborough as Military Commander
William Craig	**Enemy at the Gates**
Carlo D'Este	**Decision in Normandy**
Michael Glover	**The Peninsular War**
	Wellington as Military Commander
Winston Graham	**The Spanish Armadas**
Heinz Guderian	**Panzer Leader**
Christopher Hibbert	**Redcoats and Rebels**
Heinz Höhne	**The Order of the Death's Head**
Anthony Kemp	**The SAS at War**
Ronald Lewin	**Ultra Goes to War**
Martin Middlebrook	**The Falklands War**
	The First Day on the Somme
	The Kaiser's Battle
Desmond Seward	**Henry V**
John Toland	**Infamy**
Philip Warner	**Sieges of the Middle Ages**
Leon Wolff	**In Flanders Fields**
Cecil Woodham-Smith	**The Reason Why**